TRAFFIC SAFETY AND THE DRIVER

TRAFFIC SAFETY AND THE DRIVER

Leonard Evans

 VAN NOSTRAND REINHOLD
New York

7/93

22184468

Copyright © 1991 by Van Nostrand Reinhold
Library of Congress Catalog Card Number 90-44233
ISBN 0-442-00163-0

Manufactured in the United States of America

Published by Van Nostrand Reinhold
115 Fifth Avenue
New York, New York 10003

Chapman and Hall
2-6 Boundary Row
London, SE1 8HN

Thomas Nelson Australia
102 Dodds Street
South Melbourne 3205
Victoria, Australia

Nelson Canada
1120 Birchmount Road
Scarborough, Ontario M1K 5G4, Canada

16 15 14 13 12 11 10 9 8 7 6 5 4 3 2

Library of Congress Cataloging-in-Publication Data
Evans, Leonard.
   Traffic safety and the driver / by Leonard Evans.
      p.   cm.
   Includes bibliographical references and index.
   ISBN 0-442-00163-0
   1. Traffic safety—United States.   2. Traffic accidents—United
States.   3. Automobile drivers—United States.   I. Title.
HE5614.2.E93   1991   90-44233
363.12′51—dc20   CIP

To:

Wendy, who was involved deeply and
creatively in every phase of this book, and
without whose untiring support it would
never have been written.

Contents

Preface

Deaths, injuries, and property damage from traffic crashes—their origin and nature, and ways to prevent their occurrence and reduce their severity—form the subject of this book. Traffic crashes are perhaps the number one public health problem in the United States and in other motorized societies; more preretirement years of life are lost due to traffic crashes than from the combined effects of the two leading diseases, cancer and heart disease; almost half of the 19-year-olds who die do so as the result of traffic crashes. This book applies the methods of science to illuminate the characteristics of this major problem, both by new analyses and by synthesizing and summarizing the world's research literature on the subject.

Because at least one driver is involved in every traffic crash, there is considerable focus on the driver. While most subjects of importance in traffic safety are covered, I have covered in greater depth those areas in which I have myself performed research; one always learns more by doing, listening and reading than by just listening and reading. In covering such areas, I have tended to place a good deal of reliance on my own work, not just because of my intimate knowledge of it, but because by using it a more unified and coherent treatment is possible. The goal of quantification that characterizes my published research is one also striven for in the book. As conclusions, reflecting the essence of what was found out, are a prime focus of my own research, I have collected the major conclusions in short sections at the end of most chapters, and also in a short concluding chapter.

I have been uniquely fortunate in having the freedom to pursue those research areas that I considered to be important, fruitful, and intellectually challenging, unfettered by constraints of writing project proposals defining what I was going to find out before looking for it. In other words, within the framework of a large industrial manufacturing company, I have been doing what professors are ideally supposed to do, but in fact rarely have the opportunity to do in today's world.

The book presents the results of published research without giving the detailed computations that led to these results, such details being available in the many original sources cited. In a few cases where results are available only in this book, or are not generally available, I have included more mathematical detail. However, most of the book should be accessible to readers not expert in mathematics or statistics.

In only a few cases is it possible to make inferences or arrive at conclusions that are so assumption free, or based on assumptions so universally accepted, that there is no possibility of alternative interpretations. This being so, I must strongly stress that the judgments and opinions in this book are my own, and do not necessarily reflect those of any other individuals, institutions or organizations with which I am or have been affiliated. The book is an individual effort written in my own time to express my own thoughts on traffic safety and traffic safety research, past, present, and future. Although it is my own effort, it nonetheless depends on the efforts of innumerable professional colleagues, most of whom I have interacted with directly over the years, and many of whose contributions are reflected in the references. Even beyond the course of normal professional interactions, a number of individuals have made a variety of contributions to specific portions of this book. Among them I particularly want to thank: Wally Albers, Larry Blincoe, Peter Cairney, Bob Campbell, Ken Campbell, Alan Donelson, Kurt Dubowski, Anita Evans, David Evans, Edwin Evans, Wendy Evans, Gene Farber, Jim Fell, Mike Frick, Ray Fuller, Graham Grayson, Ann Grimm, Frank Haight, Ezra Hauer, Robin Hertz, Avram Horowitz, Denis Huguenin, Charles Kahane, Dana Kamerud, Matthijs Koornstra, Murray Mackay, Robert Mann, Greg Mucha, Göran Nilsson, Paul Olson, Susan Partyka, Raymond Peck, Brian Repa, Dick Schwing, Marge Shepard, John Siefert, Mike Sivak, David Sleet, David Viano, V.V. Vlassov, Julian Waller, Patricia Waller, Paul Wasielewski, Kathy Weber, Kenneth Welty, and Nicholas Wittner.

While expressing gratitude for all the help without which this project would not have been possible, let me stress that the errors, omissions, and opinions with which you might disagree are entirely my responsibility, so any blame is entirely mine.

TRAFFIC SAFETY AND THE DRIVER

1 Introduction

THE IMPORTANCE OF TRAFFIC SAFETY

No one who lives in a motorized society can fail to be concerned about the enormous human cost of traffic crashes. In the United States almost as many young men die as a result of traffic crashes as die from all other causes combined. From 1928 through 1988 more than two and a half million people were killed on US roads; more than half a million from 1969. Traffic deaths from 1977 through 1988 exceeded all US battle deaths in all wars from the revolutionary war through the Vietnam war. Injuries outnumber deaths by about a factor of 70. The annual monetary cost of US motor vehicle crashes is estimated at 70 billion dollars for 1988. Worldwide, about half a million people are killed annually in traffic crashes.

This book describes what has been learned by applying the methods of science to understand better the origin and nature of the enormous human and economic losses associated with automobile-based transportation systems. It attempts to illuminate the problem, in perhaps the spirit of a microbiologist trying to understand a disease; there is a need to keep some separation between the concern and the science if the science is to succeed. Understanding and action are different processes; action is more likely to produce the results sought if it is grounded in understanding. As Haight [1988] comments about efforts to improve traffic safety, "Many of us have heard demands that we 'do something,' but it is only recently that there have been suggestions that we should 'know what we are doing' before we begin to do it."

Before raising questions about the nature and sources of traffic crashes we summarize some basic facts. Information from around the world will be used in the book, although more of the information comes from the United States than from any other country. This is mainly because, with 193 million vehicles in use in 1989 [National Safety Council 1990, p. 51], the US provides more data than any other nation. In addition, the US Department of Transportation maintains data files of a size and quality unavailable elsewhere. Many relationships relating to traffic safety are of a general nature which apply beyond the jurisdiction providing the data from which they were derived. For example, there is no reason why the effectiveness of occupant protection devices such as safety belts or airbags in preventing fatalities should vary much from jurisdiction to jurisdiction; at the same wearing rates, safety belts are expected to produce a similar percent reduction in fatalities in a nation of one million as in a larger nation providing

1

sufficient data to estimate the percent reduction. Damask [1987] reports that an attorney's closing remarks to a New Jersey jury included the statement that, "The laws of physics are obeyed in the laboratory, but not in rural New Jersey." The jury, evidently moved by the force of this argument, found in favor of the attorney's client [Damask 1988]. When results presented here arise mainly from physics, human physiology and biomechanics, they are likely to apply similarly in jurisdictions other than the one providing the data. Many aspects of traffic safety are, of course, jurisdiction specific. For example, alcohol plays a quite different role in traffic safety in Sweden, Saudi Arabia, the US, and Israel.

CASUALTIES DUE TO TRAFFIC CRASHES

Fatalities

In this book we place considerable emphasis on fatalities, the most serious consequence of a traffic crash. Fatality data are more complete than data on injuries at other levels, and the definition of fatality involves less uncertainty than for any other type of loss. This is not to say that fatality data are free from uncertainties and errors. Hutchinson [1987] documents differences in the total numbers of fatalities indicated in death certificates and in police records in most countries; not all deaths are necessarily known to those responsible for data sets, and missing data can be especially numerous in less economically developed countries. For a death to be included in any fatality data set it must occur within some specified time after the occurrence of the crash. While the choice of the time interval is essentially arbitrary, the longer the period, the more all-inclusive will be the data set. A one year criterion, as used by the National Safety Council [1990], is a common choice. The disadvantage of so long a period is that the data file is not complete for an entire year after the last crash it documents, thus, theoretically, the earliest at which the data for, say, calender year 1988 could be known is January 1990. The data set that we use extensively, described in Chapter 2, defines a death as one that occurs within 30 days of the crash as a result of the crash.

Worldwide, more than half a million people are killed each year in traffic crashes [Hutchinson 1987], and approximately one person in 200 in the world's population dies from injuries received in traffic crashes [Trinca et al. 1988]. These losses are spread among the nations of the world in an uneven way, as indicated by the data from 21 large countries shown in Table 1-1. This table shows 213 517 fatalities, less than one half of the number that occured. The first column gives the number of vehicles per thousand inhabitants, which provides a measure of the nation's level of motorization; this level is generally linked to the production of economic goods. The 21 countries are listed in order of decreasing degree of motorization; they were selected from the cited sources

Table 1-1. Fatality rates for various countries based on data in
Hutchinson [1987], Trinca et al. [1988], Cerrelli [1990], and
International Road Federation [1984].

Country	Vehicles per 1000 people	Deaths per 1000 veh.	Deaths per million people	Fatalities per year	Data year
United States	778	0.24	184	45 500	1989
Canada	561	0.28	158	4 120	1984
Australia	540	0.34	186	2 821	1984
Japan	403	0.26	103	12 456	1985
Netherlands	355	0.32	113	1 625	1984
United Kingdom	322	0.32	103	5 788	1984
Greece	176	1.20	211	2 091	1984
Israel	147	0.74	109	436	1981
South Africa	123	2.5	305	9 621	1984
USSR	76	2.7	204	58 651	1989*
Chile	74	1.8	133	1 552	1983
Colombia	35	2.6	89	2 383	1981
Turkey	27	4.4	118	5 677	1984
Egypt	19	6.0	114	5 092	1982
Thailand	17	5.0	84	4 315	1985
Kenya	12	11.3	134	2 228	1980
Nigeria	7	14.5	107	9 150	1980
South Korea	5	5.2	171	6 834	1983
India	4	10.9	42	30 471	1983
Ethiopia	1	17	25	1 016	1983
Liberia	1	36	39	97	1981

*Fatality data from "Argumenti i Fakti" kindly provided by Dr. V.V. Vlassov.

to illustrate the wide variability between countries and the dependence of fatalities on motorization, a dependence captured approximately in relations presented by Smeed [1949; 1968]. The fatality data are not all for the same year—generally deaths per vehicle declines by about 5% per year, while the other quantities do not change systematically over a period of a few years.

Motorization took deep roots earlier in the US than in other countries; the relatively low population density of the US has been conducive to developing a roadway system capable of accommodating a great number of vehicles. In 1989 there were more than three motorized vehicles (mainly cars, but trucks, busses, and motorcycles are also included) for every four members of the US population (193 million vehicles for 248 million people).

As the degree of motorization increases, there is a decrease in the number of deaths per registered vehicle; the largest rate in Table 1-1 is 150 times the smallest. This same pattern occurs within an individual nation as its degree of motorization increases (Chapter 13). It is possible that differences between countries (and over time) are even greater than the data indicate, because underreporting of fatalities is likely to be greater when a country is less motorized. As motorization increases, the number of deaths per capita (and also the total number) may increase if the fatality rates decline at a lower rate than the increase of the number of vehicles.

As motorization increases, not only does the number of fatalities change, but the types of fatalities also change. In the US, 14.6% of all 1988 traffic crash fatalities were pedestrians. In only two countries, Canada and the Netherlands, do pedestrian fatalities constitute a lower fraction of fatalities. In many countries the percentage of fatalities that are pedestrians is much higher (for example, 35% in the UK, 42% in Poland, 45% in Israel, and 60% in Hong Kong) [Hutchinson 1987]. Among the states in the US, the fraction of all traffic fatalities that are pedestrians also varies widely, from a low of 3.2% in Wyoming to a high of 41.7% in the District of Columbia [National Highway Traffic Safety Administration 1989]. Fatality rates vary widely between the states; for example, 97 fatalities per million people in the District of Columbia as compared to 324 in Wyoming. Degree of motorization and degree of urbanization influence the number of fatalities, and the fraction of these that are pedestrians. Thus, while the data in Table 1-1 show some broad patterns, it is inappropriate to read too much into them, especially because definitions, reliability, and completeness vary from country to country. Fatalities will be a central consideration in later chapters.

Non-fatal Injuries

Non-fatal injury data are not as complete as are the data for fatal injuries. In contrast to fatal injuries, which conceptually involve only a yes or no discrimination, non-fatal injuries lie along a severity continuum, from minor scratches to nearly fatal injuries. The question "How many injuries?" has little meaning in the absence of some defined level of injury. Generally, the less severe the injury, the greater is its frequency of occurrence, so the total number of injuries is extremely sensitive to whether or not, say, minor scratches are included. The most widely used injury scale is the Abbreviated Injury Scale (AIS) developed by the Association for the Advancement of Automotive Medicine. Injuries for each body region are placed into six levels, $AIS = 1$ through $AIS = 6$. These are defined in terms of a detailed medical examination, and the scale undergoes continuing revision, expansion and enhancement [American Association for Automotive Medicine 1985]. The AIS level is based on the level of injury revealed by an examination soon after the crash, and not by final outcome. As a consequence, it is possible for injuries at any AIS level to subsequently prove fatal, although the life-threatening potential of the injury increases steeply with increasing AIS level. Injured occupants often sustain injuries to more than one body region. For many analyses it is convenient to use only one measure of injury severity, which is the maximum AIS. An occupant with three injured

Table 1-2. The Abbreviated Injury Scale and probability of fatality reported in the study of Malliaris, Hitchcock, and Hedlund [1982].

AIS Level	Injury description	Fraction of those injured who died
0	No injury	—
1	Minor (may not require professional treatment)	0.0%
2	Moderate (nearly always require professional treatment, but are not ordinarily life-threatening or permanently disabling)	0.1%
3	Serious (potential for major hospitalization and long-term disability, but not normally life-threatening)	0.8%
4	Severe (life threatening and often permanently disabling, but survival is probable)	7.9%
5	Critical (usually require intensive medical care; survival uncertain)	58.4%
6	Maximum (untreatable; virtually unsurvivable)	100%

regions of the body, all at AIS 1, would have a maximum AIS of 1; an occupant with one region injured at AIS 2 would have a maximum AIS of 2. The description of the AIS levels presented in Table 1-2 is sufficient for our purposes. The probability-of-death values given are not part of the definitions, nor are they expected to be closely replicated under all conditions. They are values which were observed in one study [Malliaris, Hitchcock, and Hedlund 1982] and are presented to indicate more clearly how life-threatening potential increases with AIS.

An estimate of the distribution of traffic injuries by maximum AIS level in the US is available in the National Accident Sampling System (NASS) [National Highway Traffic Safety Administration 1988]. NASS is based on detailed post-crash examination of a carefully selected sample of crashes. The sample is chosen according to a probability scheme applied to police-reported crashes—the more severe the crash, the more likely it is to be subject to detailed post-crash examination. National estimates are inferred by scaling up by factors reflecting the probability that a crash of given severity is chosen for investigation. The information in Table 1-3 is based on data on over 13 000 crashes investigated in the 1986 NASS. This table, and the next three tables, are from an updating addendum [National Highway Traffic Safety Administration 1987] to an earlier study [National Highway Traffic Safety Administration 1983] which examined in depth the cost of motor vehicle crashes. Only those who did not die from the injuries at the indicated AIS level are shown in Table 1-3. If they died they are counted in the fatality total, so the estimates for AIS 5 (and to some extent AIS 4) substantially underestimate the actual numbers sustaining injuries at these levels in view of the probabilities (Table 1-2) that they are counted in the fatality total. The data in Table 1-3 indicate 74 injuries (of at least AIS = 1) per fatality.

Table 1-3. Estimates of the number of people injured at different maximum AIS levels who did not die, and fatalities, for the US in 1986. Data from National Highway Traffic Safety Administration [1987].

Maximum AIS	Number	Percent
1	2 895 000	84.7
2	370 200	10.8
3	127 400	3.7
4	15 500	0.5
5	9 500	0.3
Total injured survivors	3 417 600	100.0
Fatalities	46 056	

However, note how large a fraction (95.5%) of these injuries are at the two lowest AIS levels.

The National Highway Traffic Safety Administration [1987] reports that a 1981 survey they conducted indicates that there might be as many as 0.27 injury crashes not reported to the police for each NASS police-reported injury crash, with essentially all of the additional injuries being AIS 1. This suggests 4.34 million (rather than 3.42 million) injuries per year, and 94, rather than 74, injuries per fatality.

The above discussion of injuries has focused on the US, and shown the difficulties associated with injury measurements. Trinca et al. [1988] write that about 15 million people per year are injured in traffic crashes, and they estimate that the average citizen of the world has about a one in seven chance of being injured in a traffic crash sometime during his or her life.

Property Damage Only

The most common type of crash involves property damage only, without any personal injury. Estimates of the total number of vehicles involved in crashes are particularly uncertain, because as the value of the property loss decreases, so does the probability that authorities will know that the crash has occurred. One report [National Highway Traffic Safety Administration 1983, p. II-14] estimates the total number of vehicles involved in crashes in 1980, based on two separate approaches. In one approach, 34 million reported incidents (reported to police, insurance, or other authorities) of vehicles involved in property-dam-age-only crashes are augmented by an estimate of an additional 11 million unreported incidents, to give 44 million. In another approach, an estimated number of reported and unreported crashes of 24 million is multiplied by an average of 1.7 vehicles per crash to give 41 million vehicles involved in all types of crashes. The National Safety Council [1989, p. 48] provides comparable,

Table 1-4. Estimates of costs of US motor-vehicle crashes in 1986 according to the maximum level of injury in the crash. Data from National Highway Traffic Safety Administration [1987].

Maximum AIS	$ (billions)	Percent
1	9.39	12.7
2	2.47	3.3
3	1.88	2.5
4	1.01	1.4
5	2.71	3.7
Fatalities	16.50	22.2
Property damage only (vehicles)	29.59	39.9
Uninvolved vehicles	10.64	14.3
Total	74.20	100.0

but lower estimates of 19.4 million property-damage-only-crashes involving 36.2 million vehicles for 1988. These values indicate that the average vehicle has about a 20% probability of being involved in some type of crash per year, or is likely to be involved in some type of crash about every five years.

Given that the number of property-damage-only crashes depends critically on the definition of a crash, and that there is much uncertainty in the number of minor crashes, it is more appropriate to consider the total monetary cost. In doing so, ignoring large numbers of very minor incidents will have less effect.

ECONOMIC LOSSES

In discussing economic losses, we confine our attention to specifically identifiable monetary losses. We do not delve into the question of how much a life is worth, which is steeped in problems of the type discussed by Broome [1978], and by Adams [1981, p. 245] in his essay ". . . . And how much for your grandmother?" Nor do we address the emotional effects on families and associates of traffic victims, ignoring also their medical costs [Miller and Luchter 1988].

Estimates of monetary costs associated with different levels of injury are shown in Table 1-4. The costs attributed to death and injury include estimates of lost earnings, medical, legal, and property damage costs; although property damage costs increase with injury severity, they become a smaller fraction of the total cost of the crash. The traffic crash costs for uninvolved vehicles reflect various fixed costs that are relatively unaffected by the number of crashes, such as the administrative costs of insurance and other activities concerned with safety.

The largest single economic cost of traffic crashes is property damage (29.6 billion dollars for the US in 1986). This arises because of the enormous number of property-damage-only crashes, even though the cost of each such crash is very small compared to that for an injury-producing crash. The next highest

Table 1-5. Estimates of the distribution of the total 74.2 billion dollars in Table 1-4. Data from National Highway Traffic Safety Administration [1987].

Cost category	$ (billions)	Percent
Property losses	27.37	36.9
Insurance expenses	20.86	28.1
Productivity losses	16.38	22.1
Legal and court costs	4.32	5.8
Medical costs	4.12	5.6
Emergency costs	0.70	0.9
Other	0.45	0.6
Totals	74.20	100.0

monetary cost is fatalities (16.5 billion dollars for the US in 1986). The divisions of cost among the various AIS levels depend on the definitions of these levels, and therefore do not have the same clear-cut meaning as the fatality or property-damage-only categories. The total monetary cost of all non-fatal injury-producing crashes is similar to the cost for fatalities.

Table 1-5 shows an estimate of the distribution of the 74.2 billion dollar cost of traffic crashes in the US in 1986. The second largest cost, insurance expenses, includes only costs spent to maintain and operate the insurance system, including marketing, administrating, adjusting, etc. A large proportion of all the costs are paid directly, or reimbursed, by insurance; such transfer payment processes do not, in idealized form, add to the cost.

TERMINOLOGY

The word *accident* is avoided in this book; Doege [1978], Langley [1988], and others have reasoned persuasively that the conceptual ambiguities encompassed by this term are sufficient to disqualify it for technical use, notwithstanding its near universal general use. Accident conveys a sense that the losses incurred are due to fate and devoid of predictability; this book is devoted to examining the factors that influence the likelihood of occurrence and resulting harm from *crashes,* the preferred term that we have been using. Some crashes are purposeful acts for which the term *accident* would be quite inappropriate even in popular use. Philipps [1979] and Bollen and Philipps [1981] indicate that suicide may contribute to traffic fatalities. Although the use of vehicles for homicide may be less frequent than in the movies, such use is certainly not zero. The chosen word, *crash,* indicates in a simple factual way what is observed in nearly all cases, while accident seems to additionally suggest a general explanation of why it occurred. There are very few traffic fatalities (the small fraction of drownings and fire-deaths not initiated by crashes) for which the term crash is inappropriate.

Collections of observed numbers are referred to as *data* and not as *statistics*. Since this latter term is the name of a branch of mathematics dealing with hypothesis testing and confidence limits, using it to also mean *data* invites needless ambiguity.

We follow common usage in indicating ages; age 20 means people with ages equal to or greater than 20 years, but less than 21 years. Strictly speaking, age 20 means those who have been alive for, on average, 20.5 years; 40-year olds are not quite twice as old as 20-year olds, which might come as good news to some!

We use the term *car,* in preference to more cumbersome terms such as *motor car,* or *passenger automobile.* Stationwagons are considered to be cars. Persons travelling in vehicles are referred to as occupants, and all occupants are either drivers or passengers. We follow customary usage in referring to the device that controls the fuel to a vehicle's engine as the accelerator pedal, although this is an unfortunate designation. The accelerator must be pressed to impart zero acceleration to a vehicle in motion, and its non-use generates an acceleration, albeit a negative one, to a vehicle in motion. Indeed, it must be applied to decelerate a vehicle at a lower level of deceleration than the vehicle's coast-down deceleration. The use of *throttle,* rather than *accelerator,* is technically incorrect for vehicles not equipped with carburetors, which now constitute the majority of all vehicles. The term *decelerate* is also enshrined in common usage, and will be used rather than the more technically coherent term *negative acceleration,* although the negative and positive values of variables are not usually given different names.

It is assumed in the text that the driver sits on the left side of the vehicle and that traffic drives on the right, as in America and Europe. Those from countries which drive on the left, including Japan, the UK, Ireland, Australia, and Hong Kong, should make the necessary transformation.

We use the terms *safety* and *risk* throughout the book without confining them to any narrow technical definition, so that their meaning will be context dependent. In accord with common usage, increased safety generally implies reductions in such quantities as the numbers of crashes, injuries, or deaths.

UNITS

Given the high level of uncertainty intrinsic in many traffic safety studies, it is important to avoid needless confusion and ambiguity from other sources. Accordingly, when questions of units arise, I have been at some pains to be as explicit as possible. The workings of nature are, of course, independent of units. An intelligent Martian visitor would correctly predict when a dropped object would strike the ground, even though the numerical values used in his, her, or its calculation would have nothing in common with numerical values we would use, because the Martian would use Martian units. However, the underlying equation would be the same as ours. Although units never affect the answer, they do influence all numerical steps in calculations, and mistakes will lead to incorrect results.

The core of science is quantification, which requires measuring the values of specific quantities, or variables. In traffic safety such concepts as fatalities per unit distance of travel should, to the extent that is practicable, be conceived of as variables defined without regard to units of measurement, rather than thought of as, for example, fatalities per hundred million miles of travel. The quantitative statement that fatalities per unit distance of travel tends to decline by about 5% per year is independent of the units in which the variable is measured. Different units may be used in different circumstances, but the variable remains the same variable. Thinking about variables without regard to the units in which they are measured is universal in science, and common in general usage. For example, one asks for a person's height and age, which are appropriate variable names; one does not ask for their inchage and yearage. The units are a crucial component of the answer, but should not appear in the question. Sometimes it is impractical to avoid the inappropriate use of units in table column headings or in names of quantities, such as fatalities per year; here the unit of time is so universal in this application that little inelegance results.

Another reason why, throughout the book, I am particularly explicit about units is the hope that by doing so I might help encourage a more unified and rational practice [Evans 1978]. Such optimism probably merits the same dismissal as Dr. Samuel Johnson's description of a second marriage as "the triumph of hope over experience." When presenting material original to this book I have nearly always used the SI system, the internationally agreed upon metric system of units which is universally accepted, if not always correctly used, throughout the world outside the US and the UK. (Their contiguous majority-English-speaking neighbors, Canada and Ireland, have embraced the SI system). Even in the US, the SI system has been adopted in some industries, such as soft drink, photographic, pharmaceutical, and automobile manufacturing.

I have advocated [Evans 1987] that the SI system should be used exclusively in all technical work, a practice to which I have adhered in my own research. However, I have departed from exclusive SI use in this book because work performed and described in one set of units may not readily translate into another. If an instruction were given to drive at about 30 mph (miles per hour), then that was the instruction. It was not to drive at about 50 km/h, and it was certainly *not* to drive at about 48 km/h, because the concept of about 48 km/h (let alone 48.28 km/h) does not exist in the context of humans attempting to produce vehicle speeds. So, when describing studies reporting material in customary US/English units that do not convert readily, I quote as in the original work, without adding any distracting, and generally unneeded, conversions in parenthesis.

Hopefully, the reader who wants the values in the other units system will have little difficulty performing the conversions, which rarely require knowing more than that one mile is approximately 1.6 km (in fact, one mile is exactly 1.609 344 km, because US customary units are now defined as multiples of SI standard units). Similarly, Y fatalities per 100 million miles is equivalent to 6.213 71 times Y fatalities per billion km (one billion = one thousand million), and Z fatalities per billion km is equivalent to 0.160 933 4 times Z fatalities per hundred million miles.

In writing numbers with more than four digits, as in the last two sentences, I follow the SI practice of inserting a space between each group of three, as in 1 000 000 for a million; for four digits the space is optional, as in 1 000 or 1000. The customary US/English use of the comma is avoided, because the same symbol is used by others to denote the decimal point.

SOME COMMENTS ON METHODOLOGY

The position of a scientist trying to understand traffic safety has more in common with that of an astronomer than with that of a more terrestrially-oriented physical or biological scientist. The traffic safety scientist must try to devise ways to extract information from a system that is to a large extent given. This is done mainly using data collected by public authorities for purposes other than addressing the specific question the scientist has in mind. The luxury of varying input variables and observing what happens, and then repeating until reliability is established is not available. Some research relating to traffic safety is done in laboratories, and on test tracks and public roads using volunteer subjects and instrumented vehicles. This provides more experimenter control, but a question arises regarding how the results relate to normal driving. Studies have also been conducted in which the behavior of drivers in actual traffic has been observed. Studies using a variety of experimental and observational methods will be described throughout the book. Although such studies can illuminate road-user behavior, they cannot address the matter of most interest—the crash. While there were an estimated 20.6 million crashes [National Safety Council 1989, p. 48] in the US in 1988, these occurred in 3200 billion km of travel, so that there was one crash per 150 000 km. If one imagined photographically observing or instrumenting a 50 m section of *random* roadway, then one would expect about one out of every three million observed vehicles to crash, most likely into another vehicle. At a typical flow of 10 000 vehicles per day, you would expect about one crash (typically involving no injury and only minor property damage) per year; the same calculation indicates one fatal crash per 400 years. Given this, it is not surprising that most of what we know about crashes is based on crash data collected by public authorities.

The Problem of Exposure

Knowledge about the numbers of persons injured at some level is rarely sufficient to answer specific traffic safety questions without some measure of *exposure*, or the numbers exposed to the risk of being injured. The difficulties of estimating exposure in traffic safety research can be illustrated by a non-traffic example. Although fewer people are killed by crocodile bites than by dog bites, one cannot conclude that it is safer to have a pet crocodile around the house than a pet dog. Even after recognizing this, the way to proceed is not all that clear. Fatalities per animal appears a better measure than a simple count of fatalities, yet such an approach is also flawed. Dogs, unlike crocodiles, tend to be close to people. Even if one normalized for proximity, the problem remains that people, even without the benefit of carefully controlled studies, exercise more care near crocodiles. So it would be very difficult to answer the question "Is it safer to keep a pet crocodile or a pet dog?" by comparing fatalities due to dog and crocodile bites.

Comparable difficulties surround some questions in traffic safety, such as the influence of occupant age and car size on fatality risk in a crash, and the effectiveness of safety belts in preventing fatalities. The approaches used to address these problems are described in Chapters 2, 4, and 9.

There is no all-purpose definition of exposure [Evans 1984]; the definition always depends on the question being addressed. If we want to know whether more males or females are killed in traffic crashes in the US, the answer is simply the count of the number of deaths; the answer is unmistakably clear— more males are killed. If we want to know how the risk per capita depends on sex—then again, using population data to normalize, or correct for exposure, we find an equally clear difference, but one which does not address the risk of crashing for the same amount of travel. To do this we compute the number of deaths per unit distance of travel, and find that only a small difference remains between the male and female rates. This provides a measure of the rate per unit distance of driving, but not per unit of driving under identical driving conditions. As it is likely that males do more driving under more risky conditions (while intoxicated, at night, in bad weather, etc.), these additional factors would have to be incorporated into the measure of exposure.

None of the above measures is more "correct" than any other. Each validly measures something important; it is crucial to always understand clearly what is measured and what it means. Crashes per year, or *accident liability*, determines insurance premiums for which it is not relevant whether increased liability arises from increased driving or increased risk while driving; because of its ready availability in data sets, this same measure is used in many studies [Peck, McBride, and Coppin 1971]. If one is interested in how fatal traffic crashes influence population projections, the appropriate measure is the simple count of fatalities. If the aim is to determine which sex is more likely to crash under the same driving conditions, then all the discussed factors, and others, would have to be incorporated in the exposure measure, a task of such difficulty that the answer to this question remains unknown.

To help clarify thinking on this, assume that it turned out that one sex did have a higher crash rate under identical driving conditions, but that it is suggested that this difference arises because of faster driving under the same conditions, and that this should be incorporated into the measure of exposure. Suppose that when this is done, a difference in fatality rates is now attributed to one sex being more vulnerable to death from the same impact, and that this factor also should be normalized. It should be apparent that this process must end with the rates being identical, and the vacuous conclusion that when you correct for everything that is different, there cannot be any differences!

Because of the above considerations, it is inadvisable to think of exposure as some narrow concept; one should not say that any measure is corrected for exposure. Throughout the book various measures and rates are used; if we are discussing, for example, crashes per unit distance of travel, this will be stated explicitly, and all inferences will apply explicitly only to crashes per unit distance of travel.

Poisson Distribution

Probability, statistics, and mathematics are kept to a minimum in this book. However, there are a number of occasions in which we use the Poisson distribution. This can be explained in an example in which we assume that drivers have some average crash rate, x, per some unit of time. If x were 0.1 crashes per year, this would mean that drivers have, on average, 1 crash per 10 years. The underlying assumption for Poisson processes is that the observed risk of crashing is the result of a uniform risk of crashing at all times (a 0.1 probability of crashing per year, or equivalently a 1/120 probability of crashing each month, and so on). If a group of drivers have the same probability of crashing each month, at the end of a year all will not have the same number of crashes because of randomness. The Poisson distribution enables us to compute the probability, $P(n)$, that a driver will have precisely n crashes as

$$P(n) = \exp{(-x)}(x)^n/n!, \qquad \text{Eqn 1-1}$$

where $n!$ (factorial n) means $1 \times 2 \times 3 \ldots \times n$. For more details see, for example, Haight [1967]. Rather than thinking of $P(n)$ as referring to the probability that an individual driver will have n crashes, we can think of it as the fraction, or percent, of drivers from a population of identical drivers who will have n crashes. Substituting $x = 0.1$ into Eqn 1-1 gives that at the end of one year 90.48% of drivers are crash free, 9.05% have one crash, 0.45% have two crashes, and 0.02% have more than two crashes. If we encountered some driver with more than two crashes, this would strongly suggest that the driver is from a different, and more crash-involved population than the one with drivers whose average risk is 0.1 per year. After 20 years, if everything remained the same, the average number of crashes would be 2.0, which, when substituted for x in Eqn 1-1 gives that 13.53% of drivers would be expected to be crash free, 27.07% to have one crash, 27.07% to have two, 18.04% to have three, 9.02% to have four, 3.61% to have five, and 1.66% to have more than five. Note that the most likely values are close to the average of 2.0. What is indicated is purely statistical variation—we are assuming here that all the drivers are identical, so the drivers with zero crashes were lucky and those with more than two were not.

An illustrative distribution of data for 148 006 California drivers in 1963, with an average police-reported crash rate of 0.0626 crashes per year [Peck, McBride, and Coppin 1971] is compared to the Poisson distribution below:

Number of crashes	Observed	Poisson distribution
0	94.135%	93.932%
1	5.500	5.880
2	0.341	0.184
3 or more	0.024	0.004

While there is broad agreement, the differences between observed and calculated distributions, which are well above what is expected by chance in so large a sample, reflect that some drivers do indeed have higher crash rates than others [Peck, McBride, and Coppin 1971]. The California rate for police-reported crashes has remained close to about 0.05 crashes per year [Gebers and Peck 1987]. In various examples we use a larger rate of 0.1 crashes per year, which is considered more reflective of other states, as indicated in, for example, the data of Evans and Wasielewski [1982] for Michigan. The police-reported crash rate is, of course, critically dependent on the threshold criterion for reporting, and on levels of police enforcement; it should not be interpreted to reflect safer driving in one jurisdiction compared to another.

Many of the results derived involve combinations of observed frequencies, such as numbers of driver fatalities, numbers of pedestrian fatalities, etc. By assuming that these frequencies arise from Poisson processes we can estimate errors. Suppose there is, on average, one crash per day, so that after n days we would expect n crashes. However, a rate of one crash per day, on average, is not going to lead to exactly n crashes because of randomness, but to a distribution with an average value of n. The standard deviation of this distribution is equal to $\sqrt{n}$, and for n reasonably large (say, more than about 6), the distribution is close to the normal distribution, which has particularly convenient properties. Thus, an observed n fatalities implies that the process generating them, if replicated many times, would produce $(n \pm \sqrt{n})$ fatalities, where the error is one standard error. The fractional error is $\sqrt{n}/n = 1/\sqrt{n}$. Applying this simple formula enables one to compute errors in quantities formed by combining observed quantities which may be assumed to arise from Poisson-like processes.

Statistical Inference

We shall not often make reference to whether something is *statistically significant,* a phrase of ubiquitous occurrence in the literature. It is generally used to discriminate between the competing hypotheses that an observed difference is likely to have occurred by chance, or had a probability less than some specified low level (written, for example, $p < 0.05$) to have occurred by chance. While answering such questions may sometimes be important in that grey area between knowing nothing about a subject and the first glimmers of information, it is just a first step towards the scientific goal of quantification. There is rarely any scientific, let alone practical, interest in knowing whether one variable affects another. Basically, just about everything in the universe influences everything else to some extent; variables investigated in most reported studies are particularly likely to have some influence on each other. For sufficiently large samples, every effect, no matter how small or unimportant, becomes statistically significant. On the other hand, for sufficiently small samples, no effect, no matter how large or important, will be found to be statistically significant. Thus statistical significance measures are really more commentaries on the experiment than on the phenomenon being studied.

To illustrate, suppose studies investigated whether two alternative paints, B and C, covered more area than a presently-used paint A. Assume results report no statistically significant difference between A and B, but that C covers more area than A, this difference being statistically significant at $p < 0.001$. Such results provide no guidance on which paint to select to minimize the cost of painting the same area. If all three cost the same per can, the results presented might mislead a decision maker to choose C. If B and C cost more per can than A, then the results do not invite any decisions, which is perhaps better than inviting an incorrect one. If the results are presented in terms of interval estimates, for example that B covered $(20 \pm 25)\%$ more area than A, and C covered $(4 \pm 1)\%$ more area than A, then the likely most economical paint can be identified. If all cost the same, B is expected to minimize cost, but with some uncertainty. If both new paints cost 10% more than A, then the results indicate clearly that the statistically significantly better C is almost certainly the most costly choice, while B is still likely the least costly, with A still an option for the risk-averse. Assuming that the errors are one standard error arising from an underlying normal distribution, one can compute that there is a 66% chance that paint B will cover a given area at less cost than paint A (compared to a 34% chance that paint A is the more economical choice).

While academic statisticians might consider the above comments and illustration trivial (a clear exposition is presented by Mood and Graybill [1963]), many papers on traffic safety publish levels of statistical significance as if they were of paramount importance. The problem illustrated in the example has an analogue in traffic safety literature, in which it is often implied that the finding that some intervention has had a statistically significant effect is sufficient reason to favor such intervention over an equally costly intervention whose effect has not been shown to be statistically significant. The goal in this book will be to express estimates quantitatively with associated errors which convey immediately the magnitude and reliability of such estimates. I follow the common practice in science of quoting plus or minus one standard error, as in $(X \pm \Delta X)$; the approximate interpretation is that the true value of X has a 68% chance of being within the indicated range, a 16% chance of being lower than $X - \Delta X$ and a 16% chance of being higher than $X + \Delta X$. In some cases the indicated error will include contributions from factors other than randomness in data, in analogue with experimental errors in the physical sciences. It is simply not true that collecting more and more data in the same way will eventually provide a numerical value of some property of nature to whatever precision is desired. In much literature 95% confidence intervals, which correspond to 1.96 standard errors, are given. Provided it is clear which is used, the choice is arbitrary. The computation of confidence intervals and the determination of whether something is statistically significantly different from zero (or some other value) are essentially identical, but as discussed above, presenting an interval estimate is nearly always more illuminating.

THREE LEVELS OF KNOWLEDGE

Because the goal of quantification with specified error limits is not always attainable, it is helpful to distinguish three levels of knowledge:

1. Not based on observational data
2. Hinted at by observational data
3. Quantified by observational data

It might seem surprising that the first level should appear in any effort focused on technical understanding. Yet there are many cases in traffic safety, and even more in other aspects of life, in which we have confident knowledge which is not based on scientific investigation. One crucial example in traffic safety is the advice to pedestrians to look both ways before crossing the road. There are no observational data showing that it is safer to look than not to look, nor is it likely that the question will ever be addressed experimentally. Even in the absence of a shred of empirical verification, I nonetheless look both ways, and consider it good public policy to vigorously encourage everyone to do likewise. Such a conclusion is based on reason and logic alone, and most people agree that it would be foolish to suspend judgment until a study satisfying strict standards of rigor is published in the scientific literature. There are other important traffic safety problems where reason is our only guide. When rational discourse is all that is available, there is nothing shameful about using it, provided that the basis for the belief is stated clearly. A major problem is that what is reasonable to one individual might not be reasonable to others. Claims which are not supported by firm evidence are naturally less satisfactory, other factors being equal, than those supported by objective data.

The second level occurs when there are data, but for various reasons the data do not support clear-cut quantitative findings. The problem at this level arises because the use of the data to make inferences requires assumptions of such uncertainty that more than one interpretation is possible. Another problem may be that the data are so few that they do not lead to definitive conclusions.

The firmest knowledge occurs at the third level, the one to which we always aspire. The goal is well stated in the often quoted words of Lord Kelvin:

I often say that when you can measure what you are speaking about, and express it in numbers, you know something about it; but when you cannot express it in numbers, your knowledge is a meagre and unsatisfactory kind. It may be the beginning of knowledge, but you have scarcely in your thoughts advanced to the stage of science, whatever the matter may be.

REFERENCES

Adams, J. *Transportation Planning—Vision and Practice*. London, UK: Routledge and Kegan Paul; 1981.

American Association for Automotive Medicine. *The Abbreviated Injury Scale, 1985 Revision*. Des Plaines, IL: AAAM; 1985.

Bollen, K.A.; Philipps, D.P. 1981 suicidal motor vehicle fatalities in Detroit: a replication. *American Journal of Sociology* 87:404–412; 1981.

Broome, J. Trying to value a life. *Journal of Public Economics* 9:91–100; 1978.

Cerrelli, E.C. *Preliminary Report—1989 Traffic Fatalities*. Washington, DC: National Highway Traffic Safety Administration, May 1990.

Damask, A.C. Forensic physics of vehicle accidents. *Physics Today* 40(3):36–44; 1987.

Damask, A.C. Personal letter, dated 10 December 1988.

Doege, T.C. Sounding board—an injury is no accident. *New England Journal of Medicine* 298:509–510; 1978

Evans, L. The why and how of the (metric) system of units. *Human Factors Society Bulletin* 21(4):3–5; 1978.

Evans, L. Driver fatalities versus car mass using a new exposure approach. *Accident Analysis and Prevention* 16:19–36; 1984.

Evans, L.; Wasielewski, P. Do accident involved drivers exhibit riskier everyday driving behavior? *Accident Analysis and Prevention* 14:57–64; 1982.

Gebers, M.A.; Peck, R.C. Basic California traffic convictions and accident record facts. Sacramento, CA: California Department of Motor Vehicles, report CAL–DMV–114; December 1987.

Haight, F.A. *Handbook of the Poisson Distribution.* New York, NY: John Wiley; 1967.

Haight, F.A. Research and theory in traffic safety. Paper presented to International Symposium on Traffic Safety Theory and Research Methods, sponsored by SWOV, Amsterdam, Netherlands; April 1988.

Hutchinson, T.P. *Road Accident Statistics.* Adelaide, Australia: Rumsby Scientific Publishing; 1987.

International Road Federation. *World Road Statistics 1979–1983.* IRF, 525 School St. SW, Washington, DC; 1984.

Langley, J.D. The need to discontinue the use of the term *accident* when referring to unintentional injury events. *Accident Analysis and Prevention* 20:1–8; 1988.

Malliaris, A.C.; Hitchcock, R.; Hedlund, J. A search for priorities in crash protection. SAE paper 820242. Warrendale, PA: Society of Automotive Engineers; 1982.

Miller, T.R.; Luchter, S. The socio–economic impacts of injuries resulting from motor vehicle crashes. SAE paper 885162. Warrendale, PA: Society of Automotive Engineers; 1988. (Also included in XXII FISITA Congress Technical Papers, volume II, SAE Publication P–211, p. 513–527; 1988).

Mood, A.M.; Graybill, F.A. *Introduction to the Theory of Statistics* (Second Edition). New York, NY: McGraw Hill; 1963.

National Highway Traffic Safety Administration. The economic cost to society of motor vehicle accidents. Document DOT HS 806 342. Washington, DC; January 1983.

National Highway Traffic Safety Administration. 1986 addendum to The economic cost to society of motor vehicle accidents. Washington, DC; September 1987.

National Highway Traffic Safety Administration. National accident sampling system 1986—a report on traffic crashes and injuries in the United States. Document DOT HS 807 296. Washington, DC; July 1988.

National Highway Traffic Safety Administration. Fatal Accident Reporting System 1988. Document DOT HS 807 507. Washington, DC; December 1989.

National Safety Council. *Accident Facts.* Chicago, IL. 1990 edition (issued annually).

Peck, R.C.; McBride, R.S.; Coppin, R.S. The distribution and prediction of driver accident frequencies. *Accident Analysis and Prevention* 2:243–299; 1971.

Philipps, D.P. Suicide, motor vehicle fatalities, and the mass media: evidence towards a theory of suggestion. *American Journal of Sociology* 84:1150–1174; 1979.

Smeed, R. Some statistical aspects of road safety research. *Journal of the Royal Statistical Society, Series A* 112:1–34; 1949.

Smeed, R. Variations in the pattern of accident rates in different countries and their causes. *Traffic Engineering and Control* 10:364–371; 1968.

Trinca, G.W.; Johnston, I.R.; Campbell, B.J.; Haight, F.A.; Knight, P.R.; Mackay, G.M.; McLean, A.J.; Petrucelli, E. *Reducing Traffic Injury—A Global Challenge.* Melbourne, Australia: A.H. Massina & Co.; 1988.

2 Effects of Sex and Age

INTRODUCTION

Most road-user factors important in traffic safety depend strongly on the sex and age of the road-user. US male fatalities outnumber female fatalities by well over a factor of two; eight 20-year-old male drivers are killed for each 65-year-old driver killed. A focus on the variables of sex and age is therefore to be expected. Another reason for emphasizing these variables is that they tend to be the only demographic variables available, as Haight [1985] has remarked. The first question we address is a basic one which is not confined to traffic, but is an important consideration in nearly all studies of fatal injury. This question is, "How does the risk of death from identical physical impacts depend on sex and age?" Although the question relates more to basic human physiology than to traffic, it has been answered using a data file collected for traffic safety applications (many examples of the use of this data file to address traffic safety questions will be described later).

THE FATAL ACCIDENT REPORTING SYSTEM (FARS)

The Fatal Accident Reporting System, which we shall refer to as FARS, is a computerized data file maintained by the National Highway Traffic Safety Administration, an agency of the US Department of Transportation. The file was set up to document every fatal crash that occurred on any US public road since 1 January 1975. A fatal crash is defined as one in which anyone dies within 30 days of the crash as a result of the crash.

Data on the crash, the people involved, and the vehicles involved are compiled mainly using information provided by police at the scene of the crash. Because the goal is to include every fatal crash, there is no possibility of post-crash physical examinations of vehicle and site to provide estimates of travel speed, or vehicle change of speed on impact, the most effective indicator of crash severity. The file is largely limited to information which can be readily recorded, such as the number and type of vehicles involved, sex and age of occupants involved, time of day, posted speed limit on the roadway, etc. More specific vehicular information can be extracted from the Vehicle Identification Number (VIN) and the driver's license number. By the end of 1988 the file had records on over half a million fatal crashes in which over 650 000 people were killed. The number of fatalities necessarily exceeds the number of crashes because there

19

must be at least one fatality for the crash to be included in FARS. A publication giving much summary information from the file is issued annually [National Highway Traffic Safety Administration 1989, and previous years].

Even though data in this file are as reliable as any available, there is still some uncertainty. There are obviously people, especially elderly victims, who die from non-trauma causes in hospital within 30 days of a crash. In such cases is not clear whether the death resulted from the crash or from other causes. The total number of fatalities in the FARS file is less than the number estimated by the National Safety Council [1989] by between 2.9% and 4.5% (average 3.9%) for the years 1975 - 1988. The main contributor to this difference is that the National Safety Council includes deaths that occur within one year of the crash; even longer periods would increase the total further, but by increasingly small amounts. Although the 3.9% difference corresponds to almost 2000 traffic deaths per year which are not coded in FARS, this is not expected to materially affect the results of the studies described here, especially as most characteristics of the excluded fatalities are expected to reasonably match those of the included fatalities. Other problems which arise because of missing, and possibly inaccurate, data will be mentioned when specific studies are described. These points are mentioned to stress that even fatality data coded in FARS are far from perfect, even though they are far more reliable than data for any other level of harm.

RISK OF DEATH FROM THE SAME PHYSICAL IMPACT

Given that a male and female of similar age are subjected to similar physical insults, or impacts, which one is more likely to die? Traditional epidemiological studies are unable to answer this question because adequate samples of sufficiently similar cases are not available. Medical treatment naturally focuses more on the injuries than on quantifying the forces that caused them. While it was well known that death and injury risk increase with increasing age [Baker, O'Neill, and Karph 1984; Verbrugge 1982; Waller 1985], the effect was not quantified. By using the method described below to make appropriate inferences from the FARS data, Evans [1988a] addressed this physiological problem using data on over 80 000 fatalities.

Double Pair Comparison Method

The double pair comparison method enables us to make inferences from the FARS data without the need for external exposure measures. Two classes of occupants, *subject* occupants and *control* occupants are used. The influence of some characteristic (sex, age, belt-wearing, etc.) of the subject occupant on his or her fatality probability in a crash, other factors being the same, is estimated using the control occupant to standardize conditions—that is, to estimate exposure. Many different subject and control occupants were used to study the influence of sex and age on fatality risk. For expository convenience the method is described below for one specific case in which the subject occupant is a car driver and the control occupant is a male passenger seated in the right-front seat.

Two sets of fatal crashes are selected. The first set consists of crashes involving cars each containing a female driver and a male passenger, at least one of whom is killed. From the numbers of female driver and male passenger fatalities, a female driver to male passenger fatality ratio is calculated. From a second set of crashes involving cars containing male drivers and male passengers, a male driver to male passenger ratio is similarly calculated. Under assumptions discussed in Evans [1986], dividing the first fatality ratio by the second gives the probability that a female driver is killed compared to the corresponding probability that a male driver is killed, averaged over the distribution of crashes that occur in actual traffic; thus we obtain the risk to the female driver compared to the risk to the male driver averaged over a wide range of impact severities.

The control occupant, the male passenger, does not enter directly into the result. Because of this key feature of the method, many separate estimates can be calculated by choosing various control occupants. This helps avoid confounding influences due to interactions between subject and control occupant; the basic assumptions of the method require that, given crashes of identical severity, the probability of a passenger death should not depend (in the present example) on the sex of the driver. This assumption would be violated if, for example, the same physical insult were more likely to kill a passenger travelling with a male driver than one travelling with a female driver. Departures from this assumption could arise if, for example, passengers travelling with male drivers tend to be older than those travelling with female drivers. The potentially biasing influences of such confounding interactions can be removed by disaggregating the passenger into age categories so that male and female drivers are examined when accompanied by passengers of similar age. Consequently, the control occupant will be disaggregated into as many categories as the data allow. It is further assumed that the information coded in the FARS data is correct; the potentially biasing effects of missing data are discussed in detail, for a number of specific cases, by Evans [1988b].

Let us give the specific example of comparing unbelted car driver fatality risk for females aged 33-37 to that for males in the same age range (call them 35-year-old drivers). For the control occupant we choose unbelted male right-front passengers aged 16-24, hereafter referred to as 20-year-old male passengers. The 1975-1983 FARS data used by Evans [1988a] show that, in the set of cars used in the first of the two comparisons, 43 female drivers aged 35 were killed while travelling with 20-year-old male passengers, while 23 male passengers aged 20 were killed while travelling with female drivers aged 35. From these values we compute the 35-year-old female driver to 20-year-old male passenger fatality ratio

$$r_1 = 43/23 = 1.870 \qquad \text{Eqn 2-1}$$

That is, for this case, 1.870 female drivers were killed per male passenger killed.

The corresponding information from the set of crashes used for the second comparison, in which the driver is male rather than female, gives a 35-year-old male driver to 20-year-old male passenger ratio

$$r_2 = 206/128 = 1.609 \qquad \text{Eqn 2-2}$$

The female to male fatality risk for 35-year-old car drivers (using 20-year-old male passengers as control occupants) is given by

$$R = r_1/r_2 = 1.162 \qquad \text{Eqn 2-3}$$

Note that any asymmetries between the safety of the driver and passenger seating positions operate in one direction in the first comparison (Eqn 2-1), but in the opposite direction in the second comparison (Eqn 2-2), so that when the Eqn 2-3 ratio is computed any such effects cancel. The driver risk far exceeds the passenger risk regardless of the sex of the driver in the specific case illustrated because of the age difference between subject and control occupants, as discussed later. Based on the raw data, the standard error in R can be calculated as described in Evans [1986; 1988c], and for this case it is 0.332. The relatively large uncertainty arises mainly from the smallest of the four frequency counts in the calculation, namely, the 23 male passengers, aged 16-24, killed travelling with 35-year-old female drivers. Inferences about relative fatality risk in crashes were made by Partyka [1984] and Kahane [1986] using the same ratios explored formally in the double pair comparison method [Evans 1986].

The above estimate of fatality risk to 35-year-old female drivers compared to 35-year-old male drivers was based on one set of control occupants—males aged 16-24. In Evans [1988a] the same calculation is applied for eight classes of control occupants (male and female passengers, each in four age categories). Each calculation provides an independent estimate of the fatality risk to 35-year-old female drivers compared to that to 35-year-old male drivers, and procedures are described in Evans [1986; 1988c] for determining a weighted average and associated standard error.

Effect of Sex on Fatality Risk

Applying the above procedure to car drivers in five-year age cells generates the results plotted in the top left graph of Fig. 2-1. The larger standard errors at

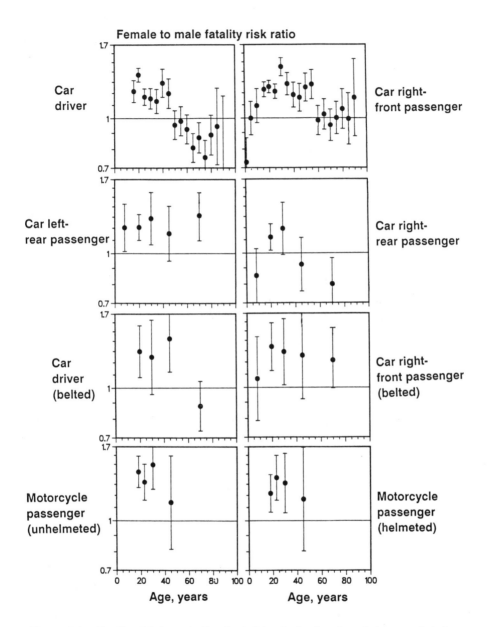

Figure 2-1. Fatality risk from similar physical insults for females relative to males of the same age versus age for eight subject occupant categories. Based on Evans [1988c].

older ages arise because of fewer fatalities to older drivers. The discussion has so far focused exclusively on drivers as subjects. However, the subject can be any vehicle occupant. The top right plot in Fig. 2-1 is for right-front passengers as subjects, using drivers as control occupants; in this case we have data for ages below the minimum for driving. The other plots in Fig. 2-1 show corresponding data for other subject occupants for which substantial numbers of male and female data are available. The rear-car-seat estimates use drivers as control occupants. Fatality risk to female and male motorcycle drivers cannot be compared because of insufficient female fatalities; motorcycle drivers (male) are used as control subjects for the motorcycle passenger comparison.

Subjects in the eight categories in Fig. 2-1 are killed by a wide range of impact mechanisms. For example, car occupant fatalities usually are associated with impact upon the vehicle interior, while motorcyclist fatalities are associated with impact upon objects not related to the vehicle. The absence or presence of steering wheels, safety belts, helmets, cushioning effects of motorcyclist drivers in front, etc. all affect the details of the injury insult. Given these differences, the extent to which the eight plots in Fig. 2-1 show similar features for ages for which there are data in common is notable. For example, for all eight cases, at average age 30, the female fatality risk exceeds the male fatality risk. The eight values range from a low of 15% (that is, $R = 1.15$) for car drivers, to a high of 49% for unhelmeted motorcycle passengers. The weighted average of the eight values is $(31 \pm 6)\%$. There is no indication that any of the eight individual estimates departs in a statistically significant way from this average value, thus supporting the interpretation that the same physical insult is 31% more likely to kill a 30-year-old female than a 30-year-old male.

The features in common in the eight plots in Fig. 2-1 suggest that the effect displayed is due essentially to differences in basic susceptibility to fatal trauma as a function of sex, with the specific nature of the traffic crash being of secondary importance. That is, we would anticipate that fatality risk would similarly depend on sex for other types of potentially fatal physical insults, such as severe falls or blows from objects (including vehicles—the present method cannot be applied to investigate pedestrian fatality risk).

Figure 2-2 presents a synthesis of all the information in Fig. 2-1. The point plotted at each age is the weighted average and standard error for all the points at the same age. The number of points contributing to the average varies between 2 and 8. From about age 15 to age 45, the same physical insult is approximately 25% more likely to kill a female than a male of the same age. By comparing outcomes for similar severity crashes, Foret-Bruno et al. [1990] find that females are about 20% more likely to be injured than are males. They further find explanations of the difference in terms of differences in bone strength measured in tests using cadavers. Figure 2-2 shows that for ages less than about 5, the risk is higher for males than for females. At ages greater than 60 there is a

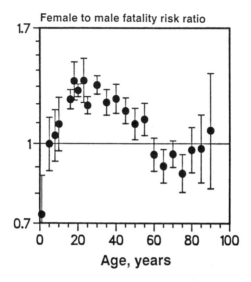

Figure 2-2. Fatality risk from similar physical insults for females relative to males of the same age versus age; averages for the eight subject occupant categories are shown in Figure 2-1. From Evans [1988c].

suggestion that the fatality risk may again become higher for males, although the uncertainty is too great to justify any definitive conclusion.

Effect of Age on Fatality Risk

Age effects are more difficult to determine than the sex effects because of extremely strong interactions between driver age and passenger age—drivers of a given age tend to travel with passengers of a similar age, but of the opposite sex. Although both tendencies facilitated the sex analysis, they make the age analysis more difficult because the cases which provide the crucial information are those less common ones in which the occupants differ in age. Further, the likelihood of finding subject and control occupants of dissimilar age decreases steeply with the magnitude of the age discrepancy. Of even greater concern is the possibility of strong unknown confounding factors. For example, crashes of cars containing two 20-year olds might differ in so many ways from crashes of cars containing a 20-year old and a 70-year old that important violations of the assumptions on which the method is based could occur. To reduce the possibility of such potentially confounding effects, the following approach was adopted, The approach will be explained in terms of male car drivers.

First, fatality risk for 25-year-old male drivers was determined relative to fatality risk for 20-year-old males. Then fatality risk for 30-year-old males was determined in the same way relative to 25-year-old males (not 20-year-olds). The ratio of fatality risk for 30-year olds relative to 20-year olds was then obtained as the product of the two ratios, and the standard error as a combination of the errors for both. The risk for 35-year- old male drivers relative to 20-year-old male drivers was then obtained by multiplying this by the 35 to 30 year ratio, and so on for all ages above (and below) 20 . In this way fatality risks for all the ages relative to age 20 are obtained without individual comparisons involving large differences in age. As the error at any age reflects contributions from each step away from the reference, it will necessarily increase as we move further from the reference age. Applying this process to the data for each of the individual subject-occupant categories generates the 10 plots shown in Fig. 2-3; the two plots more than in Fig. 2-1 are motorcycle drivers. A figure corresponding to Fig. 2-3 for females, is given in Evans [1988a].

Comments previously made regarding Fig. 2-1 apply to Fig. 2-3 (and to the corresponding data in Evans [1988a] for females). The plots are interpreted as showing the age dependence of basic physiological response to physical impact, with the specific details of the physical insult being of less central importance. There is every reason to expect that these same relationships apply to physical insults unrelated to occupant injuries; for example to people struck by vehicles, or to injuries unrelated to traffic. Additional supportive evidence for this interpretation is the finding in Evans [1988a] that age effects are relatively similar for car passengers involved in different types of crashes.

The age effects are summarized in Fig. 2-4, in which each point is the average extracted from the 10 different male occupants and 8 different female occupants. The form of both figures at young ages explains part of the increase in the number of occupant fatalities per capita with declining age for young children reported by Baker [1979]. The relations in Fig. 2-4 can be expressed analytically as

$$R_{males}(A) = \exp 0.0231 (A - 20) = 0.630 \exp (0.0231 A) \qquad \text{Eqn 2-4}$$

and

$$R_{females}(A) = 1.3 \exp 0.0197 (A - 20) = 0.877 \exp (0.0197 A) \qquad \text{Eqn 2-5}$$

for $A \geq 20$, where A is the age in years and R is the probability that a given impact will prove fatal relative to the probability that the same impact will kill a 20-year-old male. Once age exceeds about 20, fatality risk grows at an approximately uniform rate of $(2.3 \pm 0.2)\%$ per year for males and $(2.0 \pm 0.2)\%$ per year for females. At age 70 the risk is about three times what it is at age

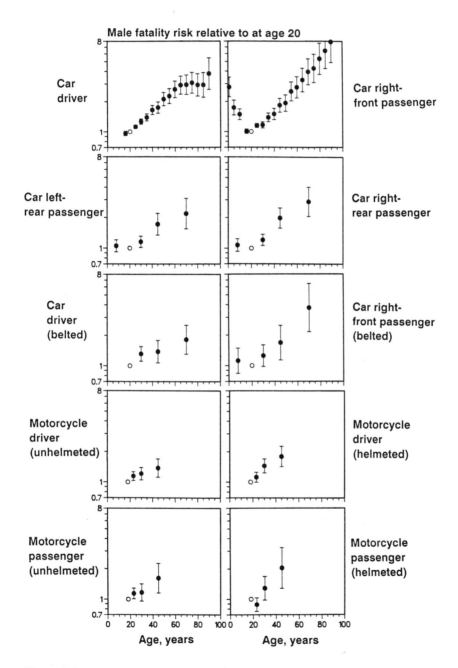

Figure 2-3.   Fatality risk from similar physical insults for males of different ages compared to that for 20-year-old males for ten subject occupant categories. Based on Evans [1988c].

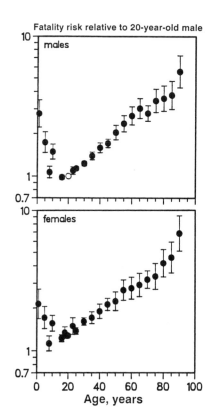

Figure 2-4. Fatality risk from similar physical insults for males and females relative to the same reference case, 20-year-old males. From Evans [1988c].

20. Dividing Eqn 2-5 by Eqn 2-4 produces the broad effect, but not the details, of the Fig. 2-2 direct comparison of female to male risk.

The data used to derive the age and sex effects were included irrespective of alcohol involvement. Because alcohol use increases the risk of death from the same impact (Chapter 7), and its use is more associated with males and the young, it is likely that the results reported above underestimate the degree to which females are more likely than males to be killed by the same physical impact, and the extent to which risk increases with age.

VARIOUS DRIVER FATALITY RATES

For the remainder of this chapter driver will be used to mean a driver of any motorized vehicle, including a motorcycle, truck, bus, etc. This choice ensures

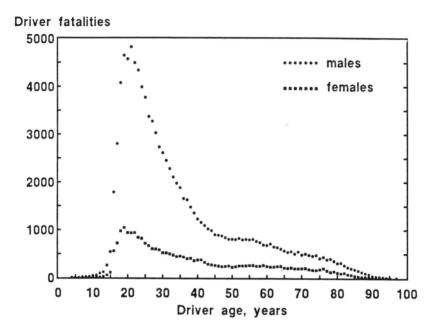

Figure 2-5. Number of driver fatalities (all motorized vehicles) versus sex and age, based on FARS 1981-1985. From Evans [1988c].

a simple categorization of all traffic fatalities as either drivers or non-drivers; pedalcyclists are considered non-drivers. The dependence of driver fatalities on age and sex examined below, which is based on Evans [1988c], thus reflects the choice of vehicle, how it is used, and what the consequences of a crash are, given that one occurs, all factors which are themselves strongly influenced by age and sex. (Some information parallel to that presented here, but for car drivers only, is given in Evans [1987]).

Figure 2-5 shows the number of driver fatalities versus age and sex for FARS 1981-1985. The pattern is very stable from year to year—the plots (with the ordinate scale to 1000 rather than 5000) for each of the individual FARS years look essentially the same as Fig. 2-5, except for an increase in random variation, or noise. The steep decline with age (the value for 65-year-old males is 0.123 times what it is for 20-year-old males) is, in part, due to the fact that there are more younger than older people in the US population.

Figure 2-6 shows the data in Fig. 2-5 normalized for population using data from the Bureau of the Census [1987] giving estimates of the resident population on July 1 by age (in 1 year increments) and sex. The point plotted in Fig. 2-6 at age 65 is the number of 65-year-old drivers killed from 1981-1985 divided

Driver fatalities per million population

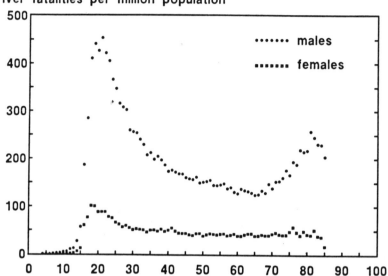

Figure 2-6. Driver fatalities (all motorized vehicles) per million population versus sex and age. Based on FARS and US Bureau of the Census data, 1981-1985. From Evans [1988c].

by the sum of the number of 65-year olds in each of these years. The plot is therefore an average, weighted by population, of graphs for individual years, all of which look similar (with more noise) to Fig. 2-6. Fig. 2-6 shows that driver deaths per capita increase with age for males over about age 65.

Figure 2-7 shows driver fatalities per licensed driver, as given by the Federal Highway Administration [1983]. The data plotted are for 1983 to ensure compatibility with the estimates of distance of travel introduced for the next graph. The general pattern in Fig. 2-7 differs from that in Fig. 2-6 only insofar as the fraction of the population holding driving licenses varies with age; in particular, older females are less likely than those in mid life (in 1983) to have driver licenses; for example, about 70% of 70-year-old females have licenses, compared to over 90% for similarly aged males or 30-year-old females [Federal Highway Administration 1983]. Thus, in contrast to Fig. 2-6, the rates in Fig. 2-7 increase with age for males and females older than about 65.

Figure 2-8 shows, on a logarithmic scale, the number of driver fatalities per unit distance of travel. This rate is estimated by dividing driver fatalities by the product of the number of licensed drivers and the average distance of travel per

Driver fatalities per million licensed drivers

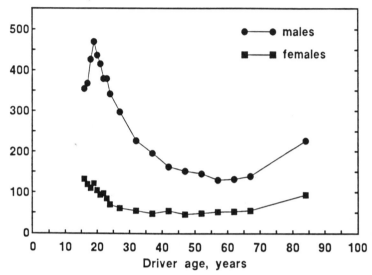

Figure 2-7.   Driver fatalities (all motorized vehicles) per million licensed drivers versus sex and age. Based on FARS and Federal Highway Administration data, 1983. From Evans [1988c].

driver as determined in the Nationwide Personal Transportation Study data [US Department of Transportation 1985] for 1983. Fig. 2-8 shows a further rise for older and younger ages above the average because older and younger drivers travel less than average drivers do. For example, the average annual distance of travel for male drivers aged 65-69, aged 35-39, and aged 16 is, respectively, 14 500 km, 31 400 km, and 2 200 km.

INVOLVEMENT RATES IN SEVERE CRASHES

Increases of various crash measures with age like those in Figs 2-7 and 2-8 have contributed to concerns regarding the driving performance of older drivers. Such concerns find additional support in research showing various changes in mental and sensory functions as humans age [Charness 1985; Reff and Schneider 1982; Welford 1981]. Declines with age have been found for such driving tasks as reading signs at night [Sivak, Olson, and Pastalan 1981], perceiving and reacting to roadway hazards [Olson and Sivak 1986], and general driver performance [Yanik 1985]. Ranney and Pulling [1989] find reaction times for skills related to vehicle control increase with age. Involvement rates in fatal crashes do not

Driver fatalities per billion km of travel

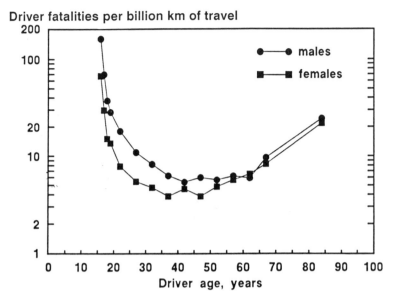

Figure 2-8. Driver fatalities (all motorized vehicles) per billion km of travel versus sex and age. Based on FARS, Federal Highway Administration and Nationwide Personal Transportation Study data for 1983. From Evans [1988c].

correctly reflect such changes, because of the strong influence of age on fatality risk when a crash occurs. The number of drivers of given age and sex killed should be considered to be the product of two factors:

1. The number of involvements in very serious crashes
2. The probability that involvement proves fatal.

The first factor reflects influences from all use and behavioral factors, such as amount and type of driving, driver capabilities, type of vehicle driven, time of day, degree of intoxication, and driving risks. The second factor can be influenced also by such behavioral factors as safety belt use and alcohol consumption. Apart from such considerations, which will be discussed in Chapters 7 and 9, the probability that a given crash results in death is essentially physiological rather than behavioral in nature, and for the present purposes can be adequately approximated by Eqns 2-4 and 2-5. When driver age is 16 to 20, we assume $R = 1$ for males an $R = 1.3$ for females; that is, the fatality risk from the same severity crash is the same as for a 20-year-old driver of the same sex.

Fatality rates focus on the outcome, not the severity of the crash that led to

Severe crash involvements per million licensed drivers

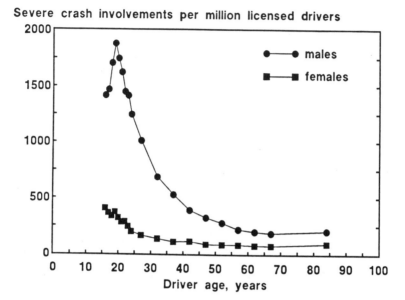

Figure 2-9.   Estimated driver involvements (all motorized vehicles) per million licensed drivers in crashes of sufficient severity to kill 80-year-old-male drivers versus sex and age. From Evans [1988c].

the death. Here we examine involvement rates in crashes of similar severity by considering crashes in a severity range greater than or equal to that sufficient to kill 80-year-old male drivers, for which case R has a value of 4.0 (Eqn 2-4). Consider a set of crashes in which N fatalities occur to 80-year-old males. If these crashes were repeated, keeping all factors the same except the drivers, then we would expect $0.25N$ fatalities for 20-year-old male drivers and $0.325N$ fatalities for 20-year-old female drivers (Eqn 2-5). In order to obtain the same number of fatalities, 4.0 times as many crashes by 20-year-old male drivers, and 3.1 times as many crashes by 20-year-old female drivers are required. In this way we can use the observed numbers of fatalities to infer involvement rates in crashes in the severity range sufficient to kill 80-year-old male drivers.

Figure 2-9 shows the number of involvements in crashes in the same severity range (that necessary to kill 80-year-old males) per licensed driver versus age and sex. In contrast to Fig. 2-7, there is now no longer any noticeable upward trend at older ages. The upward trend in Fig. 2-7 was caused by the increase in fatality risk from the same impact with increasing age, and not by an increase in involvements with increasing age.

Severe crash involvements per unit distance of travel (Fig. 2-10) increase with

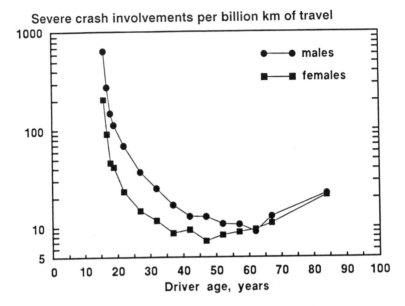

Figure 2-10. Estimated driver involvements (all motorized vehicles) per billion km of travel in crashes of sufficient severity to kill 80-year-old-male drivers versus sex and age. From Evans [1988c].

increasing driver age for ages above about 60. However, the increase is smaller than in Fig. 2-8; even at the oldest age plotted, the rates for males and females are still less than those for male drivers under age 30.

THREAT TO OTHER ROAD USERS

All the above considerations focused on how the age and sex of a driver influence the threat to the driver's own life. In many ways this risk is presumed to be largely under the control of the driver. Here we address how the risk a driver poses to other road users depends on the driver's age and sex. This question raises a host of different legal and moral issues which are relevant to discussions of driver licensing policy, in particular licensing test procedures that may make it more difficult for the elderly to obtain licenses. We investigate the threat to other road users by examining the number of crashes in which pedestrians are killed as a function of the age and sex of drivers (of any type of motorized vehicle) involved in the crashes. Attention is confined to single vehicle crashes because when more than one vehicle is involved it is not always possible to determine from the FARS data which vehicle struck the pedestrian. In addition,

Pedestrian fatality crashes

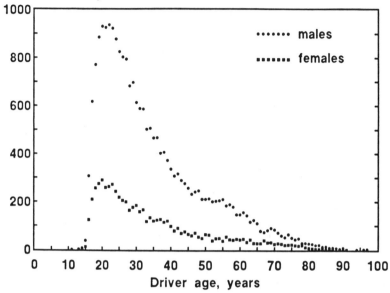

Figure 2-11. Number of single-vehicle crashes in which one or more pedestrians were killed versus the age and sex of the driver, based on FARS 1981–1985. From Evans [1988c].

involvement in multiple vehicle crashes poses threats to drivers different from those of single vehicle crashes in which pedestrians are killed; the drivers of cars in single-vehicle pedestrian-fatality crashes are themselves usually not seriously injured. No assumption is made regarding responsibility in pedestrian fatality crashes; the FARS data show about one third of fatally injured pedestrians have blood alcohol concentrations in excess of the legal limit for driver intoxication in most US states.

Figures 2-11 through 2-14 show the variables for crashes involving pedestrian fatalities corresponding to those for driver fatalities in Figs. 2-5 through 2-8. The similarity between each corresponding set of curves reflects the extent to which pedestrian fatalities are proportional to driver fatalities, the basis of the pedestrian fatality exposure approach to be discussed in Chapter 4. The only curve that suggests any increase in threat to other road users as drivers age is Fig. 2-14, which shows pedestrian fatality crashes per unit distance of travel. Here the increase is small, and applies only at ages above about 70; it is quite overshadowed by the much greater values associated with young drivers of either sex.

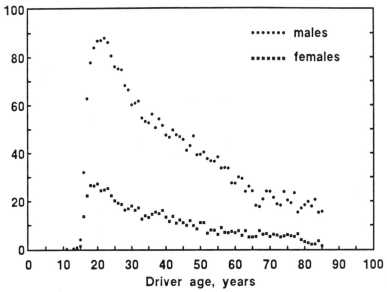

Figure 2-12. Number of single-vehicle crashes per million population in which one or more pedestrians were killed versus the age and sex of the driver. Based on FARS and US Bureau of the Census data for 1981-1985. From Evans [1988c].

HOW SERIOUS IS THE OLDER-DRIVER PROBLEM?

The ten figures (Figs. 2-5 through 2-14) show relations between driver age and a variety of measures of risk of involvement in severe and fatal traffic crashes for male and female drivers. For all 20 comparisons of values at age 65 to values at age 20 for the same sex, the value at age 65 was less than (in most cases substantially less than) the value at age 20 (numerical values are given in Evans [1988c]). For example, 65-year-old male drivers were involved in 88 percent fewer single vehicle crashes in which pedestrians died than were 20-year-old male drivers; when normalized to the same distance of driving, the older driver's rate becomes 72% less.

When 65-year-old drivers are compared to 40-year-old drivers, the only variable which is greater for the older male drivers is driver fatalities per unit distance of travel; here the rate for 65-year-olds exceeds that for 40-year-olds by 33%. For female drivers, three variables are larger at age 65 than at age 40, namely number of drivers killed per licensed driver (5% larger), driver fatalities per unit

Pedestrian fatality crashes per million licensed drivers

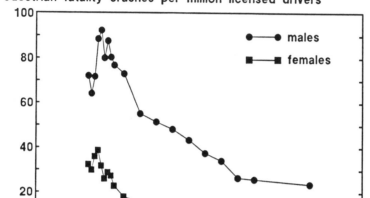

Figure 2-13. Number of single-vehicle crashes per million licensed drivers in which one or more pedestrians were killed versus the age and sex of the driver. Based on FARS and Federal Highway Administration data for 1983. From Evans [1988c].

distance of travel (77% larger), and driver involvements in severe crashes per unit distance of travel (13% larger).

Thus for some measures 65-year-old drivers are more at risk than 40-year-old drivers, though not more at risk than 20-year-old drivers. In all the cases where the risk at age 65 exceeds that at age 40, the increased risk is borne by the driver; in no case studied did the 65-year-old driver pose a greater threat to pedestrians than did the 40-year-old driver. The source data for driver licenses and distances of travel place all drivers 70 and older in the same category, which precluded any detailed examination at ages beyond the 60s. It would be desirable if organizations tabulating data such as the number of licensed drivers would avoid such broad aggregation when substantial quantities of data are available at older ages. The fatality and population data, which are available in one year increments to age 85, indicate a declining threat to other users (Fig. 2-12) through age 85 for both sexes on a per capita basis. The upward trend in the corresponding graph for male driver fatalities (Fig. 2-6) is largely explained by the greater likelihood of fatality in a crash.

The graphs which best reflect the behavioral aspects of driving, namely, driver involvements in crashes in the same high severity range per unit distance of

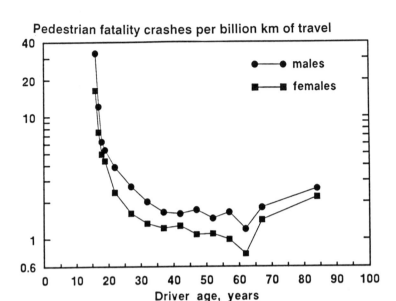

Figure 2-14.   Number of single-vehicle crashes per billion km of travel in which one or more pedestrians were killed versus the age and sex of the driver. Based on FARS, Federal Highway Administration and Nationwide Personal Transportation Study data for 1983. From Evans [1988c].

travel, and crashes in which pedestrians are killed per unit distance of travel (Figs. 2-10 and 2-14) show remarkably similar features. Drivers from about age 30 to 60 have the lowest involvement rates. As age decreases below 30, rates increase at an increasing rate. For ages greater than about 60, rates increase somewhat, but much less rapidly than as one approaches the younger ages in the graphs. Male rates are consistently higher than those for females.

Much larger than any proportionate increase in driver risk with increasing age is the decline in distance of driving. For example, male drivers 70 and over drive, on average, 9 300 km/year, compared to 31 000 km/year for 35 to 39 year-old drivers; the corresponding values for female drivers are 4 300 km/year and 12 600 km/year, respectively. The problem of aging may thus be more one of reduced mobility than of reduced safety. As mental and sensory abilities decline, the dominant response is less driving, especially under conditions of elevated risk, rather than a net increase in risk from driving; as people age, the threat they pose to other road users declines.

The above discussion has focused on how various measures depend on average chronological age. Not only do various measures of driver performance decline

Pedestrian fatalities

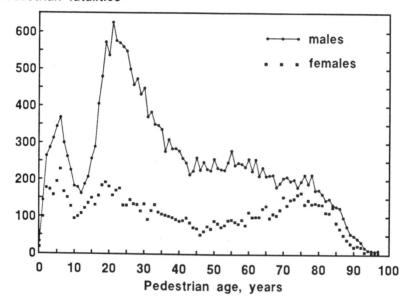

Figure 2-15.   Number of pedestrian fatalities versus sex and age, based on FARS 1981-1985. Maximum values occur at ages 6 and 21 for males and at ages 6 and 19 for females. From Evans [1987].

with age, but variability amongst individuals also increases [Ranney and Pulling 1990], underlying the importance of not judging an individual's driving ability on the basis of chronological age. As individuals age, risk of death increases rapidly, so the fraction of the total risk that is due to motor vehicle crashes declines (Fig. 14-2 and related discussion).

PEDESTRIAN INVOLVEMENTS IN FATAL AND SEVERE CRASHES

Above we examined the age and sex of *drivers* involved in crashes in which pedestrians were killed. We now examine the age and sex of the *pedestrians* involved, without regard to the characteristics of the involved drivers, using 1981-1985 FARS data [Evans 1987].

Fig. 2-15 shows the distribution of pedestrian fatalities by pedestrian age and sex. In order to make the graph easier to follow, the male data have been joined by lines, and the peak values are identified in the caption. The 1981-1985 FARS data show 596 six-year-old child fatalities (an average of 73 six-year-old boys killed per year and 46 six-year-old girls).

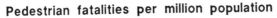

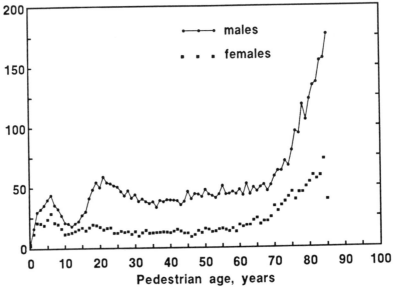

Figure 2-16. Pedestrian fatalities per million population versus sex and age. Based on FARS and US Bureau of the Census data for 1981-1985. Maximum values occur for males at ages 6 and 21, and for females at ages 6 and 18. From Evans [1987].

The same data normalized by population are shown in Fig. 2-16. In Chapter 6 (Fig. 6-5) we comment further on the large systematic difference dependent on sex, showing higher male than female pedestrian fatality rates for all ages, including the first year of life.

Part of the large increase in pedestrian fatalities per capita at older ages arises from the greater likelihood that the older person will be killed in a crash which a younger one would survive. In order to estimate the risk of involvement in a severe crash, as distinct from the outcome, we again use the relationships between risk of death from the same impact and sex and age given in Eqns 2-4 and 2-5. Fig. 2-17 shows the number of pedestrian involvements in crashes in the severity range equal to or greater than that necessary to kill an 80-year-old male pedestrian. Like the driver fatality data, the pedestrian fatality data show peaks at about age 20 for males and females. The increasing involvement in severe pedestrian crashes with increasing age at ages above about 60 probably reflects decreasing perceptual skills and agility, and also perhaps reflects increased pedestrian exposure because of less driving.

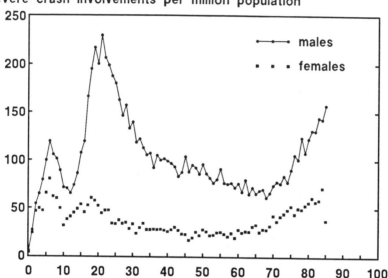

Figure 2-17. Estimated pedestrian involvements per million population in crashes of sufficient severity to kill 80-year-old male pedestrians versus sex and age. From Evans [1987].

OVERINVOLVEMENT OF YOUNG ROAD USERS

A feature common to all ten figures (Figs. 2-5 through 2-14) showing driver rates versus sex and age is the dramatically higher values for drivers in their late teens and early twenties, especially male drivers. Similarly, young male pedestrians had higher involvement rates in severe crashes than persons of either sex at any other age for which data are available (up to 85 years) (Fig. 2-17). The only rate for which young males did not have the highest value was pedestrian fatalities per capita (Fig. 2-16), a rate which increases rapidly with age largely because of increased likelihood of death from crashes which younger pedestrians would survive.

The overinvolvement of young, and male, road users is one of the largest and most consistently observed phenomena in traffic throughout the world. It is so robust and repeatable that it is almost like a law of nature. Its magnitude suggests that it must involve much more than a mere lack of driving (or road-crossing) experience. This question is of such central importance in traffic safety that various additional aspects of it will be discussed in many of the later chapters.

CONCLUSIONS

From about age 15 to age 45, the same physical insult is approximately 25% more likely to kill a female than a male of the same age. For ages less than about 5, the risk is higher for males than for females. These results were obtained by applying double pair comparison (a method which allows inferences without external measures of exposure) to 80 000 fatalities coded in the FARS data. Because effects are similar for different occupants (unbelted car drivers, helmeted motorcycle passengers, etc.), the results are interpreted to apply to physical insults in general, and not just to those sustained in traffic crashes. Applying the same approach to investigate age effects shows that for ages greater than about 20, fatality risk grows at an approximately uniform rate of $(2.3 \pm 0.2)\%$ per year for males and $(2.0 \pm 0.2)\%$ per year for females; at age 70 the risk is about three times what it is at 20.

The number of fatalities suffered by a group of road users does not measure the number of crashes in which the group is involved because the outcome (the fatality) depends on a behavioral and a physiological factor—the involvement in the crash and the probability that the impacts sustained in the crash lead to death. The dependence of the behavioral factor was inferred from the observed number of fatalities, using the relationships between probability of death from the same impact, and sex, and age. Ten measures of driver involvement in crashes (fatalities per capita, involvements in severe crashes per unit distance of travel, involvements in crashes in which pedestrians were killed, etc.) consistently show much higher rates for drivers in their late teens and early twenties, and higher values for male drivers. Male pedestrians of these same ages were overinvolved in pedestrian crashes, indicating consistently the disproportionate contribution of this group of road users to traffic crashes.

As drivers age they pose ever decreasing threats to other road users, as indicated by the number of pedestrian fatality crashes in which they are involved. One reason why they pose a reduced threat to others is a reduction in driving with increasing age. For every one of a large number of measures of crash involvement examined, 65-year-old drivers had lower rates than 20-year-old drivers. Even though by some measures 65-year-old drivers had higher rates than 40-year-old drivers, the problem of the aging driver may be more one of reduced mobility than of reduced safety.

REFERENCES

Baker, S.P. Motor vehicle occupant deaths in young children. *Pediatrics* 64:860–861; 1979.
Baker, S.P.; O'Neill, B.; Karph, R.S. *The Injury Fact Book*. Lexington, MA: Lexington Books; 1984.
Bureau of the Census. Estimates of the population of the United States, by age, sex and race: 1980

to 1985. Series P–25, no. 985. Washington, DC: US Department of Commerce, Washington, Government Printing Office; 1987.

Charness, N., editor. *Ageing and Human Performance*. New York: John Wiley; 1985.

Evans, L. Double pair comparison—a new method to determine how occupant characteristics affect fatality risk in traffic crashes. *Accident Analysis and Prevention* 18:217–227; 1986.

Evans, L. Young driver involvement in severe car crashes. *Alcohol, Drugs, and Driving* 3(3–4):63–78; 1987.

Evans, L. Risk of fatality from physical trauma versus sex and age. *Journal of Trauma* 28:368–378; 1988a.

Evans, L. Examination of some possible biases in double pair comparison estimates of safety belt effectiveness. *Accident Analysis and Prevention* 20:215–218; 1988b.

Evans, L. Older driver involvement in fatal and severe traffic crashes. *Journal of Gerontology: Social Sciences* 43:S186–S193; 1988c.

Federal Highway Administration. *Highway Statistics, 1983*. Washington, DC: US Department of Transportation, Government Printing Office; 1983.

Foret-Bruno, J.Y.; Faverjon, G.; Brun-Cassan, F.; Tarriere, C.; Got, C.; Patel, A.; Guillon, F. Females more vulnerable than males in road accidents. Proceedings of the XXIII FISITA Congress, Torina, Italy, Vol. 1, p. 941–947; 7–11 May 1990.

Haight, F.A. The place of safety research in transportation research. *Transportation Research* 19A:373–376; 1985.

Kahane, C.J. An evaluation of child passenger safety: the effectiveness and benefits of safety seats. Washington, DC: National Highway Traffic Safety Administration, report DOT HS–806 890; February 1986.

National Highway Traffic Safety Administration. *Fatal Accident Reporting System 1988*. Document DOT HS 807 507. Washington, DC; December 1989.

National Safety Council. *Accident Facts*. Chicago, IL; 1989 edition (issued annually).

Olson, P.L.; Sivak, M. Perception–response time to unexpected roadway hazards. *Human Factors* 28:91–96; 1986.

Partyka, S.C. Restraint use and fatality risk for infants and toddlers. Washington, DC: National Highway Traffic Safety Administration; May 1984.

Ranney, T.A.; Pulling, N.H. Relation of individual differences in information–processing ability to driving performance. Human Factors Society, Proceedings of the 33rd Annual Meeting, Denver, CO, p. 965–969; 16–20 October 1989.

Ranney, T.A.; Pulling, N.H. Performance differences on driving and laboratory tasks between drivers of different ages. Paper 890270, presented to the 69th Annual Meeting of the Transportation Research Board, Washington, DC; 7–11 January 1990.

Reff, M.E.; Schneider, E.L., editors. *Biological Markers of Ageing*. Washington, DC: US Department of Health and Human Services, NIH publication 82–2221; April 1982.

Sivak, M.; Olson, P.L.; Pastalan, L.A. Effect of driver's age on nighttime legibility of highway signs. *Human Factors* 23:59–64; 1981.

US Department of Transportation. Survey data tabulations; 1983–1984. Nationwide Personal Transportation Study. Report DOT–P36–85–1. Washington, DC; November 1985.

Verbrugge, L.M. Sex differentials in health. *Public Health Reports* 97:417–432; 1982.

Waller, J.A. *Injury control—A Guide to the Causes and Prevention of Trauma*. Lexington, MA: Lexington Books; 1985.

Welford, A.T. Signal, noise, performance, and age. *Human Factors* 23:97–109; 1981.

Yanik, A.J. What accident data reveal about elderly drivers. SAE paper 851688. Warrendale, PA: Society of Automotive Engineers; 1985.

3 An Overview of United States Traffic Fatalities

INTRODUCTION

The 1988 FARS data code 42 119 fatal crashes in the US in which 47 093 people were killed, for an average of 1.118 fatalities per fatal crash; 70% of those killed were male. Fig. 3-1 shows a distribution of these fatalities by different categories of road users. Percentages (of the 47 093 fatalities that occurred in 1988) are shown rather than the numbers because the pattern is fairly stable from year to year. A year to year decrease (increase) in overall fatalities tends to increase (or decrease) the number of fatalities in each cell in Fig. 3-1 in an approximately proportional way, so that the percentages shown remain fairly constant from year to year [see also Hedlund 1985; National Highway Traffic Safety Administration 1989 (and earlier years)]. For FARS data from 1975 through 1988 the annual number of fatalities varied from a low of 42 584 in 1983 to a high of 51 093 in 1979. The pattern in Fig. 3-1 would not persist over long time trends—in the 1930s about 35% of all traffic fatalities were pedestrians compared to 14.7% in 1988.

Another reason why we generally display percentages is that, in nearly all FARS categories, there are cases with some unknown variables (for example, the occupant's age, or the make of the vehicle, is unknown). When unknown cases are few, distributing them into other categories in proportion to the numbers already in those categories is appropriate. Only in cases of variables for which there are substantial numbers in the unknown category (such as safety belt use or blood alcohol concentration) will we need to address this problem more directly.

FRACTION OF FATALITIES THAT ARE DRIVERS

While every traffic crash involves at least one driver, it is important to note, from Fig. 3-1, that 42% of traffic fatalities are not drivers, with the percentage being higher for other countries because of a larger proportion of non-occupant fatalities, and higher occupancy rates in vehicles. The fraction of all traffic fatalities that are drivers depends strongly on sex and age, as shown in Fig. 3-2. Only a very small fraction of those killed at ages below the age required to obtain a driving license are drivers. The fraction of male fatalities that are drivers exceeds 70% between ages 20 and 40. The fraction of male traffic fatalities that are drivers exceeds the fraction of female fatalities that are drivers at every age, based on the 1983-1985 FARS data used to produce Fig. 3-2.

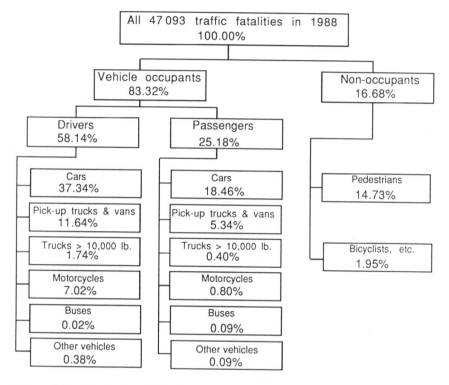

Figure 3-1.   Distribution of fatalities in 1988 according to the road user killed. The values in all boxes indicate the percent of the total 47 093 fatalities. Computed from FARS 1988.

CAR OCCUPANTS

Fig. 3-1 shows that 56% of all fatalities are occupants of cars. Of those killed in motorized vehicles, 67% are killed in cars; 64% of all drivers killed are drivers of cars. Because of the dominant role of car occupants in overall occupant fatalities we examine car occupant fatalities in some detail below. Parallel information for all occupants is less informative because of the wide range of occupants, from those in motorcycles to those in buses.

Vehicles and Objects Struck

The 26 069 car occupant fatalities in 1988 are shown in Fig. 3-3 according to the other vehicles involved. The most important factor to note here is that the most common type of crash leading to a car-occupant fatality is a single-car

(Driver fatalities)/(all traffic fatalities)

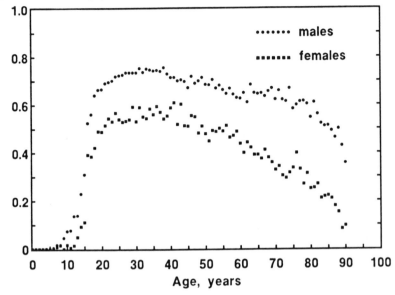

Figure 3-2. Ratio of driver fatalities (all motor vehicles) to all traffic fatalities (drivers, passengers, pedalcyclists, pedestrians) based on FARS 1983-1985. From Evans [1988].

crash; this is at variance with the popular image of a fatal crash most typically involving two cars. This misconception probably arises because the most common type of crash, without regard to injury level, is indeed a two-car crash. If we consider only minor property damage crashes, two-car crashes dominate, with rear-end *fender bender* incidents being most common. Crashes involving cars travelling in congested traffic in the same direction, although numerous, are unlikely to prove fatal. As we focus on crashes of increasing severity, the role of two-car crashes becomes less dominant, and that of single-car crashes more dominant.

Single-car crashes are either non-collisions or crashes into objects (a distribution is shown in Fig. 3-3). More than 90% of the non-collision crashes are rollovers; the remainder is the sum of occupants killed by fire, explosion, immersion in water, falling from the vehicle, injuries sustained in non-crashing vehicles, and other types of non-collisions. The most commonly struck objects which lead to car occupant deaths are trees, reflecting the large number of trees close to roadways, especially in rural two-lane roads. The "all other objects" category includes highway sign posts, boulders, walls, fire hydrants, animals, impact attenuators and many other objects which make small contributions to the total.

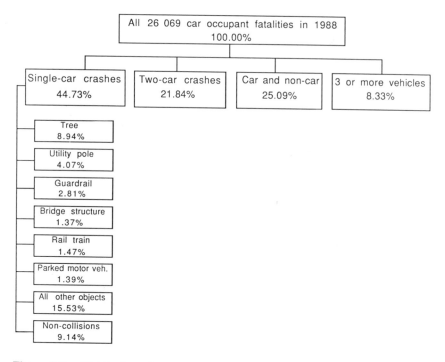

Figure 3-3. Distribution of car occupants killed in 1988 according to the number of vehicles involved. The values in all boxes indicate the percent of the total 26 069 car occupant fatalities. Computed from FARS 1988.

Fatalities According to Seating Position

Car occupants killed are shown in Fig. 3-4 distributed according to the seat in which they were travelling. This figure, in common with previous figures, uses 1988 FARS data. It therefore reflects the mix of cars by type and model year which were on the roads in 1988. Only occupants coded as occupying one of the six seats are included in the analysis—about 0.3% are coded as being in unknown seats. The distributions in Fig. 3-4 are important when considering questions of occupant protection. A device that reduces driver fatality risk by 1% would prevent a larger number of fatalities than one which reduces center-rear passenger fatality risk by 60%.

Relative Fatality Risk in Different Seats

The data in Fig. 3-4 do not enable us to address the relative risk of sitting in different seats, because a greater number of fatalities in one seat occurs mainly

	D R I V E R	Center-front passenger	Right-front passenger
All	68.1%	0.8%	23.1%
Restrained	66.0	0.2	27.5
Unrestrained	68.1	1.0	22.2

	Left-rear passenger	Center-rear passenger	Right-rear passenger
All	3.2%	1.1%	3.8%
Restrained	2.4	0.5	3.4
Unrestrained	3.5	1.3	3.9

Figure 3-4. Distribution of car-occupants killed according to seating position, and restraint use. Computed from FARS 1988. Restrained includes use of any type of safety belt, or travelling in an airbag-equipped seating position.

due to a higher occupancy rate in that seat. However, even if we could correct for different occupancy rates, many other factors that affect fatality risk would still make it difficult to isolate the influence of the seating position, as such. Cars with only one occupant are involved in crashes of different types and severity than cars with more than one occupant. Occupants in different seats have different distributions by sex and age, factors that have a substantial influence on fatality risk (Chapter 2). We thus encounter an example of the problem of exposure, referred to in Chapter 1, which arises when attempts are made to make inferences from field data.

This problem is addressed [Evans and Frick 1988a] by selecting from 1975–1985 FARS data cars in which there were drivers and passengers in specified seats. In order to avoid confounding sex and age effects, only cases in which the driver and passenger are of the same sex, and have ages within three years of each other, are included. Also, occupants coded as using any restraint system, or who were less than 16 years old, are excluded from the analysis. From data restricted in this way, the ratio R

$$R = \frac{\text{Number of passenger fatalities in specified seat}}{\text{Number of driver fatalities}} \qquad \text{Eqn 3-1}$$

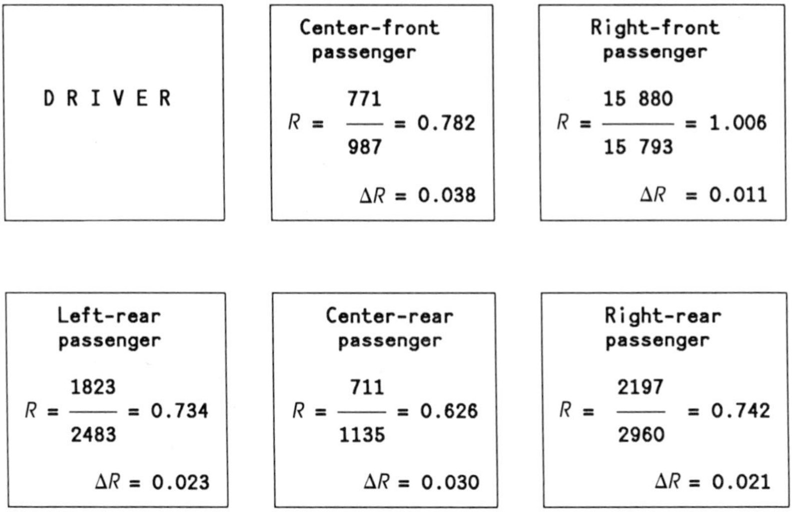

	Center-front passenger	Right-front passenger
D R I V E R	$R = \dfrac{771}{987} = 0.782$ $\Delta R = 0.038$	$R = \dfrac{15\ 880}{15\ 793} = 1.006$ $\Delta R = 0.011$

Left-rear passenger	Center-rear passenger	Right-rear passenger
$R = \dfrac{1823}{2483} = 0.734$ $\Delta R = 0.023$	$R = \dfrac{711}{1135} = 0.626$ $\Delta R = 0.030$	$R = \dfrac{2197}{2960} = 0.742$ $\Delta R = 0.021$

Figure 3-5.   Fatality risk, R, relative to that of a driver, for passengers in different seats. From Evans and Frick [1988].

is computed. Because all the occupants in Eqn 3-1 are killed in crashes in which the other occupant is also present in the car, and both occupants are of the same sex and similar age, R provides a remarkably assumption-free estimate of the difference in risk due to differences in the physical environment of the different seating positions. Thus R is essentially free from confounding effects due to occupant characteristics being correlated with the use of different seats.

Raw data and computed values of R are shown in Fig. 3-5; because all values are relative to the driver, there is no computed relative risk for the driver, for whom, by definition, $R = 1$. For cars containing a driver and a right-front passenger, there are 15 880 right-front passenger fatalities compared to 15 793 driver fatalities; thus for a right-front passenger the relative fatality risk is $R = 1.006 \pm 0.011$. The error is computed assuming that the fatalities arise from a Poisson process. Thus the finding is that, to high precision, there is no difference in fatality risk to drivers and right-front passengers. The center-front seat $R = 0.78 \pm 0.04$ indicates that this position is associated with a $(22 \pm 4)\%$ lower fatality risk than the outboard (driver or right-front passenger) front positions. The outboard-rear seats have a composite $R = 0.739 \pm 0.015$. That is, for unrestrained occupants in outboard seating positions, rear seats are associated with a fatality risk $(26.1 \pm 1.5)\%$ lower than for front seats.

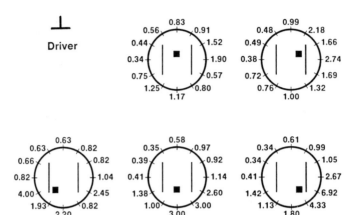

Figure 3-6.   Fatality risk, R, relative to that of a driver, for passengers in different seats as a function of principal impact point. From Evans and Frick [1988].

Seating Position and Direction of Impact

The FARS data contain a principal impact point variable, defined as the impact that is judged to have produced the greatest personal injury or property damage for a particular vehicle. The impact refers to the location on the vehicle sustaining damage, so that a principal impact point at 12 o'clock means that the damage is in the center-front of the vehicle. The actual direction of impact cannot be inferred from the damage alone—this would require a detailed post-crash investigation. The center front could be damaged by, say, an oblique impact into a tree. However, a principal impact point at 12 o'clock may be approximately interpreted as indicating, on average at least, head-on impacts.

Figure 3-6 shows the relative risk for the five passenger seating positions versus principal impact point, displayed in the same bird's eye view of the vehicle travelling up the page, used in Figs 3-4 and 3-5. All values are relative to a value of one for drivers. Focusing on the right-front passenger data, which is displayed in the right-top circle in Fig. 3-6, we note that when the impact is from the right, the right-front passenger is 2.74 times as likely to die as is the driver (as before, both occupants are of the same sex, with ages within three years of each other). When the impact is from the left, then the right-front passenger is 0.38 times as likely to die as the driver; this could also be expressed by saying that the driver is $1/0.38 = 2.63$ times as likely to die as is the right-front passenger. The essential symmetry (reflected in the closeness of the ratios 2.74 and 2.63) is to be expected on physical grounds, and increases confidence in the estimates. For principal impact point 12 o'clock, the value of R for right-front passengers is 0.988 ± 0.019. Thus the similarity of fatality risk to drivers and right-front passengers applies also to the frontal case. Drivers and right-front passengers are equally likely to be killed from rear impacts ($R = 1.00 \pm 0.10$). In frontal crashes, the advantage of rear compared to corresponding front seating positions is larger than for all crash directions combined. The general pattern in Fig. 3-6 shows that occupants near the point of impact are at much greater fatality risk than those far from the point of impact. Although rear occupants are at much greater risk than front occupants in rear-impact crashes, such crashes account for less than 5% of all fatalities. The overall 26% lower fatality risk in rear seats as compared to front seats reflects the predominance of frontal fatal crashes.

A corresponding phenomenon occurs for motorcyclists, where it is found [Evans and Frick 1988b] that fatality risk in the driver seat is $(26 \pm 2)\%$ greater than that in the passenger seat; for frontal crashes the difference is $(40\% \pm 6)\%$, again demonstrating the greater risk associated with being nearer the impact. For non-frontal crashes there is no difference between driver and passenger risk ($R = 1.01 \pm 0.04$). In the motorcycle case, the front occupant probably helps cushion the impact for the passenger.

An additional finding in the Evans and Frick [1988a] study of car occupant risk is that there are 38% more impacts of high severity from the right than from the left, a result possibly reflecting asymmetries resulting from driving on the right; it would be interesting to see if countries which drive on the left produce an opposite effect.

Passenger Compared to Driver Risk Versus Model Year

The finding that the fatality risk to right-front passengers is the same as that to drivers, to within about 1%, is surprising in view of the substantial differences between the physical environment of drivers and right-front passengers, especially the presence of the steering wheel. To explore this further, the ratio of right-front passenger risk to driver risk is examined versus model year [Evans and Frick 1989a] with the results shown in Fig. 3-7. Error limits are large for the oldest cars because few remained in use by the first year, 1975, covered by FARS data. Errors are also large for the latest model-year cars shown because the majority of crashes in which these cars are likely to be involved had not yet occurred by 1986, the last FARS year included in the study. The results suggest that fatality risk to right-front passengers is somewhat higher than that to drivers for early 1960s model-year cars, but the reverse applies for later model years. This suggests that the various vehicle modifications aimed at reducing occupant risk have generated somewhat larger fatality risk reductions for right-front passengers than for drivers [Kahane 1988].

In the past it was thought that the right-front seat had a substantially higher fatality risk than the driver seat. I suspect that this arose more because of the

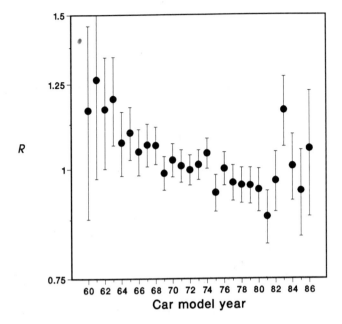

Figure 3-7.   Fatality risk, R, relative to that of a driver, for right-front passengers versus car model year. From Evans and Frick [1989].

25% increased fatality risk associated with being female (Chapter 2); in the period when the term suicide seat was used, a higher proportion of severe crashes would have involved a male driver and a female passenger. Campbell [1987] finds right-front passengers about 15% more likely to be injured than drivers in data for 1973-1981; I suspect that differential sex effects might have contributed to this.

Fraction of Deaths That Are Ejections

Figure 3-8 shows information on ejection for all six car seating positions, based on 1975-1986 FARS data [Evans and Frick 1989b]. Occupants coded in FARS as being totally ejected or partially ejected are included. According to Clark and Sursi [1985], half of ejection fatalities are through glass or open windows. The ratio, R, of fatality risk if ejected to fatality risk if not ejected is estimated by applying the double pair comparison method described in Chapter 2. The values obtained are in agreement with similar quantities estimated by others [Huelke and Compton 1983; Sikora 1986; Green et al. 1987]. Basically, an occupant

$N_e =$	44 631
R =	3.82 ± 0.28
f =	25.3 ± 0.1
F =	18.7 ± 0.5

	904
	3.38 ± 0.36
	26.5 ± 0.8
	18.7 ± 1.0

	13 554
	3.04 ± 0.22
	25.2 ± 0.2
	16.9 ± 0.6

$N_e =$	1245
R =	3.24 ± 0.31
f =	23.3 ± 0.6
F =	16.1 ± 0.8

	524
	4.07 ± 0.49
	25.5 ± 1.0
	19.2 ± 1.0

	1579
	3.89 ± 0.35
	23.8 ± 0.5
	17.7 ± 0.7

Figure 3-8. Ejection data for driver and passengers. From Evans and Frick [1989b]. N_e is the number of fatally injured ejected occupants. R is the ratio of the probability of death if ejected to the probability of death if not ejected. f is the percent of fatalities that are ejections. F is the percent reduction in fatalities from elimination of ejection.

ejected in a crash is three to four times as likely to be killed as an occupant not ejected in a similar crash.

Close to a quarter of fatalities for each seating position are ejected occupants. If these occupants had not been ejected, then a fraction $1/R$ of them would still have been killed. Thus, the percent of fatalities preventable by eliminating ejection, F, is readily computed as $f(1 - 1/R)$, where f is the percent of fatalities that are ejectees. For all seating positions, eliminating ejection would prevent about 18% of fatalities. These results are relevant to the effectiveness of safety belts, which essentially prevent ejection.

The values of the quantities displayed in Fig. 3-8 vary with occupant age as shown in Fig. 3-9. Eliminating ejection probably provides a lesser reduction in fatality risk to older occupants because of their higher fatality risk when not ejected. If ejection does occur, fatality risk is so high that the greater survivability of the young has a discounted value (it would be of no value in completely unsurvivable crashes), whereas when occupants remain in the vehicle, the greater survivability of the younger occupant translates into a real reduction in fatality risk. The lower rate of rollover crashes of older drivers discussed in the next section also contributes to declines in f and F with age.

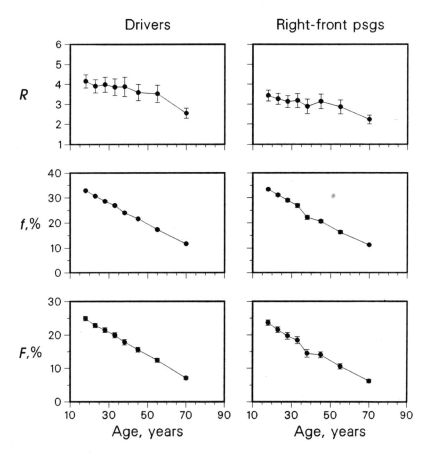

Figure 3-9. Ejection results for drivers and right-front passengers versus age. From Evans and Frick [1989b]. R is the ratio of the probability of death if ejected to the probability of death if not ejected. f is the percent of fatalities that are ejections. F is the percent reduction in fatalities from elimination of ejection.

Impact Direction and Age

Figure 3-10 shows the distribution of car-driver fatalities into principal impact categories [Evans 1991]. The definitions used are, for front, 12 o'clock; for near front, 10, 11, 1 and 2 o'clock; for side, 9 and 3; and for rear, 4 to 8. The non-collisions in the top/non-collision category are essentially all rollovers, although other rare events such as drownings and fires are included. The data in Fig. 3-10 are such that for each driver age, all five components total 100%. The most noticeable characteristic is that given a fatality, it is increasingly less likely to

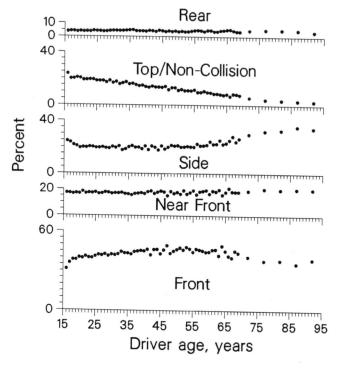

Figure 3-10.   Percent of driver fatalities according to principal impact categories; at every age the data sum to 100%. From Evans [1991].

be a rollover crash as drivers age. Also note that the fraction of deaths that are side impacts increases with driver age, supporting other studies [Viano et al. 1990] that side impact plays an increasingly important relative role in older-driver safety.

NUMBER OF FATALITIES PER DAY

Because there are about 45 000 fatalities per year in the US one occasionally hears comments to the effect that each day there are 120 deaths on our roads, or each hour there are five, or, in extreme form, every ten minutes someone is killed in traffic somewhere in the US. Fatalities do not occur in the regular pattern implicit in such comments, as the distribution of the number of fatalities per day in Fig. 3-11 shows. This is based on the 653 804 fatalities for which the day of death is coded (there are another 124, or 0.02%, with day uncoded), occurring in the 5114 days in FARS 1975 - 1988. The average is 127.8 fatalities per day.

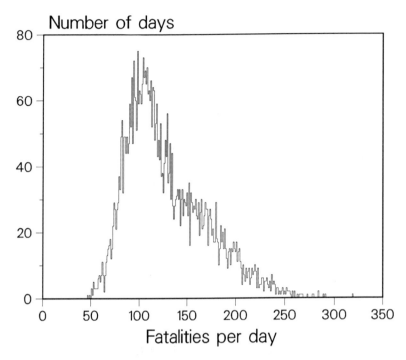

Figure 3-11.   Distribution of the number of fatalities per day for FARS data from 1975 through 1988 (based on 653 804 fatalities occurring on 5114 days, for an average of 128 fatalities per day).

The least number of fatalities in a day, 47, occurred on Monday 10 January 1977. The largest number, 319, occurred on Friday 21 December 1979. If one does not restrict the comparison to legal days (ending at midnight), then the smallest number of fatalities recorded in a 24 hour period is 39, from 7:01 a.m. on Monday 10 January 1977 to 7:00 a.m. on the following Tuesday. The largest number recorded in a 24 hour period is 400, from 1:46 p.m. on Friday 21 December 1979 to 1:45 p.m. the next day. The concurrence of weekend and Christmas celebrations, and the consequent alcohol consumption, undoubtedly contributed to this highest value, more than ten times the smallest value. Rank ordering of fatalities per (legal) day shows that the 31 days with the largest numbers of fatalities (ranging from 249 to 319) are all either Fridays or Saturdays (28 of the 31 are Saturdays). None of the 77 lowest fatality days (from 47 to 65 fatalities) contained a Friday or a Saturday. The number of fatalities on Mondays, Tuesdays and Wednesdays average about 54% of the Saturday total, and on Thursdays 60% of the Saturday total. The other two week-end days,

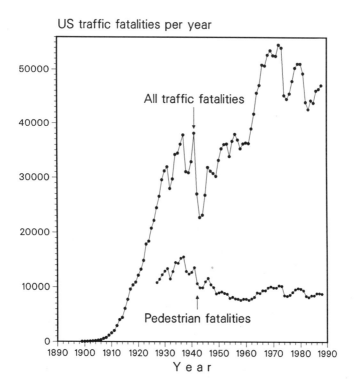

US traffic fatalities per year

Figure 3-12. Total US traffic fatalities per year, and pedestrian fatalities per year, versus year.

Friday and Sunday, have about 80% as many fatalities as Saturday, the Sunday total being concentrated on the first few hours of the day (that is late on "Saturday").

The longest fatality-free period is 6 hours 20 minutes; there were no fatalities from 4:09 a.m. to 10:29 a.m. on Sunday 23 January 1977 (fatalities occurred at 4:08 a.m. and 10:30 a.m.). There have been five fatality-free periods longer than five hours, 31 longer than four hours, 221 longer than three hours, 1364 longer than two hours. It is not possible to determine the highest rate of occurrence of fatal crashes because the time of occurrence of fatal crashes is rarely known to high precision, and in many cases known only approximately. Hence crashes tend to be coded in accord with the customary practice of estimating uncertain times. Far more are coded at whole hours than at half hours, followed by 15 minutes before and after the hour, and then in five minute gradations. The example above of a crash coded at other than a multiple of five minutes past the hour is rare. The most crashes coded as occurring at the same time is nine, a value that occurs on five occasions, but each is exactly on the hour. In Chapter 4 the variation of fatalities by month is discussed in the context of weather conditions.

LONG TERM TREND IN FATALITIES

Figure 3-12 shows the number of traffic fatalities per year in the US since 1900. The values for 1975 and later are from FARS. The earlier values are unpublished estimates by the National Highway Traffic Safety Administration. These values differ from those published by the National Safety Council [1989] because they have been corrected to reflect the same inclusion criteria as FARS, namely, death resulting from the crash within 30 days of the crash; The National Safety Council data use a one year inclusion criterion, so that their values are typically 4% higher than those plotted.

Also shown in Fig. 3-12 is the number of pedestrian fatalities, which has been declining since peaking in the mid 1930s. The fraction of all fatalities that are pedestrian fatalities has been declining, a characteristic of developing motorization observed in many countries [Hutchinson 1987].

REFERENCES

Campbell, B.J. Safety belt injury reduction related to crash severity and front seated position. *Journal of Trauma* 27:733–739; 1987.

Clark, C.C.; Sursi, P. Car crash tests of ejection reduction by glass-plastic side glazing. SAE paper 851203. Warrendale, PA: Society of Automotive Engineers; 1985.

Evans, L. Airbag effectiveness in preventing fatalities predicted according to type of crash, driver age, and blood alcohol concentration. *Accident Analysis and Prevention* 23 (in press) 1991.

Evans, L.; Frick, M.C. Seating position in cars and fatality risk. *American Journal of Public Health* 78:1456–1458; 1988a.

Evans, L.; Frick, M.C. Helmet effectiveness in preventing motorcycle driver and passenger fatalities. *Accident Analysis and Prevention* 20:447–458; 1988b.

Evans, L.; Frick, M.C. Relative fatality risk in different seating positions versus car model year. *Accident Analysis and Prevention* 21:581–587; 1989a.

Evans, L.; Frick, M.C. Potential fatality reductions through eliminating occupant ejection from cars. *Accident Analysis and Prevention* 21:169–182; 1989b.

Green, P.D.; Robertson, N.K.B.; Bradford, M.A.; Bodiwala, G.G. Car occupant ejection in 919 sampled accidents in the U.K.—1983–86. SAE paper 870323. Warrendale, PA: Society of Automotive Engineers; 1987. (Also included in *Restraint Technologies: Front Seat Occupant Protection*. SAE special publication SP-690: p. 91–104; 1987).

Hedlund, J.H. Recent U.S. traffic fatality trends. In: Evans, L.; Schwing, R.C., editors. *Human Behavior and Traffic Safety*. New York, NY: Plenum Press, p. 7–19; 1985.

Huelke, D.F.; Compton, C.P. Injury frequency and severity in rollover car crashes as related to occupant ejection, contacts and roof damage. *Accident Analysis and Prevention* 15:395–401; 1983.

Hutchinson, T.P. *Road Accident Statistics*. Adelaide, Australia: Rumsby Scientific Publishing; 1987.

Kahane, C.J. An evaluation of occupant protection in frontal interior impact for unrestrained front seat occupants of cars and light trucks. Washington DC: National Highway Traffic Safety Administration, report DOT HS 807 203; January 1988.

National Highway Traffic Safety Administration. *Fatal Accident Reporting System 1988.* Document DOT HS 807 507. Washington, DC; December 1989.

National Safety Council. *Accident Facts.* Chicago, IL; 1989 edition (issued annually).

Sikora, J.J. Relative risk of death for ejected occupants in fatal traffic accidents. Washington, DC: National Highway Traffic Safety Administration, report DOT HS 807 096; November 1986.

Viano, D.C.; Culver, C.C.; Evans, L.; Frick, M.C; Scott, R. Involvement of older drivers in multivehicle side-impact crashes. *Accident Analysis and Prevention* 22:177–199; 1990.

4 Engineering, Roadway and Environmental Factors

INTRODUCTION

Many factors are associated with every traffic crash. The word *cause* has largely disappeared from the technical literature on safety, and for good reasons. Suppose that on a dark rainy morning a young man argues with his wife about the purchase of a sofa, leaves the house late for work in a rage, drives his poorly-maintained car too fast on a badly-designed, poorly-lit curve. Suppose further that he skids, and is killed in a crash with a truck driven by an older driver. It is of little value to say that the death was *caused* by the car driver's youth or maleness, the truck driver's old age, the car's bald tires, the high cost of sofas, emotional stress, the non-use of a safety belt, inadequate police enforcement, rain, or any other of the many factors which, if different on this particular occasion, would have prevented the death.

All too often the term *cause* conveys the notion of a single cause, in the deterministic sense in which it is used in the physical sciences or engineering. The rich variety of individual factors which, if different, would alter the outcome or probability of occurrence of crashes, can be classified into broad categories using different schemes. Haddon [1972] introduced a 3 × 3 matrix classification in which all factors are classified either as human, as vehicle and equipment, or as environment. Each of these is further categorized as pre-crash, crash, or post-crash. The example which opened this chapter involved factors in more than half of the nine cells in this matrix. In this book we use a broader classification into road-user and non-road-user factors; this chapter is devoted to non-road-user factors—those relating to engineering and environment.

DIFFICULTY OF IDENTIFYING SPECIFIC FACTORS

One recurrent complexity that continually arises when attempting to understand traffic safety is that factors interact with each other—every aspect of the traffic system is in some way connected to every other aspect. If drivers know that their vehicles are in poor safety condition, they may exercise increased caution. If a hazardous section of roadway is rebuilt to higher safety standards, it is likely that drivers will travel this section faster than before the improvement, or with reduced care. Differences in crash rates on different types of roadways reflect not only effects due to the roadways as such, but also that different speed limits,

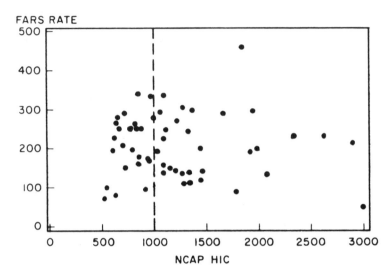

Figure 4-1. Driver fatalities per million registered cars for various specific car models versus the Head Injury Criterion, a parameter measured for an anthropomorphic dummy in a barrier crash test of the same model car. Reproduced, with permission, from Grush, Marsh, and South [1983].

driver speed choices, and driver vigilance levels are associated with different types of roadways. Any observed dependence of crashes as a function of specific engineering and environmental factors possibly reflects large contributions from interactions with other factors.

This point can be illustrated dramatically by the large differences in fatality rates for different vehicles. Figure 4-1 shows fatal crash involvements per million registered cars for many individual car models; the dependent variable (Head Injury Criterion measured in the New Car Assessment Program) is not germane to the present discussion. The highest rate is more than six times the lowest. It is implausible that such differences could be due to differences in engineering safety between the cars, especially as all are of similar model year, and all are in conformity with all applicable safety standards. The major contributor to the wide variation in rates in Fig. 4-1 is that some cars are used by different types of drivers in different ways and in different driving environments than other cars.

The pitfalls of examining simple rates and attributing the differences to engineering factors are further illustrated using insurance data [Highway Loss Data Institute 1989]. Table 4-1 shows injury-claim rates, defined here as insurance injury claims per insured car-year, relative to a value of 100 for the average of

Table 4-1. Injury claims per insured vehicle, relative to a value of 100 for all cars. Based on data from the Highway Data Loss Institute [1989]

Car size	Model years	Make	Relative claim frequency		
			Station wagon	4-door	2-door
LARGE	86–88	Chevrolet Caprice	58	64	67
	86–88	Mercury Grand Marquis	58	64	
	86–88	Ford Crown Victoria	58	63	
	86–88	Buick Electra	63	67	
	87–88	Buick LeSabre		68	92
		AVERAGE FOR LARGE	59.2	65.2	79.5
MID–SIZE	86–88	Oldsmobile Cutlass Ciera	70	89	96
	86–88	Buick Century	71	90	93
	86–88	Chevrolet Celebrity	84	95	100
	86–88	Plymouth Reliant	92	110	102
	86–88	Chevrolet Cavalier	106	129	136
	86–88	Dodge Aries	108	100	104
	87–88	Toyota Camry	59	84	
	86–88	Volvo 240	60	90	
	86–88	Mercury Sable	67	85	
	86–88	Ford Taurus	67	86	
	86–88	Pontiac 6000	71	94	
	86–88	Chrysler LeBaron	78	90	
	87–88	Oldsmobile Calais		105	110
	87–88	Pontiac Grand Am		114	120
	86–88	Buick Skyhawk		120	129
	86–88	Oldsmobile Firenza		122	137
		AVERAGE FOR MIDSIZE	77.7	100.2	112.7
SMALL	86–88	Subaru DL/GL	100	139	133
	87–88	Nissan Sentra	102	153	151
	86–88	Saab 900		77	83
	86–88	Volkswagen Golf		100	96
	86–88	Acura Integra		102	102
	88	Honda Civic		111	97
	87–88	Dodge Shadow		112	126
	87–88	Plymouth Sundance		112	121
	86–88	Mazda 323		119	106
	87–88	Volkswagen Fox		124	122
	86–88	Dodge Colt		143	130
	86–88	Plymouth Colt		152	129
	86–88	Isuzu I–Mark		164	182
	86–88	Chevrolet Sprint		164	178
	86–88	Chevrolet Spectrum		176	166
	86–88			176	
		AVERAGE FOR SMALL	101.0	129.9	128.1
		GRAND AVERAGE	76.2	107.7	118.8

all cars. All cars listed in identical ways in more than one of the categories labelled *station-wagon, four-door* or *two-door* are included; if, for example, a different restraint system is indicated for the two-door and four-door versions, this car is not included. The published data classify cars as small, midsize, or large depending on whether their wheelbase is 99 inches or less, greater than 99 inches but not greater than 109 inches, and greater than 109 inches.

Table 4-1 shows consistently lower injury-claim rates for station wagons than for non-station wagons of the same make and model years. There are 18 cases of station wagons and four-door cars of the same make; in 17 of these the station wagon has a lower injury-claim rate—the average of all 18 differences being 17.7%. In 8 of 9 cases in which there are station wagons and two-door cars of the same make, the station wagons have a lower injury-claim rate—the average of all 9 differences being 18.4%. The evidence is conclusive that station wagons have lower injury-claim frequencies than the non-station wagon versions of the same make cars, the quantitative estimate being that the station wagon rate is (18 ± 3)% lower.

The data in Table 4-1 also indicate differences dependent on the number of doors. For the two large car models available in two-door and four-door versions, the injury-claim rate for the four-door version is less than that for the two-door version. The average and standard error of the two differences, (15 ± 11)%, indicates lower rates for the four-door version (the nominal interpretation is a 91% probability that the four-door rate is really lower than the two-door rate, compared to a 9% probability of the reverse). For midsize cars, the larger number of cases of four- and two-door versions of the same model give clearer effects. In nine out of ten cases the four-door version has a lower injury-claim rate than the two-door version, with the average of the ten differences being (4.4 ± 1.5)%. For the small cars there is no consistent difference dependent on number of doors—the average value of the 15 differences is (−1.9 ± 2.4)%, a difference inconsequential in both magnitude and statistical significance. Thus we find no difference for small cars, a small but reliable difference for midsize cars, and a large but uncertain difference for large cars. With the exception of small cars, the four-door version has a lower injury-claim rate than the two-door version of the same car.

The engineering details of the different versions of the same cars, except differences specific to number of doors or whether it is a station wagon, are generally the same. Such differences are unlikely to have much influence on injury risk, especially in frontal crashes, the most common injury-producing crash impact direction. The differences do not plausibly imply that cars should be redesigned to more resemble station wagons, or that a couple of extra doors be added to larger two-door cars to increase their crashworthiness (although Kahane [1989] does find higher ejection rates associated with two-door compared to four-door cars). What the differences across the rows in Table 4-1 are more likely showing is not so much engineering differences, but differences in use and behavior. There may also be driver age effects; although the data [Highway Loss Data Institute 1989] include a correction for the number of youthful drivers listed in the insurance policy, this cannot capture the dominant influence of driver age, especially as the age of the driver involved in the crash is not used in the correction.

Much larger than the differences dependent on car body style are those dependent on car size category. Focusing on station wagons shows a 31% higher rate for midsized compared to large, and a 71% higher rate for small compared to large. For four-door cars the corresponding values are 54% and 99%, and for the two-door cars 42% and 61%. These differences suggest large increases in injury risk with decreasing car size. Indeed, much of the variation in Table 4-1 within the three car-size categories is due to the wide range of car sizes necessarily included within each of these broad categories. Station wagons are generally heavier than corresponding four-door cars, which are generally heavier than two-door versions, which probably accounts for some of the differences.

Car size effects, being among the largest and most consistently observed effects in traffic safety, are discussed in some detail below. Not only are such effects important in themselves, but they provide additionally a means to disentangle some of the interactions between engineering factors and road-user factors.

VEHICLE MASS

In investigating the influence of vehicle size on risk, we must first define *size*. As vehicles are not of identical shape, one linear dimension, such as the frequently used wheelbase, does not necessarily characterize size. The least satisfactory approach, from a technical point of view, is the one to which the public probably most readily relates, which is to categorize vehicles as subcompact cars, mid-sized cars, etc. These manufacturer designations are not based exclusively on physical dimensions, so that a new model-year version of a specific vehicle will retain its former designation even if its physical dimensions change. The data in Table 4-1 are based on wheelbase, an objective physical property of the vehicle.

For a number of reasons I consider mass (essentially weight) to be the best (but certainly not perfect) indicator of a vehicle's size for most analyses. There is no one variable which captures the pertinent safety characteristics related to size under all conditions. Mass is a clearly defined physical property of the whole vehicle; unlike wheelbase, it nearly always changes when any component in the vehicle changes. Mass is a central physical parameter in crash dynamics, especially in two-vehicle crashes. If vehicles of identical mass crash into each other head-on, the change in speed sustained by each is identical without regard to any other physical properties of the vehicles. This does not mean that the forces experienced by the occupants depend only on mass. These forces are directly influenced by the amount of time the occupants spend changing from the pre-crash speed to the post-crash speed, and by the maximum deceleration forces sustained. These are greatly influenced by the amount of crush space available, which is related to size rather than mass. Indeed, McCarthy [1989] finds that for the same wheelbase, larger mass cars actually have higher risk in single-car crashes, although this is possibly a confounding effect with engine power since a larger engine will make an otherwise identical car heavier. Apart from such specific considerations, there is a strong tendency for most linear dimensions of similarly shaped vehicles to increase with mass, so that this single quantity captures size effects to a large extent. For a crash into an immovable barrier, the quantity and characteristics of crushable material and space in front of the occupant are more important than mass. However, as crashes in the real world nearly all involve objects that will to some extent move, bend, break or distort, increased mass in the vehicle will always reduce the deceleration forces experienced within the vehicle.

Masses of specific car models are available in many sources, such as *Automotive News* [1989]. Some 1989 model-year cars at around 900 kg curb mass are the Toyota Tercel (907 kg) and the Honda Civic Hatchback (913 kg). The Ford Crown Victoria four-door station wagon (1804 kg), Mercedes Benz 560 SEL Sedan (1851 kg), and Mercury Marquis four-door sedan (1707 kg) are close to 1800 kg. While 900 kg and 1800 kg provide a fairly extreme comparison, there are still many lighter and heavier cars; for example, the Geo Metro two-door Hatchback (719 kg), the Ford Fiesta (777 kg), the Cadillac Brougham four-door sedan (1901 kg) and the Rolls Royce Bentley Continental (2422 kg). The median car mass is about 1400 kg. The above illustrative examples are all for 1989 model-year cars—older model-year cars, especially those prior to model year 1977, tended to be heavier.

Analytical relations with car mass. Another important advantage of a physical measure such as mass is that quantitative relations can be derived. Data are fitted below by a weighted least squares procedure to

$$\ln y = A + b\,m \qquad \text{Eqn 4-1}$$

where ln is the natural logarithm (to base e), y is the crash rate, m is the mass, and A and b are parameters derived from the data. The data are displayed in a linear rather than logarithmic form, so Eqn 4-1 may be conceptualized more conveniently as:

$$y = a \exp(b\,m) \qquad \text{Eqn 4-2}$$

where $a = \exp(A)$. A logarithmic relationship between m and y has a number of advantages over a linear relationship. First, the logarithmic relation generally provides a better fit to the data. Second, the logarithmic relation is a simpler and more effective way to compare the rates for cars of different masses because the comparison involves only the slope parameter, b. The other parameter, a, is merely a scaling factor which cancels when cars are compared, and is, in any event, arbitrary when relative rates are examined.

Illustrative Example—Comparing 900 kg Car to 1800 kg Car.   It is even simpler to compare rates for two cars of specific masses—one a small car and the other a large car. The specific masses we chose are 900 kg and 1800 kg. Thus, we compare the rate for a 900 kg car to that for an 1800 kg car, which, from Eqn 4-2, is given by

$$y(m = 900 \text{ kg})/y(m = 1800 \text{ kg}) = \exp{(900\ b)} \qquad \text{Eqn 4-3}$$

where b is in kg^{-1}. Choosing a specific comparison enables us to compare results summarized in the literature using different equations, such as a linear relation between mass and rates. After deriving the various car mass effects, they are summarized (Table 4-2) in terms of the 900 kg car risk compared to the 1800 kg car risk.

Two-Car Crashes

The large role of mass in two-car crashes has long been recognized. Using state injury data, Joksch [1976a], and Campbell and Reinfurt [1973] find that when cars of dissimilar mass crash into each other, the risk of injury is substantially greater in the lighter car. FARS provides more extensive data than were available when these important earlier studies were performed.

Figure 4-2 shows the number of drivers killed in cars in one mass category as a result of crashing into cars in another mass category, based on FARS data for 1975 through 1980. For example, there are 578 drivers in cars in the lightest of the six mass categories killed in crashes with cars in the heaviest category; there are 35 drivers in the heaviest cars killed in crashes with the lightest cars. All these drivers were killed in the same set of crashes—those between lightest and heaviest cars. The ratio, $578/35 = 16.51$, shows that when cars in the lightest and heaviest categories crash into each other, the driver in the lighter car is about 17 times as likely to die as the driver in the heavier car. Extending the analysis to trucks shows that drivers in small cars are about 50 times as likely to die as drivers in large trucks when these vehicles crash into each other.

To answer the more general question of how the risk of death when one pair of cars crash compares to the risk when some other pair of cars crash requires knowing the rates at which the different pairs crash. In other words, we need to estimate exposure for involvement in two-car crashes. This can be done using car j

	Mass, kg		m_1	m_2	m_3	m_4	m_5	m_6	Total
car i	500- 900	m_1	34	79	156	352	582	578	1781
	900-1100	m_2	33	86	165	396	679	693	2052
	1100-1300	m_3	36	74	171	443	684	698	2106
	1300-1500	m_4	47	79	226	604	1088	1132	3176
	1500-1800	m_5	34	95	189	558	1071	1253	3200
	1800-2400	m_6	35	70	139	415	753	878	2290
	Total		219	483	1046	2768	4857	5232	14605

Figure 4-2. Number of driver fatalities in cars of mass m_i in crashes with cars of mass m_j. From Evans and Wasielewski [1987].

an approach, to be described in the next section, in which the numbers of pedestrians killed in crashes involving cars in the six mass categories are used to estimate exposure. In this way, the relative risk of driver death for two-car crashes involving any pair of cars is calculated, as shown in Fig. 4-3. All values are expressed relative to an arbitrary value of unity for the driver at lowest risk—namely one in the heaviest car crashing into the lightest car. A driver in a car in the lightest category crashing into another in the lightest category is 7.04

car j

	Mass, kg		m_1	m_2	m_3	m_4	m_5	m_6
car i	500- 900	m_1	7.04	12.12	15.15	16.05	16.86	16.51
	900-1100	m_2	5.06	9.78	11.88	13.38	14.58	14.68
	1100-1300	m_3	3.50	5.33	7.79	9.48	9.30	9.36
	1300-1500	m_4	2.14	2.67	4.83	6.06	6.94	7.12
	1500-1800	m_5	0.98	2.04	2.57	3.56	4.34	5.01
	1800-2400	m_6	1.00	1.48	1.86	2.61	3.01	3.46

Figure 4-3. Relative likelihood of driver fatality in a car of mass m_i involved in a crash with a car of mass m_j. From Evans and Wasielewski [1987].

times as likely to be killed as is a driver in a car in the heaviest category crashing into a car in the lightest category, but is $7.04/16.51 = 0.43$ times as likely to be killed as a driver in a car in the lightest category crashing into one in the heaviest.

The data in Fig. 4-3 show that as a car's mass increases, fatality risk in that car decreases, but the risk in the other involved car increases. Thus drivers transferring to larger cars reduce their personal fatality risk, but impose increased fatality risk on occupants of other cars. This raises the question of whether a driver transferring to a larger car generates a net increase or decrease in fatality risk. The data in Fig. 4-3 can be used to address this question. Consider an example of a driver who transfers from an m_3 to an m_4 category car. If the m_3 car is in collision with, say, an m_1 car, the risk to the m_3 driver is 3.50 and that to the m_1 driver 15.15, for a combined risk of 18.65. If the m_3 car becomes an m_4 car, the corresponding risks become 2.14 and 16.05, for a total risk of 18.19, which is slightly less than the previous 18.65. Applying the comparison for each category of car into which the m_3, and later the m_4, car might crash reveals that in six out of six cases the net fatality risk is lower when the driver transfers to the heavier car. Applying the same comparison for all five cases of a driver switching to a car in the next highest mass category shows that in 26 out of 30 cases a net reduction in fatality risk results. If we do not restrict the mass increase to one mass category, but allow all possibilities (for example, an m_1 driver might switch to an m_6 category car), we find that 78 of 90 comparisons show a net fatality decrease.

Joksch [1983] fits to state injury and fatality data a relationship which can be expressed as

$$y = \exp\left(-\ 0.001\ 102\ M_1 + 0.000\ 441\ M_2\right), \qquad \text{Eqn 4-4}$$

where y is the relative risk of an injury to an occupant in a car of mass M_1 when it crashes with a car of mass M_2 (masses in kg). If we add the risk to the driver in car M_1 to the risk to the driver in car M_2 we obtain an expression for the combined risk to both drivers. Increasing the value of M_1 decreases the combined risk except when cars of over 1300 kg are replaced by heavier ones. Eqn 4-4 and Fig. 4-3 consistently indicate that substituting a heavier for a lighter car nearly always reduces the system-wide harm from two-car crashes, assuming that driver behavior remains unchanged. The exceptions are likely spurious, especially as the regions where the inversions occur are different for Eqn 4-4 and Fig. 4-3.

Fig. 4-4 shows information parallel to that shown in Fig. 4-3, but for head-on crashes only (principal impact point at 12 o'clock). About 40% of the Fig.

		car j					
	Mass, kg	m_1	m_2	m_3	m_4	m_5	m_6
	500- 900 m_1	10.14	20.41	23.12	21.70	22.10	20.70
	900-1100 m_2	6.98	17.12	17.14	22.00	19.84	20.31
car i	1100-1300 m_3	5.78	8.57	10.37	12.58	12.03	12.58
	1300-1500 m_4	2.71	3.43	6.89	8.85	9.09	9.80
	1500-1800 m_5	1.01	3.31	3.47	4.96	6.38	8.02
	1800-2400 m_6	1.00	2.30	2.35	3.35	4.56	5.07

Figure 4-4. As Fig 4-3, except confined to head-on crashes, defined as each vehicle sustaining the maximum damage in the 12 o'clock position in a 12 point scale. From Evans and Wasielewski [1987].

4-2 data are for head-on crashes. Note that the effect of mass is greater in the head-on than in the all-directions cases.

Of particular interest in Figs. 4-3 and 4-4 are the highlighted diagonal elements, which show how the risk of driver death in crashes involving cars of similar mass depends on their common mass. The data for head-on crashes are plotted in Fig. 4-5, together with data for serious injuries (including fatalities) per registered car from New York [Negri and Riley 1974] and North Carolina [Campbell and Reinfurt 1973]. These data are fitted to Eqn 4-2 to yield b = 0.000 785 kg^{-1}, with a slightly higher value of 0.000 854 kg^{-1} for the all-directions case. Thus, a driver in a 900 kg car crashing head-on into another 900 kg car is about 2.0 times as likely to be killed as is a driver in an 1800 kg car crashing head-on into another 1800 kg car. The corresponding value for the all-directions case is 2.2. Substituting $M_1 = M_2$ into Eqn 4-4 generates an equation of the same form as Eqn 4-2 with $b = -0.000\,661$ kg^{-1}. Substituting 900 kg and 1800 kg gives the result that the risk in the small-small crash is 1.8 times the risk in the large-large case.

When cars of identical mass crash into each other head-on, mass as such does not influence overall crash dynamics. The effect here is certainly due to correlates with mass, such as additional crush material and space in the occupant compartment. The much larger differences in fatality risk to occupants of light and heavy cars when they crash into each other are due mainly to differences in mass as such.

The above results are interpreted to indicate risk in a crash, given that the

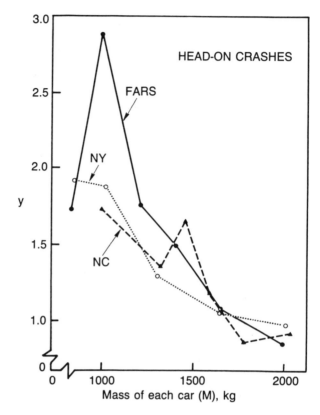

Figure 4-5. Relative likelihood, y, of driver injury (serious or fatal) when a car of mass M crashes into another car of similar mass. All values are relative to a value of one for two 1800 kg cars crashing into each other. From Evans and Wasielewski [1987].

crash occurs. Evans [1982] averaged the relative risk of death in a two-car crash over the mix of cars by mass on the roads (in 1978) and found that the driver of a 900 kg car is about four times as likely to be killed in a "typical" two-car crash as is the driver of an 1800 kg car. Direct examination of the number of fatalities sustained in two-car crashes per registered car, as discussed below, shows a considerably smaller effect.

   Partyka [1989a] derives relationships between occupant fatalities and car mass for different crash types by dividing the number of fatalities from FARS data by the number of registered vehicles as tabulated by R.L. Polk. She includes a correction factor which reflects her finding that the same car tends to be coded as about 100 pounds heavier in the registration than in the fatality data [Partyka 1990]. The relationship derived by Partyka [1989a] for cars involved in multiple vehicle crashes (two-car crashes constitute the majority of these) estimates 169.5 occupant fatalities per 900 kg car per year compared to 91.8 for 1800 kg cars, for a ratio of 1.85. In relating deaths per registered car to the probability of death given a crash, it is more appropriate to concentrate on driver fatalities per crash than occupant fatalities per crash. The larger occupancy rates associated with larger cars places more occupants at risk, which increases fatality rates. Car mass effects are generally best discussed in terms of driver risk, with the reasonable assumption that the risks scale proportionately for other occupants. If a large car is replaced by a smaller car in a specific family context, occupancy will not necessarily decline. Partyka [1989b] repeated the same analysis for drivers, deriving a relationship for cars involved in multiple vehicle crashes which estimates 113.6 driver fatalities per million 900 kg cars compared to 58.5 for 1800 kg cars, for a ratio of 1.94.

The results for relative risk in crashes (about a factor of four between 900 kg and 1800 kg cars) and fatalities per registered vehicle (about a factor of two) are not inconsistent—they measure different phenomena [Evans 1985a]. The relative risk when cars crash into each other depends only on engineering and biomechanics. The fatalities per vehicle rate depends additionally on crash involvement rates. Based on an analysis of over 100 000 police-reported two-car crashes in New York State in 1971 and 1972, Evans [1985b] finds that the number of two-car crashes per registered car increased systematically and strongly with car mass; the quantitative specifics of this study may not apply beyond the early 1970s because small cars, at that time in the US, were of a rather different nature than in later years. The early 1970s data gave that, on a per registered car basis, 900 kg cars crashed into 900 kg cars at only 30% the rate that 1800 kg cars crashed into 1800 kg cars. Thus, notwithstanding the greater fatality risk when the two small cars crash into each other, the total number of fatalities per registered car in such crashes is actually estimated to be less because the reduced crash rate more than offsets the increased fatality risk in the crash.

Single-Car Crashes

There is no simple reasoning based on elementary physics why fatality risk should depend on mass in single-car crashes. Accordingly, effects are expected to be smaller, and exposure estimates are critical. Some early studies examining quantities such as the number of injuries per crash proved inconclusive. A major problem here is that a single-car crash is included in a data file only if it is, for example, reported to the police. Yet if the vehicle is drivable after the crash, the driver may decline to inform the authorities. As larger cars are less likely than smaller cars to be immobilized by the same crash, the same physical characteristics that reduce injury would also deplete the exposure measure. The same comment applies with greater emphasis to such measures as deaths per injury-producing crash, or serious injuries per minor-injury crash; lower values may mean fewer serious injuries, or more minor injuries.

While a number of studies of single-car crashes [Partyka 1989a; b; McCarthy 1989; Evans 1982] do show that fatalities per registered vehicle decrease with increasing car mass, such measures reflect crash involvement rates as well as the risk of death in a crash.

The Pedestrian Exposure Approach. As the most common object struck in a single-car fatal crash is a tree, let us consider cars hitting trees. FARS provides the number of drivers by age and sex killed in cars of known make, model year, and mass crashing into trees. What is not known is how many car/tree crashes occur in which no one is killed, because unless there is a fatality, the crash is not coded in FARS. We get around this problem by using crashes into pedestrians as a surrogate for crashes into trees; such crashes are coded in FARS provided the pedestrian is killed. We proceed by assuming that when a car and a pedestrian crash, the probability that the pedestrian is killed is independent of the mass of the car. This is a reasonable assumption on physical grounds because the lightest car is so much heavier than the heaviest pedestrian that the car trajectory is relatively unaffected by the collision. As the crash forces on the pedestrian are independent of car mass, the number of pedestrian fatalities is consequently proportional to the number of severe crashes.

Thus we conclude that the number of pedestrian fatalities associated with cars in some category (say, in the same mass range) is a measure of the exposure of that group of cars to severe crashes in general. If the category includes more cars, proportionally more pedestrian fatalities will result. Similarly, if these cars are driven more, are associated with younger drivers, with riskier drivers, with more alcohol abuse, etc., then we would expect all these factors to increase the number of pedestrian fatalities and the number of severe crashes into trees in similar proportions. When we take the ratio of driver to pedestrian fatalities, all the factors relating to number of cars, use and behavioral factors (that is, exposure) appear as multiplicative factors in both denominator and numerator, and accordingly cancel, leaving the ratio as a measure of driver fatality risk in a single-car crash as a function of the properties of the cars in the particular category chosen.

Fig. 4-6 shows the ratio of drivers killed in single-car crashes to pedestrians killed in crashes involving similar mass cars, separated into three driver age groups. The similarity of the three plots supports the interpretation that it is mainly car-mass effects that are shown, because there is no hint of the large age effects discussed in Chapter 2.

The same approach may be applied using motorcyclist fatalities rather than pedestrian fatalities to estimate exposure. Also, the fatality risk to drivers in cars crashing with large trucks may depend on car mass in a similar manner to that

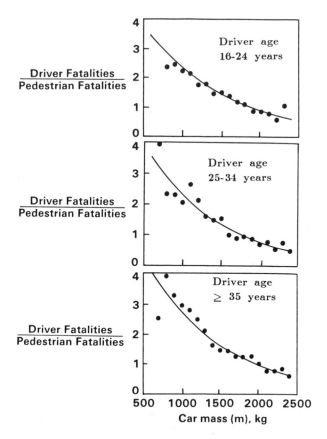

Figure 4-6.   The ratio of drivers killed in single-car crashes to the number of crashes in which pedestrians were killed versus the mass of the involved cars (FARS 1975-1980). This ratio is approximately proportional to the probability that a driver is killed given that a single-car crash occurs, so that the graphs are interpreted to reflect driver fatality risk in single-car crashes versus car mass. From Evans [1984a].

for single-car crashes. Thus we have two types of crashes in which drivers are killed (single-car and car-truck) evaluated by two exposure measures (pedestrian and motorcyclist fatalities) and three driver age categories, generating in all twelve separate relationships with car mass. The close quantitative agreement found [Evans 1984a] between all 12 plots indicates highly robust phenomena. In addition, the number of drivers killed in single-car crashes divided by the number killed in car-truck crashes is independent of mass, as is the number of pedestrian fatalities divided by the number of motorcyclist fatalities. All these results support the interpretation given that the ratio of driver deaths to pedestrian

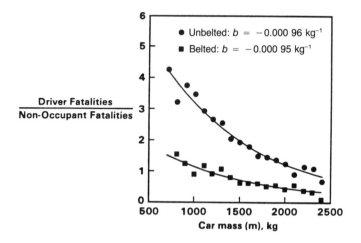

Figure 4-7. Car driver fatalities in crashes involving only one car divided by non-occupants killed in crashes involving cars in the same mass range using FARS 1975-1982 data for all driver ages. From Evans [1986].

(or motorcyclist) deaths reflects the physical effect of car mass, essentially independent of driver behavior effects.

There are sources of error. While pedestrian fatality risk does not depend on car mass, it may depend on the details of hood geometry and other car details that might be correlated with car mass. There are some indications that smaller cars may be less likely to injure pedestrians [McLean 1972] and others that the reverse may be so [Mackay 1985, p. 353]. The driver and pedestrian fatalities could take place at different times and places in ways that could invalidate the method. However, repeating the analyses for data divided by time of the day, and by rural versus urban crashes, provided essentially similar relationships with car mass [Evans 1984a]. Larger size, as such, does of course increase the probability that the car strikes the pedestrian; but the same reasoning applies equally to striking the tree.

The same pedestrian exposure approach is applied for drivers coded in the FARS data as using safety belts [Evans 1985c]. Because of fewer data, drivers killed in either single-car or car-truck crashes are included in the numerator, and pedestrian and motorcyclist fatalities are included in the denominator. The result for unbelted drivers, shown in Fig. 4-7, is computed in the same way. Note how similar the values of b are for each case, showing that the influence of car mass on fatality risk is essentially the same for belted and unbelted occupants. The difference between these curves, although related to belt effectiveness, should not be interpreted to measure belt effectiveness because of large reporting biases, which are assumed to not depend on car mass. As belts are not exclusively a vehicle factor—they only have influence when worn—we discuss them, together with related passive restraint systems, in Chapter 9.

The data in Fig. 4-7 indicate that in single-car crashes a driver in a 900 kg car is 2.4 times as likely to be killed as is a driver in an 1800 kg car, assuming both drivers are unbelted. When both drivers are belted, the corresponding ratio is 2.3. Subject to the assumptions of the pedestrian exposure approach, this result arises from differences in the cars and is unrelated to driver behavior. If, in a pedestrian crash, the pedestrian is more likely to die if the car is large, then the estimated mass effects will be too large.

We compare the number of deaths per registered car in the same way as was previously done for two-car crashes. Partyka's [1989a] equation for occupants estimates 112.6 fatalities per million 900 kg cars per year compared to 79.3 for 1800 kg cars, for a ratio of 1.42, which may be compared to the value 1.48 reported by Evans [1982]. Partyka's [1989b] equation for drivers estimates 79.3 fatalities per million 900 kg cars compared to 53.9 for 1800 kg cars, for a ratio of 1.47, which may be compared to the value 1.68 reported by Evans [1982]. The higher values in the earlier study reflect the discrepancy in the mass definitions which are corrected for in the later estimates.

As with two-car crashes, the finding that the estimate for the physical effect is larger than that for the fatalities per registered vehicle does not imply inconsistency, but rather points to differences in crash rates (and other factors) dependent on car size. Such effects are directly measured [Evans 1984b] using data for all crashes from North Carolina (1979), New York State (1971 and 1972) and Michigan (1976). For each state the data are partitioned into three driver age categories, thus providing nine crash involvement rate versus car mass relationships; all nine indicate higher crash rates for larger cars. The average result is that, when driven by drivers of the same age, 900 kg cars are involved in 28% fewer crashes per unit distance of travel than are 1800 kg cars. Let us assume that this result, based on all crashes, most of which are minor property damage crashes involving two cars, applies also to single-car crashes. If one takes the physical effect as being a 2.4 ratio, the expected number of fatalities per registered car is given by $2.4 \times (1 - 0.28) = 1.72$, which may be compared to the directly measured 1.47 ratio. There is direct observational evidence that larger cars are associated with higher levels of driver risk-taking, as indicated by higher travel speeds and closer following headways [Wasielewski and Evans 1985].

It is not quite correct to assume that the risk of death in a crash times the number of crashes per unit distance of travel gives the number of crashes per registered vehicle, because a number of other factors are also related to car mass. Although I am unaware of quantitative estimates, it is recognized that smaller cars tend to travel less and be more associated with urban driving than larger cars; both these effects will reduce the relative number of driver fatalities in smaller cars. On the other hand, small cars are more likely to be driven by younger drivers [Evans 1985d] who have higher crash rates, but the effect of this will be somewhat lessened by the higher survivability of the younger drivers.

Rollover. Partyka [1989a; b] partitions single-vehicle crashes into those which involve rollover and those which do not. The regression equation for crashes with rollover estimates 39.5 driver fatalities per million 900 kg cars compared to 21.4 for 1800 kg cars, for a ratio of 1.84. The effect for crashes not involving rollover is smaller (37.2 for 900 kg compared to 32.5 at 1800 kg for a ratio of 1.15) but still statistically significantly different from zero (the corresponding difference for occupants rather than drivers is not statistically different from zero [Partyka and Boehly 1989]). For the 900 kg car, almost half of the single-car fatalities involve rollover. Further evidence of the relationship between mass and rollover is provided in findings that the fraction of fatalities that would be prevented by eliminating ejection is larger for smaller cars [Evans and Frick 1989a].

Rollover risk does not arise from mass as such. One vehicle manufactured from materials which are a constant fraction more dense than another vehicle would have the same rollover resistance under the same conditions. Likewise, a vehicle that is the same shape, but smaller, than another vehicle would similarly have the same rollover resistance. However, small vehicles are not simply scaled down versions of larger ones because of the need to accommodate their human occupants. Thus, as vehicles become smaller, the height of the center of gravity above the ground must remain relatively constant, whereas the track width, the distance between the paths of the left and right wheels, decreases. Simple physics indicates that rollover resistance should be related to the ratio of the track width to the height of center of gravity above the ground. Stonex [1962] defined a *stability factor* as half this ratio, namely, the distance from the point under the vehicle's center of gravity to a line along which the wheels travel, divided by the height of the center of gravity above the ground. Mengert et al. [1989] find that the fraction of all single-vehicle crashes that are rollovers is related strongly to this stability factor, with observed values of the fraction of single-vehicle crashes that are rollovers varying from below 10% for vehicles with a stability factor of over 1.4 to over 30% for vehicles with stability factors under 1.1. Robertson [1989] finds that rollover crashes per registered vehicle also increases with decreasing stability factor.

For vehicles of fixed mass, those with lower stability factors have less rollover resistance; for the same stability factor, heavier vehicles provide more crash protection. As for the case of car mass in two-vehicle crashes, it is not surprising that vehicles obey the laws of physics. One interesting difference is that there has been advocacy for regulation to restrict the height of the center of gravity above the ground for a vehicle of given track width [Robertson 1989], yet none to place lower limits on car mass. The mass and center of gravity of a vehicle are chosen based on many considerations and constraints. Knowing that a higher center of gravity or a lighter vehicle implies a reduction in safety is hardly sufficient reason to justify an arbitrary cut-off criterion.

Summary of Vehicle-Mass Effects

The above vehicle mass effects are summarized in Table 4-2 in terms of the example of a small 900 kg car and a large 1800 kg car. The results for these cars crashing into each other are based on simple interpolations from the data in Figs 4-3 and 4-4 [Evans 1986]. The result that for all crashes the fatality risk in a 900 kg car is 2.8 times what it is in an 1800 kg car is a simple weighting (by 0.75 and 0.25) of the single-car and two-car effects to reflect the relative occurrence of non-two-car crashes and two-car crashes [Evans 1989]. The value of 1.7 for driver fatalities per registered car [Partyka 1989b] is not materially different from the value of 1.8 for occupants (drivers would have been a more appropriate choice, as discussed above) used in Schwing, Evans, and Schreck [1983], which is based on Evans [1982].

In order to be in compliance with Corporate Average Fuel Economy (CAFE) standards mandated by the Energy Policy Conservation Act of 1975, the average mass of US vehicles declined. Using some of the relationships in Table 4-2, Crandall and Graham [1989] estimated that as a result of these mass reductions, 1989 model-year cars would be responsible for 2200 to 3900 additional fatalities in the ten years following their introduction.

OTHER VEHICLE CHARACTERISTICS

Many vehicle modifications aimed at increasing safety have been introduced over the years. In many cases the modifications were first introduced by one vehicle manufacturer, but were later required by Federal Motor Vehicle Safety Standards (FMVSS), often in modified form, to apply to all vehicles sold in the US. The effectiveness of specific FMVSS in reducing fatalities can be estimated by comparing fatality rates for vehicles of the model year before the introduction of the standard, to the corresponding fatality rates after the introduction. The estimates discussed below are all by the National Highway Traffic Safety Administration [Kahane 1984], the agency responsible for the standards.

Federal Motor Vehicle Safety Standards (FMVSS)

There are three main categories of standards that apply to cars; those numbered in the 100s apply to crash avoidance, those numbered in the 200s apply to

Table 4-2. Summary of car mass effects, expressed as the risk associated with a 900 kg car compared to that associated with an 1800 kg car

Number of cars involved	Quantity measured	Description of crash	900 kg to 1800 kg ratio
TWO-CAR CRASHES	Driver fatalities per crash	Into each other: All directions Head on	 13 14
	Driver serious injuries (including fatalities) per crash	Into car of similar mass All directions Head on	 2.2 2.0
	Driver fatalities per crash	Into "average" car in 1978 car mix	4
	Driver fatalities per registered car	All driver fatalities in two-car crashes	1.9
	Police-reported crashes per registered car	Into car of similar mass	0.3
SINGLE-CAR CRASHES	Driver fatalities per crash	Unbelted drivers	2.4
	Driver fatalities per registered car	Belted drivers	2.3
	Police reported crashes per registered car	All single-car crashes Rollover only Non-rollover only Assumed to be the same as for all crashes	1.5 1.8 1.15 0.72
ALL CAR CRASHES	Driver fatalities per crash	All crashes	2.8
	Driver fatalities per registered car	All crashes	1.7
	Police-reported crashes per registered car	All crashes	0.72

occupant protection, given that a crash occurs, and those in the 300s apply to immediate post-crash considerations. The National Traffic and Motor Vehicle Safety Act of 1966 directed that all vehicles manufactured in 1968 or later satisfy a number of these standards; additional standards continue to be promulgated.

The largest fatality reductions are from the combined effects of FMVSS 203 and FMVSS 204; FMVSS 203 required energy absorbing steering columns designed to cushion the driver's chest impact in a frontal crash, and FMVSS 204 limited the rearward displacement of the steering wheel towards the driver. These standards, which became effective in 1968, were intended to reduce driver fatality risk in frontal crashes, but were not intended to change passenger risk, or driver risk in non-frontal crashes. Hence, their effect might be detected in two ways; by comparing right-front passenger to driver fatality risk, or by comparing driver risk in frontal crashes to driver risk in non-frontal crashes. Kahane [1981; 1982a] used FARS data from 1975 through 1979 to perform such analyses, obtaining estimates of 13% and 11%, respectively. Although these estimates are not independent, in that each uses the same driver fatalities, the agreement nonetheless

Table 4-3. Fatality reductions estimated by Kahane for various Federal Motor Vehicle Safety Standards (FMVSS)

Description	FMVSS	Occupants protected	Fatalities prevented Protected occupant	Fatalities prevented Average over all occupants
Energy absorbing column	203	Driver	6.6%	4.4%
Column displacement	204			
Instrument panels	201	Front passengers	7%	1.7%
Side structure	214	All	1.7%	1.7%
Door locks	206	All	1.5%	1.5%
Roof crush resistance	216	All	0.43%	0.43%
Windshield glazing	212	All	0.39%	0.39%
Head restraints	202	Driver and right-front passengers	0.36%	0.33%
Braking improvements	105	All	0.9%	0.9%

suggests a fairly robust effect. Thus Kahane's [1981] conclusion of a 12.1% effectiveness, with confidence bounds from 8.5% to 15.5%, seems well supported by the data and analysis presented, although Evans and Frick [1989b] suggest that the estimate could be somewhat high because of possible concurrent changes in the control crashes. A 12.1% reduction in fatality risk in frontal crashes, which in the definition used in Kahane [1981] constitute about 54% of all fatal crashes, implies a net 6.6% reduction in driver fatalities, or, when averaged over all car occupants, a 4.4% reduction (Table 4-3).

Kahane [1988] estimates that improvements in instrument panels in the 1965-1975 era reduced fatality risk by about 13% for unrestrained front passengers in frontal crashes, a 7% reduction for all crashes. As right-front plus center-front passengers constitute 24% of all car-occupant fatalities (Fig. 3-4), this reduces car-occupant fatalities by about 1.7%.

Side door beams (FMVSS 214) are estimated by Kahane [1982b] to prevent 480 fatalities, or, based on the number in 1980, about 1.7% of car-occupant fatalities. Head restraints for drivers and right-front passengers are estimated to reduce overall injury risk in rear impacts by 12% [Kahane 1982c]. Let us make the very approximate assumption that this applies also to fatalities, about 3% of which result from rear (principal impact point 6 o'clock) impact, so we obtain a net reduction in outboard-front occupant fatalities of 0.36%, or 0.33% of all occupant fatalities. Adhesive bonding is estimated [Kahane 1985] to halve windshield bond separation and occupant ejection through the windshield, thereby preventing 105 fatalities. As an approximation, we express this as an average risk reduction of 0.39% for all occupants. Kahane [1989] estimates that improved door locks and door retention components (FMVSS 206) and improved roof crush resistance (FMVSS 216) reduced occupant fatalities by 400 and 110 per year, or 1.5% and 0.43%, respectively. One measure aimed at crash prevention rather than occupant protection, namely dual master brake cylinders, is estimated [Kahane 1983] to prevent 260 fatalities, or 0.9%.

Combined Effect of All Standards

Although summing the last column in Table 4-3 gives an approximate estimate of the total reduction in occupant fatalities from the combined effects of all the changes listed, from a formal point of view, it is an inappropriate calculation which would lead to serious errors if the percent reductions were larger. If better brakes prevent a crash, then the contribution of the energy absorbing steering column must not be included for the crash which did not occur. The application of two measures which successively reduce something by 50% does not eliminate it, but reduces it by 75%.

In order to address the combined effects of all the measures, one must compute the effect for each occupant in the vehicle, and then compute a weighted sum over all occupants. Seven of the eight items in Table 4-3 reduce driver fatalities. Their combined effect is to reduce driver fatalities by

$$1 - (1-0.066)(1-0.017)(1-0.015)(1-0.0043)(1-0.0039)(1-0.0036)(1-0.009)$$

$$= 11.43\%. \qquad \text{Eqn 4-5}$$

Applying similar reasoning gives that the combined effects of all the standards reduce fatalities to right-front, center-front and all rear passengers by 11.8%, 11.5%, and 4.8%. These passengers are 23%, 1%, and 8%, respectively, of all occupant fatalities, drivers being the remaining 68% (Fig. 3-4). By weighting each reduction by the corresponding occupancy, the combined effect of the six measures in Table 4-3 is estimated to reduce car occupant fatalities by 10.9%.

Table 4-3 does not include all changes which may have reduced car-occupant fatalities, but only those for which fatality reductions have been estimated. Other FMVSS may be associated with fatality reductions too small to have been measured, yet important in terms of total numbers. Much engineering attention has been focused on energy management during crashes, with finite element techniques being applied to design vehicle structure so that it crushes in ways that transmit the least damaging forces to occupants. The requirements that the forces on belted anthropomorphic dummies in barrier crash tests (FMVSS 208) be within specified limits has helped stimulate developments in these areas, although the performance on such tests has not been found to be related to field fatality rates [Grush, Marsh, and South 1983]. Many changes addressing specific injury modes in specific crashes have been made based on engineering judgment. If such a change prevents, say, 10 fatalities per year, it is exceedingly unlikely that it will be detected in field data. If the 10.9% estimate is increased by half of its estimated value to capture all the effects missed, this implies that vehicle changes have reduced occupant fatality risk by 16%. Many automotive engineers consider that the cumulative effect of vehicle changes from the early 1960s to the present have reduced car-occupant risk by somewhere in the range of 10% to 20%, a range consistent with the above discussion.

Attempts to Estimate Aggregate Effects of FMVSS Directly

Rather than estimating the aggregate effect of the standards by combining contributions from specific standards, it would be desirable to examine the overall effect by a more general change in fatalities from pre-regulation to post-regulation vehicles. Such a task is rendered difficult because the earliest calender year for FARS data is 1975, by which time the newest cars which were unaffected by changes incorporated in FMVSS, namely 1966 model-year (MY) cars, were already eight years old. Thus any study using FARS data must necessarily focus on very old cars, which have use and ownership patterns that differ from those for new cars by larger amounts than are expected to be associated with vehicle design standards.

Robertson [1981] estimates the combined effects from all changes by comparing fatalities per unit distance of travel for pre-1964 MY cars, 1964–1967 MY cars, and 1968–1977 MY cars, as estimated by applying multivariate analysis to 1975–1978 FARS data. Robertson [1981, p. 820] concludes, "The numbers of deaths avoided by the federal safety standards amount to 26,500 occupants, 7,600 pedestrians, 1,000 pedalcyclists and 2,000 motorcyclists—for a total of about 37,000 people who would have died without the standards in those years" (the four years 1975–1978).

The same 1975–1978 FARS data used in Robertson's analysis show 4665 motorcyclists (3975 drivers and 690 passengers, more wearing helmets than not wearing them) killed in crashes involving model year 1968 or later cars; these fatalities constitute less than a third of all motorcyclist fatalities—the most common crash mode involves no vehicle other than the motorcycle. Robertson's conclusion thus implies that without the regulations, motorcyclist fatalities in crashes with MY 1968 or later cars would have been about 6665 instead of 4665; a 30% reduction in motorcyclist fatalities is therefore attributed to changes in these cars. An inference that car safety standards had reduced motorcyclist fatality risk by 30% should have immediately brought into question the face-validity of the model fitted to the data.

Orr [1984] addresses the validity of the model directly by performing additional multivariate analyses on Robertson's data and concludes that most of the reduction in fatalities is more appropriately attributed to car age; older cars, which are driven by younger drivers, have substantially higher crash-involvement rates than do newer cars. Orr estimates that the total fatality reductions attributable to vehicle changes are in the range of zero to 9200, less than one quarter of those found by Robertson. Lower crash-involvement rates for newer, post-regulation, cars provide a more plausible explanation for their substantially lower involvement rates in pedestrian, pedalcycle, and motorcycle fatality crashes than do federal regulations aimed mainly at protecting car occupants. Orr [1984] also points out the inappropriate inclusion of trucks, which were not subject to regulatory changes, and other methodological problems. In response, Robertson [1984] applies a different model, this time reporting even larger effects; for example, fatality reductions of 15 311 in 1979 and 15 909 in 1980. Orr [1985] responds by claiming that the new estimate contains the same basic flaw as the original—it is primarily a car-age effect that has nothing to do with the regulations. Indeed, Robertson's [1984, p. 1392] own Figure 1 showing fatality rate versus model year shows no indication of any decline from MY 1966 to MY 1968 sufficiently in excess of the trend to generate the claimed reductions. Robertson [1985] responds by citing, "irrefutable evidence of the effectiveness of seat belts, energy absorbing steering mechanisms, etc." Given that safety belts were preventing less than one thousand fatalities in 1980 [Partyka 1988; Evans 1987], and that Kahane [1981] estimates that all cars having energy absorbing columns and limited column displacement would reduce fatalities by 1300, it is difficult to see how the "etc." is going to account for the more than 13 000 additional fatalities alleged to have been prevented!

Simple graphical presentations by Adams [1985a] further demonstrate the absence of any large change in occupant fatality risk coincident with the introduction of the safety standards. Applying the pedestrian exposure approach to compare post-1968 and pre-1966 MY cars shows rates incompatible with any change of the magnitude claimed by Robertson.

Another attempt to estimate the aggregate effect of federal regulations on fatalities is that of Peltzman [1975], who uses data from 1947 to 1965 to project fatality rates for the first seven years of federal safety standards, and then compares those estimates to actual values. He concludes that the net effect of the standards is essentially zero; a small reduction in deaths to car occupants is balanced by a corresponding increase in deaths to non-occupants. Unlike the Robertson [1981; 1984] estimates, a mechanism is offered to explain the alleged effect. The explanation contends that safer vehicles increase driver risk-taking, thereby reducing, but not eliminating, the benefits to car occupants, but increasing the risk to non-occupants. Chapter 11 discusses such behavioral feedback responses to safety measures—suffice it to comment here that the changes associated with the safety standards are so invisible to most drivers that any large behavior response to them is unlikely. Peltzman's [1975] paper has been much discussed in the literature [Joksch 1976b; 1976c; Robertson 1977; Peltzman 1976; Graham 1984; Crandall and Graham 1984; Graham and Garber 1984; Zlatoper 1984], and the same, or similar, data have been shown to lead to a wide variety

Table 4-4. Traffic fatalities and fatalities per billion km of travel on various types of roads in 1988. Data from Table 1 of Federal Highway Administration [1990]

	Fatalities			Fatalities per billion km		
Highway system	Rural	Urban	Total	Rural	Urban	Total
NON-INTERSTATE:						
Federal aid primary (arterial)	10 748	4 252	15 000	21.7	9.7	16.1
Other Federal aid urban	—	8 726	8 726	—	12.2	12.2
Federal aid secondary collector	6 771	—	6 771	24.0	—	24.0
Non-federal aid arterial	295	299	594	50.9	7.2	12.6
Non-Federal aid collector	2 214	313	2 527	25.0	7.9	19.7
Non-Federal aid local	4 839	3 509	8 348	32.1	12.0	18.8
NON-INTERSTATE TOTAL	24 867	17 099	41 966	24.3	11.2	16.4
INTERSTATE	2 826	2 301	5 127	9.7	5.5	7.2
ALL ROADS TOTAL	27 693	19 400	47 093	21.0	10.0	14.4

of conclusions in the hands of others. This illustrates what seems to me to be an intrinsic problem with complicated multivariate analyses. There are so many choices of variables and of transformations at the discretion of the analyst that the detached reader rarely has any way of knowing whether the analysis is performed to discover new information or to buttress prior beliefs. The reader cannot generally check the calculation, or get a clear sense of the origin of the claimed effects. Differences in interpretation often do not arise from different assumptions that can be discussed in terms of plausibility, but from such abstract issues as whether to use the logarithm or the square of the dependent variable in the model specification.

The two estimates discussed above, one that the safety standards prevented zero deaths, and the other that they prevented over 37 000 deaths, both probably reflect the triumph of zeal over science, or perhaps even common sense. An enthusiastic editorial in the *American Journal of Public Health* [Yankauer 1981] states, "It is good to know that in 1975-1978, the automobile safety standards laid down by the federal government some years earlier resulted in the saving of 37,000 lives." There has been no subsequent editorial to set the record straight.

EFFECTS OF ROADWAY

Table 4-4 shows the number of fatalities (all road users), and the rates per unit distance of vehicle travel for different types of roads. The distinction between federal-aid and non-federal aid is based on the manner in which the roads are financed, rather than strictly on physical characteristics. The same road can be changed from one classification to another administratively, without any physical changes in the road. Generally, the more major the road, the more likely it is to receive federal aid. The classifications for the roadways are the same as those coded in FARS data, the source of the fatality data. The Interstate category represents the most homogeneous physical system, with all Interstate roads being limited access freeways, with at least two lanes of traffic in each direction being well separated from each other.

For all roadways for which a comparison can be made, rural fatality rates are substantially higher than urban rates. By far the lowest fatality rate, 5.5 deaths per billion km, occurs on the urban Interstate system. The rate on the rural system, 9.7 deaths per billion km, is 76% higher. This difference is primarily due to different use patterns on the two types of roads. Much of the travel on the urban system is high flow commuting travel under congested conditions which constrain speed. Alcohol is not prevalent during commuting hours. In contrast, lower traffic densities and less commuting traffic on the rural system permit higher speeds. The 65 mph speed limit on some portions of the rural system compared to 55 mph on the urban system also contributes to the difference; however, from 1974 to 1986, when the maximum speed limit throughout the entire system was 55 mph, the rural rate still exceeded the urban rate by substantial amounts, though less than the proportionate difference for 1988.

After controlling for the urban compared to rural difference, the differences in fatality rates are much more linked to the physical nature of the roadway. The much higher fatality rates on two-lane roads are associated with head-on crashes involving cars travelling in opposite directions, with striking trees and other objects close to the trafficway, with intersection crashes, and with pedestrian impacts. All these crash-types are absent from Interstate (or other) freeways. Each of the non-Interstate categories in Table 4-4 contains a mix of types of roadways, some with lower and some with higher fatality rates than the average.

The highest fatality rate in Table 4-4 is 825% above the lowest. If one confines the comparison to rural travel only, then the highest rate is 425% above the lowest; for urban only, the highest rate is 120% above the lowest. If the rate on the urban Interstate system applied for all travel, then the total fatalities would be 18 019 instead of 47 093, a reduction of 62%. If all urban and all rural travel were at the same fatality rate as the corresponding Interstate rate, then fatalities would be 23 491, a reduction of 50%.

These calculations show the enormous influence of roadway characteristics on safety. They do not imply that if all roadways were upgraded to Interstate standards, the calculated reductions would occur. To start with, a world without local streets would be hard to imagine. More specifically, the upgrading of a roadway does not simply substitute a new lower fatality rate for a prior higher fatality rate. Upgrading roads reduces congestion and delay, which, in time, generates increased travel [Mackie and Bonsall 1989], with consequent higher than calculated fatalities if the fatality rate remains unchanged. Although interactive effects unquestionably occur and are substantial, the differences between fatality rates on different types of roads are so great that it is beyond reasonable doubt that replacing, say, a well-travelled rural two-lane road with a limited access freeway will reduce traffic deaths and injuries.

Traffic Engineering

Traffic engineering changes, such as installing traffic lights or stop signs, have many motivations in addition to safety. Surprisingly, the influence of such devices on safety is not all that clearly established [Persaud 1988; Hauer 1988; 1989]. There is a general theme in the traffic engineering literature that traffic control devices enhance safety, but definitive evidence is difficult to generate. An intrinsic problem is that at any particular site, traffic crashes are rare events, so that it is extremely difficult to get enough *before* and *after* data to support reliable conclusions. Sites selected for treatment generally have much higher than average crash rates; because of *regression to the mean,* these rates would tend to be lower in subsequent years regardless of treatment [Hauer 1980], thus adding to the problem of satisfactorily evaluating the safety effect of treatments. One change for which there is clear evidence of large reductions in crash rates is replacing two-way by four-way stop signs [Hauer 1985].

ENVIRONMENTAL FACTORS

Weather—Variations by Season

Figure 4-8 shows the number of fatalities per calender month for the six years 1983-1988. A clear cyclical pattern is apparent. Total fatalities typically peak in August or September, and have minima in February. Pedestrian fatalities are greatest in December, and least in January. Motorcycle drivers contribute to the cyclical pattern for drivers—the pattern for car drivers is more like that for pedestrians than for all drivers.

Part of the reason for the cyclical pattern is, of course, that travel is greater in the summer months. Fig. 4-9 shows the data in Fig. 4-8 for all fatalities divided by total distance of travel. Nominally, this normalization should remove effects due to different amounts of travel, and due to different numbers of days in different months. Note that while total traffic fatalities were on an upward trend in the six years (Fig. 4-8), the trend for the fatality rate is downwards.

In order to illustrate better the cyclical behavior of fatalities, Fig. 4-10 shows the fatality rate for each month relative to the yearly average; the average for the 12 values for each year is one. A highly regular pattern is apparent. The lowest fatality rates occur consistently in the winter months, notwithstanding the increased adverse factors of darkness, snow, and ice. The highest rates occur in the summer and fall months.

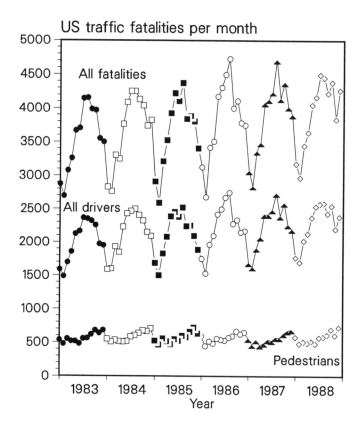

Figure 4-8. US traffic fatalities per month. The first point plotted is for January 1983, and the last for December 1988. FARS data.

FARS data for 1988 show that 8.3% of fatal crashes occurred in rain, 1.9% in snow, and 1.5% in fog or other unusual atmospheric conditions; thus the vast majority (88.3%) of fatal crashes occurred in the absence of any adverse atmospheric conditions. In addition, 83.6% of fatal crashes occurred on dry roadway surfaces; the remainder are 12.8% on wet surfaces, 1.6% on snow, 1.8% on ice, and 0.3% on sand or other surface. A study of injury-producing crashes in Leeds, UK, finds that 81% occurred under fine weather conditions, 69% occurred in daylight, and 61% occurred when the road was dry [Carsten, Tight, and Southwell 1989]. Information on the amount of travel as a function of roadway surface or atmospheric conditions is unavailable, so it is not possible to determine directly how these factors influence fatality risk.

Adams [1985b] presents data on how injuries and fatalities in Ontario, Canada

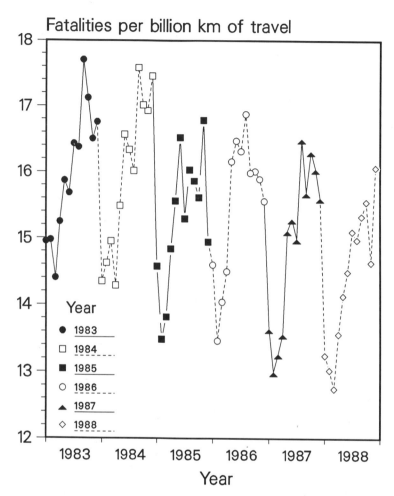

Figure 4-9. US traffic fatalities per unit distance of travel versus month. The first point plotted is for January 1983, and the last for December 1988. Calculated using FARS and FHWA data.

depend on the month of the year. There, where the winter is much more severe than the average for the US, the seasonal variation is greater. The numbers of fatalities in the summer months are about 100% higher than in the winter months (compared to 30% for the US). Adams [1985b] also plots the ratio of fatality to injury crashes for Ontario as a function of month, with the results shown in Fig. 4-11. The data in Adams [1985b] are further tabulated by road surface condition, as reproduced in Table 4-5. Mueller, Rivara, and Bergman [1987] find that,

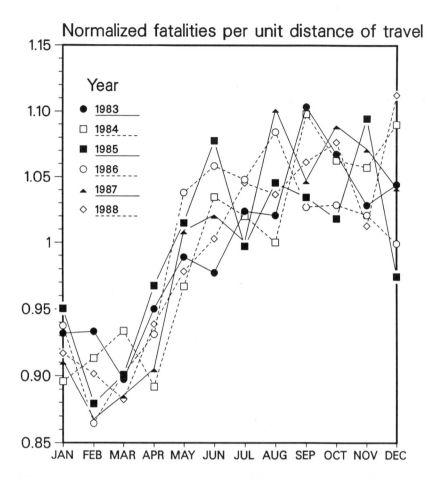

Figure 4-10. The fraction of yearly traffic fatalities in a given month divided by the fraction of yearly distance of travel in the same month, using the data in Figure 4-9.

given a pedestrian injury crash, the probability that the pedestrian is killed is greatest when the road surface is dry, and least when it is ice covered; when the visibility is clear, pedestrian fatality risk in a crash is twice what it is when it is snowing.

The above data associate highest fatality rates with dry roadway surfaces and favorable atmospheric conditions. There are insufficient exposure data to determine to what extent crash rates depend on roadway surface, but crash rates almost certainly are higher with reduced roadway friction and visibility. Driver responses to inclement weather and slippery roadways, especially reduced speeds,

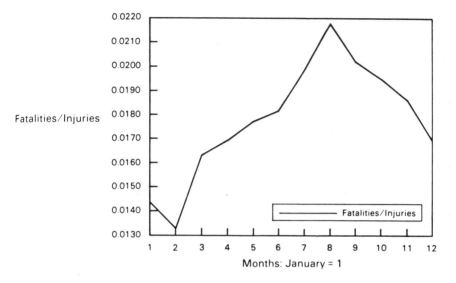

Figure 4-11. The number of fatality crashes divided by the number of injury crashes, based on 1974-1980 data for Ontario, Canada. Reproduced, with permission, from Adams [1985b].

lead to more but less severe crashes, with consequent reductions in fatalities. Thus through road-user responses, to be discussed more fully in Chapter 11, environmental factors reduce mobility but, in terms of fatalities, actually increase safety.

Darkness—Variations by Day and Hour

Schwing and Kamerud [1988] examine traffic fatality risk for each of the 7 × 24 = 168 hours in the week (Fig. 4-12). The top graph shows the distribution

Table 4-5. Fatal and personal injury crashes in Ontario, Canada in 1974–1980. From Adams [1985b].

Road surface condition	Number of crashes		Fatal/injury (%)
	Fatal	*Injury*	
Dry	6494	274 873	2.36
Wet	1878	113 051	1.66
Loose snow	214	16 448	1.30
Slush	179	11 000	1.63
Packed snow	226	12 413	1.82
Ice	289	19 446	1.49

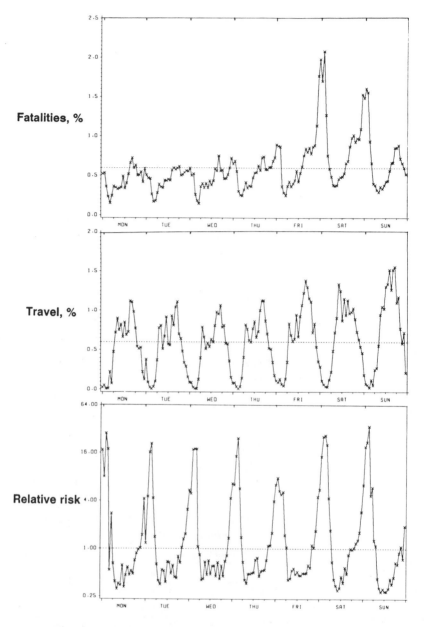

Figure 4-12. The distribution of occupant fatalities, travel by vehicle occupants, and occupant fatalities per unit distance of travel by each hour of the week. From Schwing and Kamerud [1988].

of fatalities to occupants of cars and light trucks, based on FARS data for 1983. If fatalities were equally likely at all times, then 1/168, or 0.595% (indicated by a dotted line), would occur in each hour of the week. Fatalities are in fact distributed in a far from uniform manner, with particularly large peaks on late Friday/early Saturday and late Saturday/early Sunday. Other days have smaller peaks in the afternoon and around midnight. Fatalities are lowest between 4:00 a.m. and 5:00 a.m. on weekdays, and 8:00 a.m. and 9:00 a.m. on weekends.

The center graph shows the distribution of travel (total distance travelled by vehicle occupants). This is derived from a survey [Horowitz 1986] of the travel activities in 2000 households during a one week period. Each household member recorded the starting time, duration, purpose, whether a driver or passenger, etc. for each trip taken. The cycles in the two curves are essentially out of phase—the greatest numbers of fatalities tend to occur at times associated with the least amount of travel.

The bottom graph shows the fatalities per unit distance of travel relative to a value of unity for the average rate over the entire week. The variations are so large that the data are shown in a log representation. The 168 values of relative risk vary from a low of 0.32 (between 10:00 a.m. and 11:00 a.m. on Sunday morning) to a high of 43 (between 3:00 a.m. and 4:00 a.m. on Sunday morning); the ratio between these indicates that the most dangerous hour is 134 times as dangerous as the safest hour.

Many factors contribute to the wide variation in risk. Another study [Mortimer and Fell 1988] finds that drivers in different age categories, including those older than 65 years, have higher crash rates between midnight and 6:00 a.m. than during daytime periods. As alcohol is less of a factor for older drivers this finding could point to darkness as a possible contributing factor. However, the data in Fig. 4-12 show that weekend rates at 3:00 to 4:00 a.m. are well over ten times greater than are the rates at the similarly dark period 10:00 to 11:00 p.m., so that darkness is not the main contributor to the pattern. Local minima in risk occur during the morning and afternoon rush periods, in part because congestion, through speed reduction, reduces fatality, though not crash, risk.

The risk pattern refers to the relative risk sustained by the mix of drivers, by age, purpose of trip, alcohol use, etc. who are driving at the indicated times; it does not indicate how the risk varies for an individual driver. Let us imagine a specific individual driver with unvarying sober careful behavior, and ignore possible influences from the effects of darkness, fatigue, etc. The crashes that contribute to the peaks are nearly all single-vehicle crashes. There is no reason why our hypothetical driver should dramatically increase single-vehicle crash risk just because it is 3:00 a.m. on Sunday morning. It seems plausible to presume that for this driver, the single-vehicle crash risk would remain constant, and low. His risk of being killed in a multiple-vehicle crash is proportional to the probability that another vehicle strikes his. This can be assumed to be proportional to the probability that the other vehicle is involved in any type of serious crash, which, if measured by fatalities, is given by the top graph in Fig. 4-12. If we assume that our hypothetical driver is so careful that the risk of a single-vehicle crash is zero, then his fatality risk depends on time and day in a similar manner to the top graph in Fig. 4-12. Thus his fatality risk at 3:00 a.m. on Sunday is about three times its average value provided his own driving style remains unchanged.

What Fig. 4-12 shows with dramatic clarity is a large variation in risk in a system in which the engineering is largely constant. Environmental factors may contribute to the variation, but cannot come close to explaining it all. There can be little doubt that the main contributor to the risk pattern is road-user rather than engineering in origin, with such factors as alcohol (Fig. 7-5) and youthful driving playing crucial roles.

STUDIES TO IDENTIFY FACTOR CONTRIBUTIONS DIRECTLY

In the 1970s two major studies, one in the US and one in the UK, were performed to identify factors associated with a large sample of crashes. The US study was performed by Indiana University, and is often referred to as the *Tri-Level Study* because crashes were examined in one of three levels of depth, depending mainly on their severity; the study has been described in many detailed reports, with Treat [1980] providing a succinct description of the methods and results. The British study was performed by the Transport and Road Research Laboratory, and is described by Sabey and Taylor [1980] and Sabey and Staughton [1975]. In both studies a team of multi-disciplinary experts conducted a detailed post-crash examination of crashes satisfying specified selection criteria. The crash site was examined for physical evidence, the vehicles involved were examined by an engineer, and the participants in the crash were interviewed in depth. Based on such information, factors contributing to the crashes were identified.

Rumar [1985] elegantly summarized the results from both studies in one figure reproduced as Fig. 4-13. The interpretation is that, for example, in the US study, the vehicle is identified as the sole factor in 2% of crashes, the interaction between vehicle and road user is identified as a factor in 6% of the crashes; the interaction between vehicle, road user, and environment is identified as a factor in 3% of crashes, and the interaction between vehicle and road is identified as a factor in 1% of crashes; the corresponding values for the UK study are 2%, 4%, 1%, and 1%, respectively.

The studies were performed independently—indeed it appears that neither study group was aware of the activities of the other. The results are remarkably consistent. Each finds that the non-road-user factors of vehicle and environment are rarely the sole factors associated with a crash—the British study finding 5% of crashes not linked to the road user, and the US study 6%. In both studies,

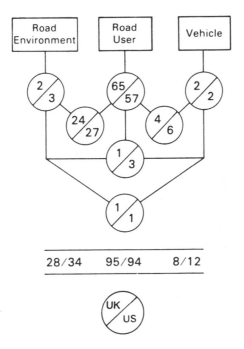

Figure 4-13. Percent contributions to traffic crashes as obtained in British and US in-depth studies. Reproduced, with permission, from Rumar [1985].

when only one factor is identified, it is overwhelmingly the road user (65% in the British study, 57% in the US study). The British study finds that road user factors are present as sole or contributory factors in 95% of crashes, the US study 94%.

Carsten, Tight, and Southwell [1989] use a somewhat similar approach to study injury-producing crashes in Leeds, UK. Their exclusively urban sample of injured road users contained 24% pedestrians or pedalcyclists. While differences in categorization and method make it impossible to compare their results directly with the two previous studies, their data do suggest that vehicle factors played an even smaller role (about 1%). They associate perceptual or judgment errors with essentially all of the crashes.

Many words of caution have been offered [for example, Shinar 1985, p. 166] about interpreting the findings of studies such as the three discussed above. The identification of factors implies only that if a particular factor, or combination of factors, had been absent on a specific occasion, this particular crash would not have occurred. Suppose a head-on collision resulting from improper overtaking at too high a speed occurred on a dry, well-lit roadway. It is unlikely that any factors other than road-user factors would be associated with this crash; yet such a crash would not occur on a divided highway. If a driver's neglect of vehicle upkeep culminated in a tire failure that preceded a crash, it is unlikely that any factors other than vehicle factors would be associated with this crash. Also, outcomes are not identified in Fig. 4-13; the same crash, with identical factors, might have different outcomes dependent on vehicle size and belt use.

Identifying the mix of factors is not the same as identifying the mix of countermeasures. This point can be illustrated building upon the example, invoked by Haddon [1972], of sending fragile packages in the mail. If some fraction of these arrived damaged, multi-disciplinary investigation would doubtless discover that in almost all cases the damage resulted from improper handling by postal employees. However, this does not logically imply that the most effective remedy is to attempt to upgrade the handling practices of the employees by training and motivation. Better packaging might achieve larger benefits at less cost. No general principal can be inferred from this example; in each case countermeasures must be evaluated in terms of potential safety benefits and the costs required to achieve them. Data such as those presented in Fig. 4-13 neither contain, nor suggest, benefit or cost information.

The consistent findings in the above studies of the dominant role of road-user factors does complement other results which were derived in this chapter showing that attempts to measure the influence of non-road-user factors often encounter much larger influences from road-user factors. The recurrent central role of the road-user as a factor in traffic safety leads us to treat this subject in detail in the next two chapters.

CONCLUSIONS

Traffic crashes are best examined in terms of factors, which, if different, would have altered the probability of occurrence or severity of outcome of the crash; it is generally less illuminating to focus on causes, especially single causes. It is difficult to identify the influence of specific engineering and environmental factors because of large confounding influences from road-user factors. For example, station wagons have about 18% fewer injury claims per insured vehicle than non-station wagon versions of the same model cars; larger model four-door cars tend to have lower injury claim rates than two-door versions of the same models. Such differences are due more to different use and behavior patterns than to differences in occupant protection.

One vehicle characteristic which does exercise a major influence on occupant protection in crashes is vehicle size, which is best represented by vehicle mass, or weight. When 900 kg and 1800 kg cars crash into each other, the risk of death in the small car is about 13 times what it is in the large car. A driver in a 900 kg car crashing into another 900 kg car is about twice as likely to be killed as a driver in an 1800 kg car crashing into another 1800 kg car. In a single-car crash, the risk in a 900 kg car is about 2.4 times that in an 1800 kg car. Fatalities per registered car show weaker mass effects because smaller cars are involved in fewer severe crashes. Driver fatalities per registered car decreases steeply with increasing car mass for single-car rollover crashes, and weakly for non-rollover crashes. General principles of physics and many studies using data support the following two *laws*. When a crash occurs, other factors being equal

1. The lighter the vehicle, the less risk posed to other road users.
2. The heavier the vehicle, the less risk posed to its occupants.

These laws are expected to apply over the entire spectrum of vehicle masses, from pedacycles, through motorcycles, small cars, medium cars, large cars, small buses, large buses, trains, etc.

Fatality reductions have been associated with vehicle changes related to various Federal Motor Vehicle Safety Standards (FMVSS). The largest change, a driver fatality reduction of 6.6%, is associated with the energy absorbing steering column and related alterations in the maximum rearward displacement of the steering column. The combined effect of all quantitatively evaluated FMVSS is to reduce car-occupant fatalities by 11%. Taking into account other changes, it seems that vehicles now have occupant fatality risks about 15% to 20% lower than pre-regulation cars.

The magnitudes of the differences in fatality rates between different types of roads, in some cases more than a factor of nine, show conclusively that, say, replacing a stretch of rural two-lane roadway by a divided freeway will substantially reduce casualties. Fatalities per unit distance of travel are lower in the winter months, and fatality risk is less on wet and snow-covered roads than on dry roads. The effect of inclement weather is more to reduce mobility by deterring travel or reducing speeds than to change safety. Fatality rates are dramatically higher at night, an effect largely due to road-user characteristics such as alcohol consumption. Multi-disciplinary post-crash investigations in the US and UK identify road-user characteristics as factors in 94% and 95% of crashes, respectively, while only 6% and 5% of crashes are associated only with the non-user factors of environment and roadway. Nearly all attempts to examine engineering and environmental factors encounter larger driver behavior influences.

REFERENCES

Adams, J.G.U. *Risk and Freedom—The Record of Road Safety Regulations.* Nottingham, UK: Bottesford Press; 1985a.

Adams, J.G.U. Smeed's law, seat belts and the emperor's new clothes. In: Evans, L.; Schwing, R.C., editors. *Human Behavior and Traffic Safety.* New York, NY: Plenum Press, p. 193–238; 1985b.

Automotive News. *1989 Market Data Book Issue*. Detroit, MI: Crain Communications; 31 May 1989.

Campbell, B.J.; Reinfurt, D.W. *The Relationship Between Driver Crash Injury and Passenger Car Weight*. Chapel Hill, NC: Highway Safety Research Center, University of North Carolina; 1973.

Carsten, O.M.J.; Tight, M.R.; Southwell, M.T. *Urban Accidents: Why Do They Happen?* Basingstoke, UK: AA Foundation for Road Safety Research; 1989.

Crandall, R.W.; Graham, J.D. Automobile safety regulation and off-setting behavior; some new empirical estimates. *American Economic Association Proceedings* 74:328–330; 1984.

Crandall, R.W.; Graham, J.D. The effect of fuel economy standards on automobile safety. *Journal of Law and Economics* 32:97–118; 1989.

Evans, L. Car mass and likelihood of occupant fatality. SAE paper 820807. Warrendale, PA: Society of Automotive Engineers; 1982.

Evans, L. Driver fatalities versus car mass using a new exposure approach. *Accident Analysis and Prevention* 16:19–36; 1984a.

Evans, L. Accident involvement rate and car size. *Accident Analysis and Prevention* 16:387–405; 1984b.

Evans, L. Driver behavior revealed in relations involving car mass. In: Evans, L.; Schwing, R.C., editors. *Human Behavior and Traffic Safety*. New York, NY: Plenum Press, p. 337–352; 1985a.

Evans, L. Involvement rate in two-car crashes versus driver age and car mass of each involved car. *Accident Analysis and Prevention* 17:155–170; 1985b.

Evans, L. Fatality risk for belted drivers versus car mass. *Accident Analysis and Prevention* 17:251–271; 1985c.

Evans, L. Driver age, car mass and accident exposure—a synthesis of available data. *Accident Analysis and Prevention* 17:439–448; 1985d.

Evans, L. Car size and safety: results from analyzing U.S. accident data. *Proceedings of the Tenth International Technical Conference on Experimental Safety Vehicles*, Oxford, UK; 1–4 July 1985. National Highway Traffic Safety Administration, report DOT HS 806 916. Washington, DC, p. 548–556; February 1986.

Evans, L. Estimating fatality reductions from increased safety belt use. *Risk Analysis* 7:49–57; 1987.

Evans, L. Passive compared to active approaches to reducing occupant fatalities. Paper No. ESV 89-5B-0-005, presented to the Twelfth International Technical Conference on Experimental Safety Vehicles, Gothenburg, Sweden; 29 May–1 June 1989. To be published in proceedings of the meeting.

Evans, L.; Frick, M.C. Potential fatality reductions through eliminating occupant ejection from cars. *Accident Analysis and Prevention* 21:169–182; 1989a.

Evans, L.; Frick, M.C. Relative fatality risk in different seating positions versus car model year. *Accident Analysis and Prevention* 21:581–587; 1989b.

Evans, L.; Wasielewski, P.F. Serious or fatal driver injury rate versus car mass in head-on crashes between cars of similar mass. *Accident Analysis and Prevention* 19:119–131; 1987.

Federal Highway Administration. Fatal and injury accident rates on public roads in the United States. Publication FHWA-SA-90-029, Washington, DC; 1990.

Graham, J.D. Technology, behavior and safety an empirical study of occupant-protection regulation. *Policy Sciences* 17:141–151; 1984.

Graham, J.D.; Garber, S. Evaluating the effects of automobile safety regulation. *Journal of Policy Analysis and Management* 3:206–224; 1984.

Grush, E.S.; Marsh, J.C.; South, N.E. Comparison of high speed crash test results with fatality rates. *American Association for Automotive Medicine, 27th Annual Proceedings*, San Antonio, TX, p. 189–206; 3–6 October 1983.

Haddon, W. Jr. A logical framework for categorizing highway safety phenomena and activity. *Journal of Trauma* 12:193–207; 1972.

Hauer, E. Selection for treatment as a source of bias in before-and-after studies. *Traffic Engineering and Control* 20:418–421; 1980.

Hauer, E. *Review of Published Evidence on the Safety Effect of Conversion from Two-way to Four-way Stop Sign Control*. University of Toronto, Department of Civil Engineering, publication ISBN: 0-7727 7069 7; 1985.

Hauer, E. The reign of ignorance in road safety: a case for separating evaluation from implementation. In: Moses, L.N.; Savage, I, editors. *Transportation Safety in an Age of Deregulation*. Oxford, UK: Oxford University Press, p. 56–69; 1989.

Hauer, E. A case for science-based safety design and management. In Stammer, R.E., editor. *Highway Safety: At the Crossroads*. Washington, DC: American Society of Civil Engineers, p. 241–267; 1988.

Highway Loss Data Institute. *Insurance Injury Report: Passenger Cars, Vans, Pickups, and Utility Vehicles*. Arlington, VA: Research report HLDI I88-1; September 1989.

Horowitz, A.D. *Automobile Usage: A Factbook on Trips and Weekly Travel*. Warren, MI: General Motors Research Laboratories, research publication GMR-5351; 2 April 1986.

Joksch, H.C. Analysis of the future effects of the fuel shortage and increased small car usage upon traffic deaths and injuries. Report DOT-TSC-OST-75-21; January 1976a.

Joksch, H.C. Critique of Sam Peltzman's study: The effects of automobile safety regulation. *Accident Analysis and Prevention* 8:129–137; 1976b.

Joksch, H.C. The effects of automobile safety regulation: Comments on Peltzman's reply. *Accident Analysis and Prevention* 8:213–214; 1976c.

Joksch, H.C. Light-weight car safety analysis, phase II, part II: occupant fatality and injury risk in relation to car weight. Performed under contract CEM-8102C1160, Center for the Environment and Man, Hartford, CT; June 1983.

Kahane, C.J. An evaluation of Federal Motor Vehicle Safety Standards for passenger car steering assemblies: Standard 203—impact protection for the driver; Standard 204—rearward column displacement. Washington, DC: National Highway Traffic Safety Administration, report DOT HS-805 705; January 1981.

Kahane, C.J. Evaluation of current energy-absorbing steering assemblies. SAE paper 820473. Warrendale, PA: Society of Automotive Engineers; 1982a. (Also included in: *Occupant Crash Interaction with the Steering System*. SAE special publication SP-507, p. 45–49; 1982a).

Kahane, C.J. An evaluation of side structure improvements in response to Federal Motor Vehicle Safety Standard 212. Washington, DC: National Highway Traffic Safety Administration, report DOT HS 806 314; November 1982b.

Kahane, C.J. An evaluation of head restraints—Federal Motor Vehicle Safety Standard 202. Washington, DC: National Highway Traffic Safety Administration, report DOT HS-806 108; February 1982c.

Kahane, C.J. A preliminary evaluation of two braking improvements for passenger cars—dual master cylinders and front disc brakes. Washington, DC: National Highway Traffic Safety Administration, report DOT HS-806 359; February 1983.

Kahane, C.J. The National Highway Traffic Safety Administration's evaluations of Federal Motor Vehicle Safety Standards. SAE paper 840902. Warrendale, PA: Society of Automotive Engineers; 1984.

Kahane, C.J. An evaluation of windshield glazing and installation methods for passenger cars. Washington, DC: National Highway Traffic Safety Administration, report DOT HS-806 693; February 1985.

Kahane, C.J. An evaluation of occupant protection in frontal interior impact for unrestrained front seat occupants of cars and light trucks. Washington, DC: National Highway Traffic Safety Administration, report DOT HS 807 203; January 1988.

Kahane, C.J. An evaluation of door locks and roof crush resistance of passenger cars—Federal

Motor Vehicle Safety Standards 206 and 216. Washington, DC: National Highway Traffic Safety Administration, report DOT HS 807 489; November 1989.

Mackay, M. Comment on p. 353 of Evans, L; Schwing, R.C., editors. *Human Behavior and Traffic Safety*. New York, NY: Plenum Press; 1985.

Mackie, P.J; Bonsall, P.W. Traveller response to road improvements: implications for user benefits. *Traffic Engineering and Control* 29:411–416; 1989.

McCarthy, R.L. An examination of the relationship between vehicle mass, wheelbase and safety. Paper presented to the Winter Annual Meeting of the American Society of Mechanical Engineers, San Franscisco, CA; 12–15 December 1989.

McLean, A.J. Car shape and pedestrian injury. In: *National Road Safety Symposium*, Canberra, Australia, p. 179–192; March 1972.

Mengert, P.; Salvatore, S.; DiSario, R.; Walter, R. Statistical estimation of rollover risk. Cambridge, MA: National Highway Traffic Safety Administration, Transportation Systems Center, report DOT-HS-807-446/DOT- TSC-NHTSA-89-3; August 1989.

Mortimer, R.G.; Fell, J.C. Older drivers: their night fatal crash involvement and risk. Association for the Advancement of Automotive Medicine, 32nd Annual Proceedings, Seattle, WA, p. 327–206; 12-14 September 1988.

Mueller, B.A.; Rivara, F.P.; Bergman, A.B. Factors associated with pedestrian-vehicle collision injuries and fatalities. *Western Journal of Medicine* 146:243–245; 1987.

National Highway Traffic Safety Administration. *Fatal Accident Reporting System 1988*. Document DOT HS 807 507. Washington, DC; December 1989.

Negri, D.B.; Riley, R.K. *Two Car Collision Study II*. Report DOT-HS- 245-2-478-4. Albany, NY: State of New York, Department of Motor Vehicles; June 1974.

Orr, L.D. The effectiveness of automobile safety regulation: evidence from the FARS data. *American Journal of Public Health* 74:1384–1389; 1984.

Orr, L.D. Auto safety regulation variable: a reply to Robertson. *American Journal of Public Health* 75:789–790; 1985.

Partyka, S.C. *Lives Saved by Seat Belts from 1983 through 1987*. National Highway Traffic Safety Administration. Washington, DC; June 1988.

Partyka, S.C. Registration-based fatality rates by car size from 1978 through 1987. In: *Papers on Car Size—Safety and Trends*, National Highway Traffic Safety Administration, report DOT HS 807 444, p. 45–72; June 1989a.

Partyka, S.C. Recomputation of results in Partyka [1989a] for drivers only rather than all occupants. Private communication 1989b.

Partyka, S.C. Differences in reported car weight between fatality and registration data files. *Accident Analysis and Prevention* 22:161–166; 1990.

Partyka, S.C.; Boehly, W.A. Passenger car weight and injury severity in single vehicle nonrollover crashes. Paper ESV 89-2B-0-005, presented to the Twelfth International Technical Conference on Experimental Safety Vehicles, Gothenburg, Sweden; 29 May-1 June 1989. To be published in proceedings of the meeting.

Peltzman, S. The effects of automobile safety regulation. *Journal of Political Economy* 83:677–725; 1975.

Peltzman, S. The effects of automobile safety regulation: reply. *Accident Analysis and Prevention* 8:139–142; 1976.

Persaud, B.N. Do traffic signals affect safety? Some methodological issues. Paper 870610, presented to the 67th Annual Meeting of the Transportation Research Board, Washington, DC; 11–14 January 1988.

Robertson, L.S. A critical analysis of Peltzman's "The effects of automobile safety regulation." *Journal of Economic Issues* ll:586–600; 1977.

Robertson, L.S. Automobile safety regulations and death reductions in the United States. *American Journal of Public Health* 71:818–822; 1981.

Robertson, L.S. Automobile safety regulation: rebuttal and new data. *American Journal of Public Health* 74:1390–1394; 1984.

Robertson, L.S. Rejoinder from Robertson (to Orr 1985). *American Journal of Public Health* 75:790–790; 1985.

Robertson, L.S. Risk of fatal rollover in utility vehicles relative to static stability. *American Journal of Public Health* 79:300–303; 1989.

Rumar, K. The role of perceptual and cognitive filters in observed behavior. In: Evans, L; Schwing, R.C., editors. *Human Behavior and Traffic Safety*. New York, NY: Plenum Press, p. 151–165; 1985.

Sabey, B.E.; Staughton, G.C. Interacting roles of road environment, vehicle and road user in accidents. Presented to the Fifth International Conference of the International Association for Accident and Traffic Medicine, London, UK; 1975.

Sabey, B.E.; Taylor, H. The known risks we run: the highway. In: Schwing, R.C.; Albers, W.A., editors. *Societal Risk Assessment—How Safe is Safe Enough?* New York, NY: Plenum Press, p. 43–63; 1980.

Schwing, R.C.; Evans, L.; Schreck, R.M. Uncertainties in diesel engine health effects (a comment on two papers). *Risk Analysis* 3:129–131; 1983.

Schwing, R.C; Kamerud, D.B. The distribution of risks: vehicle occupant fatalities and time of the week. *Risk Analysis* 8:127–133; 1988.

Shinar, D. Comment on p. 166-167 of Evans, L; Schwing, R.C., editors. *Human Behavior and Traffic Safety*. New York, NY: Plenum Press; 1985.

Stonex, K.A. Vehicle aspects of the single-car accident problem. *Second Regional Conference on Single-car Accidents,* Flint, MI; October 1962.

Treat, J.R. A study of precrash factors involved in traffic accidents. *The HSRI Research Review,* Ann Arbor, MI; May-August 1980.

Wasielewski, P.F.; Evans, L. Do drivers of small cars take less risk in everyday driving? *Risk Analysis* 5:25–32; 1985.

Yankauer, A. Deregulation and the right to life. *American Journal of Public Health* 71:797–798; 1981.

Zlatoper, T.J. Regression analysis of time series data on motor vehicle deaths in the United States. *Journal of Transport Economics* 18:263–274; 1984.

5 Driver Performance

INTRODUCTION

One of the most remarkable features about vehicle driving is that a very large fraction of the human race can do it. Not only can most people do it, but they learn to perform it in a rudimentary fashion in a matter of weeks or months, and without expending large amounts of time or energy. This remarkable state of affairs can not be predicted from any known general principles of how people learn, or on the difficulty of performing the component skills which collectively constitute driving. In 1901 Carl Benz thought that the global market for the automobile was limited because, "There were going to be no more than one million people capable of being trained as chauffeurs" (as quoted by Mackay [1990]; also cited in slightly different form by Macrae [1988, p. 18]). If automobiles and stringed musical instruments did not exist, but were suddenly invented, there is no theory which would predict that most people could learn to use one, but only a few would be able to use the other, and then only after years of dedicated effort. Indeed, given that music is about as old as humanity, it would seem natural to expect people to quickly realize that if a note is flat, you just slide your finger up the string until it sounds right. In contrast, it is only in the last few hundred years that humans have been able to travel at speeds exceeding those produced by muscle power. A common sense guess might be that just about everyone could rattle off many tunes on a stringed instrument after an hour's instruction, but only the gifted few, after years of dedicated training, could reliably keep a 1500 kg car travelling at 100 km/h within a 4 m freeway lane surrounded on all four sides by other vehicles.

More than 30 years after *human factors* became a formal discipline, with journals and organizations, questions are still posed [Boff 1988], with some frustration and anguish, regarding how all the knowledge acquired can be distilled into coherent models of how people learn and perform. Notwithstanding the lack of any effective overall model of how people drive, a great deal has been learned about various specific aspects of the driving task. The techniques for studying driver capabilities and performance have included observing actual drivers in traffic, experiments using instrumented vehicles, and studies using driving simulators of varying degrees of sophistication and realism. Below we skim the surface of this large body of literature.

THE ACQUISITION OF DRIVING SKILL

Although there are no effective models to predict the rate of learning and proficiency of one task compared to another, some patterns have been observed common to the acquisition of complex skills in general. Fitts and Posner [1967] consider that such acquisition occurs in three phases:

1. Early, or cognitive phase
2. Intermediate, or associative phase
3. Final, or autonomous phase

This categorization fits well the acquisition of driving skill.

In the early, or cognitive phase, the person learning the task tries to understand the components. For driving, the location of the controls and what vehicle responses they produce must be learned. In the intermediate phase, different strategies are explored, and the learner is acutely attentive to feedback. The learner-driver devotes full attention to the task, and increases skill by responding to feedback either from observed consequences of inputs, or from directions from an instructor. The skill of knowing what output is required in specific traffic situations develops together with the skill of knowing what input produces the desired output. In the third, or autonomous phase, the task is performed at a high level with minimal effort, in part because behavior becomes rather fixed and inflexible. In this autonomous phase, the task can be performed using a small fraction of the driver's attention. Other tasks, such as navigation, looking for specific addresses, conversation, admiring the scenery, listening to the radio, or thinking about other matters, can be performed. In this autonomous stage, the mental capacity assigned to the driving task, although small, is still such that if a threatening incident occurs, all attention is quickly switched to the driving task. Most drivers have personally experienced this many times when, for example, driving along awaiting some specific portion of a radio broadcast. An incident occurs in traffic, the driver responds, and later realizes that the sought after radio information, although broadcast, has not been perceived.

The Beginning Driver

A clear indication of the changes that occur as driving skill increases is provided by research on eye movements which identifies the location in the visual field on which the subject is fixating. Fig. 5-1 shows data from an experiment conducted by Zell in 1969, as reported by Mourant and Rockwell [1970]. The density of eye fixations superimposed on a schematic representation of the lane markings on a straight section of freeway is displayed. In the first hours of

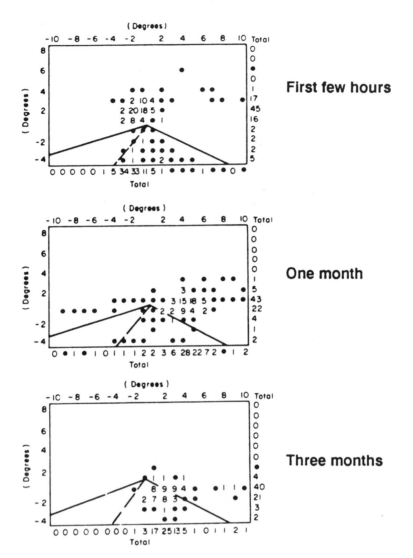

Figure 5-1. Eye fixations of novice drivers as a function of driving experience for driving on an open road at 50 mph. Reprinted from Mourant and Rockwell [1970] with permission © 1970 Society of Automotive Engineers, Inc.

driving experience, the driver scanned over a wide area, including points well above the horizon. After about a month's driving experience, the fixations are more confined in the vertical direction, but still vary horizontally. After three months' experience, fixations are more concentrated at the focus of expansion of the roadway, with a much greater reliance on peripheral vision for cues to control the vehicle's lateral position in the lane. When they compared fixations of novice and experienced drivers, Mourant and Rockwell [1972] found additional evidence that as drivers gain experience they concentrate their eye fixations in a smaller area. Novice drivers looked closer in front of the vehicle and more to the right of the vehicle's direction than did experienced drivers. It appears that the novice drivers frequently sample the curb to estimate the vehicle's lane location. The novice drivers sample the rear-view mirrors much less frequently than the experienced drivers. The results suggest that the novice drivers are unskilled and overloaded in their visual acquisition task.

These results indicate that the first few times behind the wheel almost all of the information processing capacity is absorbed in simply maintaining the car's position in the lane. As experience is gained, peripheral vision is used more to locate the vehicle in the lane, with fixations focused further down the road to allow more time to process information that becomes of increasing relevance as the vehicle's speed increases. The relative ineffectiveness of scanning patterns of the novice drivers probably accounts for Summala and Näätänen's [1974] finding that, even when specifically instructed to pay attention to road signs, inexperienced drivers miss significantly more signs than experienced drivers. Brown [1982] reports that young drivers are relatively poor at identifying distant hazards, although they compare well with older drivers in identifying near hazards. Psychophysical performance at many of the component tasks of driving are found to develop rapidly during early stages of learning to drive [Rockwell 1972, p. 149].

The early stages of learning to drive are characterized by substantial levels of fear. As driving skill increases, fear decreases. Job [1990] comments that training courses focusing on skill, and on producing relaxed and confident drivers, may provide desensitization of fear in more risky situations. Although driving remains one of the riskiest activities, it soon becomes relatively unconnected with fear. We retain greater fear of objectively safer situations. As Rumar [1985] discusses, evolution imparted us with a natural fear of heights which is so ingrained that we retain it in the absence of reinforcing experiences. We do not lean far out of a window on the third floor, from which height a freely falling object would strike the ground at 50 km/h. Yet we travel at much higher vehicle speeds without feelings of anxiety. As smooth locomotion through the environment is not part of our evolutionary heritage, we have no built-in basic fear of it. After we acquire basic driving skills, driving becomes relaxing and unassociated with danger. We largely lose that protection described by Shakespeare [Hamlet, Act I, Scene 3], "Best safety lies in fear."

Early Stages of Driving and Crash Rates

Although crash data show consistently that the youngest drivers have the highest crash rates (Chapter 2), it is difficult to attribute all of this to lack of skill [Summala 1987]. If skill were the sole factor, then the observed lower crash rates for 40-year-old drivers than for 30-year-old drivers would imply important additional skill acquisition even decades after first learning to drive. While such a sustained learning curve is not impossible, it is a learning curve not encountered for other perceptual-motor skills.

While skill is not the only important factor, crash data nonetheless provide indications that lack of skill in novice drivers contributes to crashes. Fig. 3-10 shows that rollover crashes (the main component of the top/non-collision category) account for a larger fraction of fatalities to 16-year-old drivers than to drivers of any other age; a rollover crash may result from an inability to steer effectively. In contrast, frontal crashes account for a smaller fraction of fatalities to 16-year-old drivers than to drivers of any other age; frontal fatal crashes, typically into fixed objects such as trees, generally suggest high speeds. There is high reliability in the measured differences between the 16-year-old and older drivers because the data are many and do not involve external exposure measures; indeed, the effect is equally clear if the analysis is confined to single-vehicle crashes [Evans 1991]. The noticeably larger difference that occurs from age 16 to 17 compared to (say) from age 17 to 18 suggests effects due to lack of driving experience. Lack of skill is likely a more dominant factor in the beginning driver's high rate of involvement in minor crashes. Smiley, Reid, and Fraser [1980] find changes in steering control strategy as novices begin to learn to drive, but of a less clear nature than observed in visual search patterns.

Fuller [1988] considers that young drivers are overinvolved for three reasons; they are exposed to more risky conditions, they are more likely to experience risk as intrinsically rewarding, and they are inexperienced. Objections can be raised to the exposure explanation; the main factor causing high risk to be associated with nighttime driving, is the very presence of young drivers. In any event, Jonah [1986, p. 257] concludes that, "Even when one controls for the quantity and quality of exposure to risk, young drivers are still at greatest risk of casualty accident involvement." The seeking of risk, or intrinsic nature of youth, seems to me the main factor, although experience is also important. Evidence hinting at an important influence of experience is provided by Polus, Hocherman, and Efrat [1988] who find that female drivers on rural roads in Israel were more involved in single-vehicle crashes, but less involved in multiple-vehicle crashes than male drivers, even though the females drove more slowly.

The Israeli female drivers (unlike female drivers in the US) obtained driving licenses at considerably older ages than the male drivers. The authors interpret the absence of a net difference in crash rate, notwithstanding greater caution, to less driving experience by the female drivers. A similar interpretation might apply to the finding of Carsten, Tight, and Southwell [1989] that judgment errors were more frequently coded for female than male drivers in injury producing crashes in Leeds, UK.

Driver Education and Training

If increased rates of crashing were due to lack of skill, then training and education would appear to be a natural countermeasure. Although there have been many studies of the influence of driver education on crash rates, none with acceptable methodology has shown that those who receive driver education have lower crash rates than those who do not. Indeed, Lund, Williams, and Zador [1986], in analyzing data from the largest evaluation of driver education to date, in DeKalb County, Georgia, conclude that the most noticeable effect is to enable those who take it to acquire licenses at an earlier age. Having acquired the licenses, these drivers then experience crash rates typical for their age, and as a consequence end up with more crashes than if they had not received driver education. In an earlier study, Robertson [1980] comes to a similar conclusion. Brown, Groeger, and Biehl [1987] conclude that there is no reliable evidence of safety benefits from driver training. Potvin, Champagne, and Laberge-Nadeau [1988] find no effect on crash rates from driver training in Quebec, Canada.

Helander [1984] provides convincing evidence that crash-involved drivers subject to certain intervention strategies are about 20% less likely to have subsequent crashes than are untreated drivers. Although the interventions involve training, it is not clear whether the mechanism producing the crash reduction is the knowledge acquired, or the experience of detailed interaction with the authorities. The effect may be more in the realm of enforcement and deterrence rather than education and training. Post-licensure training programs have not been shown to reduce crash rates. Lund and Williams [1985] review 14 controlled studies of the effects of defensive driving course training programs. They conclude that, while the methodologically strong studies show a decrease in the frequency of traffic violations, no consistent effect on crashes is apparent. Some states require drivers with multiple citations or crashes to attend such courses. Others require automobile insurers to give discounts to graduates of approved training courses. Clearly, if there were convincing evidence that such courses reduced crash rates, then discounts would be given as part of the actuarial process without the need for compulsion. There are presently widespread efforts to increase training programs for older drivers, with a move to provide compulsory insurance reductions for graduates without any evidence that the programs do indeed reduce crash rates. A possible reason why training and education do not lead to clear changes in safety is that so much of the skill and knowledge they aim to impart will be learned by trial and error, and by experience. Without instruction, drivers will learn how to negotiate corners, park, reverse, and perform all the repetitive tasks based on experimentation and feedback.

Further indications that increased knowledge does not translate into reduced crash rates is provided by Conley and Smiley [1976] who trace the four year driving records of over 22 523 licensed drivers in Illinois. No relationships are found between performance on a pencil and paper license test and subsequent violation and crash rates.

It is often claimed that crash involvement itself plays a crucial role in education, and that older drivers have lower rates because the crashes they had when they were younger taught them a lesson, or as Shakespeare [King Lear, Act III, Scene 1] put it, "The injuries that they themselves procure must be their schoolmasters." While such effects almost certainly occur, there seems little possibility of empirical investigation.

Motorcycle riding requires learning specific control and balancing skills beyond those required for driving vehicles with more than two wheels. McDavid, Lohrmann, and Lohrmann [1989] provide evidence from their own study, and from their review of many prior studies, that motorcycle training does appear to lead to somewhat lower motorcyclist crash rates.

The absence of proven safety benefits from driver education does not prove that training cannot increase safety, but merely that none of the methods so far applied have been demonstrated to be successful. The importance of traffic safety justifies continuing searching aimed at discovering more effective training techniques. Michon [1989] claims that rule-based approaches rooted in cognitive psychology have promise.

Although there is an absence of evidence from countries in mature stages of motorization that traditional driver education or the possession of specific knowledge is associated with lower crash rates, Trinca et al. [1988, p. 68] invite caution in assuming that this necessarily applies to countries in early stages of motorization. I share this caution, especially as crash rates are so much higher in less motorized countries, and some fraction of the excess might be due to insufficient knowledge or skill. In motorized countries, pre-driving-age teenagers already have a large body of information about the rules of the road and how to behave in traffic. They have been riding in, and getting out of the way of, motorized vehicles since infancy. Rockwell [1972, p. 150] writes that much of driving skill development greatly depends on exposure both as a driver and passenger in the family automobile environment. The few weeks of driver education makes but a modest increment to this large pool of knowledge. People not growing up surrounded by motorization, who start with a lesser pool of knowledge, might possibly acquire in driver education programs specific knowledge that is already well known by children in motorized countries. Any specific conclusion about the value of driver education in less motorized countries must await specific evaluation studies.

Longer Term Experience

Although crash rates are minimum at about age 40, this does not necessarily imply that driver performance reaches a maximum at this age. Factors other than skill contribute to crash rates. Little of a specific nature is known about the development of higher level driving skills beyond the changes in the very early stages of learning, although much is known about the reduced sensory capability with ageing that contributes to increased crash rates with increasing age beyond about 40. There are no directly measured indications of changes in driver skill from, say, one year's experience to 10 or 20 years' experience. While skill at the components of driving increases rapidly in early learning, the ability to identify and extract relevant information from a complex cluttered traffic environment appears to come more slowly. Perhaps a distinction should be drawn between perceptual-motor skills and total performance which additionally incorporates more advanced and complex information processing capacities. These additional abilities, which might be described as road sense, or good traffic judgment, develop over many years.

It is almost impossible to investigate such phenomena experimentally. On the one hand, it is not feasible to compare drivers with, say, one year's experience to those with ten years' experience because, if done at one time, differences between the two samples of drivers would probably overwhelm any possible difference due to experience; the thought in the title of Brown's [1982] "Exposure and experience are a confounded nuisance in research on driver behaviour" applies. On the other hand, longitudinal studies, using the same drivers tested nine years apart, are also infeasible; even if there were a commitment to such ongoing research, and a sufficient number of subjects returned for retesting, changes in roadways, vehicle and traffic characteristics, and traffic volumes would make it difficult to attribute any observed changes to increased driver skill.

Although there is no specific evidence available, and unlikely to be any, I share the view of most observers that higher level driving skills do continue to increase with driving experience even over time frames of the order of decades. The ability to extract and correctly process relevant information from a complex visual field appears to increase, and there appear to be ongoing increases in driver abilities to project further in time. We saw above that the novice driver is grimly focused on the present location of the vehicle, whereas as skills increase, visual attention focuses more on the vanishing point ahead—where the vehicle will be in the future. As each task becomes more overlearned, the driver acquires more spare mental capacity which, through learning by feedback, focuses further ahead.

Driving seems to abound with examples in which events more and more in the future can beneficially influence present decisions. For example, a driver with a few years experience will likely approach a car stopped at a red light on a straight road in a manner that is independent of how many vehicles are stopped, or when the light turned red; all attention is on the vehicle ahead to the exclusion of other cues. A more experienced driver may slow down gently a long way from the light if it has just turned red or if there is a long line of stopped vehicles, but maintain a higher speed if the light has been red for some time and there are only a few vehicles waiting. The more experienced driver is more likely to have learned that in the first case stopping is essentially inevitable, whereas in the second case stopping, or even slowing down, may not be required. Which of these cases applies depends on events well in advance of the decision to slow down now or continue to monitor the situation further before acting.

The less experienced driver tends to use turn signals more as part of the ceremony of turning or changing lanes, rather than to warn other road users of intent. For turn-signal information to be really useful, it should be the first indication of an intended maneuver; providing corroborative information after the vehicle has initiated the maneuver is of minimal value. As some drivers increase in experience, the warning time they provide other road users of intending maneuvers increases. It should be emphasized that some less experienced drivers exhibit the more advanced behavior in the above examples, while some experienced drivers exhibit the less advanced behavior—there are large variations amongst drivers at each stage of experience.

Even drivers with high crash rates still complete the vast majority of trips without crashing; a driver with a crash rate ten times the average would still, on average, drive about a year, or ten thousand miles, between crashes. Even for such a high risk driver, a crash is a rare event. For such a driver, even the frequency of near-misses would still be insufficient to teach which actions are likely to lead to crashes. Drivers learn to negotiate corners skillfully by practicing such maneuvers hundreds of times; each time it is done badly, corrections can be planned for the next time. Thus driving skills are learned and polished largely by experimentation and direct feedback. In contrast, safety can be learned only by more indirect means, benefiting from the experience of the whole society rather than each driver learning from individual experience. Aspects of safety will not be learned by experience in the same sense that people are unlikely to learn by experience that the earth is spherical.

THE COMPONENTS OF THE DRIVING TASK

When decomposed into fine detail, the driving task has much complexity, involving as it does the simultaneous control of lateral and longitudinal position through the use of steering wheel, accelerator and brakes, together with many pattern recognition and other higher level cognitive skills, such as estimating future situations from present information. McKnight and Adams [1970] identify about 1500 different perceptual-motor tasks in driving. Although I consider the task to be more holistic in nature, such a taxonomy is useful in helping establish its complexity.

Basically, the driving task is a 'closed-loop compensatory feedback control process, meaning that the driver makes inputs (to the steering wheel, brake and accelerator pedal), receives feedback by monitoring the results of the inputs, and in response to the results, makes additional inputs; an open loop process is one, such as throwing a baseball, in which once the process is initiated no corrections are possible based on later knowledge about the trajectory. Below some comments about the major building blocks that comprise the driving task are presented.

Predominance of Visual Feedback

The feedback used to monitor driving is overwhelmingly visual. I see no reason to dissent from Rockwell's [1972, p. 150] statement that vision in driving is believed to constitute over 90% of information input to the driver. A questionnaire administered by Gardner and Rockwell [1983] revealed that most drivers relied on their own judgment rather than signs when making decisions about speed and lane changes when encountering freeway construction and maintenance zones. Indeed, an extensive body of research on sign perception reviewed by Näätänen and Summala [1976, p. 115–130] indicates that drivers generally ignore signs if the information conveyed by them can be extracted directly from the visual environment. This is further substantiated by Shinar and Drory [1983], who find that in daylight drivers had little recall of signs they had just passed on a road in Israel. It appeared they placed more reliance on their own observation and judgment of impending danger, taking little note of the existence of the sign. In contrast, at night, when potential hazards are less visible, recollection of the same signs was much greater. Although viewed through the windshield, the signs could, conceptually at least, be presented in other ways, such as an on-board display. The driver's preferred mode of operation is to pursue a visual search, and only resort to other information sources when problems arise.

The preponderance of visual information over that from all other senses, while always high in driving, probably increases yet further with increasing skill levels. For example, proprioceptive cues (those from the force and position of hands and arms in supplying control inputs) are of minor importance, and, surprisingly, are even less likely to be noticed by more experienced than less experienced drivers. A skilled driver is relatively unaware of the gain in the steering system (the amount the steering wheel must be turned to alter the vehicle's direction by a given angle). When transferring to cars with higher (or lower) steering system gains, experienced drivers do not travel more (less) sharply around corners, or have difficulty maintaining lane position. Instead, they react to the visual information by making the steering input necessary to achieve the desired visual result without being much aware how much they moved the wheel and in such a manner that there are no observable changes in the behavior of the vehicle. Similar comments apply to different force characteristics, or, in the extreme, to power versus manual steering. Less experienced drivers are more aware of changes in steering system gain or force-feel characteristics, and their driving can be noticeably influenced by transferring to a different vehicle. The dominance of visual feedback in driving is similar to dominance of aural feedback in playing a stringed musical instrument. Intonation (playing in tune) is not controlled by the proprioceptive sense of remembering where to place the fingers, but by listening to what comes out. A learner training on an instrument of one size will play one of a different size (on which all the finger placings are different) more out of tune, whereas a skilled player will be less aware that there is even a difference, just as in the steering gain case.

Visual Performance

Given the predominance of the visual sense in driving, one might expect that visual performance and crash risks would be intimately related. Such is not the case, because when driver visual acuity and contrast sensitivity are highest, in the earliest years of driving, so are crash rates. Crash rates decline to a minimum at about age 40 years, by which time visual acuity and contrast sensitivity have already begun to decline, as have other visual capabilities relevant to driving, such as the ability to withstand glare [Sturgis and Osgood 1982]. At older ages visual performance declines further at such driving tasks as reading signs at night [Sivak, Olson, and Pastalan 1981]. Concern has increased that such changes might seriously detract from the abilities of older drivers to drive safely [Yanik 1985].

Because the relationship between visual performance and age is quite different from the relationship between traffic crash rates and age, one must conclude that visual performance alone is not the key to driver safety. This view is further reinforced by such information as does exist on the safety of monocular drivers. Liessma [1977, p. 31], using data from 1021 drivers stopped by traffic police, conclude that "The monocular driver is not an above average source of accidents." Data collected by the District of Columbia Department of Motor Vehicles [Medically Handicapped Drivers 1973] show 20 crashes per 1000 for monocular drivers, about a quarter of the average rate. So the available literature [see also Thalmann 1971] provides little evidence that so specific a vision deficiency as the loss of one eye is associated with elevated crash rates. A related finding is the absence of any important correlations between crash rates and static visual acuity, dynamic acuity, visual field, glare recovery and recognition in low illumination for groups of subjects under 25 years and over 54 years [Davison 1978].

Higher level visual search and pattern recognition skills are probably more important in driving than optimum performance at simple visual tasks. From the loosely structured, but stimuli-rich, visual environment the driver must select the relevant, a task so central that the driver has been considered [Shinar 1978] to be an information processor. One of the few indications in the literature of a link between driver performance measures and crash involvement rates relates to driver information-processing abilities [Avolio, Kroeck, and Panek 1985].

Judgment of Speed

Of the various quantities a driver is called upon to judge, speed is the only one for which instrumented quantitative feedback is provided on a regular basis. Each time a driver consults a speedometer, a comparison can be made between perceived and actual speed. Such consultations are additionally motivated by the need to obey speed limits. The overlearning of this task might suggest that drivers would become very good at it.

The ability of drivers to estimate speed without the use of a speedometer has been investigated in a number of studies. Denton [1966] instructed drivers of cars with obscured speedometers to double or halve an initial speed of magnitude unknown to the subject, set by following experimenter instructions. The subjects' attempts to decelerate or accelerate to halve or double these speeds were biased by large amounts in the direction of the initial speed. For example, the goal of doubling an initial speed of 30 mph produced an average speed of 44 mph, rather than the nominally correct 60 mph. The goal of halving 60 mph produced, on average, 38 mph. Noguchi [1990] instructed subjects to drive at their chosen speeds on closed roads; when the speedometer was concealed, speeds were consistently higher (in all of 14 comparisons) than when the speedometer was visible, with the overall average difference being 3 km/h.

In other studies, subjects in passenger seats have estimated the speed of a car in which they were travelling. The car was driven by an experimenter, and the speedometer could not be seen by the subject. Noguchi [1990] instructed subjects to keep their eyes on the focus of expansion, and finds that travel speeds are consistently underestimated (the subjects thought they were travelling slower than they were). Milosevic [1986] and Evans [1970a] asked subjects to estimate speed without specifying where they should look, and find that subjects estimated normal driving speeds without large average systematic errors; errors averaged over all subjects tested are typically less than 5 km/h. When hearing is restricted, both studies find systematic speed underestimation, typically by about 8 km/h. Further evidence of the importance of hearing in judging speed is provided by

Evans [1970a] who finds that blindfolded subjects could judge speed without systematic error, and by McLane and Wierwille [1975] who find that depriving subjects in a driving simulator of auditory cues increased inaccuracy at maintaining instructed speeds.

The importance of auditory information in judging speed motivated Triggs and Berenyi [1982] to mask this cue. They were interested in how drivers would estimate speed in conditions, such as negotiating a freeway ramp, in which looking at the speedometer is unlikely. They reasoned that the auditory information would be likely masked by other sounds, such as a radio playing. Subjects were given one second glimpses of the roadway using an occlusion helmet. Under daylight conditions speeds were systematically underestimated by about 10 km/h; judgments made at night were more accurate. Subjects viewing a silent movie [Evans 1970b] photographed looking forward from the passenger seat of a moving car underestimated the car's speed to a degree similar to that found for the hearing-deprived subjects making judgments from this same car. Noguchi [1990] finds that subject estimations of speeds of video scenes shot from a moving car are consistently underestimated by substantial amounts, which might also be related to auditory cues.

While the above experiments indicate that hearing plays a contributory role in estimating speed, it is still the movement of objects in the visual field that provides the main cues to motion, and variations in these can generate different sensations of motion. Shinar, McDowell, and Rockwell [1974] find that drivers instructed to maintain a nominal speed of 60 mph without the aid of a speedometer drove at an average speed of 57 mph on an open road segment compared to an average speed of 53 mph on another tree-lined segment of the same road. Denton [1973] used a geometric pattern of bars with decreasing spacing on a roadway to induce vehicles to reduce speed; the pattern is such that at constant speed it generated a sensation of increasing speed.

Although there are indications in the literature, as discussed by Shinar [1978, p 82], that peripheral vision provides most of the cues to motion, the situation is probably rather complex and involves learned geometrical relationships. In the movie film study by Evans [1970b], subjects at the rear of the auditorium judged speeds to be $(11 \pm 3)\%$ higher than those at the front, notwithstanding that the rates of visual angle change are clearly less at the rear. For every picture, there is only one viewing distance which preserves the original perspective, and therefore, even more, the original motion cues in their correct geometrical relationship to the scene. Those standing further away from the screen than this viewing distance will sense faster motion, and those nearer will experience slower motion. We are all very familiar with this phenomenon in long focus (telephoto lens) pictures of racing cars approaching the camera. The racing car seems almost motionless when viewed on the screen. To preserve a non-distorted sense of the car's speed, the screen would have to be viewed from a distance increased in proportion to the ratio of the focal length of the lens photographing the picture to that of a more typical lens. Viewed from such a distance the picture would be free from motion distortion, but too distant to convey useful information.

Speed Adaptation

Another sensation we are all probably familiar with is that after prolonged driving at highway speeds, lower speeds seem even lower than they really are. This phenomenon, referred to as speed adaptation, is examined by Schmidt and Tiffin [1969] who had subjects drive at 70 mph for specified distances, after which they were instructed to slow down to 40 mph. They find that the longer the exposure to 70 mph, the higher is the speed later produced to represent 40 mph. After driving 40 miles at 70 mph, the average driver decelerated only to 53 mph in response to the request to produce 40 mph. Denton [1976] finds that a subject's selection of a target speed is highly influenced by the subject's previous speed. After simulated driving at about 70 mph for three minutes, subjects underestimated a simulated 30 mph by between 5 to 15 mph; the perception that the speed is lower than actual persisted for at least 4 minutes. Matthews [1978] measured speeds of vehicles traveling in each of two directions on a four-lane divided highway. One direction of traffic had been exposed previously to expressway speeds of about 60 mph, while vehicles in the other direction had been exposed to about 40 mph. For each of seven categories of vehicles examined, higher speeds are observed for those exposed to the higher prior speed. The magnitude of the effect is that those previously exposed to 60 mph travelled about 7% faster than those exposed to 40 mph. It is not possible to determine to what extent this difference is due to speeds being perceived differently, or to drivers merely tending to continue driving close to their prior speeds because of behavioral inertia. Casey and Lund [1987] address this distinction by choosing sites which required drivers to slow down or stop prior to entering the section of roadway on which their speeds were measured. They find, typically, effects about half of the 7% effect observed by Matthews [1978], but are able to attribute them more unambiguously to prior speeds influencing the perceptual sensation of subsequent speeds. It is, however, worth noting that the act of slowing down after prolonged freeway driving may itself influence the speed adaptation phenomenon, in that the prior speed becomes not the freeway speed, but (for a short exposure), a slow or zero speed.

The tendency to drive faster on a given road because of prior high speeds on a different road, regardless of the extent to which it is due to perceptual biases in speed estimation or to speed perpetuation, has important safety implications. Through this phenomenon, speed limits, and changes in speed limits, may have spillover effects that influence safety on roads other than the ones directly affected. Indeed, Brown, Maghsoodloo, and McArdle [1989] find evidence that property damage crashes increased on stretches of Alabama Interstate highway on which the speed limit remained fixed at 55 mph when the speed limit on other sections was increased from 55 mph to 65 mph.

Speed adaptation appears to be largely a perceptual illusion not unlike many optical illusions in which how part of a simple drawing is perceived is greatly influenced by adjacent parts of the drawing. As visual training and experience do not make optical illusions disappear, it seems unlikely that experience or training would make speed adaptation disappear. This underlines the importance of speedometer use, especially when exiting from a freeway after prolonged travel, or when travelling on streets with low speed limits after travelling at higher speeds. The speedometer is thus an example of an instrument providing important information beyond that obtained by the driver by just looking out of the car.

Judgment of Relative Speed

Judgments of speed arise mainly in isolated, relatively unconstrained driving. Most driving is spent constrained by a vehicle in front, although there does not appear to be any quantitative estimate of the fraction of driving spent following vehicles. The car-following situation has been the focus of much investigation, and elegant mathematical descriptions of it have been developed [Herman and Potts 1961]. Each vehicle (except the lead) in a platoon of vehicles reacts, after a time delay, to a stimulus arising from its relationship with the vehicle in front. The reaction is an acceleration or deceleration. Various forms of the stimulus have been explored, but the one most successful at explaining a great deal of experimental data is the relative speed divided by the spacing. One of the least successful is the spacing between the vehicles. It appears that the following driver does not attempt to, or is unable to, maintain a desired spacing by accelerating or decelerating when the actual spacing becomes larger or smaller than desired. Rather, when the vehicles move apart, the driver accelerates, and when they approach, the driver decelerates.

There have been many studies of perceptual thresholds of the stimuli that drivers use in car following, as summarized by Evans and Rothery [1977]. In keeping with the results from the car-following experiments, it is found that the ability to judge relative speed is approximately inversely proportional to inter-vehicle spacing. This shows that the primary cue, at least within the distance range of car following (up to about 150 m), is not simply the change in the angle the target car subtends at the subject's eye; if this were so, then a simple geometrical calculation shows that sensitivity would be inversely proportional to the square of the spacing. At greater distances, the cue may be changes in the angle the target subtends, as suggested by Michaels [1965], with the implication that for the same probability of detection, the speed must increase as the square of the spacing; Michael's suggested threshold value of 6×10^{-4} rad/s is provided by a speed of 100 km/h at a viewing distance of 300 m.

Evans and Rothery [1974] investigated the ability to judge the sign of relative motion in a car-following situation by placing an occlusion device (Fig. 5-2) in front of the eyes of subjects who rode in the right-front-passenger seat of an instrumented car. This car followed another instrumented car on a freeway. When the experimenter in the following car judged that the relative speed between the vehicles was sufficiently close to zero to make judging its sign difficult, he pressed a button which opened the occlusion device to allow the subject to view the lead car for four seconds. The subject's task was to move a lever forward if the cars were judged to have come closer (negative relative speed) and backwards if thy were judged to have moved further apart. Instructions called for a "forced choice"—one or the other response was required for each stimulus. As is common in forced choice experiments, even for stimuli so small that subjects indicated that they were only guessing, they were in fact scoring well above the chance level.

One surprising result of this experiment is a highly consistent response bias in favor of judging the relative speeds to be more negative than they were; for example, when the spacing was between 100 m and 200 m, there was a 75% probability that zero relative speed was perceived as negative relative speed [Evans and Rothery 1973]. This bias, in the direction of increased safety, is likely induced by motion cues resulting from the subject's speed (about 70 km/h) relative to the roadway environment, and may be some type of dynamic optical illusion worthy of further laboratory study. Its existence makes it unlikely that estimates from a moving vehicle of the speed of another vehicle would depend simply on the change in the angle subtended at the viewer's eyes, even at large spacings. Because of the bias, which increased in magnitude with inter-vehicle spacing, it is not possible to express the results in terms of one threshold value because different values for positive and negative relative speed pertained at each spacing. However, the experiment showed high capabilities at judging the sign of relative motion. For example, if a lead car 60 m away is approaching the following car at 5 km/h, the following driver's probability of correctly identifying the relative motion as negative is 0.99.

The results show that inability of attentive drivers to judge that they are approaching a lead car is an unlikely explanation of rear-end crashes. The study did not ask subjects to estimate the magnitude of relative speed, but only its sign. A driver could perceive correctly that a lead car was coming closer, but realize too late that the closing speed was much greater than thought. Violation of expectancy is probably a more important factor in rear-end crashes than limitations in the ability to perceive the sign or magnitude of relative speed. It is not so much that the following driver has too slow a reaction time, or misjudges closing speed, but that the cognitive process is dominated by the expectation

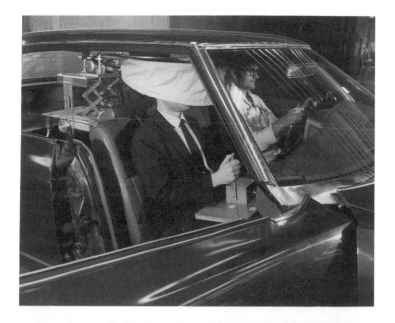

Figure 5-2.   Eye occlusion device used in experiments to determine perceptual thresholds in detecting relative speed [Evans and Rothery 1973; 1974]. The top picture shows occluded vision, and the bottom picture shows unobstructed vision.

that the lead car will continue to travel at constant speed, or, in the case of a stationery car on a freeway, will travel at a speed appropriate for the roadway. Repeated experience builds robust expectancies for many driving situations. If, over many years, a driver exiting from a home driveway on the way to work finds little traffic on the main street, and essentially all of this coming in the predominant commuting direction, the tendency to check the other direction may erode. The unexpected nature of such events as another commuter speeding back home to retrieve a forgotten item, rather than the exiting driver's inability to perceive fast uncoming cars, could explain why so many crashes of this type occur [Campbell 1990].

Judgment of Spacing

People tend to be able to judge distance reliably over a wide distance range [Sedgwick 1986]. The short distance cues of accommodation (the focusing of the eye's lens) and binocular disparity (the eyes having to aim more towards each other as viewed objects become nearer) are of little consequence in judging distances of objects outside a vehicle one is driving. Most distances that require judgment are in the range of 5 m to 500 m. Many factors have been shown to influence spacing judgments. For example, size constancy, the built-in knowledge we have about the size of familiar objects. Enlarged pictures, placed the same distances from subjects, of different-sized well-recognized coins are judged to be at different distances; the larger the size of the real coin, the further away it is judged to be [Sedgwick 1986, p. 21–13].

Judgment of factors influencing spacing in car following was investigated by Evans and Rothery [1976a] using projected views of the rear of a lead car photographed from the driver's eye position of a following car. Subjects judged whether a particular view represented a greater or lesser inter-vehicle spacing than a standard view representing a spacing of 20 m. It is found that the spacing judgment is uninfluenced by whether the lead car is a large or small car. Thus, although the large car subtends a larger angle at the subjects' eyes, this did not make it appear nearer. Spacing judgments are influenced by characteristics of the car from which the pictures were taken (the following car). Identical spacings were judged to be greater when viewed from a small than from a large car. The view from the small car exposed a greater distance of roadway between the two cars—that is, the hood being smaller and lower, allowed the driver to see the roadway at distances closer to the front of the following vehicle. The amount of visible roadway was further established as an important cue in judging distance by having an additional condition in which the rear of the lead car was raised so that, for the same spacing, yet more roadway was exposed to the view of the camera at the driver's eye position. It was found that the same spacing, judged from the same car, is perceived to be greater when more roadway is visible. The target car is the same distance from the camera in both photographs in Fig. 5-3.

The finding that the same spacing is judged to be larger when perceived from the smaller car offers an explanation of a number of field and experimental observations that small cars follow at closer headways than larger cars [Herman, Lam, and Rothery 1973]. In order to maintain the same subjective spacing in large and small cars, a smaller spacing (which seems larger) would have to be chosen when driving the smaller car. To maintain equal protection in the event of a crash would require larger, not smaller, following distances in the smaller cars. Drivers reacting to a lowered sense of security in the smaller car could cause them to choose a greater spacing than for the larger car, with the perceptual bias either reducing the magnitude of their desired increased safety margin, or even reversing it.

Overtaking

On a two lane roadway the task of overtaking a lead car in the face of an oncoming car involves judging the distance of the oncoming car, and the relative speed between the oncoming car and the driven car, which may be in excess of 200 km/h. Farber and Silver [1967] performed an extensive experimental investigation of the influence of many factors on drivers' judgments and decisions in overtaking. Tests were conducted on one side of a completed but unopened four-lane section of Interstate freeway. Subjects in one car followed another car, while a third car approached in an adjacent lane. It is found that while drivers make reliable estimates of the distance to the oncoming car, they are insensitive to its speed. Basically, at the distances required for this task, the cues to relative speed (mainly the angle subtended at the driver's eyes by the oncoming car) provide minimal information. When the subjects were informed of the speed of the oncoming car, passing occurred at smaller, and less varying, spacings. In a follow-up study, Farber [1969] finds that unsuspecting drivers on two-lane rural roads passed slower moving cars with greater likelihood the greater the available passing distance, and the lower the speed of the lead car. At night, drivers were more conservative and variable in the passing distances they were willing to accept than in daytime driving. The inability of drivers to estimate oncoming speed leads them to decline safe passing opportunities when the oncoming car is travelling slower than expected, and to initiate unsafe passing maneuvers when the oncoming car is travelling faster than expected. Technology to inform the driver of the oncoming vehicle's speed could therefore increase both traffic efficiency and safety.

REACTION TIMES

From the point of view of driving, the two most important characteristics of reaction time are, first, the number of stimuli and the number of possible re-

Figure 5-3.   The perception of inter-vehicular spacing. Which picture shows a closer following distance?

sponses, and second, expectancy [Näätänen and Summala 1976]. If a subject is instructed to fixate on an unlit lamp, and press a switch as soon as possible after it lights, then simple reaction times of the order of 0.15 s are generally recorded. If the number of stimuli and responses increase (say a number of lights, each with its own associated switch), then choice reaction times become progressively longer. As the uncertainty about when the light is going to come on increases, so does the reaction time [Fitts and Posner 1967].

Reaction times in driving involve identifying a variety of events in a complex environment, so it is not surprising that reaction times bear little resemblance to the minimum possible in laboratory tests. Indeed, it is convenient, conceptually, to divide the time from stimulus to driver response into two phases, decision or perception reaction time (time to decide to brake, for example), and response or movement reaction time (time to place foot on brake pedal), even though they are generally observed as one composite reaction time. Although there is a fairly extensive literature on reaction times relating to driving [Shinar 1978; Näätänen and Summala 1976], the most difficult factor to investigate, especially as it relates to crashes, is that of expectancy.

The average reaction time which produced the best fit to the previously discussed car-following data is 1.6 s. It should be noted that this is for drivers specifically focusing on the car ahead in a test track experiment. Wierwille, Casali, and Repa [1983] measured steering reaction times to abrupt-onset crosswinds in a moving-base driving simulator, finding reaction times between 0.30 s and 0.59 s. As the drivers hands are already on the steering wheel, there is minimal movement reaction time for this task compared to braking.

Olson and Sivak [1986] measured the perception and response times of young and old drivers to an object suddenly encountered when driving an instrumented station wagon over a crest-vertical curve. On the first trial, the drivers had been driving the vehicle for about 10 to 15 minutes, and the object was unexpected. In subsequent trials subjects knew the goal of the experiment, but the location of the object changed. Perception and response times are considerably longer for the unalerted trial than for the subsequent ones. The older subjects have longer perception and reaction times than the younger, in keeping with much research that shows that reaction times increase with age. For all the subjects combined, the 95th percentile total reaction time for the unalerted trials is 1.6 s. However, the authors point out that after driving an instrumented vehicle with an experimenter present, a driver may be more alert than an average driver. They recommend the continued use of a reaction time of 2.5 s for the surprised driver; this value is a common choice in US traffic engineering practice for such purposes as computing sight distances in freeway design.

Perhaps the most realistic measurement of reaction times in actual driving is that of Summala [1981], who used an instrumented vehicle parked on a roadway shoulder to present an unexpected stimulus to actual drivers in Finland. When it was safe to do so, the door of this vehicle was opened presenting an oncoming motorist with a view of the door close to, but not encroaching upon, the lane on which he or she was travelling. By means of eight pairs of infrared photocells, the moment at which the oncoming vehicle's trajectory first changed in response to the stimulus of the opened door was measured for 1326 oncoming drivers. It is found that the average response time is about 2.5 s, with most responses being between 1.5 s and 4.0 s. Thus the 2.5 s value mentioned above finds additional support in this study, and is used in the following example constructed to bring out the importance of reaction time and stopping time.

An Example Illustrating Reaction Time and Braking

Suppose a car travelling at speed v_1 drives over the crest of a crest-vertical curve (a straight road travelling over a hill), and is confronted by a large object completely blocking the roadway (say, an overturned truck blocking all lanes). After an assumed reaction time, the driver applies maximum braking, which imparts a constant deceleration, A, to the vehicle. From Newton's laws of motion, the vehicle's speed, $v(d)$, will decline as a function of distance along the roadway according to

$$v(d) = \sqrt{v_1{}^2 - 2\,A\,d}, \qquad \text{Eqn 5-1}$$

where d is the distance along the roadway since braking commenced. Assuming braking continues until the vehicle stops, then it will stop a distance $v_1{}^2/(2A)$ from the point at which the brakes were first applied, coming to rest at the point marked d_1 in Fig. 5-4. This figure shows schematically the trajectory for this vehicle, and also for another vehicle arriving similarly at the crest of the hill, but at a higher speed, v_2, and coming to a stop at a point marked d_2. If the obstruction is located at a distance greater than d_2 from where it is first seen, neither car will strike it. If it is located between d_1 and d_2, the faster car will crash into it, but the slower one will not. If it is located nearer than d_1, then both cars will strike it. However, the first car will strike it at a lower speed. The lower curve shows the kinetic energy dissipated by the lower-speed car expressed as a percent of the kinetic energy of the higher-speed car. Injury risk and severity probably increase much more than linearly with kinetic energy.

   Figure 5-4 is plotted using the following specific values; $v_1 = 55$ mph (89 km/h, or 24.6 m/s); $v_2 = 70$ mph (113 km/h, or 31.3 m/s); and reaction time $= 2.5$ s. The constant deceleration, A, is taken to be 5 m/s^2, a reasonable value for good tires on dry level pavement, even though a few exceptional vehicles under ideal conditions can even exceed the value of the acceleration due to gravity of 9.8 m/s^2. We ignore the hill which was for expository convenience only. During the 2.5 s reaction time the two vehicles travel 61 m and 78 m

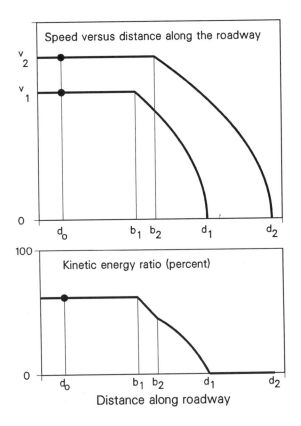

Figure 5-4.   Schematic representation of how the speed of a vehicle varies along the roadway from the location d_o, at which a need to brake can first be perceived (top) and the relative kinetic energy of the vehicle with the lower initial speed relative to the kinetic energy of the vehicle with the higher initial speed (bottom).

respectively. During the braking phases they travel 60 m and 98 m, for total stopping distances of 121 m and 176 m respectively.

If the obstacle is so close that the slower car strikes it before beginning to brake, then the ratio of the kinetic energies for the two cars is $55^2/70^2 = 0.62$; that is, the kinetic energy dissipated in the crash of the slower car is 62% of that dissipated in the crash of the faster. Whether the driver of even the slower car could survive so severe a crash will depend on many factors, such as the stiffness of the object struck, the size of the striking car, restraint system use (lap/shoulder belt plus airbag maximizes survival—Chapter 9), and driver age. As the distance between the point at which the first car begins to brake and the struck object increases, the chances of the first driver surviving compared to the second increase rapidly.

This simple example illustrates a number of central themes, in all cases assuming that other factors except those discussed are equal. First, the probability of the crash occurring increases with speed. Second, given that the crash occurs, the injury risk increases steeply with the initial driving speed. Third, reductions in reaction time can reduce the probability and severity of crashes. Empirical relations (Eqns 6-1 to 6-3) between actual speeds and fatality risk are given in the next chapter.

Rear Impact Crashes

As motorization develops, a greater fraction of driving is spent following other vehicles, with consequent risk of rear impact crashes; rear-end crashes account for approximately 15% to 20% of all vehicles damaged in crashes in the US [O'Day et al. 1975; Campbell 1990]. The first major technological countermeasure was the development of brake lights. In the early 1980s there were over one million police reported crashes annually in the US in which a car is struck in the rear, this representing 19% of all police reported crashes [Kahane 1989]. Because small reductions in reaction time promise large reductions in crash rates, there has been much research on rear-lighting approaches to reduce reaction times. Such factors as light configuration, color, and brightness [Mortimer 1977] have been examined, as well as methods of indicating the magnitude of deceleration of the lead car [Mortimer and Kupec 1983]. Babarik [1968] examined the ratio of simple reaction time (finger pressing in response to a light) to jump reaction time (moving the hand 12 inches in response to a light) for 127 Washington, DC taxicab drivers. He finds that higher than average values of this ratio are associated with a greater tendency to be struck in the rear, given that the driver is involved in a crash. A possible interpretation is that an increased delay before perceiving the need for braking, followed by a faster movement of the foot to the pedal and subsequent larger deceleration, will increase the risk of being struck in the rear.

Center High Mounted Stop Lamps

Motor Vehicle Safety Standard FMVSS-108 required all new cars sold in the United States since 1 September 1985 to be equipped with a red stop lamp mounted on the centerline of the rear of the car, generally higher then the other two stop lamps mounted on the sides (Fig. 5-5). This configuration was identified in an experiment involving a fleet of Washington, DC taxicabs fitted with this type of device or other innovative stop lamps, while a control group matched in makes and models, and in driver characteristics, had conventional stop lamps

Figure 5-5. Two typical implementations of center high mounted stop lamps.

[Kohl and Baker 1978]. Drivers reported details of all crash involvements. The study analyzed changes in the number of impacts on the rear during braking—the only type of crash subject to potential influence from changing stop lights; in the field tests, 67% of the taxis struck in the rear were struck while braking. The key finding in the experiment is that the Washington taxicabs with center high mounted stop lamps were struck in the rear while braking 54% less often for the same distance of driving as the taxis in the control group.

In a follow-up study, Reilly, Kurke, and Buckenmaier [1981] used 5400 telephone company passenger vehicles driven 55 million miles during a 12 month period in locations scattered widely throughout the US. The 2500 vehicles equipped with center high mounted stop lamps are found to be struck in the rear while braking 53% less than those not so equipped, for the same distance of driving, a result in close agreement with the 54% for the taxicabs. In another study, Rausch, Wong, and Kirkpatrick [1982] find a 51% reduction. By examining driver eye fixations, Sivak, Conn, and Olson [1984] provide a possible behavioral explanation of the efficacy of the center high mounted stop light in terms of the driver being more likely to fixate in the region of the center of the vehicle, rather than its extremities.

The effectiveness of center high mounted stop lamps in actual use was investigated by Kahane [1989] using 1987 police reported data for 11 states. He compared the ratio of rear impacts to non-rear impacts for 1986 and 1987 model year cars, all of which were equipped with center high mounted stop lamps, to the same ratio for model year 1980 to 1985 cars, very few of which were so equipped. In estimating effectiveness, three corrections are applied reflecting the following three effects. First, about 10% of the 1980–1985 cars were built or retrofitted with center high mounted stop lamps. Second, newer cars involved in crashes are more likely to be struck in the rear than are older cars (presumably because they use higher levels of braking [Evans and Rothery 1976b]). Third, because the device is only relevant if braking occurs, the earlier finding that the effectiveness in reducing crashes in which braking does occur is approximately 1.5 times the effectiveness in reducing all rear impact crashes is used to infer the effectiveness when braking did occur. The result Kahane [1989] obtained is that the center high mounted stop lamp reduced rear impacts to cars that are braking by $(17 \pm 2)\%$, where the error is one standard error. This reduction is estimated to provide property damage loss reductions about nine times as great as the estimated cost of the devices.

The above studies collectively provide one of the clearest examples of crash reduction from an intervention. The main remaining uncertainty about an intervention of this type is what might be called the "novelty effect." Anything unusual on the rear of a vehicle might invite a following driver to fixate on that vehicle and thereby reduce the chances of crashing into it. If this were the only mechanism at work, then, when all vehicles were so equipped, the benefit would disappear. Kahane [1989] discusses this question using the empirical information so far collected; the experimental evaluations indicated 50% effectiveness, his earlier study [Kahane 1987] of actual effectiveness using 1966 data (specially collected within the National Accident Sampling System program) gave 22%, while the 1989 study gave 17%. Further evaluations are planned. About 25% of the cars in the 1989 study were equipped. The precision with which differences can be determined is greatest when half of the sample is equipped and half is not, which will occur soon. Later, when most cars are equipped, estimates of the effectiveness of the device will become more and more imprecise as the sample of control cars becomes more depleted each year, so that it does not seem possible to obtain an estimate when all cars are equipped, and all drivers expect the device. There are indications that drivers sometimes monitor cars ahead of the one they are following directly through windows. In such cases the center high mounted stop lamp would be perceived more reliably than those on the sides, which would militate against the effectiveness reducing to zero. Even if effectiveness does decline in time, which is certainly not known to be the case, the benefits that accrue in the interim are real and would still count for much in any benefit-cost analysis in which the benefits are assumed to decline, even to zero, in time.

DRIVING SIMULATORS

The difficulty, expense, lack of reproducibility, and danger of conducting various types of driver behavior research in actual traffic provide the main impetus for developing driving simulators, devices which, while remaining within the safety and control of the laboratory, represent driving with varying degrees of fidelity. While such devices have produced much valuable information, some of which is cited above, some intrinsic limitations should be kept in mind. The discussion above on reaction time showed the primacy of expectancy; even in real-world experiments, reaction times of participating subjects are substantially shorter than unalerted drivers. Thus, any estimate of reaction time using a simulator, no matter how realistic, would be suspect unless the subject drove for many hours to establish arousal and anxiety levels characteristic of normal driving, thus limiting data collection rates to a few per day.

The success of sophisticated moving-base aircraft simulators has encouraged the application of similar technology to the driving case. There is little in common between the two situations. The aircraft simulator is a 30 million dollar device representing a 150 million dollar aircraft. For the automobile case, it seems harder to justify a 30 million dollar simulator, when the real article can be purchased for about 10 thousand dollars. High realism simulators appear to offer little for driver training, although rudimentary low-cost simulators can be useful in initial instruction of location and function of controls. An accompanied learner driver can practice starting and stopping a real car 5 times per minute; a simulator offers little difference in training rate or safety. In contrast, it would be difficult to fit in more than a few real aircraft take-offs and landings in an hour, not to mention the fuel cost, equipment cost, and danger. The simulator allows take-offs, followed by take-offs without intervening landings, to be repeated under varying conditions. While the performance skills learned in simulators can be critical in emergencies in the air, car driving emergency situations usually arise because of expectancy violations.

The notion of driving simulators is far from new. A survey published 20 years ago [Kuratorium für Verkehrssicherheit 1970, as cited by Hulbert and Wojcik 1972] lists 28 devices then in use, 17 of them in the US. For well over 20 years driver simulators have incorporated moving bases and multiple movie projectors to provide visual information, including information to the rear view mirror. Hulbert and Wojcik [1972] list 30 driver performance topics they consider could be successfully researched using simulators. Included on their list are such items as alcohol and drug effects, fatigue effects, rear lighting systems, reduced visibility in fog, and passing zone markings and signs. While some progress has been achieved on a few items on their list using simulators, a basic question must remain about the majority. Can the lack of progress be traced specifically to insufficient realism in the simulator, thus justifying a more sophisticated simulator? Any decisions regarding major investments in additional driver simulators should identify what specific problems they can be used to solve, and why they can solve them when only slightly less sophisticated simulators could not.

The following thought experiment helps address such questions. Consider a make-believe simulator consisting of an actual car, but with the remarkable property that after it crashes a reset button instantly cancels all damage to people and equipment. What experiments could be performed on such make-believe equipment which would increase our basic knowledge about driving? The answers provide an upper limit on what might be done using improved simulators. Defining subject areas, such as alcohol and driving, should not be confused with defining specific questions; in Chapter 7 we note that there are already over 500 technical papers on how alcohol affects performance. Increased knowledge about driving is most likely to be discovered using the normal processes of science. In these, problems are first defined, and if they can be solved using existing equipment, they are. If they cannot be solved using existing equipment, new equipment is developed only if it is considered likely to contribute to the solution, and not for its own sake.

CONCLUSIONS

As driving skill increases from the first time behind the wheel, both the ability to project the present state of a vehicle into the near future, and the ability to judge the future effects of control inputs increase. The amount of mental capacity that must be assigned to the driving task decreases, although in emergency situations, the driver re-directs full attention to the driving task. Many studies have failed to show that crash rates are influenced by car driver education, training, or knowledge, though there are indications that motorcycle safety is increased by such programs. Driving is essentially a closed-loop compensatory feedback process in which the driver makes control inputs in response to what is perceived. Once the task is well learned, such vehicle characteristics as steering system gain have little effect; indeed, the driver may not even be aware that one vehicle requires more steering wheel rotation or torque than another to produce the same consequence. It is the consequence, as perceived through the windshield, that is the controlling signal, not the intermediate steps that produce it. Although vision is central to driving, those with the best vision do not have the lowest crash rates. Errors in subjectively estimating speed are sufficiently great that drivers should consult speedometers. Attentive drivers have high sensitivity to judging that they are approaching vehicles ahead, so that instruments to augment this ability appear to have limited potential. Drivers are poor judges of speeds of oncoming cars, as required in overtaking maneuvers; technological innovations providing such information could increase traffic efficiency and safety. While violations of expectancy play an important role in many crashes rather than limitations of drivers ability to judge such stimuli as relative speed, small reductions in reaction time can still reduce the probability and severity of crashes in many cases. One approach to reducing reaction time in car following, the center high mounted stop lamp, has been effective in reducing rear-end crashes. While driver simulators can be useful in some areas of driver performance research, any decisions regarding major investments in additional driver simulators should identify what specific problems they can be used to solve, and why they can solve them when only slightly less sophisticated simulators could not.

Overall, while various aspects of driver performance are related to safety, there is not a coherent pattern. The finding of no effect from driver education and knowledge, and that younger drivers, with the best visual acuity and shortest reaction times, have the highest crash rates, suggests that driver performance is not the driver characteristic which has the largest influence on traffic safety.

REFERENCES

Avolio, B.J.; Kroeck, K.G.; Panek, P.E. Individual differences in information-processing ability as a predictor of motor vehicle accidents. *Human Factors* 27:577–587; 1985.

Babarik, P. Automobile accidents and driver reaction pattern. *Journal of Applied Psychology* 52:49–54; 1968.

Boff, K.R. The value of research is in the eye of the beholder. *Human Factors Society Bulletin* 31(6):1–4; 1988.

Brown, D.B; Maghsoodloo, S; McArdle, M.E. The safety impact of the 65 mph speed limit: a case study using Alabama accident data. Washington, DC: National Highway Traffic Safety Administration, Report no. DOT HS 807 425; April 1989.

Brown, I.D. Exposure and experience are a confounded nuisance in research on driver behaviour. *Ergonomics* 14:345–352; 1982.

Brown, I.D.; Groeger, J.A.; Biehl, B. Is driver training contributing enough towards road safety? In: Rothergatter, J.A.; de Bruin, R.A., editors. *Road Users and Traffic Safety*. Assen/Maastricht, Netherlands: Van Gorcum, p. 135–156; 1988.

Campbell, K.L. Personal communication based on preliminary analyses of CARDfile data, 1990.

Carsten, O.M.J.; Tight, M.R.; Southwell, M.T. *Urban Accidents: Why Do They Happen?* Basingstoke, UK: AA Foundation for Road Safety Research; 1989.

Casey, S.M.; Lund, A.K. Three field studies on driver speed adaptation. *Human Factors* 29:541–550; 1987.

Conley, J.A.; Smiley, R. Driver licensing tests as a predictor of subsequent violations. *Human Factors* 18:565–574; 1976.

Davison, P.A. The role of drivers' vision in road safety. *Lighting Research and Technology* 10:125–139; 1978.

Denton, G.G. A subjective scale of speed when driving a motor vehicle. *Ergonomics* 9:203–210; 1966.

Denton, G.G. *The Influence of Visual Pattern on Perceived Speed at Newbridge M8 Midlothian.* Transport and Road Research Laboratory, Crowthorne, Berkshire, UK; 1973.

Denton, G.G. The influence of adaptation on subjective velocity for an observer in simulated rectilinear motion. *Ergonomics* 19:409–430; 1976.

Evans, L. Speed estimation from a moving automobile. *Ergonomics* 13:219–230; 1970a.

Evans, L. Automobile speed estimation using movie-film simulation. *Ergonomics* 13:231–237; 1970b.

Evans, L. Airbag effectiveness in preventing fatalities predicted according to type of crash, driver age, and blood alcohol concentration. *Accident Analysis and Prevention* 23 (in press) 1991.

Evans, L.; Rothery, R. Experimental measurement of perceptual thresholds in car-following. *Highway Research Board Record* 464:13–29; 1973.

Evans, L.; Rothery, R. Detection of the sign of relative motion when following a vehicle. *Human Factors* 16:161–173; 1974.

Evans, L.; Rothery, R. Comments on effects of vehicle type and age on driver behaviour at signalized intersections. *Ergonomics* 19:559–570; 1976a.

Evans, L.; Rothery, R. The influence of forward vision and target size on apparent inter-vehicular spacing. *Transportation Science* 10:85–101; 1976b.

Evans, L.; Rothery, R. Perceptual thresholds in car-following—a comparison of recent measurements with earlier results. *Transportation Science* 11:60–72; 1977.

Farber, E.I.; Silver, C.A. Knowledge of oncoming car speed as a determiner of driver's passing behavior. *Highway Research Record* 195:52–65; 1967.

Farber, E.I. Passing behavior on public highways under daytime and nighttime conditions. *Highway Research Record* 292:11–23; 1969.

Fitts, P.M.; Posner, M.I. *Human Performance*. Belmont, CA: Brooks/Cole; 1967.

Fuller, R. Psychological aspects of learning to drive. In: Rothergatter, J.A.; de Bruin, R.A., editors. *Road Users and Traffic Safety*. Assen/Maastricht, Netherlands: Van Gorcum, p. 527–537; 1988.

Gardner, D.J.; Rockwell, T.H. Two views of motorist behavior in rural freeway construction and maintenance zones: the driver and state highway patrolman. *Human Factors* 25:415–424; 1983.

Helander, C.J. Intervention strategies for accident-involved drivers: an experimental evaluation of current California policy and alternatives. *Journal of Safety Research* 15:23–40; 1984.

Herman, R.; Potts, R.B. Single-lane traffic theory and experiment. In: Herman, R., editor. *Theory of Traffic Flow*. Amsterdam, Netherlands: Elsevier, p. 120–146; 1961.

Herman, R; Lam, T; Rothery, R. An experiment on car size effects in traffic. *Traffic Engineering and Control* 15:90–93,99; June 1973.

Hulbert, S.; Wojcik, C. Driving task simulation. In: Forbes, T.W., editor. *Human Factors in Highway Traffic Safety Research.* New York, NY: Wiley-Interscience, p. 44–73; 1972.

Kahane, C.J. The effectiveness of center high mounted stop lamps: a preliminary evaluation. Washington, DC: National Highway Traffic Safety Administration, report DOT HS 807 076; March 1987.

Kahane, C.J. An evaluation of center high mounted stop lamps based on 1987 data. Washington, DC: National Highway Traffic Safety Administration, report DOT HS 807 442; July 1989.

Kohl, J.S.; Baker, C. Field test evaluation of rear lighting systems. Washington, DC: National Highway Traffic Safety Administration, report DOT HS 803 467; 1978.

Kuratorium für Verkehrssicherheit. Verkerspsychologie IV, Vienna, Austria, p. 149–184; May 1970.

Job, R.F.S. The application of learning theory to driving confidence: the effect of age and the impact of random breath testing. *Accident Analysis and Prevention* 22:97–107; 1990.

Jonah, B. A. Accident risk and risk-taking behaviour among young drivers. *Accident Analysis and Prevention* 18:255–271; 1986.

Liessma, M. The influence of a driver's vision in relation to his driving. First International Congress on Vision and Road Safety, organized by La Prevention Routiere Internationale, p. 31–34; 1977.

Lund, A.K.; Williams, A.F. A review of the literature evaluating the defensive driving course. *Accident Analysis and Prevention* 17:449–460; 1985.

Lund, A.K.; Williams, A.F.; Zador, P. High school driver education: further evaluation of the DeKalb county study. *Accident Analysis and Prevention* 18:349–357; 1986.

Mackay, M. Towards a unified traffic science. *IATSS Research—Journal of International Association of Traffic and Safety Sciences* 14 (in press) 1990.

Macrae, N. The next ages of man. London, UK: *The Economist*, p. 5–20; 24 December, 1988.

Matthews, M.L. A field study of the effects of drivers' adaptation to automobile velocity. *Human Factors* 20:709–716; 1978.

McDavid, J.C; Lohrmann, B.A.; Lohrmann, G. Does motorcycle training reduce accidents? Evidence from a longitudinal quasi-experimental study. *Journal of Safety Research* 20:61–72; 1989.

McKnight, A.J.; Adams, B.D. *Driver Education Task Analysis, Volume 1, Task Descriptions.* Alexandria, VA: Human Resources Research Organization, 1970.

McLane, R.C.; Wierwille, W.W. The influence of motion and audio cues on driver performance in an automobile simulator. *Human Factors* 17:488–501; 1975.

Medically Handicapped Drivers. Today's traffic. *Traffic Safety* 73:20; November, 1973.

Michaels, R.M. Perceptual factors in car following. In: Almond, J., editor. *Second International Symposium on the Theory of Traffic Flow.* Paris, France: OCDE, p. 44–59; 1965.

Michon, J.A. Explanatory pitfalls and rule-based driver models. *Accident Analysis and Prevention* 21:341–353; 1989.

Milosevic, S. Perception of vehicle speed. *Revija za psihologijy* (Yugoslavia) 16:11–19; 1986.

Mortimer, R.G. A decade of research in vehicle rear lighting. What have we learned? American Association for the Advancement of Automotive Medicine, 21st Annual Proceedings, p. 101–112; September 1977.

Mortimer, R.G.; Kupec, J.D. Scaling of flash rate for a deceleration signal. *Human Factors* 25:313–318; 1983.

Mourant, R.R.; Rockwell, T.H. Visual information seeking of novice drivers. SAE paper 700397. Warrendale, PA: Society of Automotive Engineers; 1970; included in the proceedings of the 13th FISITA conference, p. 704–711, 1970 International Automobile Safety Conference compendium, 1970.

Mourant, R.R.; Rockwell, T.H. Strategies of visual search by novice and experienced drivers. *Human Factors* 14:325–335; 1972.

Näätänen, R.; Summala, H. *Road-User Behavior and Traffic Accidents*. Amsterdam, Netherlands: North Holland; 1976.

Noguchi, K. In search of optimum speed: from the users viewpoint. *IATSS Research—Journal of International Association of Traffic and Safety Sciences* 14(1): (in press) 1990.

O'Day, J.; Filkins, L.D.; Compton, C.P.; Lawson, T.E. Rear impacted vehicle collisions: frequencies and casualty patterns. Contract no. UM-HSRI-SA-75-2, Motor Vehicle Manufacturers Association, Highway Safety Research Institute, University of Michigan: Ann Arbor, MI; July 1975.

Olson, P.L.; Sivak, M. Perception-response time to unexpected roadway hazards. *Human Factors* 28:91–96; 1986.

Polus, A.; Hocherman, I.; Efrat, E. Evaluation of the accident rates of male and female drivers. Paper 870302, presented to the 67th annual meeting of the Transportation Research Board, Washington, DC; 11–14 January 1988.

Potvin, L.; Champagne, F.; Laberge-Nadeau, C. Mandatory driver training and road safety: the Quebec experience. *American Journal of Public Health* 78:1206–1209; 1988.

Rausch, A.; Wong, J.; Kirkpatrick, M. A field test of two single, center high mounted brake light systems. *Accident Analysis and Prevention* 14:287–291; 1982.

Reilly, R.E.; Kurke, D.S.; Buckenmaier, C.C. Validation of the reduction of rear-end collisions by a high-mounted auxiliary stoplamp. SAE paper 810189. Warrendale, PA: Society of Automotive Engineers; 1981.

Robertson, L.S. Crash involvement of teenaged drivers when driver education is eliminated from high school. *American Journal of Public Health* 70:599–603; 1980.

Rockwell, T.H. Skills, judgment and information acquisition in driving. In: Forbes, T.W., editor. *Human Factors in Highway Traffic Safety Research*. New York, NY: Wiley-Interscience, p. 133–164; 1972.

Rumar, K. The role of perceptual and cognitive filters in observed behavior. In: Evans, L; Schwing, R.C., editors. *Human Behavior and Traffic Safety*. New York, NY: Plenum Press, p. 151–165; 1985.

Schmidt, F; Tiffin, J. Distortion of drivers' estimates of automobile speed as a function of speed adaptation. *Journal of Applied Psychology* 53:536–539; 1969

Sedgwick, H.A. Space perception. Chapter 21 in Boff, K.R.; Kaufman, L; Thomas, J.P., editors. *Handbook of Perception and Human Performance, Volume 1, Sensory Processes and Perception*. New York: John Wiley; 1986.

Shinar, D. *Psychology on the Road—The Human Factor in Traffic Safety*. New York, NY: John Wiley; 1978.

Shinar, D.; McDowell, E.D.; Rockwell, T.H. Improving driver performance on curves in rural highways through perceptual changes. The Ohio State University, Engineering Experiment Station, report EES 428B; 1974.

Shinar, D.; Drory, A. Sign registration in daytime and nighttime driving. *Human Factors* 25:117–122; 1983.

Sivak, M.; Conn, L.S.; Olson, P.L. Driver eye fixations and the optimal locations for automobile brake lights. Report no. UMTRI-84-29, University of Michigan Transportation Research Institute, Ann Arbor, MI; November 1984.

Sivak, M.; Olson, P.L.; Pastalan, L.A. Effect of driver's age on nighttime legibility of highway signs. *Human Factors* 23:59–64; 1981.

Smiley, A.; Reid, L.; Fraser, M. Changes in driver steering control with learning. *Human Factors* 22:401–415; 1980.

Sturgis, S.P.; Osgood, D.J. Effects of glare and background luminance on visual acuity and contrast sensitivity: implications for driver night vision testing. *Human Factors* 23:347–360; 1982.

Summala, H. Driver/vehicle steering response latencies. *Human Factors* 23:683–692; 1981.

Summala, H. Young driver accidents: risk taking or failure of skills? *Alcohol, Drugs, and Driving* 3(3–4):79–91; 1987.

Summala, H.; Näätänen, R. Perception of highway traffic signs and motivation. *Journal of Safety Research* 6:150–153; 1974.

Thalmann, H. Der Einaugige im Strassenverkehr (The monocular driver in street traffic.) *Schweizerische Medizinische Wochenschrift* 101:981–987; July 1971.

Triggs, T.J.; Berenyi, J.S. Estimation of automobile speed under day and night conditions. *Human Factors* 24:111–114; 1982

Trinca, G.W.; Johnston, I.R.; Campbell B.J.; Haight, F.A.; Knight, P.R.; Mackay, G.M.; McLean, A.J.; Petrucelli, E. *Reducing Traffic Injury—A Global Challenge.* Melbourne, Australia: A.H. Massina; 1988.

Wierwille, W.W.; Casali, J.G.; Repa, B.S. Driver steering reaction time to abrupt-onset crosswinds, as measured in a moving-base simulator. *Human Factors* 25:103–116; 1983.

Yanik, A.J. What accident data reveal about elderly drivers. SAE paper 851688. Warrendale, PA: Society of Automotive Engineers; 1985.

6 Driver Behavior

INTRODUCTION

Driver performance, as discussed in Chapter 5, refers to the driver's perceptual and motor skills, or what the driver *can* do. Driver behavior refers to what the driver in fact *does* do. The example represented in Fig. 5-4 illustrates how the distance covered depends on driver reaction time and vehicle speed. What is not encompassed in this figure is why one driver chooses to travel at one speed, while another chooses a different speed. The ability to judge the speed, control the vehicle at that speed, and react to hazards are all in the realm of driver performance. The speed chosen is in the realm of driver behavior.

As driver performance focuses on capabilities and skills, it can be investigated by many methods, including laboratory tests, simulator experiments, tests using instrumented vehicles and observations of actual traffic. As driver behavior indicates what the driver actually does, it cannot be investigated in laboratory, simulator or instrumented vehicle studies. As a consequence, information on driver behavior tends to be more uncertain than that about driver performance.

The distinction between performance and behavior is one of the most central concepts in traffic safety. This is because driving is, in Näätänen and Summala's [1976] phrase, a "self-paced" task. That is, drivers choose their own desired levels of task difficulty. The acquisition of increased skill is likely to lead to an increase in the level of task difficulty, such as driving faster, overtaking in heavier traffic, or accepting additional secondary tasks like listening to the radio, rather than simply to an increase in safety. When task difficulty is maintained constant, increases in skill are likely to lead to increases in safety. Häkkinen [1979] finds that the crash rates of Helsinki bus and streetcar drivers are strongly correlated with a series of performance-measuring tests. He also finds that the drivers' crash rates are stable over long periods; the time span for the entire study is 1947–1973. More recently, Lim and Dewar [1989] find higher information processing ability, as measured in laboratory tests, is associated with lower on-the-job crash rates for bus drivers in Calgary, Canada. McKenna, Duncan, and Brown [1986] find no statistically significant effect in a similar study of British bus drivers, although the nominal effect is in the same direction. The basic distinction between the professional drivers in the studies above and drivers in general is that the schedules, and other aspects of driving behavior for professional drivers, is specified. Constraints militate against such driving being self-paced, so that increased skill can be expected to produce fewer crashes, as is found. Car driving in a regulated structured environment has much in common with the task of piloting a commercial air liner. For both tasks, increased skill, knowledge and performance are expected to increase safety. However, this may not be so for the self-paced task of normal driving.

RACING DRIVERS COMPARED TO AVERAGE DRIVERS

The belief that increased skill would lead to lower crash involvement rates seems to many so intuitively obvious that it should be superfluous even to investigate it. Such a belief nurtures the view that driver education necessarily increases safety. It is widely held by driving aficionados, especially the racing fraternity, that race drivers have fewer crashes than the average driver. For example, in discussing the on-the-road experience of race drivers, an editor of *Road and Track* magazine writes, "I have for many years claimed that the licensed racer is far safer than ordinary chaps, on grounds of practiced skills, mental ability, cognizance of hazards in driving, keen interest in driving well, and so on." [Girdler 1972, p. 98, as cited by Williams and O'Neill 1974] The belief that superior skills lead to reduced crashes led to the concept of a *Master Driver's License* which would entitle those with proven high driving skills to various privileges denied the average driver. The National Highway Traffic Safety Administration [1972] at one time addressed harnessing this concept in its efforts to reduce crashes.

In order to discover if unusually skilled drivers really did have different on-the-road driving records from the average driver, Williams and O'Neill [1974] obtained names and addresses of national competition license holders from the Sports Car Club of America. They compared the on-the-road driving records of these license holders (referred to in their paper as racing drivers) in Florida, New York, and Texas, to comparison groups of drivers in the same states matched in such characteristics as sex and age. There are minor variations in the details of the matching procedures between the states.

The results of the study are summarized in Fig. 6-1, which displays the rate for the racing drivers divided by the corresponding rate for the comparison drivers. If there were no differences between the groups of drivers, then these ratios would all be close to one, whereas if the racing drivers had lower crash and violation rates, the ratios would be less than one. What in fact is found is that in all 12 cases studied, the rates for the racing drivers exceed those for the comparison drivers, in most cases by considerable amounts. Thus, on a per year basis, the racing drivers had substantially more crashes, and more violations, especially speeding violations. Self-reported estimates of distance of travel indicate that the racing drivers travelled more than the comparison drivers; however, additional analyses by Williams and O'Neill [1974] indicate that this does not explain all of the difference observed. What is unambiguous from the study

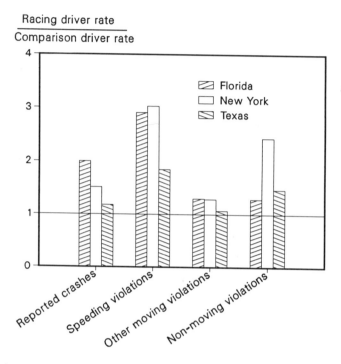

Figure 6-1. The number of incidents per year for racing drivers compared to the values of the same quantities for comparison drivers matched in age and sex. Based on the values in Williams and O'Neill [1974].

is that the possession of a national competition license is associated with higher crash and violation rates per year.

In interpreting the difference between the driving records of the race drivers and the comparison drivers, it is not possible to determine whether the effect flows from the use of the additional skill acquired by the drivers to drive more aggressively, or whether it is simply high-risk drivers who are attracted to racing. Perhaps, without the additional skills acquired in pursuit of their advanced license, they might have had yet higher crash rates. The study does show that higher skill levels are not necessarily associated with lower crash rates.

SEX AND AGE DEPENDENCE

The dependence of various traffic-related quantities on driver sex and age offers an indirect probe of the relationship between skill, behavior and safety. These variables have the advantage that they are unambiguously known for large num-

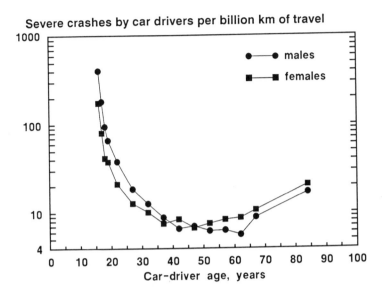

Figure 6-2. Car-driver involvements in severe crashes per unit distance of travel versus car-driver sex and age.

bers of individuals. Jonah [1986] gives an excellent review of much more material relating to the relationship between crash risk and risk-taking behavior than presented below.

Crash Rates

Figure 6-2 shows car driver involvements in severe crashes (sufficient severity to kill an 80-year-old male driver) per unit distance of travel versus sex and age; this figure differs from Fig. 2-10 only in that it refers to car drivers only rather than to drivers of any vehicle. At all ages less than 40, involvement rates are higher for males than for females. The higher levels of interest in cars and driving traditionally exhibited by males does not lead to lower crash rates even though it may lead to higher levels of skill and knowledge. The crash rate at age 40 is about one sixth what it is at age 20. Although some increase in skill, especially higher level information processing, may contribute to a decreased crash rate with age, it seems implausible that it could generate more than a small fraction of this large effect. In terms of such performance measures as visual acuity and reaction time, the performance of younger drivers is markedly superior to that of older drivers. The higher involvement rates of younger, and male, drivers seem more related to how they are choosing to drive, particularly their propensity to take driving risks, than to their abilities at the driving task.

Marital status has been shown to have a large influence on number of crashes per year. Peck, McBride, and Coppin [1971] find that single males have higher crash rates than married males of the same age, based on analyzing 1961–1963 California data. An even larger and more systematic effect is found for females— the unmarried female rate exceeds the married female rate at all ages, typically by a factor of between one and a half and two. The unmarried female rate is still less than that for the married male. Essentially similar patterns are observed for traffic violations. Part of these differences is almost certainly due to differences in amounts of driving—in the early 1960s married females probably drove substantially less than unmarried ones.

Observational Effects

Driver propensity to take risk as indicated by chosen speed and following headway (gap between a driver's vehicle and one in front) was measured in a series of observational studies [Wasielewski 1984; Evans and Wasielewski 1983] in which oncoming cars were photographed from freeway overpasses. The license-plate number, read from the photograph, was used to extract from state files the driving record, sex, and age of the registered owner. A photographed driver judged not to differ in age or sex from the registered owner was assumed to be the owner.

Figure 6-3 shows results for Wasielewski's [1984] study, in which the measured variable associated with risk taking is travel speed on a rural two-lane road. A systematic decline in speed with increasing age is apparent. Figure 6-4 shows results from Evans and Wasielewski's [1983] study in which the measured variable associated with risk taking is following headway. The quantity plotted is the reciprocal of headway, so that, as for the speed case, larger values indicate higher levels of risk taking. Again, a decrease in the measure of risk taking is apparent with increasing age. The observational data are insufficient to permit plotting separate relations for males and females. However, analyses in each of the original papers cited find higher levels of risk taking associated with male than with female drivers. A study examining factors present in urban crashes in Leeds, UK, finds, "Driving too fast was more common for males than for females, and more common for younger drivers than older drivers" [Carsten, Tight, and Southwell 1989].

Sex Differences in Activity Level or Risk Taking

Evidence of clear differences between the behavior of males and females is provided in Fig. 6-5. What is shown is the number of male pedestrian fatalities

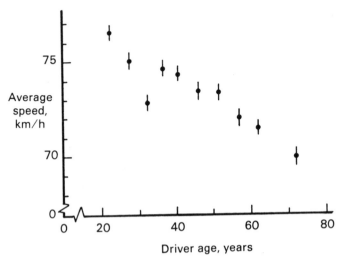

Figure 6-3. Observed travel speed versus driver age. From Wasielewski [1984].

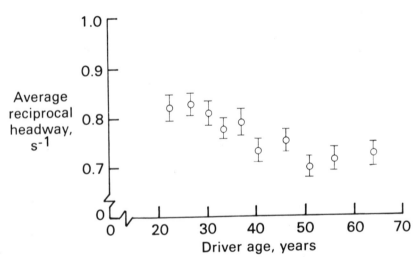

Figure 6-4 Observed tendency to follow closely, as indicated by the reciprocal of inter-vehicular headway. From Evans and Wasielewski [1983].

Male to female pedestrian fatality ratio

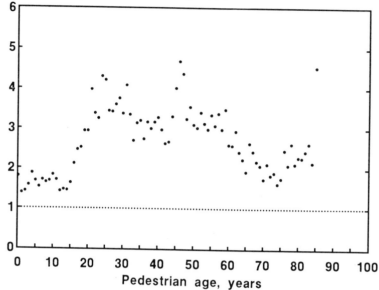

Figure 6-5. Number of male pedestrian fatalities per capita divided by female pedestrian fatalities (of the same age) per capita based on FARS and census data for 1981 through 1985. From Evans [1987a].

per capita divided by the number of female pedestrian fatalities per capita, based on FARS data from 1981 through 1985 and US census data for the same years; there is accordingly very little uncertainty in the data. At all ages, male pedestrian fatalities per capita exceed those of females. For the first point plotted, for age from birth to 11 months 31 days, there are 32 male compared to 17 female pedestrian fatalities; for the second point, from age 1 year to age 2 years, there are 144 male compared to 99 female pedestrian fatalities. These proportionate differences far exceed any difference in numbers in the population (already corrected for in the comparison in Fig. 6-5), and are larger than can be explained by the greater vulnerability of male than female babies to death from the same impact (Chapter 2).

It is not possible to infer from Fig. 6-5 whether the differences between the sexes result from differences in exposure, or differences in risk taking for each exposure. Either interpretation points to large differences in behavior between the sexes. Either males cross roads more often than females, or else they are subject to a greater risk per crossing. Howarth [1985] provides clear evidence based on UK data that boys do in fact have higher risks of being involved in a

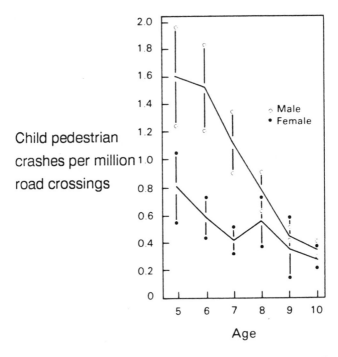

Child pedestrian crashes per million road crossings

Figure 6-6. Child-pedestrian crash involvements per million road crossings in UK traffic. Reproduced, with permission, from Howarth [1985].

pedestrian crash per road crossing than do girls. His results (Fig. 6-6) show the number of children involved in pedestrian crashes divided by an estimate of the number of children crossing roads, based on extensive observations of child-pedestrian behavior.

It is not possible to determine the extent to which the large systematic differences in Fig. 6-5 reflect intrinsic differences between males and females as distinct from socially induced differences. It is, for example, possible that higher pedestrian fatality rates for males at age 0, 1, 2, 3, . . . 12 reflect different parental treatment of boys and girls. Although such an explanation is logically possible, I find it implausible for the case of babies. After the mid-teen years differences in Fig. 6-5 become much larger, being typically a factor of three between age 20 and 60. These differences could reflect the greater social freedom which society has traditionally afforded males, enabling them to spend more time as pedestrians and also as drivers. Such differences might diminish, or disappear, as distinctions between the roles of the sexes in society change; there is already evidence of increased female arrests for drunk driving even as male arrests decline [Popkin et al. 1986]. The differences in Fig. 6-5 appear to reflect some greater activity level, and/or greater propensity to take risk, by males compared to females. Although the data have nothing to do with driving risk, as such, the interpretation in terms of greater activity level or risk taking on the part of males supports a similar interpretation of the earlier data showing higher driver crash rates for males than for females.

RELATIONSHIP OF CRASH RATES TO CRIME RATES

Figure 6-7 (top) shows involvements in severe (sufficient severity to kill an 80-year-old-male driver) single-car crashes per million population. Single-car crashes are chosen because they are most representative of the behavioral aspects of crash involvement, in that they involve no driver other than the subject driver. The lower figure shows the number of arrests per thousand population versus sex and age, based on data from FBI Uniform Crime Reports [US Department of Justice 1985]. The data plotted refer to crimes unrelated to driving—data on such offenses as driving while intoxicated are excluded. Hence, activity nominally unrelated to anything to do with driving is displayed. Top and bottom curves both show incidents per capita per year. One of the reasons why the male crash rate is so much higher than the female crash rate is that males are more exposed to the risk of the crash because they drive greater distances than do females. Presumably, the reason more males than females are arrested is because they also are exposed more, in that they presumably commit more crimes. Figure 6-7 should not be interpreted to mean that males are more likely than females to be arrested per burglary; likewise, it does not imply that males have crash involvements per unit distance of travel greater than those of females in the proportion shown in the figure.

The similarity between the two plots suggests that involvement in severe crashes and being arrested for offenses unrelated to traffic both flow in large measure from common explanatory factors. No one would suggest that the lower arrest rate for 40-year olds compared to 20-year olds occurs because the 40-year olds have at long last learned how to not commit burglaries! This should invite a parallel caution against interpreting lower crash rates for 40-year-old drivers compared to those for 20-year-old drivers to mean that the 40-year-old drivers have simply learned how to not crash. It has been facetiously suggested that the crime rate curve is not reflecting decreased involvement in crime with increasing age, but increased skill at avoiding arrest. The most compelling and common-sense interpretation of the similarity between the two curves in Fig. 6-7 is that involvement in severe crashes and being arrested for offenses unrelated to driving each have explanatory factors in common, and that increasing skill and knowledge is not the major factor in the large decline in crash rates with increasing age.

Severe crash involvements per million population

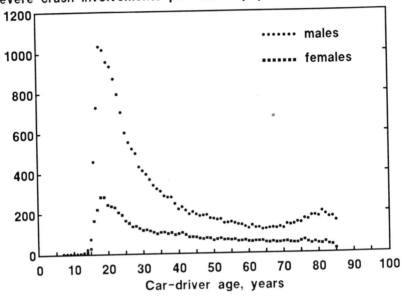

Arrests per thousand population

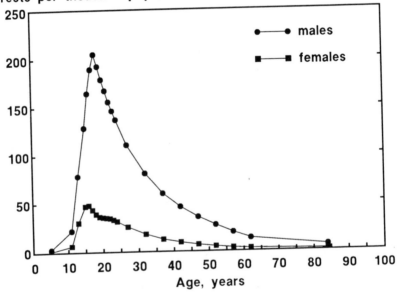

Figure 6-7. *Top:* Estimated car-driver involvements in single-car severe crashes per capita. *Bottom:* Number of arrests (for all offenses except those related to traffic laws) per capita. From Evans [1987a].

The type of age dependence shown in Fig. 6-7 seems fairly intrinsic to criminal activity, and also applies to homicide victims [Baker, O'Neill, and Karph 1984]. Gottfredson and Hirschi [1986] write: "The propensity to commit criminal acts reaches a peak in the middle to late teens and then declines rapidly throughout life. Further, this distribution is characteristic of the age-crime relation regardless of sex, race, country, time, or offense. Indeed, the persistence of this relation across time and culture is phenomenal." Although Steffensmeier et al. [1989] document much variability around the claimed pattern (for example, more fraud is committed by 50-year olds than by 20-year olds), the pattern does reasonably well fit a whole range of criminal activity, and also involvement in severe traffic crashes.

Direct association between criminal involvement and traffic crashes is provided by Haviland and Wiseman [1974] who compare the driving records of 114 jailed criminals with those of the general population They find that, compared to average drivers, the criminals have 3.25 times as many citations for traffic violations, 5.5 times as many property damage and injury producing crashes, and 19.5 times as many involvements in fatal crashes. They further write, "Criminals who were involved in major traffic offenses were likely to have been involved in major crimes and those involved in minor traffic offenses in a minor crime," suggesting that "the degree of an individual's deviation from societal norms is similar in divergent areas" (p. 432). A crucial point not addressed by Haviland and Wiseman [1974] is the extent to which the crimes for which the criminals were in prison were for the same traffic offenses on which their analysis is based. It is possible that some of the strength of the effects they noted is due to correlating traffic offenses with traffic offenses.

O'Toole [1990] compares criminal records of Australian army veterans killed in traffic crashes (mainly as drivers) to the records of a control group of surviving veterans. He finds that those killed in traffic crashes had, when they entered military service, almost twice as many non-traffic criminal offenses per capita as had the control group. They also had higher involvement rates in traffic offenses, but the difference was smaller.

Additional evidence that crash involvement is correlated with more general criminal involvement is provided by Sivak [1983], who finds that a state's homicide rate can be used to predict its traffic fatality rate. Whitlock [1971] finds relationships between road fatalities and homicide deaths, suicide deaths, and total violent death in data for 27 countries, mostly in Europe.

The general association between crash involvement and crime involvement invites the speculation that various factors known to be associated with crime involvement (socioeconomic, race) might also be associated with crash involvement; such variables are unavailable in nearly all traffic crash data files. However, UK data [Office of Population Censuses and Surveys 1978] suggest that involvement in all types of fatal injuries, including those from driver and pedestrian crashes, is strongly linked to social class; Adams [1985, p. 4] infers from such data, "An unskilled manual worker is four and a half times more likely to be killed in a motor vehicle accident than a self employed professional, and sixteen times more likely to be killed when walking." Further evidence of strong relationships between fatality risk and social class is provided by Keeling, Golding, and Millier [1985], who analyze non-natural child deaths in two English communities. Data for total injury deaths per capita show different rates for different racial groups in the United States, with native Americans having the highest rates and American Asians having the lowest [Baker, O'Neill, and Karph 1984, p. 27]. For pedestrian fatalities per million population, Mueller, Rivara, and Bergman [1987] report rates of 24 for whites, 38 for blacks and 148 for native Americans.

Few would suggest that criminal activity arises because of insufficient study of ethics, and that instruction in this discipline would much reduce crime. The associations noted here between criminal activity and crash involvement suggest likewise that lack of knowledge about correct driving procedures is not the main factor in traffic crashes; this observation helps illuminate the lack of demonstrated association between driver education and reduced crash rates.

The above comparisons are presented to attempt to gain insight into processes underlying traffic crashes, and to show that they involve much more than inadequate perceptual motor skill performance. The relationships should not be interpreted to suggest that those involved in traffic crashes generally possess criminal traits.

PERSONALITY FACTORS

The above findings suggest that broad psychological characteristics of the driver may play central roles in the propensity towards crash involvement. A number of studies have attempted to gain more specific information on the relationship between personality and driving.

The First Study Indicating "We Drive as We Live"

One of the earliest studies to examine the relationship between crash involvement and broad psychological characteristics is that of Tillmann and Hobbs [1949]. They compared characteristics of 96 Canadian taxicab drivers who had four or more crashes with a matched (age, sex and driving experience) group of 100 taxicab drivers who had no previous crash record, with the results shown in Table 6-1.

Tillmann and Hobbs [1949, p. 329] conclude:

It would appear that the driving hazards and the high accident record are simply one manifestation of a method of living that has been demonstrated in

Table 6-1. Relative frequency of contact with social agencies for
96 taxicab drivers with four or more crashes and for
100 with zero crashes. Table entries are percents

	Adult court	Juvenile court	Public health	Social service	Credit bureau	At least one agency
Four or more crashes	34	17	14	18	34	66
Crash-free drivers	1	1	0	1	6	9

Data from Tillman and Hobbs [1949]

their personal lives. Truly it may be said that a man drives as he lives. If his personal life is marked by caution, tolerance, foresight, and consideration for others, then he would drive in the same manner. If his personal life is devoid of these desirable characteristics then his driving will be characterized by aggressiveness, and over a long period of time he will have a much higher accident rate than his stable companion.

Although the methodology of the Tillmann and Hobbs [1949] study has been criticized on many counts, most recently by Grayson [1990], this study was the first to provide specific evidence of a strong link between broad personality characteristics and crash involvement. A major deficiency of the study is that much of the interpretation is based on psychiatric-type interviews conducted while riding in the taxicabs; this procedure is personal and subjective in nature, and given the extreme differences between the groups of drivers, it was not possible for the interviewer to remain unaware of the group to which the driver being interviewed most likely belonged, thus raising the possibility of potential bias. The comparison is between extremes (some of the high-crash-rate drivers verged on the psychopathic), so it could be argued that the results may not necessarily be applicable to a more moderate degree of crash over-involvement.

Psychiatric Profiles of Fatally Injured Drivers

Finch and Smith [1970] applied an imaginative technique to obtain psychiatric profiles of 25 deceased male drivers judged to be at fault in the crashes in which they were killed in Houston from 1967–1968. The profiles were produced by conducting in-depth interviews with family members and associates of the deceased. These profiles were compared to profiles of 25 control subjects selected from the same voter precincts in which the deceased had lived, and matched in such characteristics as age (all were males). Many criticisms of this study are

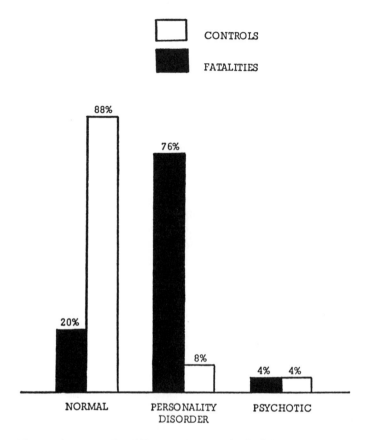

Figure 6-8.   Basic personality differences between fatally injured and control drivers. Reproduced from Finch and Smith [1970], Courtesy of Charles C. Thomas, Publisher, Springfield, IL.

possible; the information gathering processes were necessarily quite different for the deceased and the control subjects, and the sample sizes are small. However, the differences found are much larger than any that appear likely to be due to possible biases in the technique. Figure 6-8 shows the basic differences in personality factors found between the fatally injured and the control drivers. Only 20% of the fatally injured drivers were found to be free of psychosis or personality disorders, compared to 88% in the control population. Even the few abnormal personalities amongst the control population were found to be less deviant, and to have more adequate coping mechanisms which helped compensate for their psychiatric-driving liability. The study provided evidence supporting Waller's

[1967] suggestion that sociopathic personalities are overrepresented in the high-risk driving population, at least amongst fatalities.

Other Studies on the Relationship Between Personality and Crash Risk

McGuire [1976] reviews a substantial number of additional studies examining the relationship between driver personality and crash involvement (see also Shinar [1978] and Näätänen and Summala [1976]). In one study, McGuire [1956] administered a paper-and-pencil test to two groups of 67 male subjects in military service; one of the groups reported at least one crash in recent months, whereas the other group reported no crashes throughout their driving careers. McGuire [1956] summarized his findings as follows: "When compared with the 'safe' driver the accident-haver is less mature, less intellectual in his tastes and interests (but not necessarily less intelligent), has a lower aspiration level, expresses 'poorer' attitude toward the law and driving, is not as socially well adjusted, and is the product of a less happy childhood."

In a later work, McGuire [1972] administered a variety of tests and questionnaires to 2727 Mississippi driver license applicants whose driving records were derived in confidential interviews after a two-year exposure period. This study, not based on extreme groups, indicated that crashes correlate with having interests which are less intellectually oriented and less aesthetic in nature, and with a tendency not to deny open feelings of hostility. Higher crash frequency is associated with increased aggression, prestige seeking, and the seeking of social roles which are oriented towards authority and/or competition in preference to those which emphasize closeness to people and social service. Those with crash involvements are more likely to have family histories and current family relationships reflecting higher degrees of disruption and conflict. In a review of more recent literature, Tsuang, Boor, and Fleming [1985] conclude that certain personality characteristics and psychopathology—such as low tension tolerance, immaturity, personality disorder, and paranoid conditions—appear to be risk factors for traffic crashes.

O'Toole [1990] finds that men entering the Australian army who scored low on an intelligence test (equivalent to a less than 85 IQ score) were involved, as veterans, in fatal traffic crashes at about three times the rate of veterans who had above average scores. It is difficult to know whether this effect arises as a result of below average abilities at cognitive aspects of driving, or whether it more reflects influences from correlates with intelligence test scores, such as socioeconomic status. No relationship is found between crash involvement rate and intelligence test scores for those with above average scores.

An indication that avoidance of traffic crashes is related to health-producing habits in general is provided in a study by DiFranza et al. [1986] which finds that smokers have 50% more traffic crashes and 46% more violations than nonsmokers. The additional finding that the excess crashes and violations remained when differences in alcohol consumption, age, driving experience and education are taken into account led the authors to suggest that the differences might reflect more frequent general risk taking by smokers. Waller [1986] mentions that smoking may induce physiological changes, such as vision impairment, which could play a direct role in increasing crash risk.

Left-handedness has been shown to be related to shorter life, and to involvement in a whole range of injury-producing events. Coren [1989] finds that 180 left-handed drivers self-reported 19 traffic crashes in the previous two years compared to 103 self-reported crashes for 1716 right-handed drivers; that is, the left-handed drivers have a 76% higher crash involvement rate. Left-handed males have higher rates than right-handed males, and left-handed females have higher rates than right-handed females. Such an effect could possibly arise because traffic driving on the right (the study was conducted in British Columbia, Canada) might provide a safety advantage to right-handed drivers. This could be examined by repeating the study in a jurisdiction in which traffic drives on the left. (There are a number of studies for which replication in jurisdictions driving on the other side of the road could provide illumination; for example, in US traffic, Evans and Frick [1988] find 38% more impacts of high severity from the right side than from the left.) If it turned out that left-handed drivers had lower crash rates in left-drive jurisdictions, this would argue in favor of universal driving on the right, because most drivers are right-handed. My own guess is that explaining why higher crash risk is associated with left-handedness is as formidable a task as explaining why higher artistic and mathematical talent is associated with left-handedness. I would expect any performance difficulties to be adequately compensated for—recall the absence of evidence that monocular drivers have higher crash rates than binocular drivers.

Emotional Stress

Personality denotes stable character traits that do not change over short time periods. Emotional stress may produce short or medium term departures from an individual's long term average driving behavior. McMurray [1970] provides rather clear evidence that the risk of a driver being involved in a crash, or a traffic violation, increases just prior to divorce proceedings. Finch and Smith [1970] find evidence that drivers killed in crashes are more likely than control drivers to be undergoing periods of personal stress, and also that driving is used as an outlet to handle stress. Keeling, Golding, and Millier [1985] find a clustering of child pedestrian deaths around the time of the child's birthday, and suggest that the excitement engendered by the birthday overrides the child's normal caution.

NON-TRANSPORT MOTIVES

Without stating so explicitly, it is assumed in most writing on traffic safety, including this book, that the reason for driving is transportation. While such a motivation describes much of the use of the automobile, it does not describe all of its use.

Pleasure and Thrill Seeking Motives

Näätänen and Summala [1976, p 42] discuss "extra motives" that often impinge upon driving. These include competitiveness, sense of power and control, or more generally, hedonistic objectives—the pursuit of sensual pleasure for its own sake. They write, "Speed, and especially its acceleration, appears to produce pleasurable excitement even when no specific destination lies ahead and there is no point in haste . . . Driving a car or other motor vehicle affords us basically the same sort of thrills as those experienced on the roller coaster" [p. 46]. Näätänen and Summala [1976] further quote extensively from the British study by Black [1966], who interviewed 25 subjects, mainly young people, under hypnosis and not under hypnosis. When not under hypnosis, responses to traffic-safety related questions were in conformity with accepted good safety practice. Under hypnosis, the subjects expressed reduced concern about crashes and the consequences of fast driving. Whitefield [1967] considers that much of the material in Black's [1966] book lacks rigor. In a treatment not aspiring to technical rigor, Bayley [1986] links the pleasures of fast driving to more traditional pleasures.

Extra motives likely play an important role in the enhanced crash rates of younger drivers, especially the higher rates of male drivers. Although not established by controlled studies, which are bound to be difficult, there are copious anecdotal examples of the use of vehicles to show-off, to attract and impress members of the opposite sex, to provide excitement and to display competitive prowess. Such use is enshrined in our culture, and figures in many youth-cult movies (*Rebel Without a Cause, American Graffiti,* to name only two). Jessor [1984; 1987] discusses an "adolescent problem behavior syndrome" in which cars are used as an outlet for the independence, rebelliousness, and peer acceptance needs of newly licensed adolescents. Another non-transport use of vehicles is *scutting*—gaining a ride on the back of a moving vehicle by holding onto it by any means possible. Casserly and O'Brien [1989] report that this pastime is responsible for more deaths occurring in a hospital in Dublin, Ireland than is any other type of traffic crash involving children.

Suicide

Another non-transportation use of vehicles is suicide. Suicide in a single-occupant single-vehicle crash provides the most undiscoverable and honorable method of self destruction in motorized societies. It minimizes guilt in those left behind, and avoids insurance complications. It appears as an *accident,* unrelated to any decisions or deficiencies on the part of the deceased or his or her family or friends. Not only can the automobile be used for a premeditated suicide, but it may just happen to be available at the instant of a momentary, and perhaps otherwise temporary, impulse towards self destruction. It is a near-perfect instrument with which to indulge the "death instinct" postulated by Freud.

The use of vehicles for suicide unquestionably occurs, and has been discussed in the literature for decades. Indeed, Tabachnick et al. [1973] devote a book, *Accident or Suicide?—Destruction by Automobile,* to the subject. In the introduction they write: "This book revolves around a specific theory of the etiology of accident—namely, that in many, perhaps even most accidents, suicide or suicide-like factors are in evidence." Much of the book is devoted to describing a study in which psychiatric examination and questionnaire data were obtained from three groups of Los Angeles hospital patients; 25 drivers recovering from injuries sustained in severe single-vehicle traffic crashes; 29 recovering from suicide attempts; and 31 recovering from appendectomies. The most specific finding is of high alcohol use amongst the traffic-crash group, a result to be expected (Chapter 7). I find little in the 20 tables or the extensive discussion that demonstrates convincingly that some specific fraction of traffic crashes were due to suicide; the quoted claim in the introduction is not supported. The study however does find some similarities between characteristics of those involved in crashes and those attempting suicide. Additional suggestions of a link between suicides and traffic crashes are provided by Whitlock [1971], who finds that countries with high traffic fatality rates also have high suicide rates, and Bollen [1983], who finds similarities in the day-to-day variations of suicides and traffic fatalities in the US.

A novel approach to determining the role of suicide in traffic crashes is that of Bollen and Phillips [1982], who find that extensive news coverage of suicides of famous people is followed by increases in traffic fatalities. The excess is attributed to suicides, based on findings [Phillips 1979; Bollen and Phillips 1981] that media coverage of suicides leads to increases in suicides in general. To date, there is no quantitative estimate of the fraction of all traffic fatalities attributable to suicide. The method of Bollen and Phillips [1982] may be able to make such a determination, especially when coupled with the more detailed information about traffic fatalities now available in FARS. One would expect suicides preferentially to influence single-vehicle, single-occupant fatal crashes, and also, perhaps, pedestrian fatalities. Indeed, if these increased while other fatalities remained unaffected after major news coverage of suicides, this would provide particularly solid evidence for the approach used by Phillips [1979], and if enough data were combined, might offer a quantitative estimate of the fraction of all traffic fatalities that are suicides. Such a study might also provide important information on the ability of the media to influence behavior. Such information has implications for other aspects of traffic safety. An estimate of the fraction of traffic fatalities attributable to suicide is of considerable interest, because such countermeasures as better occupant protection, improved roads, or increased law enforcement are unlikely to influence this component of traffic fatalities.

DIFFICULTIES IN RESEARCHING THE ROLE OF BEHAVIOR FACTORS IN CRASHES

Although there is a large body of evidence showing that behavior is of crucial importance in traffic safety, most of the evidence is indirect, non-quantitative, and subject to differing interpretations. There are intrinsic barriers that conceal the type of direct information one would ideally like to have. One problem is that crash rates vary by large amounts based on specific known factors, such as age and alcohol use. Hoxie [1985] reports car occupant fatality rates differing by a factor of 200, while the hypothetical *high-risk* driver in Evans, Frick and Schwing [1990] has a fatality risk 1000 times that of the *low-risk* driver (differences in occupant protection contribute part of the effect).

The largest and most unmistakable behavior effects (as distinct from demographic, etc. factors) are obtained in comparing extreme cases, such as comparing taxi drivers with four or more crashes to taxi drivers with no crashes [Tillmann and Hobbs 1949], or fatally injured drivers [Finch and Smith 1970] to more typical drivers. Since the comparisons are between such extremes, bordering on comparing psychopathic to normal drivers, it could be argued that the results may have no validity when interpolated to the more moderate degrees of over-involvement which contribute to most traffic crashes. This problem has similarities to the dose-response problem in toxicology. Does a large, easily measured, deleterious effect associated with a massive dose of exposure to some substance support the inference that (say) one tenth of the dose would still produce some deleterious effect, such as about one tenth the effect of the initial dose? Or is there some threshold below which the substance produces no deleterious effect? Given that most crashes involve drivers who are not at the fringes of society, it is important to know whether moderate variations within the normal ranges of behavior can explain variations in crash rates. As in the toxicology case, the smaller the dose, the more difficult it is to measure the response.

There are methodological problems inherent in comparing those with moderately-above-average crash rates to those with below-average crash rates. Let us assume an average crash rate of one crash per ten years, or 0.1 per year. In a seven-year period, a *better than average* driver therefore expects to have no crashes, while one crash, which exceeds the expected average number of 0.7, nominally indicates a *worse than average* driver. Even a driver whose behavior is such as to double crash risk would still have a 25% chance of having no crashes in a seven-year period (assuming a Poisson distribution). On the other hand, a driver whose crash rate is half the average would still have a 30% chance of having one or more crashes in a seven-year period. The specific mix of drivers, by propensity to crash, in a sample of crash-free drivers and a sample of drivers with one or more crashes, depends on the distribution of propensity to crash in the population, which is difficult to determine. What is, however, very clear is that the crash-free population contains many drivers with above average propensity to crash, and the crash-having population contains many with below average propensity to crash. Thus any relationship between driver characteristics and propensity to crash is going to be difficult to discover in a study based on comparing the personal characteristics of the drivers assigned to each of these two groups. Accordingly, even if crash risk were strongly related to personality factors, such relationships would manifest themselves clearly only in groups of drivers with crash rates many times above the average rate.

There does not appear to be any way out of this dilemma. Even if data were available for periods of many decades, the propensity to crash may vary and therefore introduce other unwanted sources of variation. The best that probably can be done is to evaluate judgmentally the considerable body of evidence. My own intuition is that the dose-response relationship is not of a threshold type, so that the finding that large deviations in certain directions from normal behavior are associated with large increases over normal crash risk strongly suggests that small deviations in the same direction from normal behavior are likely to be associated with important increases in crash risk. Such a conclusion is supported weakly by research on non-extreme comparisons. However, as discussed above, even if such associations are in fact strong, they would appear diluted in any study seeking correlations.

I see no reason to dissent from McGuire's [1976] conclusion, which was based on a study of the extensive literature on the relationship between personality factors and traffic crashes, "It may be said that highway accidents are just another correlate of being emotionally unstable, unhappy, asocial, anti-social, impulsive, under stress and/or a host of similar conditions under other labels."

DRIVER SPEED CHOICE AND CRASH RISK

Among the factors contributing to drivers' speed choice is a systematic underestimation of the probability that they will be killed [Lichtenstein et al. 1978]. Another factor is that speed is desired for its own sake, for sensuous pleasure rather than just for utilitarian motives such as saving time. Noguchi [1990]

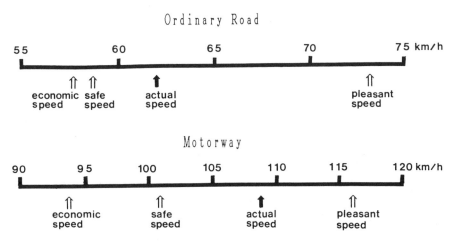

Figure 6-9. Subjects' estimates of the actual speed at which they would travel on a highway with a 50 km/h speed limit and on a motorway with a 100 km/h speed limit, together with their estimates of economic, safe, and pleasant speeds. Reproduced, with permission, from Noguchi [1990].

examines various aspects of driver's speed choice by having interviewers (a psychologist, a sociologist, and others) conduct in-depth interviews with 26 Japanese drivers selected for possessing average driver characteristics. The subjects were asked to imagine themselves driving on a highway or on a motorway with speed limits of 50 km/h and 100 km/h, respectively, and both without traffic jams. They were asked at what *actual* speed they would drive, and also what they considered to be *economic, safe,* and *pleasant* speeds. The results are shown in Fig. 6-9. The fact that they place the safe speed above the speed limit is consistent with other parts of the same study which find that subjects judged speed limits to be too low. The chosen speed appears to represent a compromise between competing desires for pleasure and safety.

Chosen speed has a large influence on the risk of crash, injury, and death. Nilsson [1982; 1990] examined changes in crashes and casualties associated with changes in travel speeds following increases or decreases in speed limits in Sweden. In many cases, speeds on roads with altered speed limits were compared to speeds on similar roads which did not have their limits changed. Nilsson finds that if mean or median speeds change (upwards or downwards) to new values, v_b, from previous values, v_a, the following relations estimate approximately the ratio of crash events before and after the speed change:

$$\text{(Crash rate after)/(Crash rate before)} = v_b/v_a \qquad \text{Eqn 6-1}$$

(Injury crash rate after)/(Injury crash rate before) $= (v_b/v_a)^2$ Eqn 6-2

(Fatality crash rate after)/(Fatality crash rate before) $= (v_b/v_a)^4$.   Eqn 6-3

These relationships have plausible physical interpretations. Crash rate is clearly related to speed, so the simplest relationship, that of direct proportionality reflected in Eqn 6-1, is a natural starting point. If, when a crash occurs, the risk of injury is proportional to speed, then injury crash rate will be proportional to speed squared. If the probability that an injury proves fatal is proportional to the energy dissipated in the crash (which is proportional to the speed squared), then the probability of a fatal crash is proportional to the fourth power of the speed.

The plausibility of these relationships is supported further by increases in fatality rates when rural Interstate speed limits in the US were increased from 55 mph to 65 mph in 1987. Miller [1989] reports that this legislative change led to an increase in average speeds from 60.8 mph to 62.2 mph. Substituting these values into Eqn 6-3 gives $(62.2/60.8)^4 = 1.10$; that is, a 10% increase in fatal crashes is estimated. Freedman and Esterlitz [1990] estimate a larger increase of "nearly 3 mph"; if we interpret this to mean a 2.5 mph increase over an initial 60 mph we compute an 18% fatality rate increase. These predictions are in reasonable agreement with observed fatality increases associated with the speed limit change of 16% [National Highway Traffic Safety Administration 1989], 15% [Garber and Graham, 1990], 15% [Baum, Lund, and Wells 1989], and 11%, by inference, from McKnight and Klein [1990].

When the 55 mph nationwide speed limit was introduced in the US in 1974, average speeds on rural Interstates, which previously had maximum speed limits of 70 mph, decreased from 63.4 mph to 57.6 mph (Federal Highway Administration data used in Evans [1987b]). Substituting these values into Eqn 6-3 estimates a reduction in the fatal crash rate of 32%; the observed reduction is 34% (Fig. 13-4).

The above discussion ignores distinctions between fatalities and fatal crashes, and in some cases between fatalities and fatality rates. Such differences are minor considering the approximate nature of the discussion, and the exclusive focus on percent changes.

The observation that fatalities per unit distance of travel on German Autobahns are similar to those on US Interstate freeways has led to questioning of the safety effects of speed. Lenz [1990] reports that average speeds on Autobahns have been increasing at about 1 km/h per year, reaching 132 km/h, or 82 mph, in 1988. Substituting into Eqn 6-3, and assuming 60 mph for US Interstates, estimates a German fatality rate 3.5 times that for the US. Such simple comparisons of rates between jurisdictions are to be approached with extreme caution, a point also made by O'Neill [1986], because there are many other important factors, including the four below. First, car ownership is concentrated in a narrower economic segment of society in Germany than in the US; there are indications of strong relationships between socioeconomic status and crash rate. Second, German anti-drunk-driving laws are stricter than those of the US. Third, the minimum age for a German driving license is 18, compared to, generally, 16 in the US; even at 18, German teenagers have less opportunity to drive than do American youths. Fourth, safety belt use in Germany is about 95%, compared to about 45% in the US. Apart from the fourth factor, which generates a fatality ratio of 1.4 (Chapter 10), these factors are difficult to quantify. However, it is not implausible that their combined effect produces a factor of 3.5, and that increases in speed are cancelling an expected large reduction in fatality risk.

While the discussion has been made in terms of average speed, the majority of harm is done by those traveling at speeds above the average. However, the fraction of drivers exceeding any speed is strongly linked to average speeds; for example, when the speed limits on US rural Interstate freeways increased from 55 mph to 65 mph, the proportion of cars exceeding 70 mph nearly doubled [Freedman and Esterlitz 1990].

Speed Variance

The importance of variability around average speeds has been recognized to be important in safety, especially since Solomon [1964] and Cirillo [1968] used crash data to show that the driver travelling at close to the average speed has a lower crash risk than drivers travelling at higher or lower than average speeds. Hauer [1971] derives such a U-shaped relationship by considering crashes to be proportional to the number of times a vehicle is overtaken or overtakes, which is at a minimum when the vehicle is travelling at the average speed. Intuitively, identical vehicles driven by identical drivers at identical speeds would provide optimum safety for a given average speed.

From time to time there are claims that speed variance is more important than speed, based on the above findings and the truism that vehicles travelling at identical speeds in the same direction cannot crash into each other. It is even periodically claimed that speed as such does not affect safety, and that instead of setting speed limits the goal should be to require all traffic to move at the same speed. While it is true that vehicles travelling slower than average have above average crash rates, the reason they are travelling more slowly is that the driver chooses to travel slower, most likely because of driver or vehicle inadequacies. If such a driver is encouraged or compelled to speed up to the average speed, an increase in crash risk seems more likely than a decrease. Even if slower than average drivers have crash rates similar to faster than average drivers, their injury and fatality rates will still be substantially less. Figure 3-3 shows that 45% of car occupants who are killed are killed in single-car crashes; speed variance is irrelevant unless vehicles travelling at different speeds interact in some way with one another. Speed variance is an unlikely contributor to many head-on or side-impact crashes, the main source of two-vehicle fatalities; only about 5% of fatally injured car occupants are killed as a result of any type of rear impact. Thus speed variance as such can play, at most, only a minor role in fatalities, and contrary suggestions based on regression analyses [Appendix C, p. 200, of Transportation Research Board 1984] provide another example of how just about any desired conclusion can be coaxed out of data by using such methods. It is because of the large influence of speed on casualties that Summala [1985] concludes that control of driver speed should be the primary focus of traffic safety interventions.

CAN SAFE DRIVING BE TAUGHT?

Driver education is, in some regards, one of the most successful educational endeavors. Students who cannot drive take a short course, at the completion of which they can drive. While safety is a primary consideration in all aspects of such training, much of the beginning driver's attention must be devoted to acquiring driving skills, and on learning the rules of the road. In Chapter 5, and in this chapter, we find no convincing evidence that driver education, or increased driving skill and knowledge, increase safety. Although driver education speeds up the process of learning driving skills, the main way such skills are acquired and honed is through direct feedback. Drivers learn, for example, to execute right turns correctly only after many errors such as riding over the curb, cornering too wide, or entering too quickly or slowly. With minimal instruction most people could probably learn to drive by trial and error.

In contrast, safety cannot be learned by direct feedback, but requires the absorption of accumulated knowledge and the experience of interactions with others. The main reason people buy smoke-detector fire alarms is not that their last house burned down; similarly, experiencing crashes is an ineffective way to learn how to avoid them. The difference between skillful driving and avoiding crashes is so basic as to suggest a course focused more specifically on safety, perhaps with a title like *Safe-driving education*. Such a course would be predicated on the assumption that all the students know how to drive, are good drivers, and are getting better all the time as they continue to practice. In the US, such a course might be appropriate in the last year of high school.

While there are many specific items (Chapter 12) that could be covered in such a course, a main emphasis would be on class discussions of broad safety issues, building on the growing interest in many other hazards which receive widespread media coverage. While the interest in reducing risks seems widespread, the public has acquired a distorted view that many improbable risks pose much greater dangers than they actually do, while at the same time the public largely discounts much more likely hazards [Lewis 1990]. The US population seems subject to frequent bouts of extreme fear over the astronomically improbable, or even the impossible.

In contrast, the possibility of commonplace events, such as a child, without warning or good cause, running onto a roadway is dismissed. Observational research in the UK shows that motorists behave as if they consider it the responsibility of the child, not the driver, to avoid child-pedestrian crashes [Howarth 1985]. Motorists have passed hundreds of children who have not run out in front of their vehicles, so experience has taught them that such events do not occur. Traffic fatality data leave little doubt that such *unexpected* events not only happen, but happen often. FARS data (Fig. 2-15) show that more than 100 six-year-old pedestrians are killed per year (and, of course, many more are injured). Most drivers have not sufficiently considered or discussed the harm that they may cause others even while driving legally, and at their normal safety margins and levels of risk-taking.

If drivers adopted safer driving practices, and allowed larger margins of safety, by the end of their driving careers it would not have made much difference in most cases; this follows from the statistical nature of crashes, which are rare events. But such a behavior change would spare large numbers of individual drivers the burden of having to claim, with legal correctness, that the six-year-old child was killed because it was the child's fault. The comment, "There was nothing I could do to prevent it," might be the subject of fruitful abstract discussions about hypothetical crash scenarios. Drivers who take extra care when near pedestrians, bicyclists, and motorcyclists, greatly reduce the probability that they will be the legally innocent and physically unharmed agent of some fellow human's death or permanent injury.

Here it is appropriate to point out that if a young person has a desire to help others, the most immediate expression of such a desire can be to take rather obvious steps to halve or quarter the chances that he or she will kill or permanently injure some innocent bystander in a crash. This is an area in which the young person has the chance to directly control events. The irresponsible use of vehicles, rather than being cool or admirable, might be viewed as being self-indulgent, similar to polluting the air to make money, an action in which the innocent pay for the behavior of the guilty. Perhaps appealing to the altruism of good driving might be more effective than appealing to the more traditional, and selfish, motive of self-preservation. It might be an uphill battle to persuade young people that they should not admire or emulate other young people who use automobiles to risk their own lives in the pursuit of pleasure and the defiance of authority. It may possibly be more fruitful to persuade them that risking the lives of innocent bystanders, especially young children, is hardly admirable conduct. Education emphasizing why people drive the way they do, and the potential consequences of such behavior to themselves and to others, might make a contribution to safer driving.

The problem of traffic crashes is much more one of drivers doing things that they know they ought not to do, than of drivers not knowing what to do. This does not imply that the problem is simply an ethical one, with the solution of the problem being to change vice into virtue; the history of the human race offers little hope of progress towards this goal. Characterizing the problem in simplistic good versus evil terms has led some to conclude that nothing can be accomplished by education or media campaigns because "You can't change human nature." Reducing traffic crashes requires a change not in human nature, but in behavior. The evidence is overwhelming that norms of behavior regarding many factors important in public health (including, in the traffic safety area, increased use of safety belts and motorcycle helmets, and decreased drunk driving) may indeed change. One dramatic change is the decline in smoking. Over the last two decades smoking has gradually become more associated with chemical dependency and negative qualities rather than with glamour and success. A large change in traffic safety could occur if the life threatening use of vehicles became more associated with immaturity and failure than with glamour and excitement. Education that emphasizes safe and considerate driving as a public health concern [Sleet 1984] may have potential, even though it is bound to be difficult to dissuade young people from doing what gives them pleasure.

CONCLUSIONS

Racing drivers, young drivers, and male drivers, the very groups with the highest levels of perceptual-motor skills and the greatest interest in driving, are groups which have higher than average crash involvement rates. This demonstrates that increased driving skill and knowledge are not the most important factors associated with avoiding traffic crashes. What is crucial is not how the driver *can* drive (driver performance), but how the driver *does* drive (driver behavior).

The overinvolvement of youth, and males, in traffic crashes is quantitatively similar to the overinvolvement of youth, and males, in criminal activity unrelated to traffic. Observations of actual drivers show higher levels of risk taking, as indicated by higher speeds and closer following distances, to be associated with young, and male, drivers. At all ages, males have larger pedestrian fatality risk than females of the same age, suggesting an intrinsically greater activity level, or propensity to take risk, which leads to greater involvement in traffic crashes.

Many studies provide evidence supporting the general contention that people drive as they live. Involvement in traffic crashes is correlated with being emotionally unstable, unhappy, asocial, anti-social, impulsive, aggressive, and being under stress. Educational initiatives which attempt to increase understanding about why people drive the way they do, and the potential consequences of such behavior to themselves, and more especially to others, such as young children, might make a contribution to safer driving.

REFERENCES

Adams, J.G.U. *Risk and Freedom—The Record of Road Safety Regulations.* Nottingham, UK: Bottesford Press; 1985.

Baker, S.P.; O'Neill, B.; Karph, R.S. *The Injury Fact Book.* Lexington, MA: Lexington Books; 1984.

Baum, H.M.; Lund, A.K.; Wells, J.K. The mortality consequences of raising the speed limit to 65 mph on rural Interstates. *American Journal of Public Health* 79:1392–1395; 1989.

Bayley, S. *Sex, Drink and Fast Cars.* London, UK: Farber and Farber; 1986.

Black, S. *Man and Motor Cars: An Ergonomic Study.* New York, NY: W.W. Norton; 1966.

Bollen, K.A. Temporal variations in mortality: a comparison of U.S. suicides and motor vehicle fatalities, 1972–1976. *Demography* 20:45–59; 1983.

Bollen, K.A.; Phillips, D.P. Suicidal motor vehicle fatalities in Detroit: a replication. *American Journal of Sociology* 87:404–412; 1981

Bollen, K.A.; Phillips, D.P. Imitative suicides: a national study of the effects of television news stories. *American Sociological Review* 47:802–808; 1982.

Carsten, O.M.J.; Tight, M.R.; Southwell, M.T. *Urban Accidents: Why Do They Happen?* Basingstoke, UK: AA Foundation for Road Safety Research; 1989.

Casserly, H.B.; O'Brien, T. Scutting: a dangerous pastime? *Injury* 20:337–338; 1989.

Cirillo, J.A. Interstate system accident research study II, interim report II. *Public Roads* 35:71–75; 1968.

Coren, S. Left-handedness and accident-related injury risk. *American Journal of Public Health* 79:1040–1041; 1989.

DiFranza, J.R.; Winters, T.H.; Goldberg, R.J.; Cirillo, L.; Biliouris, T. The relationship of smoking to motor vehicle accidents and traffic violations. *New York Journal of Medicine* 86:464–466; 1986.

Evans, L. Young driver involvement in severe car crashes. *Alcohol, Drugs, and Driving* 3(3–4):63–78; 1987a.

Evans, L. Factors controlling traffic crashes. *Journal of Applied Behavioral Science* 23:201–218; 1987b.

Evans, L.; Frick, M.C. Seating position in cars and fatality risk. *American Journal of Public Health* 78:1456–1458; 1988.

Evans, L.; Frick, M.C.; Schwing, R.C. Is it safer to fly or drive?—a problem in risk communication. *Risk Analysis* 10:239–246; 1990.

Evans, L.; Wasielewski, P. Risky driving related to driver and vehicle characteristics. *Accident Analysis and Prevention* 15:121–136; 1983.

Finch, J.R.; Smith, J.P. *Psychiatric and Legal Aspects of Automobile Fatalities.* Springfield, IL: Charles C. Thomas; 1970.

Freedman, M.; Esterlitz, J.R. *The Effect of the 65 mph Speed Limit on Speeds in Three States.* Arlington, VA: Insurance Institute for Highway Safety; January 1990.

Garber, S.; Graham, J.D. The effects of the new 65 mile-per-hour speed limit on rural highway fatalities: a state by state analysis. *Accident Analysis and Prevention* 22:137–149; 1990.

Girdler, A. About the sport. *Road and Track* 23(6):97–98; 1972.

Gottfredson, M.; Hirschi, T. The true value of lambda would appear to be zero: an essay on career criminals, criminal careers, selective incapacitation, cohort studies and related topics. *Criminology* 24:213–234; 1986.

Grayson, G. Individual and social factors in accident liability: a review of the literature. Paper presented to International Symposium on Driving Behaviour in a Social Context, Paris, France; 16–18 May 1989. To be published in proceedings of the meeting (1990).

Häkkinen, S. Traffic accidents and professional driver characteristics: a follow-up study. *Accident Analysis and Prevention* 11:7–18; 1979.

Hauer, E. Accidents, overtaking and speed control. *Accident Analysis and Prevention* 3:1–12; 1971.

Haviland, C.V.; Wiseman, H.A.B. Criminals who drive. American Association for Automotive Medicine, 18th Annual Proceedings, Toronto, Ontario, p. 432–439; 12–14 September 1974.

Howarth, C.I. *Interactions Between Drivers and Pedestrians: Some New Approaches to Pedestrian Safety.* In: Evans, L.; Schwing, R. C., editors. *Human Behavior and Traffic Safety.* New York, NY: Plenum Press, p. 171–182; 1985.

Hoxie, P. *Transportation Fatalities: A Risk Assessment.* SAE paper 851225. Warrendale, PA: Society of Automotive Engineers; 1985.

Jessor, R. Adolescent development and behavioral health. In: Matarazzo, J.D.; Weiss, S.M.; Herd, J.A.; Miller, N.E., editors. *Behavioral Health: A Handbook of Health and Disease Prevention.* New York, NY: John Wiley; 1984.

Jessor, R. Risky driving and adolescent problem behavior: an extension of problem-behavior theory. *Alcohol, Drugs, and Driving* 3(3–4):1–11; 1987.

Jonah, B.A. Accident risk and risk-taking behaviour among young drivers. *Accident Analysis and Prevention* 18:255–271; 1986.

Keeling, J.W.; Golding, J.; Millier, H.K.G.R. Non-natural deaths in two health districts. *Archives of Disease in Childhood* 60:525–529; 1985.

Lenz, K.H. Effects of speed. *IATSS Research—Journal of International Association of Traffic and Safety Sciences* 14(1):(in press) 1990.

Lewis, H.W. *Technological Risk.* New York, NY: Norton; 1990.

Lichtenstein, S.; Slovic, P.; Fishoff, B.; Layman, M.; Combs, B. Judged frequency of lethal events. *Journal of Experimental Psychology: Human Learning and Memory* 4:551–577; 1978.

Lim, C.S.; Dewar, R.E. *Driver Cognitive Ability and Traffic Accidents.* University of Calgary, Calgary, Alberta, Canada; 1989.

McGuire, F.L. The safe-driver inventory: a psychological test for selecting the safe automobile driver. *U.S. Armed Forces Medical Journal* 7:1249–1264; 1956.

McGuire, F.L. A study of methodological and psycho-social variables in accident research. *JSAS Catalog of Selected Documents in Psychology.* Ms. no. 195; 1972.

McGuire, F.L. Personality factors in highway accidents. *Human Factors* 18:433–442; 1976.

McKenna, F.P.; Duncan, J.; Brown, I.D. Cognitive abilities and safety on the road: a re-examination of individual differences in dichotic listening and search for embedded figures. *Ergonomics* 29:649–663; 1986.

McKnight, A.J.; Klein, T.M. The relationship of the 65 mph limit to speeds and fatal accidents. Paper 890711 presented to the 69th Annual Meeting of the Transportation Research Board, Washington. DC; 7–11 January 1990.

McMurray, L. Emotional stress and driving performance: the effects of divorce. *Behavioral Research in Highway Safety* 1:100–114; 1970.

Miller, T.R. 65 mph: does it save time. Association for the Advancement of Automotive Medicine, 33rd Annual Proceedings, Baltimore, MD, p. 73–90; 2–4 October 1989.

Mueller, B.A.; Rivara, F.P.; Bergman, A.B. Factors associated with pedestrian-vehicle collision injuries and fatalities. *Western Journal of Medicine* 146:243–245; 1987.

Näätänen, R. and Summala, H. *Road-user Behavior and Traffic Accidents.* Amsterdam, Netherlands: North Holland; 1976.

National Highway Traffic Safety Administration. Transcript of proceedings: Workshop on Advanced Driver Education Techniques, Washington, DC; January 1972.

National Highway Traffic Safety Administration. Interim report on the safety consequences of raising the speed limit on rural Interstate highways. Washington, DC; 1989.

Nilsson, G. The effect of speed limits on traffic accidents in Sweden. VTI Report No. 68. Linkoping, Sweden: National Road and Traffic Research Institute, S-58101, p. 1–10; 1982.

Nilsson, G. Personal communication describing results published in Swedish; publication in English is planned; 1990.

Noguchi, K. In search of optimum speed: from the users viewpoint. *IATSS Research—Journal of International Association of Traffic and Safety Sciences* 14(1):(in press) 1990.

Office of Population Censuses and Surveys. Information from the Registrar General's decennial supplement on occupational mortality, 1970–1972, Series DS No. 1. London, UK: Her Majesty's Stationery Office; 1978.

O'Neill, B. Autobahns vs. U.S. Interstates. *Insurance Institute for Highway Safety, Status Report* 21(13):2–2; 1986.

O'Toole, B.I. Intelligence and behaviour and motor vehicle accident mortality. *Accident Analysis and Prevention* 22:211–221; 1990.

Peck, R.C.; McBride, R.S.; Coppin, R.S. The distribution and prediction of driver accident frequencies. *Accident Analysis and Prevention* 2:243–299; 1971.

Phillips, D.P. Suicide, motor vehicle fatalities, and the mass media: evidence towards a theory of suggestion. *American Journal of Sociology* 84:1150–74; 1979.

Popkin, C.L.; Rudisill, L.C.; Geissinger, S.B.; Waller, P.F. Drinking and driving by women. American Association for Automotive Medicine, 30th Annual Proceedings, Montreal, Quebec, p. 1–14; 6–8 October 1986.

Shinar, D. *Psychology on the Road—The Human Factor in Traffic Safety.* New York, NY: John Wiley; 1978.

Sivak, M. Society's aggression level as a predictor of traffic fatality rate. *Journal of Safety Research* 14:93–99; 1983.

Sleet, D.A. Reducing motor vehicle trauma through health promotion programming. *Health Education Quarterly* 11:113–125; 1984.

Solomon, D. Accidents on main rural highways related to speed, driver, and vehicle. Washington, DC: Federal Highway Administration, US Department of Transportation, July 1964.

Steffensmeier, D.J.; Allan, E.A.; Harer, M.D.; Streifel, C. Age and the distribution of crime. *American Journal of Sociology* 94:803–31; 1989.

Summala, H. Modeling driver behavior: a pessimistic prediction? In: Evans, L.; Schwing, R.C., editors. *Human Behavior and Traffic Safety.* New York, NY: Plenum Press, p. 43–61; 1985.

Tabachnick, N.; Gussen, J.; Litman, R.E.; Peck, M.I.; Tiber, N.; Wold, C.I. *Accident or Suicide? Destruction by Automobile.* Springfield, IL: Charles C. Thomas; 1973.

Tillmann, W.A.; Hobbs, G.E. The accident-prone automobile driver. *American Journal of Psychiatry* 106:321–331; 1949.

Transportation Research Board. 55: a decade of experience. TRB Special Report 204. Washington, DC: National Research Council; 1984.

Tsuang, M.T.; Boor, M.; Fleming, A.A. Psychiatric aspects of traffic accidents. *American Journal of Psychiatry* 142:538–546; 1985.

US Department of Justice, Federal Bureau of Investigation. Washington, DC: Uniform crime reports: crime in the United States; 28 July 1985.

Waller, J.A. Identification of problem drinking among drunken drivers. *Journal of the American Medical Association* 200:114–120; 1967.

Waller, J.A. On smoking and drinking and crashing. *New York Journal of Medicine* 86:459–460; 1986.

Wasielewski, P. Speed as a measure of driver risk: observed speeds versus driver and vehicle characteristics. *Accident Analysis and Prevention* 16:89–103; 1984.

Whitefield, W. Review of *Man and Motor Cars* by S. Black. *Ergonomics* 10:363–364; 1967.

Whitlock, F.A. *Death on the road: a study of social violence.* London, UK: Tavistock; 1971.

Williams, A.F.; O'Neill, B. On-the-road driving records of licensed race drivers. *Accident Analysis and Prevention* 6:263–270; 1974.

7 Alcohol's Role in Traffic Crashes

INTRODUCTION

Beverage alcohol has figured in human affairs since the beginning of recorded history. Beer making is described in Egyptian hieroglyphics. The use of wine at special occasions is referred to early in the Old Testament when Isaac's son, in anticipation of being blessed, "brought him wine, and he drank" (Genesis 27:25). Alcoholic beverages have been often associated with health as well as with pleasant mood alterations. From antiquity their freedom from the disease-producing contaminants which were present in other beverages has been recognized. Adverse effects from alcohol consumption, especially in large quantities, have also been recorded for thousands of years. For example, in the Old Testament: "For the drunkard and the glutton shall come to poverty," (Proverbs 23:21) or "Who hath babbling? Who hath wounds without cause? Who hath redness of eyes? They that tarry long at the wine, they that go to seek mixed wine," (Proverbs 23:29–30). Waller [1985, p. 511] quotes the following from an Egyption papyrus:

> Make not thyself helpless in drinking in the beer shop. For will not the words of thy report repeated slip oft from thy mouth without thy knowing that thou hast uttered them? Falling down thy limbs will be broken, and no one will give thee a hand to help thee up. As for thy companions in the swilling of beer, they will get up and say, "Outside with this drunkard."

Being so long established in human societies, it is not surprising that beverage alcohol became an important concern in motor-traffic safety immediately after the invention of the automobile. Indeed, there is probably no traffic safety subject given more attention in the technical and popular literature than the role of alcohol. A review by the National Highway Traffic Safety Administration [1985] cites over 550 technical articles relevant to alcohol and driving. Moskowitz and Robinson [1987] identify 557 citations on the influence of alcohol on skills performance.

Today we can distinguish three conceptually distinct ways in which alcohol consumption influences traffic safety. These are its effects on

1. Survivability
2. Performance
3. Behavior

The first of these three effects was unknown until recently. The basic new finding, which we discuss later, is that, other factors being equal, the same physical impact tends to produce more injury for higher levels of alcohol consumption; this is counter to earlier conventional wisdom that, by relaxing the body, alcohol consumption reduced injury risk. Thus the old adage that God protects drunks and babies appears false; from the same impact, drunks and babies (as shown in Chapter 2) are both more likely to die.

The main influence of alcohol consumption on traffic safety is that it increases crash risk. This occurs through the combined influence of the second and third of the above listed three effects. Although the effects on performance and behavior are conceptually distinct, it is impossible to use crash data to assign the relative role each plays in increasing crash risk. For example, a higher involvement rate for drunk drivers in rollover crashes could be due to performance degradation (lowered ability to control a vehicle on curves) or behavior change (choice of a higher speed). Most laboratory research on the effect of alcohol focuses on its effect on performance. Although its effect on behavior may be the more important factor in traffic safety, this factor is, in principle, extremely difficult to study in laboratory experiments.

In this chapter we first discuss the measurement of alcohol use and intoxication, and then discuss the recent experiments which show that injury risk from the same impact increases with alcohol consumption. We then describe some laboratory experiments showing how alcohol affects performance. Rather than discussing the effect on behavior as such, we proceed directly to the influence on crash risk, which incorporates both performance and behavior influences. This background then sets the scene for estimates of how many crashes and fatalities would be prevented if alcohol were absent as a factor.

MEASUREMENT OF ALCOHOL

Alcohol denotes ethyl alcohol, or ethanol, the active ingredient in distilled spirits, wine, and beer; it is the second simplest member of a family of compounds chemically classified as alcohols, the simplest member being methanol. Alcohol is a colorless liquid which boils at a somewhat lower temperature (78.5° C) than water, and freezes at a considerably lower temperature (−117.3° C) than water. It is miscible with water (that is, it can be mixed in any proportion to generate a homogeneous liquid mixture). The specific gravity of alcohol is 0.79—that is, the mass (or weight) of a given volume of alcohol is 21% less than the mass of the same volume of water. Thus a solution made by combining equal volumes of alcohol and water will contain 44% alcohol and 56% water by mass, but 50% of each by volume. When indicating the proportion of a solution, such as blood or an alcoholic beverage, that is alcohol, it is therefore crucial to know whether it is the proportion of the volume or the proportion of the mass that is indicated.

Measurement of Amount Consumed

Although alcoholic beverages come in a wide variety of forms, colors, flavors, and bouquets, their chief constituents are water and alcohol. Other components appear to have only minor pharmacological significance in general [Wallgren and Barry 1970], although mold and other constituents in specific beverages may trigger allergic reactions in some individuals, while other ingredients may add to the severity of the hangover [Waller 1985, p. 512]. Most US beers contain about 4.5% alcohol by volume, with premium beers having 5.0%. Light beers can be as low as 3%, and low-alcohol beers around 2%. Alcohol content is not indicated on beer containers in the US; apparently manufacturers wanted to avoid using alcoholic content as a component in marketing and advertising because of concerns that such competition would lead to escalating alcoholic content. Canadian beers typically have 5.0% alcohol by volume. In Europe, alcohol content is indicated on some beer containers; 6% by volume is not uncommon; some lagers, referred to in the trade as *super strongs,* have alcohol content as high as 9% by volume, which is higher than the content of some wines.

The percent by volume of alcohol in wine and spirits is normally indicated directly on the label. Wines tend to be between about 8% to 14%, with the majority being in the range from 11.5% to 13.8%. Fortified wines, like sherry and port, tend to be close to 20% alcohol by volume. Wine coolers are nearly all 4.0%, with a few at 5.0% or slightly higher.

In Europe the alcohol content of all alcoholic beverages is indicated in terms of the percent alcohol by volume. In the US, for distilled spirits, alcohol content is given in terms of *proof,* which, by a strange sort of logic, indicates twice the percent alcohol content by volume. Proof originated in ignition tests to determine alcohol content. In Britain (and previously in Canada) the term proof is used, but with a different meaning than in the US. The UK proof is now defined to be directly proportional to the percent alcohol by volume, and therefore is also directly proportional to the US proof; specifically, US proof = UK proof × 8/7. Thus 80 US proof is equivalent to 70 UK proof. With increased integration with Europe, the British proof measure is gradually being replaced by the simple percent alcohol by volume, sometimes referred to in Europe as the Gay-Lussac system, named after the French chemist who introduced it. Gins, whiskies and vodkas are typically about 40% alcohol by volume (80 proof in the US system), while liqueurs tend to be lower in proof, and in some cases much lower.

Fluid measure in the US is usually in terms of fluidounces, with the US fluidounce defined as 1/16 of a US pint, and the pint defined as 1/8 of a US gallon. The US gallon is legally defined as 231×2.54^3 ml (231 cubic inches). This gives that one fluidounce is equal to 29.574 ml. The Imperial, or British, fluidounce is 1/20 of 1/8 of an Imperial gallon, which is defined as the volume of ten pounds of water at 60 degrees Fahrenheit; one Imperial gallon is measured to be 1.20095 US gallons. Hence the British fluidounce is equal to 28.413 mL, sufficiently close to the US fluidounce that no distinction need be made for most practical purposes.

A *typical* drink contains about half a fluidounce of alcohol. This quantity of alcohol is, approximately, contained in 1.25 fluidounces of 80 proof spirit (the most common US measure is larger than this, at 1.5 fluidounces), 2.5 fluid ounces of 20% alcohol-fortified wine, four ounces of 12.5% alcohol wine, 12 fluidounces of 4.5% alcohol beer or 12 fluidounces of 4.0% wine cooler. All these drinks provide approximately equal amounts of alcohol, and, if consumed within similar time periods, produce fairly similar pharmacological effects.

Content in the Human Body—Blood Alcohol Concentration (BAC)

After consumption, alcohol is absorbed rapidly through the stomach and is distributed widely throughout the body, including the brain. The amount of alcohol in the body can be determined by analysis of the alcohol content of samples of blood or breath.

The alcohol content of blood is commonly measured in terms of the *mass* of alcohol in a given *volume* of blood. In common usage, weight is often used to indicate mass. Although such use is unlikely to lead to any practical errors, it is formally quite incorrect in this case [Evans 1978]; if we ever investigate alcohol effects in space, the weight of alcohol per volume of blood is always zero, independent of consumption! In the US, laws pertaining to alcohol are commonly based on the measure grams of alcohol per milliliter of blood (g/mL) [National Highway Traffic Safety Administration 1985; 1989]. However, a milliliter of blood has a mass very close to one gram. Indeed, if blood had a density, or specific gravity, identical to that of water, a milliliter of blood would have a mass of almost exactly one gram, as this was once the definition of the gram. In fact, blood is about 5% more dense (the difference is temperature dependent) than water [US Department of Transportation 1968]. If this difference is ignored as inconsequential for the present purposes, then the measure grams of alcohol per milliliter of blood is, for all practical purposes, the same as grams of alcohol per gram of blood. More generally, the measure is simply the mass of alcohol per mass of blood, a dimensionless ratio, which is consequently not related to any specific set of units. This is the measure of Blood Alcohol Concentration (BAC) we use in this book. Since a typical value indicating intoxication is 1 part alcohol per 1000 parts blood, or 0.001, it is convenient to multiply by 100, and express the result in terms of a percent. Thus 1 part alcohol per 1000 parts blood (by mass) is represented as a BAC of 0.1%. Note that the definition of BAC is therefore simply the percent, by weight, of alcohol in the blood. It is technically correct to substitute weight for mass, because ratios of weights are identical to ratios of masses.

Although a plethora of measures representing the amount of alcohol in the blood appear in the literature, these can essentially all be converted to BAC without numerical change (apart from moving the decimal), with, at most, an inconsequential error of a few percent. The present diverse units, many of which are repeatedly qualified by such reminders as w/w, w/v and v/v (the symbols indicating weight or volume), often pose barriers to understanding, even though they are conceptually and numerically closely related to the BAC definition above. In many countries (for example, Sweden, Norway, Finland, Denmark and West Germany), legal statutes are defined directly in terms of mass of alcohol per mass of blood [Jones 1988], which, when expressed as a percent, is identical to BAC as defined above. Other measures occur; for example, in order to obtain a more convenient numerical value than provided by g/mL, the unit grams per deciliter of blood (g/dL) is used (dL = L/10). A measurement of 0.1 g/dL is identical to 0.001 g/mL, which, as discussed above, is for all practical purposes the same as a BAC of 0.1%. The unit mg/g, indicating milligrams of alcohol per gram of blood, also appears. Although such nomenclature helps remind the reader that it is masses being compared, it violates the normal practice in science of cancelling identical items in numerator and denominator. Numerically, 1 mg/g is identical to a BAC of 0.1%.

Closely related to the amount of alcohol in the blood is the amount of alcohol in breath, which has the advantage that it can be measured by less intrusive means. The earliest practical breath-alcohol measuring instrument, the *Drunkometer,* was developed in 1938 by Rolla N. Harger. The best known breath-alcohol instrument, the *Breathalyzer,* was invented in 1954 by Robert Borkenstein [Borkenstein 1985] and has been used extensively in Canada and in parts of the US [Jones 1987]. Breath alcohol is closely related to BAC, the conversion factor varying only slightly from individual to individual. A BAC level of 0.1% is approximately equivalent to 1 gram of alcohol per 2100 liters of breath [Jones 1988]. In Britain, the legal limit of alcohol in breath, adopted in 1983, is 35 µg of alcohol per 100 mL of breath, which corresponds to 0.08% BAC based on a conversion factor of 2300 [Walls and Brownlie 1985]. A breath measurement in g/L is converted to BAC in percent by multiplying by a factor in the range of 210 to 230.

There is no agreed definition of intoxication, nor any specific BAC threshold defining intoxication. Intoxicated, or *drunk,* or a host of synonyms or near synonyms given in any large dictionary, indicate large changes in conduct associated with the consumption of alcoholic beverages. Legal usage covers a wide variety of terminology and criteria. *Impaired* is used to indicate effects which, while still observable, are less than those indicating intoxication. As alcohol effects increase gradually with increased consumption, there are no clear-cut boundaries between sober, impaired, and drunk; such designations necessarily embody arbitrary criteria.

In summary, BAC is here defined simply as the percent, by weight, of alcohol in the blood. Not only is this measure the most convenient from a technical point of view, being independent of units of measurement, it is also a measure easily understandable by laymen, two advantages that support its universal use.

ABSORPTION OF ALCOHOL INTO THE HUMAN BODY

As discussed by Donelson [1988], the pharmacology of beverage alcohol is well understood in large measure because of its importance in traffic safety. When consumed, alcohol is readily and rapidly absorbed from the stomach, and especially from the small intestine, and does not have to be digested before entering the blood. Alcohol readily distributes throughout the tissues and fluids of the body in a manner similar to that of water. Alcohol is eliminated from the body mostly through metabolism (enzymatic breakdown). A very small percentage of alcohol is excreted unchanged in breath, urine, and sweat. After consumption, the amount present at a given time in body fluids, organs, and other tissues is determined by rates of absorption, distribution, and elimination. The rate of absorption depends on the quantity drunk, its concentration, and especially the other contents of the gastrointestinal tract [National Highway Traffic Safety Administration 1985]. Food in the tract delays absorption, so that the conventional wisdom that drinking on an empty stomach increases the rate of onset of intoxication is well founded. When alcohol is taken with a heavy meal, up to six hours may be required for complete absorption [Wallgren and Barry 1970].

The greater the concentration of alcohol in a drink, the more rapid is the absorption [US Department of Transportation 1968]. Thus, alcohol in straight liquor enters the blood stream more rapidly than does the same amount of alcohol contained in a larger volume of wine, which in turn enters more rapidly than the same amount contained in beer (or wine cooler). Such differences have led to an erroneous impression that beer is substantially less likely to cause impairment than hard liquor, an impression that has in many cases been used to support less stringent controls on the sale and advertisement of beer (and wine) than of hard liquor. However, the differences in peak levels of intoxication associated with different levels of concentration when the same amount of ethyl alcohol is consumed are minor compared to the main influences which are related to the actual amount of ethyl alcohol consumed, regardless of concentration [Waller 1985, p. 511].

Fig. 7-1 shows a schematic representation of the absorption and elimination

BAC

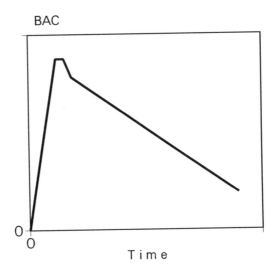

Time

Figure 7-1. Schematic representation of absorption and elimination after consuming some quantity of alcohol at time zero.

pattern that tends to be followed by most people, based on the pioneering studies conducted by Erik Windmark in Sweden in the 1920's and 1930's [Andreasson 1986]. The dependence of BAC on such factors as amount of alcohol consumed and body weight are expressed in what are referred to as Windmark laws. For example, the linear portion in Fig. 7-1 can be used to extrapolate a previous BAC level if measurements are available only some time after drinking has ended.

While the pattern in Fig. 7-1 provides a good generalization, Dubowski [1985] stresses that there is much individual variability. Fig. 7-2 shows actual data, based on breath analysis, for four subjects. While subjects A and B fit reasonably well the pattern in Fig. 7-1, subjects C and D do not. Dubowski [1985] indicates with an arrow the peak BAC; for subjects C and D this does not occur until 2 and 3 hours, respectively, have passed since the end of alcohol ingestion, which is indicated by the dotted lines. Such differences indicates that the various tables that have been produced to assist individuals in estimating their BAC as a function of number of drinks consumed and body weight can do no more than give a rough indication. Devices that attempt to measure BAC directly are of course not affected by such variability as far as indicating whether a driver is legally above a proscribed level. Various devices have been marketed, including coin-operated ones for establishments selling alcoholic beverages. These devices provide estimates of BAC, or indications of whether BAC exceeds some limit [Voas 1988].

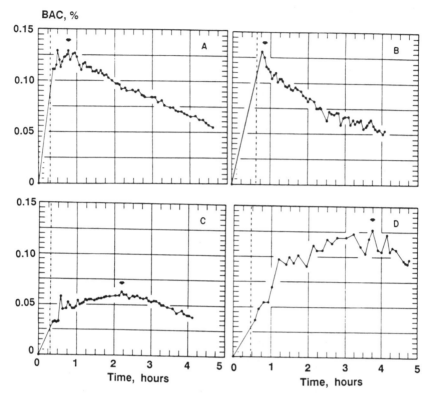

Figure 7-2. Absorption and elimination data for four subjects. Adapted from Dubowski [1985], and used with permission (copyright by Journal of Studies on Alcohol, Inc., Rutgers Center of Alcohol Studies, New Brunswick NJ 08903.)

THE EFFECT OF ALCOHOL ON HUMANS

The behavioral and emotional effects of alcohol arise from its effect on the brain. Measuring BAC is really an attempt to measure the amount of alcohol in the brain. The behavior changes associated with the same BAC vary from individual to individual, and different amounts of alcohol induce acute intoxication in different individuals. Relevant variables are body mass, body fat, stomach contents, speed of drinking, physical health, and the tolerance the individual has developed to alcohol [National Highway Traffic Safety Administration 1985]. BACs as low as 0.02% to 0.03% affect the performance of some individuals. At a BAC of 0.1%, about half of all people show signs of intoxication. Alcohol has a slightly greater effect on performance during the absorption phase than during the elimination phase. This is known as the Mellanby effect [Moskowitz,

Daily, and Henderson 1979]. There may be residual effects on behavior also during *hangover*, after all the alcohol has been eliminated from the system [Laurell and Tornros 1982].

There is no general theory to explain the mechanisms by which alcohol alters mood, performance, behavior, or susceptability to injury. The components of the central nervous system most affected by alcohol have yet to be adequately identified [US Department of Health, Education and Welfare 1971]. The main conclusion that can be drawn from existing research is that we do not yet have a good model to explain the many ways in which alcohol influences human physiology and brain function. Although we lack unifying theories and predictive models, we still have a large and increasing body of empirical knowledge on alcohol's effects. Some of that knowledge is described below.

Effect on Susceptability to Injury

Until recently, it was generally believed that the presence of alcohol reduced the likelihood of injury, given an impact (or physical insult) of specific severity. This fitted a common notion that, by being more relaxed, drunks were more likely to *roll with the punches*; more importantly, it appeared to be supported by some clinical studies. In general, these studies monitored the progress of sets of *drunk* and *sober* patients who were admitted to hospitals with injuries of similar severity. It was generally observed that the drunks exhibited higher rates of recovery or survivability. It now appears that such studies were methodologicaly flawed [Waller 1987] because the agent being studied, namely alcohol, played a crucial role in subject selection. If alcohol increases the probability of dying at the scene of a crash, then subjects whose injuries prove fatal because of alcohol use are excluded from the comparison in the hospital tests. Similarly, if being sober compared to being drunk were to reduce injury to below that requiring hospitalization, this would similarly negate any conclusions based exclusively on those admitted to hospital. Indeed, instead of examining how alcohol influences injury risk, such studies are examining secondary and unimportant details of the non-normalized distributions of injury versus recovery curves for drunk and sober drivers.

Waller et al. [1986] use a quite different approach to examine whether alcohol increases or decreases injury risk in a crash. They analyze traffic crash data to examine injury outcome for drunk and sober drivers involved in crashes matched in a sufficient number of important characteristics that they could be judged to be of similar severity, using data on 1 126 507 drivers involved in 1979–1983 North Carolina crashes.

Three major sets of analyses are conducted. The first two rely on the investigating police officer's judgment as a measure of alcohol involvement, two levels (not drinking, and drinking-impaired) being used; for deceased drivers

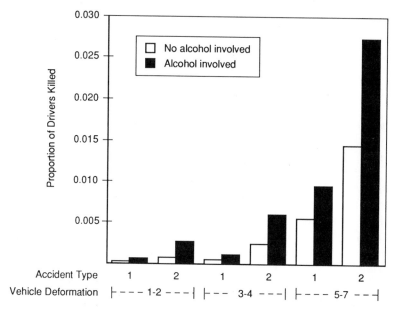

Figure 7-3.   Predicted values of the proportion of drivers killed as a function of vehicle deformation, crash type, and driver alcohol consumption. Solid bars indicate alcohol involved, and open bars indicate not alcohol involved. Type 1 accident is angle, rear-end, or other single vehicle; type 2, overturn, head-on, or hit fixed object. Reproduced, with permission, from Waller et al. [1986]. (Copyright 1986. American Medical Association.)

these data were supplemented with medical examiner records. The third set of analyses is restricted to drivers with objective BAC measurements. In the first set of analyses, the proportion of drivers killed is analyzed as a function of driver alcohol status, while taking into account other factors associated with the extent of injury. The second set of analyses uses various levels of injury as subjectively indicated by the police officer, thus yielding a much larger number of cases.

The results of fitting log-linear models to the data indicate that, in all cases, injury risk was greater when alcohol was present. The results for the first analysis— on the effect of alcohol on fatality risk, are shown in Fig. 7-3. The overall conclusion [Waller et al. 1986] is that the alcohol-impaired driver was 3.85 times as likely to die as the alcohol-free driver in crashes of comparable severity. A recent analysis using FARS data finds that alcohol increases fatality risk in the same crash by a factor of (1.9 ± 0.2) for BAC = 0.1% drivers and by a factor of (3.3 ± 0.5) for BAC = 0.25% drivers [Evans and Frick 1991]. Additional evidence that alcohol increases injury risk is provided by Anderson and Viano [1987], and by Dischinger et al. [1988], who find that an intoxicated person might be at greater risk of immediate death due to increased vulnerability to shock and therefore decreased time available for emergency medical intervention.

Effect on Performance

The alcohol effect that traditionally has been considered most relevant to traffic safety is the influence on task performance. Inability to walk a straight line, or slurred speech, have long been interpreted to indicate intoxication. There has been much scientific investigation of how alcohol consumption affects human abilities to perform a variety of tasks. The basic experimental approach common to most of the investigations is to obtain first some performance measure, such as reaction time, for a subject when the subject is alcohol-free. The subject is then administered a specified dose of alcohol, and after some appropriate delay to allow absorption, the performance is measured again. In this way variations in performance are measured as a function of alcohol consumption. When appropriate precautions are exercised, such experiments do not place subjects at risk, and consequently do not involve intractable ethical questions.

Moskowitz and Robinson [1987] identify 557 citations in the technical literature on the influence of alcohol on skills performance. They analyze the results of 159 of these, the criteria for a study to be included in their analysis being that it provides enough information to infer a BAC, and it finds alcohol effects on the performance of tasks judged to be relevant to the driving task. Most of the studies compared performance at some task at just one level of BAC with performance at zero BAC. Some of the studies used more than one level of BAC—the average number of BAC levels per study is 1.9.

They find that 45% of the studies indicate impairment at 0.04% BAC or less. The majority of the studies find impairment at below 0.07% BAC. Based on the descriptions in the original papers, the studies are separated into nine behavioral categories to determine if the BAC at which impairment began differed as a function of behaviors. The results are shown graphically in Fig. 7-4.

The nine categories are:

1. *Reaction time*. This factor appeared to show more variability than other measures for unknown reasons.
2. *Tracking*. Fifteen of 28 tracking studies demonstrated impairment at 0.05% BAC.
3. *Vigilance or concentrated attention*. This appeared among the least sensitive variables, with no study showing impairment below 0.05% BAC.
4. *Divided attention*. Subjects performed multi-tasks which placed competing demands on their attention. Impairment is reported with BAC as low as

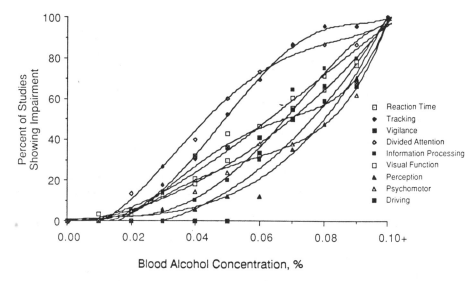

Figure 7-4. Percent of studies showing impairment at or below indicated BAC level for nine behavioral categories. Reproduced, with permission, from Moskowitz and Robinson [1987].

0.02%, with 60% of the studies reporting impairment at or below 0.05% BAC.

5. *Information processing.* It appeared that information processing skills are impaired at relatively low BAC, with 75% reporting impairment at or below 0.08%.

6. *Visual functions.* These refer to functions likely to be tested by an optometrist in contrast to performance with more complex information processing. Results suggested that retinal functions are least likely to show alcohol impairment, whereas eye movement factors are quite sensitive at low BAC.

7. *Perception.* Twenty-one studies of perception included auditory functions, visual illusions, etc., and in general are not particularly sensitive to alcohol until 0.08% BAC.

8. *Psychomotor Skills.* Most of 29 studies of psychomotor functions which were examined indicated impairment at 0.07% BAC, although some showed impairment at or below 0.05% BAC. Tasks which required skilled motor performance and coordination, including standing steadiness, are more likely to be impaired at lower BAC.

9. *Driving.* Twenty-two studies of driving simulator and on-the-road testing varied widely in results.

The large body of literature summarized by Moskowitz and Robinson [1987] shows unmistakably that a variety of performance measures show degradation with alcohol consumption, and that such degradation becomes clearly observable at relatively low levels of BAC, such as 0.04%. In contrast, twenty years earlier, effects had not been demonstrated at levels below about 0.1% BAC [US Department of Transportation 1968], a finding that contributed to the 0.1% BAC level being used to indicate intoxication in US traffic laws. As more research is conducted, it seems to me inevitable that impaired performance will be associated with ever decreasing levels of BAC for the reasons which are discussed below.

Underlying all experiments like the above is an implicit response versus dose (that is, performance versus BAC) curve, that indicates how performance changes as BAC is increased continuously from zero to higher levels. Simple experiments choose a small number (usually one) of values of BAC, and measure a few points on this curve to a precision limited by the number of subjects and other factors. To date, no experiments have been performed to explore in fine detail, and to high precision, the performance versus BAC curve for any task. However, on theoretical grounds, such a curve must be one of two types. Either it is characterized by a threshold BAC, below which there is no response, followed by a response which increases with dose, or else the response is a strictly monotonically increasing function (that is, a greater dose always leads to a greater response) of dose passing through the origin. If the former pertains, additional research may identify the threshold, which we already have convincing evidence is, for most tasks, below 0.04% BAC. On the other hand, if the response increases strictly monotonically with BAC, and there is certainly no general theoretical or other argument why it should not, then more precise research using more subjects will identify lower and lower limits of impairment. If such a response-dose curve were linear, then the performance degradation at a BAC of 0.02% would be half that at 0.04%, and at 0.01% half that at 0.02%, and so on.

It should be stressed that, in the above discussion, impairment means any demonstrated reduction in performance associated with alcohol, without regard to magnitude. Many factors in addition to alcohol are associated with reduced performance, including the aftermath of a poor night's sleep, fatigue, tension, stress, and growing older. Such differences pale in significance compared to differences between individuals; a somewhat inebriated, sleep-deprived, fatigued, tense, over-the-hill, former professional tennis player will hit a ball a lot better than I can at my peak performance.

Thus, although performance clearly degrades with the consumption of even small quantities of alcohol, the specific role of such effects in increasing crash risk are far from obvious. What is probably even more important than alcohol's effect on performance is alcohol's effect on behavior.

Effect on Behavior

In contrast to the case of performance, there is no extensive literature describing alcohol's effect on behavior, largely because it is not possible to investigate such effects in a laboratory setting. The mood alteration and reduction in inhibitions associated with alcohol consumption usually occur in social conditions quite different from those in which a laboratory technician administers carefully controlled doses of ethyl alcohol in an arid hospital environment. There are formidable ethical barriers to investigating directly the extent to which alcohol increases willingness to risk life, limb, and property in a traffic crash. Laboratory or closed-roadway tests in which subjects perform tasks that simulate risk, with relatively high probabilities of losing a few dollars or crashing into a soft traffic cone, are much more tests of performance risk-estimation capabilities than representations of the risks of real driving. One of the most celebrated of such tests is that of Cohen, Dearnaley, and Hansel [1958] who find that at very low BAC levels bus drivers were more willing to drive their vehicles through unacceptably small spaces, but at the same time were less able to drive successfully through adequate but difficult spaces; the driving errors did not, of course, actually damage the busses. There is modest evidence from real traffic situations that drivers with BAC in the range 0.08% to 0.15% may drive faster than drivers without alcohol [Damkot 1977]. House, Waller, and Stewart [1982] also report higher speeds to be associated with alcohol use, but additionally find that as BAC increased to higher levels more crash-involved drivers were travelling at slower speeds.

Although difficult to quantify in controlled tests, there is copious indirect evidence that alcohol has large effects on behaviors important in traffic safety. It is well recognized that alcohol increases aggressive behavior and general bravado. Its role in violence results not from reduced skill, but from changed behavior. It seems that this is also its larger influence on traffic safety. However, the large quantity of traffic crash data, which, as discussed below, show large influences of alcohol on traffic safety, still do not enable us to infer how much of the effect is due to mood alteration and behavior effects, and how much is due to performance degradation.

OTHER DRUGS, ILLNESS, AND SLEEP DEPRIVATION

There has been a great deal of concern about the influence of drugs other than alcohol on traffic safety; such concerns involve ethical (that is, prescription), over-the-counter nonprescription, and, perhaps most importantly of all, illegal drugs, and the combination of drug and alcohol use. Shinar [1978, p. 50] lists the therapeutic and negative side effects of a number of drugs. Although the possible adverse effect of various drugs on traffic safety has generated some descriptive papers in the literature, little of a quantitative nature is known. The quarterly journal, *Alcohol, Drugs, and Driving* is devoted almost exclusively to alcohol, reflecting the mix of research activity; similarly, many conferences devoted to alcohol and drugs focus almost entirely on alcohol. One of the basic impediments to researching the effects of drugs other than alcohol is that alcohol is the only one in which behavior and mood alteration are strongly linked to an objective chemical measure, BAC. The influence of alcohol is directly linked to its presence in the body, with such factors as time since consumption or whether the amount in the body is increasing or decreasing being only of secondary importance [Moskowitz, Daily, and Henderson 1979]. In contrast, the chemical traces of many other drugs remain in the body a number of days after their effects on performance and behavior have become unnoticeable. Thus, finding chemical traces of such drugs in the bodies of those fatally injured in traffic crashes offers little information on their influence on crash risk. Indeed, our current knowledge [Waller 1985, p. 522; Simpson 1987] is not much greater than that described much earlier by Buttigliere, Brunse, and Case [1972], who, in summarizing the pharmacology of a list of drugs, note that very little of a specific nature is known about their effects on driving. As so little of a definitive nature is known about this subject, it is not discussed further here. However, it should still be kept in mind that drug use is probably of great importance in traffic safety.

Doege [1988] finds evidence in the literature suggesting that 1700 injury producing crashes and as many as 1500 fatalities may be due to drivers' illnesses or medical conditions other than alcohol intoxication, though he stresses that the methodology in many of the studies did not inspire confidence. Morris, MacKenzie, and Edelstein [1990] report that preexisting chronic conditions, such as cirrhosis or heart disease, increase the risk that adult trauma patients will die. Popkin and Waller [1989] report that drivers known by the North Carolina Division of Motor Vehicles to be undergoing treatment for epilepsy have crash rates 40% higher than the general driving public. Findley, Unverzagt, and Suratt [1988] find that 29 patients with obstructive sleep apnea, which is associated with severe daytime sleepiness, have crash rates seven times greater than a control group of drivers. Seven of the 29 patients report falling asleep at least once a week while driving! Even without sleep disorders, drivers who have normal sleeping patterns which have been disrupted have increased fatal-crash risk [Hertz 1988; McDonald 1989].

TRAFFIC CRASH RISK AND ALCOHOL CONSUMPTION

From the earliest days of motorization, alcohol has been recognized as a factor leading to increased crash risk. The earliest known reference in the technical literature [identified and quoted in US Department of Transportation 1968, p.

146] is to a study reported in the *Quarterly Journal of Inebriety* in 1904 regarding fatal crashes involving "automobile wagons" which reads:

We have received a communication containing the history of twenty-five fatal accidents occurring to automobile wagons. Fifteen persons occupying these wagons were killed outright, five more died two days later, and three persons killed. Fourteen persons were injured, some seriously. A careful inquiry showed that in nineteen of these accidents the drivers had used spirits within an hour or more of the disaster. The other six drivers were all moderate drinkers, but it was not ascertained whether they had used spirits preceding the accident. The author of this communication shows very clearly that the management of automobile wagons is far more dangerous for men who drink than the driving of locomotives on steel rails. Inebriates and moderate drinkers are the most incapable of all persons to drive motor wagons. The general palsy and diminished power of control of both the reason and the senses are certain to invite disaster in every attempt to guide such wagons.

Case-control Studies

Case-control studies compare BACs of a group of crash-involved drivers to those of a control group of non-crash-involved drivers. Both groups of crashes are matched as closely as is practical in such characteristics as day of week, time of day, and location. The use of the control group is critical, because a finding of high levels of alcohol use in crash-involved drivers would not imply that alcohol is associated with increased risk if equally high levels were present in the control group. The first case-control study was performed in Evanston, Illinois from 1935 to 1938 by Holcomb [1938], who finds that 25% of crashed drivers had BAC > 0.1%, whereas 2% of control drivers had BAC > 0.1%. Since then, a number of other studies have been performed, all with fairly consistent results. By far the largest scale and most quoted such study is that of Borkenstein et al. [1964] in which reliable BAC levels were measured for 5985 crash-involved drivers and 7590 control drivers in Grand Rapids, Michigan, in 1962–1963. It is unlikely that a study on this scale will be performed again in the US, because, among other reasons, civil rights concerns make it increasingly difficult to obtain breath tests from the large numbers of randomly selected drivers comprising the control group. In the Borkenstein et al. [1964] study, which is also described in Borkenstein et al. [1974], the control sample was obtained by police stopping vehicles at pre-selected sites and times, after which members of the research team requested a voluntary breath sample exclusively for research purposes.

Interpreting Case-control Data. The data obtained in case-control studies fit within the framework indicated in Table 7-1. The first BAC range, or category,

Table 7-1. The form of data obtained from case-control studies to estimate the role of alcohol in crash involvement

BAC category	Number of drivers providing BAC values	
	Crash-involved, A(i)	Control, C(i)
1	A(1)	C(1)
2	A(2)	C(2)
.	.	.
.	.	.
i	A(i)	C(i)
.	.	.
.	.	.
n	A(n)	C(n)
All	T_A	T_C

with $i = 1$, is always BAC $= 0$, or BAC between zero and some low value. Such data are interpreted in terms of the risk of crash involvement when the driver has BAC in the ith category compared to zero BAC, defined more formally as

$$r(i) = \frac{\text{Risk that a driver with BAC in range } i \text{ is involved in a crash}}{\text{Risk that a driver with BAC} = 0.0 \text{ is involved in a crash}}.$$

Eqn 7-1

Values of $r(i)$ are readily obtained from data like that in Table 7-1 as

$$r(i) = \frac{A(i)}{C(i)} \times \frac{C(1)}{A(1)},$$

Eqn 7-2

where $A(i)$ and $C(i)$ represent the number of crash-involved and control drivers, respectively.

Although values of $r(i)$ are readily inferred from observational data, they must be interpreted with some care. This is because there are two quite distinct concepts, namely

1. Involvement in crash
2. Responsibility for crash.

Some blurring of the difference between these distinct concepts has contributed to a general sense that alcohol plays a less important role in multiple-vehicle crashes than it in fact does. The following (extremely hypothetical) construct illustrates the distinction between involvement and responsibility.

Imagine a population of drivers who never crash. Now, let some very small fraction of these drivers consume a substance which makes them likely to crash into the next object they encounter, be it a tree or another vehicle. Examination of a sample of drivers involved in single-vehicle crashes would find that 100% of them had consumed the substance; examining a sample of drivers involved in two-vehicle crashes would find that only about half of them had consumed the substance. The finding that 50% of drivers involved in the two-vehicle crashes had consumed the substance, compared to 100% for the single-vehicle crash drivers, does not imply any lesser responsibility of the substance for the two-vehicle crashes. For each case the substance is responsible for 100% of the crashes.

From data such as those in Table 7-1 it is therefore not, in general, possible to determine the specific risk-increasing role of alcohol. It is possible if the data refer exclusively to single-vehicle crashes, but, as single-vehicle crashes are rare, such data are difficult to obtain. Even for the Borkenstein et al. [1964] study, which provides BAC values for over 13 000 drivers, there are still only 622 drivers involved in single-vehicle crashes. In response to this problem, Borkenstein et al. [1964] present in their Table 43, page 230, and Chart XV, the BAC levels of drivers judged to have been responsible for crashes. In Table 7-2 these data are shown divided into six BAC categories that will be used later. For expository convenience, the first category is designated BAC = 0, rather than the more strictly technically correct BAC < 0.001%. The additional space before BAC ≥ 0.1% in Table 7-2 is included to identify better those in violation of most US drunk driving laws.

In order to make the distinction between involvement and responsibility we define a separate risk factor, R, as

$$R(i) = \frac{\text{Risk that a driver with BAC in range } i \text{ causes a crash}}{\text{Risk that a driver with BAC } = 0.0 \text{ causes a crash}}, \quad \text{Eqn 7-3}$$

where the term *cause* is used for convenience and consistency with Borkenstein et al. [1964] while avoiding it in general for the reasons discussed in Chapter 4.

The relative risk factors, $R(i)$, are inferred immediately from the Borkenstein et al. [1964] data using Eqn 7-2. The errors in R are derived by assuming the data arise from a Poisson process, to give

$$\Delta R(i) = R(i)\sqrt{1/C(i) + 1/A(i) + 1/A(1) + 1/C(1)}. \quad \text{Eqn 7-4}$$

All errors are standard errors, so there is a 68% probability that the true value is within the one standard error, and a 95% probability it is within two standard

Table 7-2. Estimates of $R(i)$ using data from Borkenstein et al. [1964] for drivers judged to have caused the crashes. $R(i)$ is the risk that a driver in BAC range i causes a crash compared to the risk for a driver with BAC $= 0$

		Number of drivers				Lower limit	Upper limit
i	BAC, %	Crash-causing	Control	$R(i)$	$\Delta R(i)$	$R - \Delta R$	$R + \Delta R$
1	0	2604	6756	1	—	—	—
2	0.001 − 0.049	200	589	0.88	0.075	0.81	0.96
3	0.050 − 0.099	143	187	1.98	0.22	1.76	2.21
4	0.100 − 0.149	172	44	10.1	1.7	8.4	11.9
5	0.150 − 0.199	123	10	31.9	10.5	21.4	42.4
6	≥ 0.200	63	4	40.9	21.1	19.8	62.0
	Totals	3305	7590				

errors. The lower than unity value of $R(2)$ is probably an artifact of the data [Allsop 1966]. The Borkenstein et al. [1964] study was widely discussed in the media as it was being conducted, so it is likely that some drivers who had consumed small amounts of alcohol were being unusually cautious to avoid attracting police attention. Note that, notwithstanding the sample of over 13 000 BAC measurements, there is still high uncertainty in some of the estimates of R because of sample size limitations.

The data in Table 7-2 have been discussed in some detail because they are considered to reflect best how an individual driver's risk of causing a crash increases with increasing BAC, in contrast to crash involvement. These results are compared in Table 7-3 to derivations from a number of other case-control studies. Apart from the derivations from Borkenstein et al. [1964], the other risk values are as provided by Reed [1981]. The table is structured so that as we move to the right, the causative contribution of alcohol may be presumed to decline. A large fraction of all fatal crashes are single-vehicle, so that a sample of fatally injured drivers will consist mainly of those responsible for the crash. The rightmost column is for all police-reported crashes, which are mainly two vehicle crashes, so we expect lower values of $r(i)$, in accord with the discussion above. Overall, there is fair agreement between all the studies, when sample size and varying interpretation are taken into account. The phenomenon being investigated, namely how crash risk depends on BAC, is not expected to vary much over the years, as it results from the effects of alcohol on behavior and performance. A reduction in the amount of overall drinking should not affect the relationship, although it would make a larger sample size necessary to observe it to the same precision. The evidence

Table 7-3. Relative risk of driver involvement in various types of crashes as determined in case-control studies

i	BAC, %	A	B	C	D	E	F
		IDENTIFIER—see key below					
1	0	1	1	1	1	1	1
2	0.001 – 0.049	0.88	1.02	0.82	1.34	3.82	0.93
3	0.050 – 0.099	1.98	3.27	1.27	2.02	2.90	1.52
4	0.100 – 0.149	10.1	21.1	3.2	2.7	12.7	5.7
5	0.150 – 0.199	32	53*	40*	13*	54*	17
6	≥ 0.200	41					22

*For BAC ≥ 0.15%.

Key:

A. Drivers judged responsible for police reported crashes, Grand Rapids, Michigan, 1962–1963 (sample size of crash-involved drivers, N = 3305) [Borkenstein et al. 1964].

B. Drivers killed in crashes, Vermont, 1967–1968 (N = 106) [Perrine, Waller, and Harris 1971].

C. Drivers killed in crashes, New York, New York, 1959–1960 (N = 34) [McCarroll and Haddon 1962].

D. Drivers involved in injury-producing crashes, Huntsville, Alabama, 1974–1975 (N = 599) [Farris, Malone and Lilliefors 1976].

E. Drivers involved in crashes resulting in hospitalization, Evanston, Illinois, 1935–1938 (N = 270) [Holcomb 1938].

F. Drivers involved in police reported crashes, Grand Rapids, Michigan, 1962–1963 (N = 5985) [Borkenstein et al. 1964].

(see also Hurst [1985]) is very clear that crash-involvement risk increases steeply at high BAC levels.

Approximate Estimates of the Fraction of Crashes Attributable to Alcohol

For drivers with zero BAC, the ratio, k, of crash-involved to control drivers,

$$k = A(1)/C(1) \qquad \text{Eqn 7-5}$$

reflects the average crash risk and the frequency of sampling of the crash-involved drivers. If alcohol did not change crash risk, the number of crash-involved drivers expected in BAC range i is simply $k \times C(i)$, or the total number of expected crash-involved drivers is the sum over all BAC ranges, or $k\, T_C$. Any excess of the actual number of crash-involved drivers, T_A, over this expected number is due to alcohol, so the fraction of crashes attributable to alcohol is given by

$$F = 1 - k\, \Sigma C(i)/\Sigma A(i) = 1 - k\, T_C/T_A. \qquad \text{Eqn 7-6}$$

Substituting the data in Table 7-2 gives

$$F = 1 - (2604/6756) \times (7590/3305) = 0.1148. \qquad \text{Eqn 7-7}$$

Table 7-4. Approximate estimates of the fraction of different types of crashes attributable to alcohol in 1961–1962 inferred from data of Borkenstein et al. [1964]

Type of harm	Percent attributable to alcohol
Fatal or visible signs of serious injury	22
Other visible injury	19
No visible injury but complaint of pain	9
No indication of injury	10
All crashes	11

That is, for the sample of drivers in Grand Rapids, Michigan in 1962–1963, and subject to the assumptions, especially the attribution of responsibility, 11.5% of the crashes were attributable to alcohol.

If the data for all crashes in Borkenstein et al. [1964] are substituted into Eqn 7-6 the result is 6.3%, in contrast to the 11.5% value obtained when only drivers judged responsible for the crashes are included. Thus, ignoring the question of responsibility reduces the estimate by about one half, in keeping with the hypothetical construct at the beginning of this section, when two-vehicle crashes are involved. This result can be useful in making approximate estimates when there is no way to assign responsibility—simply do the calculation based on all the data and double the result; in fact, below we will multiply by the empirically determined ratio 11.5/6.3 = 1.8, rather than 2. An advantage of the calculation reflected in Eqns 7-5 and 7-6 is that it does not require the detailed breakdown of the data by BAC level, but just the total number of cases, and the numbers of those that were alcohol free.

The above estimates refer to all crashes, which are overwhelmingly property damage only. In order to determine the fraction of losses at different injury levels we use data in Borkenstein et al. [1964, p. 232] showing drivers categorized by injury level and BAC. Quantities computed by applying Eqn 7-6 to these data do not estimate the fraction of injuries attributable to alcohol, because the data do not indicate whether the driver was responsible for the crash. The best estimate of that actual fraction attributable to alcohol is obtained by multiplying the value given in Eqn 7-6 by 1.8, in analogy with the case for all crashes. For all the crash severities, the overwhelming majority of crashes involve more than one vehicle, as is true for the case that generated the 1.8 factor.

The results of applying Eqn 7-6 and multiplying by 1.8 are shown in Table 7-4. It should be stressed that these results are, given the method of calculation, clearly approximations; more satisfactory estimates are not apparent in the literature. These results do show a clear pattern in which alcohol plays an increasing role as crash-severity increases, a finding that is supported by many other studies.

The estimates apply to Grand Rapids, Michigan in 1961–1962. There are indications that the role of alcohol in traffic safety has been declining. However, there is no way to monitor the contribution of alcohol to crashes of different severities on a national level from year to year because BAC is not measured in any systematic nationwide way for all crash-involved drivers. The situation is different for fatal crashes, which is the subject of the next section.

THE FRACTION OF TRAFFIC FATALITIES ATTRIBUTABLE TO ALCOHOL

The availability of FARS data makes it possible to determine the fraction of all fatalities in the US that are attributable to alcohol, although, surprisingly, the literature did not contain even a moderately satisfactory estimate of this prior to 1990. The press often reports that alcohol is involved in about half of all fatal crashes. While true, this does not address what role alcohol plays. Undoubtedly coffee is involved in nearly all fatal crashes, yet eliminating coffee is unlikely to have much of an effect on traffic crashes. A widely quoted study performed under the auspices of the National Academy of Sciences [Reed 1981] estimated that eliminating alcohol would reduce traffic fatalities by 23.7%.

The estimate described below [Evans 1990] uses FARS data from 26 states which recorded BAC for over 84% of fatally injured drivers. Because alcohol influences the number of fatalities in different ways depending on the types of crashes, it is necessary to treat separately single-vehicle crashes, two-vehicle crashes, and three- or more vehicle crashes, and to also consider fatalities to non-occupants of vehicles. The data used are shown in Table 7-5. Driver means a driver of any motorized vehicle; non-occupants are nearly all pedestrians. The analysis uses the risk factors in Table 7-2.

Single-Vehicle Crashes

Assume that $F(i)$ drivers in BAC range i are killed in single-vehicle crashes. If these drivers had been at zero BAC, then a lesser number, namely $F(i)/R(i)$, would have been killed. Summing this quantity over the six BAC categories gives the number of fatalities prevented by eliminating alcohol, and dividing this by the original number gives the fraction eliminated. Applying this calculation to the data in Table 7-5 gives the fraction of single-vehicle fatalities attributable to alcohol as 55.2%.

Single-vehicle driver fatalities are overwhelmingly a nighttime phenomenon, as is clear from the data in Fig. 7-5 [Stein 1989]. This figure uses FARS data for 15 states with high levels of BAC reporting, and is for three years combined (1983, 1984, and 1985).

Table 7-5. Distributions of Blood Alcohol Concentrations (BAC) of fatally injured persons in the 26 states* in 1987 FARS data with BAC known for over 84% of fatally injured drivers. All values, except those in the bottom row, are percents. From Evans [1990]

i	Blood Alcohol Concentration, BAC, %	Drivers killed in crashes involving:				Non-occupants of vehicles
		One vehicle	Two vehicles	Three vehicles	> Three vehicles	
1	0.00	35.23%	65.67%	75.17%	72.41%	58.48%
2	0.001 − 0.049	3.35	4.22	3.55	6.21	3.54
3	0.050 − 0.099	6.75	5.24	5.24	3.45	4.27
4	0.100 − 0.149	12.11	5.61	3.55	5.52	4.63
5	0.150 − 0.199	16.80	7.31	3.72	4.14	6.89
6	⩾ 0.200	25.76	11.95	8.78	8.28	22.19
	All with known BAC	100.00	100.00	100.00	100.00	100.00
	BAC unknown	10.55	14.06	13.32	12.12	27.08
	Number of fatalities	5677	5016	683	165	3405

*The 26 states, identified by their postal codes, are: CA CO CT DE HI ID IL IN ME MD MA MN MT NE NV NJ NM NC OR SD VT VA WA WV WI WY

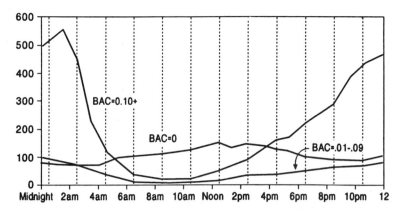

Figure 7-5. The numbers of drivers killed in single-vehicle crashes versus BAC and time of day (all days of the week combined). Based on FARS data for 15 states with high BAC recording rates (data for 1983–1985). Reproduced, with permission, from Stein [1989].

Multiple-Vehicle Crashes

The much lower alcohol use by those involved in two-vehicle crashes compared to those involved in single-vehicle crashes, as is apparent in Table 7-5, has often contributed to a general impression that the role of alcohol in driver fatalities is primarily a single-vehicle-crash phenomenon. This impression can be quite deceptive because, while none of the zero BAC drivers killed in single-vehicle crashes died because of alcohol, many of the zero-BAC drivers killed in multiple vehicle crashes did. It is accordingly necessary to model the multiple-vehicle crash process to deduce the contribution of alcohol from the data in Table 7-5. This is done in Evans [1990] by assuming that the number of crashes between drivers in the ith and jth BAC categories is proportional to the number of vehicles in the ith category times the risk factor for the ith category times the corresponding quantities for the jth category. Applying this model to the data in Table 7-5 gives the result that 45.0% of driver deaths in two-vehicle crashes are attributable to alcohol. The 45% consists of a 17.0% contribution from drivers with BAC = 0 and a 28.0% contribution from drivers with BAC > 0. The use of alcohol by other drivers increases the number of zero-BAC drivers killed in two-vehicle crashes by 35%.

An extension of the model to three-vehicle crashes gives the result that 43.8% of drivers killed in such crashes would not have died if alcohol had not been present. The same value is assumed to apply to the small numbers of drivers killed in crashes involving four or more vehicles.

Non-Occupants

The question of non-occupants (essentially pedestrians) is more uncertain. If one assumes that the distribution in time of pedestrian risk is similar to that for driver fatalities in single-vehicle crashes, and that vehicles strike pedestrians in proportion to the rate they strike other objects (the assumption used in the pedestrian exposure approach described in Chapter 4), then eliminating alcohol would reduce pedestrian fatalities in the same proportion it reduces single-vehicle driver fatalities, namely, 55%. However, pedestrian deaths tend to occur at times more like those for driver deaths in two-vehicle, not single-vehicle, crashes. It might therefore be more appropriate to consider drivers crashing into pedestrians at the same rate they crash into other vehicles. Such a calculation estimates that eliminating driver alcohol use would reduce pedestrian fatalities by 26%. However, this calculation ignores alcohol use by pedestrians, an assumption that the data in the last column of Table 7-5 unmistakably refute. Clearly, alcohol use by pedestrians contributes to pedestrian fatality risk, as has been shown in a case-control study by Blomberg and Fell [1979]. Further evidence is provided from Leeds, UK, where pedestrian alcohol use was a factor in 11% of pedestrian

Table 7-6. Fractions of fatalities attributable to alcohol (based on 46 386 traffic fatalities in 1987). From Evans [1990]

Source of fatalities	Percent of all fatalities	Percent due to alcohol		Number of fatalities preventable by eliminating alcohol
		26 states	All USA	
Occupants killed in:				
One-vehicle crashes	40.24%	55.2%	52.6%	9 818
Two-vehicle crashes	37.00	45.0	42.9	7 363
⩾ Three-vehicle crashes	6.03	43.8	41.8	1 168
Non-occupants	16.73	45.0	42.9	3 329
Total (or average)	100.00	(49.0%)	(46.7%)	21 678

injury crashes [Carsten, Tight, and Southwell 1989], and from Irish data which indicate almost one in ten fatally injured drunk pedestrians appeared to have been lying on the roadway prior to being struck [An Foras Forbartha 1985]. The similarity of the distributions of alcohol use for pedestrians and for drivers killed in two-vehicle crashes suggests that the fraction of pedestrian deaths attributed to alcohol is similar to the fraction for two-vehicle crashes, namely 45%, though it is more likely higher than lower than this value.

Overall Fatality Reductions if Alcohol Use Were Zero

The estimates of the fraction of driver fatalities attributable to alcohol for single-vehicle crashes, two-vehicle crashes, three- or more vehicle crashes based on data from 26 states are shown in Table 7-6. Also shown is the distribution of all 1987 fatalities into these same categories; it is assumed that passenger risk changes in proportion to the risk of their drivers. By weighting the percent attributable to alcohol in each category by the fraction of all fatalities due to that crash category we compute that 49% of the fatalities in the 26 states are attributable to alcohol. In order to obtain an estimate for the US, a correction factor is applied based on discriminant factor analyses [Klein 1986; Fell and Klein 1986; Fell and Nash 1989] which showed that in 1987 in the US 46.6% of fatally injured drivers had BAC > 0. The corresponding value for the 26 states is 48.9% (Table 7-5). The closeness of this to the fraction of fatalities attributable to alcohol suggests that a simple multiplicative factor should provide a satisfactory rescaling. Accordingly, all the estimates based on the 26 states are multiplied by 46.6/48.9 = 0.953 to generate the values shown in Table 7-6. Thus the fraction of US fatalities that would be prevented by eliminating alcohol is estimated to be 46.7%, or (47 ± 4)% based on the error analysis in Evans [1990]. Eliminating alcohol in 1987 would therefore have prevented about 22 000 of the 46 386 fatalities.

The estimate is based on the assumption that if drivers with a given BAC level did not consume alcohol, they would drive at the same risk level as average drivers with BAC = 0 observed at similar places on similar occasions. Although there are clear indications that heavy users of alcohol differ from the general public in ways other than their alcohol use [Donovan, Marlatt, and Salzberg 1983; Stutker, Brantley, and Allain 1980], and that such differences could lead to different crash rates even when such drivers are alcohol-free [McCord 1984], there does not appear to be sufficiently firm quantitative information to modify the above estimate. Any such effect would tend to lower the fatality reductions associated with eliminating alcohol.

Other studies report that alcohol has a large role in traffic fatalities. Donelson et al. [1989] conclude that 50% of fatal crashes in British Columbia, Canada, were due, at least in part, to alcohol use by drivers and pedestrians. Data in Stein [1989, Table 13; also see Fig. 7-5] indicate that 66% of single-vehicle driver fatalities are attributable to alcohol, somewhat higher than the values in Table 7-6 for such crashes. A higher value is to be expected in the Stein [1989] data because it refers to an earlier period (1983–1985) when alcohol played a larger role (as discussed in a later section).

Effect of Eliminating Drunk Driving Rather than Alcohol

The 47% fatality reduction is calculated by comparing the population of drivers with their current levels of BAC and associated risks, R, to an assumed population in which $R = 1.0$ for every driver. The calculation is repeated [Evans 1990] assuming that high BAC drivers reduce their risks not to $R = 1.0$, but to the level corresponding to the highest alcohol category still legal in most (but not all) US states, namely 0.05% to 0.099%, for which $R = 2.98$ (Table 7-2). Decreasing all R values higher than 2.98 to 2.98 rather than decreasing all R values to 1.0 leads to an overall reduction in fatalities of 41%. That is, all drivers with illegal levels of BAC acquiring a distribution of BAC similar to that presently observed for drivers with BAC between 0.050% and 0.099% reduces traffic fatalities by 41%. Setting the maximum risk level at other values generates the following percent declines in fatalities: 44% for a maximum risk of 1.5; 39% for a maximum risk of 3; 34% for a maximum risk of 6; 26% for a maximum risk of 10. The results of Borkenstein et al. [1964] suggest that a driver at 0.10% BAC has a risk of causing a crash about 6 times that of a zero BAC driver, suggesting that if all legally drunk drivers changed to marginally legal levels of just under 0.10% BAC, traffic fatalities would decline by 34%.

Changes in the Role of Alcohol

The simple multiplicative approach used to extrapolate from the 26 states to the US can be used also to monitor changes in the role of alcohol in traffic fatalities.

The previously mentioned discriminant analysis applied to 1982 FARS data shows 53.1% of fatally injured drivers had BAC > 0 (compared to 46.6% in 1987). From these data Evans [1990] estimates that eliminating alcohol would have prevented 53.2% of 1982 fatalities compared to 46.7% of 1987 fatalities. Hence, in 1982, alcohol increased fatalities to 2.14 times the zero-alcohol number, compared to 1.88 times in 1987, implying a reduction in fatalities of $0.26/2.14 = 12.1\%$ from 1982 to 1987 attributable to reduced alcohol use. The decline in the crashes specifically attributable to alcohol (all minus those not attributable to alcohol), from 1.14 to 0.88, represents a 23% decline. The reduction, equivalent to 6400 fewer fatalities in 1987, helps explain why national fatalities did not increase during a time of economic expansion, as predicted by the multivariate model of Partyka [1984]. This reduction is much larger than the 2%–3% decline that Hedlund et al. [1984] find associated with reduced alcohol involvement in an earlier period (1980 to 1982) before grass-roots activism became so prevalent.

Any measure which reduces the fraction of fatalities attributable to alcohol from the 1987 value of 47% to, say, 42% (that is, a reduction of 10% in the 1987 value) is calculated to generate an overall fatality reduction of 8.6%. Approaches to reduce the magnitude of the contribution of alcohol to traffic losses form the subject of the next chapter.

CONCLUSIONS

The psychological effects of alcohol are related strongly to the amount of alcohol (ethyl alcohol, or ethanol) present in the body, which can be measured conveniently from samples of blood or breath. Alcohol content in the body is expressed in terms of Blood Alcohol Concentration, or BAC, defined as the percent, by weight, of alcohol in the blood. As BAC increases, the likelihood of injury or death from the same impact increases, performance at a whole range of tasks deteriorates, and behavior (mood, aggression, bravado, risk-taking, etc.) changes. There are wide differences between individuals.

Traffic crash risk increases steeply with increasing BAC, though it is not possible to determine how much of this is due to degraded performance and how much to changed behavior. Alcohol contributes importantly to traffic crashes, with its contribution increasing as crash severity increases. About 10% of property damage, 20% of injuries and 47% of fatalities from traffic crashes are attributable to alcohol. Alcohol is therefore, by a huge margin, the largest single factor contributing to traffic-crash losses. The reductions in traffic crash losses from reducing crashes attributable to alcohol far exceed reductions from any other potential countermeasure.

REFERENCES

Allsop, R.E. Alcohol and road accidents. Report no. 6. Crowthorne, Berkshire, UK: Transport and Road Research Laboratory; 1966.

An Foras Forbartha. Road accident facts Ireland, 1984. Dublin, Ireland: National Institute for Physical Planning and Construction Research; 1985.

Anderson, T.E.; Viano, D.C. Effect of acute alcohol intoxication on injury tolerance and outcome. In: Noordzij, P.; Roszbach, R., editors. *Alcohol, Drugs and Traffic Safety—T86.* Amsterdam, Netherlands: Excerpta Medical Elsevier Science Publisher; pp. 251–254, 1987.

Andreasson, R. *Windmark's Micromethod and Swedish Legislation on Alcohol and Traffic.* Stockholm, Sweden: The Information Center for Traffic Safety; 1986.

Blomberg, R.D.; Fell, J.C. A comparison of alcohol involvement in pedestrians and pedestrian casualties. American Association for Automotive Medicine, 23rd Annual Proceedings, Louisville, KY, p. 1–17; 3–6 October 1979.

Borkenstein, R.F. Historical perspective: North American traditional and experimental response. *Journal of Studies on Alcohol Supplement* 10:3–12; 1985.

Borkenstein, R.F.; Crowther, R.F.; Shumate, R.P.; Ziel, W.B.; Zylman, R. *The Role of the Drinking Driver in Traffic Accidents.* Department of Police Administration, Indiana University; 1964.

Borkenstein, R.F.; Crowther, R.F.; Shumate, R.P.; Ziel, W.B.; Zylman, R. The role of the drinking driver in traffic accidents. *Blutalkohol* 11 (supplement 1); 1974.

Buttigliere, M., Brunse, A.J.; Case, H.W. Effect of alcohol and drugs on driving behavior. In: Forbes, T.W., editor. *Human Factors in Highway Traffic Safety Research,* p. 303–330. New York, NY: Wiley; 1972.

Carsten, O.M.J.; Tight, M.R.; Southwell, M.T. *Urban Accidents: Why Do They Happen?* Basingstoke, UK: AA Foundation for Road Safety Research; 1989.

Cohen, J.; Dearnaley, E.J.; Hansel, C.E.M. The risk taken in driving under the influence of alcohol. *British Medical Journal,* p. 1438–1442; 21 June 1958.

Damkot, D.K. On-the-road driving behavior and breath alcohol concentration. Washington, DC: National Highway Traffic Safety Administration, report DOT-HS-802-264; 1977.

Dischinger, P.C.; Soderstrom, C.A.; Shankar, B.S.; Cowley, R.A.; Smialek, J.E. The relationship between use of alcohol and place of death in vehicular fatalities. Association for the Advancement of Automotive Medicine, 32nd Annual Proceedings, Seattle, WA, p. 299–311; 12–14 September 1988.

Doege, T.C. Illness and crashes—is there a relationship? *Journal of Safety Research* 19:145–150; 1988.

Donelson, A.C. The alcohol-crash problem. In: Laurence, M.D.; Snortum, J.R.; Zimring, F.E., editors. *Social Control of the Drinking Driver.* Chicago, IL: University of Chicago Press, p. 3–40; 1988.

Donelson, A.C.; Beirness, D.J.; Hass, G.C.; Walsh, P.J. *The Role of Alcohol in Fatal Traffic Crashes: British Columbia, 1985–1986.* Ottawa, Canada: Traffic Injury Research Foundation of Canada; 1989.

Donovan, D.M.; Marlatt, G.A.; Salzberg, P.M. Drinking behavior, personality factors and high-risk driving—a review and theoretical formulation. *Journal of Studies on Alcohol* 44:395–428; 1983.

Dubowski, K.M. Absorption, distribution and elimination of alcohol: highway safety aspects. *Journal of Studies on Alcohol,* supplement no. 10:98–108; July 1985.

Evans, L. The why and how of the (metric) system of units. *Human Factors Society Bulletin* 21(4):3–5; 1978.

Evans, L. The fraction of traffic fatalities attributable to alcohol. *Accident Analysis and Prevention* 22:587–602; 1990.

Evans, L.; Frick, M.C. Alcohol's influence on fatality risk, given that a crash has occurred. Report available from GM Research Laboratories, Warren, MI. To be published in 1991.

Farris, R.; Malone, T.B.; Lilliefors, H. A comparison of alcohol involvement in exposed and injured drivers. Phases I and II. Washington, DC: National Highway Traffic Safety Administration, report DOT-HS-801-826; 1976.

Fell, J.C.; Klein, J.M. The nature of the reduction in alcohol in US fatal crashes. SAE paper 860038. Warrendale, PA: Society of Automotive Engineers; 1986.

Fell, J.C.; Nash, C.E. The nature of the alcohol problem in U.S. fatal crashes. *Health Education Quarterly* 16:335–343; 1989.

Findley, L.J.; Unverzagt, M.E.; Suratt, P.M. Automobile accidents involving patients with obstructive sleep apnea. *American Review of Respiratory Diseases* 138:337–340; 1988.

Hedlund, J.; Arnold, R.; Cerrelli, E.; Partyka, S.; Hoxie, P.; Skinner, D. An assessment of the 1982 traffic fatality decrease. *Accident Analysis and Prevention* 16:247–261; 1984.

Hertz, R.P. Sleeper berth use as a risk factor for tractor-trailer driver fatality. *Accident Analysis and Prevention* 20:431–439;1988

Holcomb, R.L. Alcohol in relation to traffic accidents. *Journal of the American Medical Association* 111:1076–1085; 1938.

House, E.G.; Waller, P.F.; Stewart, J.R. *Blood Alcohol Level and Injury in Traffic Crashes.* American Association for Automotive Medicine, 26th Annual Proceedings, Ottawa, Ontario, p. 349–373; 1982.

Hurst, P.M. Blood alcohol limits and deterrence: is there a rational basis for choice? *Alcohol, Drugs and Driving. Abstracts and Reviews* 1(1–2):121–130; 1985.

Jones, A.W. History, present status and future prospects of breath-alcohol analysis. In: Noordzij, P.; Roszbach, R., editors. *Alcohol, Drugs and Traffic Safety—T86.* Amsterdam, Netherlands: Excerpta Medical Elsevier Science Publisher, p. 349–353; 1987.

Jones, A.W. Enforcement of drink-driving laws by use of 'per se' legal alcohol limits: blood and/or breath concentration as evidence of impairment. *Alcohol, Drugs, and Driving* 4:99–112; 1988.

Klein, T.M. A method for estimating posterior BAC distributions for persons involved in fatal traffic accidents. Washington, DC: National Highway Traffic Safety Administration, document DOT HS 807 094; July 1986.

Laurell, H.; Tornros, J. Hang-over effects of alcohol on driver performance. Linkoing, Sweden: National Road and Traffic Research Institute, VTI Report 222A; 1982.

McCarroll, J.R.; Haddon, W., Jr. A controlled study of fatal automobile accidents in New York City. *Journal of Chronic Diseases* 15:811–826; 1962.

McCord, J. Drunken drivers in longitudinal perspective. *Journal of Studies on Alcohol* 45:316–320; 1984.

McDonald, N. Fatigue and driving. *Alcohol, Drugs, and Driving* 5:185–192; 1989.

Moskowitz, H.; Daily, J.; Henderson, R. The Mellanby effect in moderate and heavy drinkers. In: Johnston, I.R., editor. *7th International Conference on Alcohol, Drugs and Traffic Safety,* Melbourne, Australia; 23–28 January 1977. Canberra: Australian Publishing Service, p. 184–189; 1979.

Moskowitz, H.; Robinson, C. Driving-related skills impairment at low blood alcohol levels. In: Noordzij, P.; Roszbach, R., editors. *Alcohol, Drugs and Traffic Safety—T86.* Amsterdam, Netherlands: Excerpta Medical Elsevier Science Publisher, p. 79–86; 1987.

Morris, J.A.; MacKenzie, E.J.; Edelstein, S.L. The effect of preexisting conditions on mortality in trauma patients. *Journal of the American Medical Association* 263:1942–1946; 1990.

National Highway Traffic Safety Administration. Alcohol and highway safety 1984: a review of the state of the knowledge. Document DOT-HS-806-569. Washington, DC; February 1985.

National Highway Traffic Safety Administration. Fatal Accident Reporting System 1988. Document DOT HS 807 507. Washington, DC; December 1989.

Partyka, S.C. Simple models of fatality trends using employment and population data. *Accident Analysis and Prevention* 16:211–222; 1984.

Perrine, M.W.; Waller, J.A.; Harris, L.S. Alcohol and highway safety: behavioral and medical aspects. Washington, DC: National Highway Traffic Safety Administration, report DOT-HS-800-599; 1971.

Popkin, C.L.; Waller, P.F. Epilepsy and driving in North Carolina: an exploratory study. *Accident Analysis and Prevention* 21:389–393; 1989.

Reed, D.S. Reducing the costs of drinking and driving. In: Moore, M.H.; Gerstein, D.R., editors. *Alcohol and Public Policy—Beyond the Shadow of Prohibition.* Washington, DC: National Academy Press, p. 336–387; 1981.

Shinar, D. *Psychology on the Road—The Human Factor in Traffic Safety.* New York, NY: John Wiley; 1978.

Simpson, H.M. The epidemiology of traffic injuries involving alcohol and other drugs. In: Noordzij, P.; Roszbach, R., editors. *Alcohol, Drugs and Traffic Safety—T86.* Amsterdam, Netherlands: Excerpta Medical Elsevier Science Publisher, p. 87–96; 1987.

Stein, S.K. Risk factors of sober and drunk drivers by time of day. *Alcohol, Drugs, and Driving* 5(3):215–227; 1989.

Stutker, P.B.; Brantley, P.J.; Allain, A.N. MMPI response patterns and alcohol consumption in DUI offenders. *Journal of Consulting and Clinical Psychology* 48:350–355; 1980.

US Department of Health, Education and Welfare: National Institute of Alcohol Abuse and Alcoholism. First special report to the US Congress on alcohol and health, from the Secretary of Health, Education and Welfare. Washington, DC: US Government Printing Office; 1971.

US Department of Transportation. 1968 Alcohol and highway safety report. Report from the Secretary of Transportation to the US Congress, Washington, DC; 1968.

Voas, R.B. Emerging technologies for controlling the drunk driver. In: Laurence M.D.; Snortum J.R.; Zimring F.E., editors. *Social Control of the Drinking Driver.* Chicago, IL: University of Chicago Press, p. 321–370; 1988.

Waller, J.A. *Injury Control—A Guide to the Causes and Prevention of Trauma.* Lexington, MA: Lexington Books; 1985.

Waller, J.A. Methodologic issues in hospital based injury research. American Association for Automotive Medicine, 31st Annual Proceedings, New Orleans, LA, p. 95–108; 28–30 September 1987.

Waller, P.F.; Stewart, J.R.; Hansen, A.R.; Stutts, J.C.; Popkin, C.L.; Rodgman, E.A. The potentiating effects of alcohol on driver injury. *Journal of the American Medical Association* 256:1461–1466; 1986.

Wallgren, H.; Barry, H. *Actions of Alcohol.* Amsterdam, Netherlands: Elsevier; 1970.

Walls, H.J.; Brownlie, A.R. *Drink, Drugs and Driving,* 2nd edition. London, UK: Sweet and Maxwell; 1985.

8 Drunk Driving Countermeasures

INTRODUCTION

In Chapter 7 we conclude that alcohol's role in increasing traffic crashes far exceeds that of any other single factor. The quotations which introduce that chapter further document that alcohol abuse has been recognized as being responsible for various ills for thousands of years, and that the most basic countermeasure, namely, exhorting the individual abuser to not indulge in such reprehensible behavior, has also been attempted for thousands of years. When motorization greatly amplified the amount of harm an intoxicated individual could do, especially to others, the need increased for a richer armory of countermeasures. These have focused either on correcting the behavior of the individual abusing driver, or on the broader social context in which the driver drinks. Measures focused on the individual driver include criminal sanctions, on-board screening devices, and server intervention; measures focused at the societal level include economic influences, restriction of the availability of alcohol, and inputs to institutions, such as the media, which influence social norms.

CRIMINAL SANCTIONS

The earliest attempts to control drunk driving involved denying or withdrawing the license to operate vehicles from individuals who were known to be alcohol abusers, or individuals whom the police apprehended driving while drunk [National Highway Traffic Safety Administration 1985, p. 52]. It was not until just before World War I that statutes were passed which specifically made drinking and driving a criminal act. The State of New York passed a drinking-driving law in 1910; and in 1924, the State of Connecticut jailed 254 drivers for driving while intoxicated. These early drinking-driving statutes described the offense as *drunken driving* and later, as it became apparent that individuals who did not appear drunk still could be sufficiently impaired to be a risk on the road, the term became modified to *driving under the influence of alcohol* or *driving while impaired*. Arrest on these charges depended largely on the subjective judgment of the police officer, and the subsequent trial focused on vague definitions of the offense.

Per-se Laws and the British Road Safety Act of 1967

The advent of instruments to measure objectively alcohol content in the body gave rise to *per-se* laws, which proscribe driving with alcohol content exceeding specified legal limits. The first such law, enacted in Norway in 1936, criminalized driving with a BAC in excess of 0.05% [Glad 1987]. The other Scandanavian countries, Sweden and Denmark, adopted similar laws. The term *Scandanavian approach* indicates per-se laws enforced by severe punishments. This approach is generally considered successful in reducing drunk driving [Snortum 1988], although Ross [1975; 1988] does not find the evidence convincing.

Prior to per-se laws, and throughout much of the world until recently, the offense of driving while intoxicated was prosecuted based on such evidence as the smell of drink on the breath, erratic driving, inability to walk a straight line, or slurred speech. Such evidence is always open to subjective interpretation, and eventually comes down to which side is more convincing. Under *per-se* laws, the alcohol present in the body while driving is the offense, and if the defense cannot discredit the measurement, conviction is essentially assured.

The first *per-se* law outside the Nordic countries (the three countries of Scandanavia plus Finland) was included in the British Road Safety Act of 1967 [Ross 1984]. The act, which became effective on 9 October 1967, and applied only to England and Wales, made it an offense to drive, or attempt to drive, a vehicle on a road or other public place "having consumed alcohol in such a quantity that the proportion thereof in his blood, as ascertained by a laboratory test for which he subsequently provides a specimen . . . exceeds the prescribed limit." The limit was set at 0.08% BAC. Blood samples are required when preliminary breath tests indicate the presence of alcohol. Drivers involved in crashes, or observed driving erratically, are administered the breath tests by the police. An earlier proposal to test randomly selected drivers was abandoned in the face of vigorous political opposition.

The effect of the act is most clearly illustrated in Fig. 8-1, which shows weekend night fatalities and serious injuries in England and Wales [Ross 1984]. The 66% reduction following the act [Ross 1984, page 30] is one of the largest changes associated with any intervention observed in traffic safety, and Ross [1988, p 66] comments that the 1967 British Road Safety Act appears in some ways to have been the most successful deterrence-based measure ever launched against drunk driving. Further evidence of the influence of this intervention is provided by a time series analysis by Broughton [1988] which finds that in 1968 all traffic fatalities per unit distance of travel declined 11% below the long term trend, but resumed along the trend line thereafter; the data in Fig. 8-1 also drift back to their previous trend.

The apparent success of the British Road Safety Act of 1967 played a role in the thinking of other legislative bodies. The Canadian Criminal Law Amendment

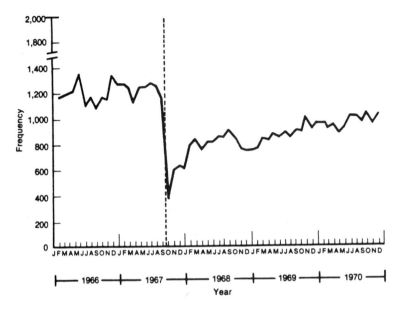

Figure 8-1. Fatalities and serious injuries in England and Wales. Combined for Friday, 10 p.m.–midnight; Saturday, midnight–4 a.m.; Saturday, 10 p.m.–midnight; Sunday, midnight–4 a.m.; corrected for weekend days per month and with seasonal variations removed. Reproduced, with permission, from Ross [1988, p. 67]. © 1988 by the University of Chicago.

Act of 1969, which made it an offense to drive anywhere in Canada with a BAC in excess of 0.08%, was directly inspired by it. Although this law was at the federal level, enforcement was in the hands of the provinces. The law does not appear to have been as successful as that in Britain, perhaps because of less public controversy (and consequently less news coverage), and less threatening enforcement [Ross 1988].

In the US, as of January 1990, 45 states and the District of Columbia had per-se laws; in the other states drivers are presumed to be driving drunk if their BAC exceeds the specified legal limit unless they can prove otherwise. Apart from five exceptions, all the states plus the District of Columbia have set their legal limit at 0.1% BAC; the five exceptions are Georgia, which has a limit of 0.12%, and California, Maine, Oregon, and Utah, which have limits of 0.08% BAC. There are efforts underway in many states to adopt lower limits. The Association for the Advancement of Automotive Medicine has a November 1987 policy recommending that 0.08% BAC should be the per-se legal limit, with 0.05% BAC considered presumptive evidence of driving impairment.

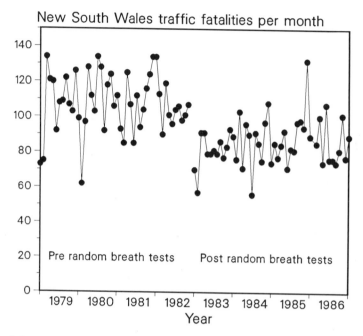

Figure 8-2. Traffic fatalities per month in New South Wales, Australia, three years before and after the introduction of mandatory breath testing on December 17, 1982. The value 84, for December 1982, is not plotted. Data from p. 7 of Roads and Traffic Authority [1989].

Random Breath Testing in New South Wales, Australia

Random breath testing was introduced in New South Wales, one of the states in Australia, on 17 December 1982; as in the US, traffic law in Australia is largely a matter for the individual states. The program in New South Wales, with its legal limit of 0.05% BAC, gave rise to the slogan "under .05 or under arrest" [Job 1990]. About 1.3 million tests were conducted annually on a driving population of 3.2 million; in other words, about a third of all drivers were tested each year (many were tested more than once). Fig. 8-2 shows a time series of the number of fatalities per month; a drop of about 19%, one of the clearest and largest changes in traffic safety associated with a specific intervention, followed the introduction of random breath testing.

An examination of the fraction of fatal crashes that involved alcohol [Roads and Traffic Authority 1989, p. 21] shows a corresponding drop downwards, from about 28% to 22%. Such a change implies that in the pre-testing period, there were 39 crashes involving alcohol for every 100 not involving alcohol, compared to 28 crashes involving alcohol to every 100 not involving alcohol in the post-testing period. If one assumes, as an approximation, no change in the number of crashes not involving alcohol, and that fatalities are proportional to crashes, then the indication is that fatalities decreased, to within a scaling constant, from 139 to 128, an 8% decline. Although this calculation rests on uncertain assumptions, the difference between the 8% effect estimated and the 19% decline apparent in Fig. 8-2 suggests strongly that part of the reduction in fatalities is due to factors other than reductions in driving while intoxicated. A likely explanation is that the increased likelihood of interacting with the police administering the testing program exercised a controlling influence on other types of driving behavior also likely to lead to fatal traffic crashes, or that driving, especially by high risk groups, was reduced. Similar effects could have contributed to Fig. 8-1.

Regardless of the specific mechanism, the fatality reductions in Fig. 8-2 resulted from the random breath testing program. Arthurson [1985] estimates that the annual reductions in casualties attributable to the program were 205 fatalities, 1125 serious injuries, 1270 minor injuries, and 1897 tow-away crashes not involving injuries. In monetary terms, he estimates the benefits of the program exceed its cost by well over a factor of 30.

What is an Appropriate Legal BAC Limit?

Jurisdictions throughout the world have written different BAC limits into per-se laws. In the late 1980s Sweden considered making the limit zero BAC—that is, making it an offense to drive with any detectable alcohol in the body, thus reflecting a Swedish social norm of "no alcohol in your blood when driving" [Klette 1990]. For various practical reasons, the zero BAC law was not accepted, but instead a 0.02% BAC law was passed by the Swedish Parliament in February 1990 to take effect in July 1990. The trend to lower legal BAC limits is in part propelled by the increasing body of research documenting skill reductions at ever lower BAC values. However, as pointed out in Chapter 7, unless the response versus dose curve for alcohol consumption is of a threshold type, it is inevitable that better measurements will provide evidence of impairment at ever lower amounts of alcohol consumption. The move to lower legal limits is inspired partly by a view that increased risk from alcohol use is more morally reprehensible than increased risk from other sources, such as driving while fatigued, upset, distracted, or slightly ill. Driving at 65 mph when the speed limit is 55 mph increases the risk of involvement in a fatal crash by a factor of 2.0 (Eqn 6-3), the same risk increase associated with driving with BAC between 0.05% and 0.099% compared to zero BAC (from Table 7-2).

While eliminating alcohol entirely would reduce US traffic fatalities by 47%, changing all road users with BACs equal to or above 0.1% to the range 0.05% to 0.099% would still produce a 41% reduction (Chapter 7). Part of the reason why BACs in fatal crashes are extremely high is the apparent large role of problem drinkers and alcoholics rather than social drinkers [Waller 1985, p. 518; Vingilis 1983]. Thus, while it could be argued that there are advantages in terms of clarity of principle for a zero BAC limit, the direct safety benefits of zero or very low BAC limits are modest compared to the benefits of enforcing higher ones. It seems to me that a modest degree of risk above the minimum similar to that acceptable for many other characteristics, such as hours of continuous driving, vehicle condition, and driver age, should also be acceptable for the case of alcohol in the private driver. The much stricter standards applied to commercial drivers (of trucks, busses, or airplanes), requiring rigorous standards of equipment inspection, driver testing, narrower age-limits, limits on hours of continuous service, etc., seem to encompass zero BAC limits as a more natural and justifiable component. Zero, or very low (say, less than 0.04%), BAC limits for private drivers appears to be an inconsistent component of any overall approach to driver risk, and one unlikely to produce much, if any, safety benefit. Indeed, such policies could increase sympathy for serious violators of drunk-driving laws, with consequences which could be counterproductive to traffic safety.

Objections to Per-se Laws

Three objections have been raised to the types of approaches described above; they have only short term effects, per se criteria are intrinsically unfair, and monitoring motorists is a violation of civil rights.

The pattern in Fig. 8-1 is common to many enforcement interventions; a sharp change followed by a drift back towards previous levels. It is difficult to determine quantitatively the long term effect, because the further in time from the introduction of the intervention, the greater is the uncertainty in any comparison. For Fig. 8-1 there is no way to tell whether the late 1969 data are, say, 10% higher or lower than they would have been in the absence of the intervention. If the measure has a 10% residual long-term effect, then this would be of the utmost importance, though not observable. Even if the crash level returns eventually to the level it would have been without the intervention (in my view, not the most plausible possibility), all the harm prevented between intervention and reversion to previous level still adds up to a considerable benefit.

One main reason why crash rates tend to drift back to previous levels after the introduction of interventions is that the objective risk of detection is small. The intervention is introduced with much publicity, convincing motorists that if they transgress, they will be subject to well advertised penalties. Later, people observe directly and by exchanging experiences with others that there is not a policeman at every corner, nor outside every drinking establishment. The New South Wales data (Fig. 8-2) suggest that when detection levels are maintained at an objectively high level, harm reductions persist.

It has been argued that making it an offense to drive with BAC above some arbitrary level is basically unjust, given the widespread variability in how alcohol degrades driving performance [Donelson 1988]. This seems parallel to the issue of driving at unsafe speeds. In the early days of driving there were general prohibitions against "driving at unsafe speeds," without specific speeds necessarily being defined, nor measuring equipment being available. Today, speeding laws throughout the industrialized world are essentially all per se. A speed limit is posted, and if a driver violates it, objective evidence (often from radar) is sufficient to ensure conviction. It is rarely argued that per-se speed limits are intrinsically unjust because some drivers are safer driving well above the speed limit than others are driving below it.

While conceding the success of the New South Wales random breath testing program in reducing harm from traffic crashes, Ross [1988, p. 75] expresses concerns regarding its intrusiveness, and reduction of civil rights of the average driver, and further considers it an unlikely policy for application to other jurisdictions, especially the US. Yet a survey by Cairney and Carseldine [1989] finds 95% support for random breath testing; even 87% of those charged with an alcohol-related driving offense expressed support for continuance of the program. The intrusiveness and civil rights issues seem somewhat parallel to those involved in screening passengers for bombs and firearms before boarding aircraft; in the US about 400 million such screenings are performed per year for expected harm reductions which are small compared to the effects shown in Fig. 8-2.

ON-BOARD DRIVER MONITORING DEVICES

On-board devices to evaluate fitness to drive have been discussed since the late 1960s [Voas 1969]. Nearly all the devices developed to date have focused on monitoring the driver before driving begins rather than continuously during driving. Pre-driving testing is less difficult technically, and promises more immediate results. The testing device may be coupled to the ignition circuit so that test failure renders the car undrivable, or it may simply advise the driver, or others, of impairment.

There are two approaches to detecting intoxication. The first is to monitor some performance characteristic which degrades with intoxication. This approach has the appeal that it focuses directly on performance degradation, rather than on the cause of performance degradation. It should therefore be equally effective at identifying drivers who are unfit for driving because of the use of any drug, or for that matter for non-drug related factors, such as fatigue.

The second approach is to measure the presence of intoxicating substances in the body. This has the appeal that it ties in directly with per-se laws. Recently, advances in solid state devices have led to progress in developing on-board devices to measure breath alcohol content. Each of these approaches has distinctive advantages and disadvantages. As the performance approaches were the initial focus of on-board devices, we first discuss these.

Driver Performance Monitors

A number of the tasks shown in the previous chapter to degrade with alcohol consumption have been used as the basis of on-board alcohol detectors. The first such device, the Phystester [Jones and Tennant 1972], momentarily presented random digits which the subject attempted to recall later by pressing control pad buttons. This device depended upon a deterioration of short-term memory with alcohol consumption, the effect being amplified by a concurrent secondary task. Although the probability of failing the test increases with increasing BAC, the only way to ensure that a large fraction of high BAC subjects fail is to set the pass-fail criterion sufficiently low that many sober subjects also fail [Thompson, Tennant, and Repa 1975]. This problem of relatively poor discrimination is intrinsic to all performance based devices—some sober subjects will fail, and some drunk ones will pass. Discrimination is improved if the pass-fail criterion is made different for each subject, which of course requires customizing the device for each user. Various other tasks [Voas 1988] were explored to seek ones with the greatest discrimination. The more complex, and the more pressure involved in the task, the greater is the decrement in performance with increasing alcohol. Another desirable criterion for vehicle on-board use is that the task control devices integrate well with equipment already in the vehicle, and that the task bear some resemblance to tasks required in driving. This led to the use of the steering wheel as the test control input device.

The task which has received most attention as an on-board monitoring device, and which has been field evaluated, is the critical tracking task [Tennant and Thompson 1973]. The critical tracking task is basically a psychomotor tracking task which was developed in the mid-1960s for testing astronaut visual motor capability [Jex, McDonnell, and Phatak 1966]. The subjects' task is to maintain the position of a pointer close to a zero, or neutral position, as an electronic random-noise signal generator drives the pointer back and forth. When the pointer departs more than a set amount from the zero position, the trial terminates. The speed with which the pointer is driven back and forth is progressively increased, thereby increasing the task difficulty until the subject inevitably fails. The time to failure is the measure of performance. The task has been likened to balancing a broom handle on the palm of the hand; the task is easy when the broom handle is long, but becomes more difficult, and eventually impossible, as the broom handle becomes shorter.

Figure 8-3. Photograph of a BAC monitoring ignition interlock system. (Courtesy of Guardian Technologies).

An on-board alcohol testing device based on the critical tracking task was evaluated by Allen, Stein, and Jex [1984] using 24 drivers who were convicted for a second time for drunk driving and assigned by a municipal court judge in California to be subjects in lieu of an alternate penalty. Each was permitted to drive only a specific car equipped with a critical tracking task monitoring device which was custom-calibrated for that particular driver. When the driver failed the test, the car's emergency flasher system was activated, and, if driven above 10 mph, the horn sounded once per second. All these events were recorded on magnetic tape. The general finding from the evaluation is that the device appeared to inhibit drunk driving among the 24 subjects. The study findings are interpreted to show the feasibility of an on-board alcohol-detection device based on performance degradation.

Devices Based on Measuring BAC

The National Highway Traffic Safety Administration evaluated three models of commercially available in-vehicle alcohol test devices [Frank 1988]. The alcohol sensor for each device was enclosed in a hand held unit (Fig. 8-3). All three were set at a threshold BAC of 0.03%, and tested using mechanically produced breath samples containing different alcohol concentrations. In nearly all cases, samples below 0.03% passed, whereas those above, even by small amounts, essentially all failed. Thus all three devices achieved their design goals to a considerable extent—they fairly accurately measured BAC in an on-board environment, leading Compton [1988] to conclude that the technology is feasible. Indeed, 12 states have active interlock programs and an additional 12 states have passed legislation which allows judges or state agencies to use ignition interlock systems as optional sanctions in drunken driving cases, generally only for second offenders. It is reported that there is a less than 1% re-arrest rate, indicating that ignition interlock systems can be effective in selected applications.

Some Problems with On-board Detection Devices

For performance monitoring devices the largest technical problem is the ability to discriminate with sufficient reliability between the impaired and the sober. Even after calibration for a specific individual, the devices still sometimes indicate impairment when the driver is alcohol-free, and they sometimes indicate no impairment when the driver is intoxicated. The only way one of these errors can be made smaller is by allowing the other to become larger. Errors can be somewhat reduced by increasing the number of trials, or the duration of the test, but such fixes have their own disadvantages. However, increasing the amount of testing cannot reduce either type of error to arbitrary small amounts, and substantial discrimination errors appear intrinsic to any device based on measuring performance.

Devices directly measuring BAC largely solve the problem of discrimination, but they have so far not satisfactorily solved the problem of driver cheating. In the performance-based tasks, the task was customized to the individual driver, who became overtrained at it; as a random driver could not perform the task at the passing level, there was little possibility that a drunk driver could solicit the help of someone sober to start his or her vehicle. As the BAC measuring devices are based on a breath sample, which could be provided by anyone, it becomes more difficult to prevent cheating. Sober breath stored in a balloon or plastic bag could also be used to fool the device. Various technological countermeasures have been developed. For example, one of the devices described by Frank [1988] measures the temperature and pressure of the injected air and requires it to be within appropriate limits for the test to be passed. However, the war between the ingenuity of the tested and the technology of the testing has not yet been decided. As discussed by Voas [1988] and Jones and Joscelyn [1978], there are many other practical and legal problems which need to be solved, even if the basic technical problems could be mastered, before widespread breath monitoring would be feasible.

Even if all the practical problems could be solved, on-board detection is bound to remain applicable to only a small fraction of the drinking and driving problem because of the question of driver acceptance. In the evaluation above, the convicted subjects participated in lieu of conventional punishment. It is difficult to foresee any circumstances in which many drivers would voluntarily subject themselves to another procedure before starting their vehicles, even if the procedure were error free, and the hardware were to cost nothing. The benefits of installing such devices on the vehicles of those convicted of drunk driving is necessarily limited to the harm done by such drivers. Reed [1981, p. 352] estimates that drivers with previous drunk driving arrests comprise 10% of all alcohol-influenced drivers in fatal crashes, 15% in injury crashes, and 20% in property-damage-only crashes. Combining these with the percent of harm attributable to alcohol in each category (47% for fatalities, 20% for injuries and 10% for property damage, as determined in Chapter 7) gives that preventing all drivers arrested for drunk driving from ever driving drunk again would reduce fatalities by 5%, injuries by 3%, and property damage by 2%.

SERVER INTERVENTION

The advent of so-called *dram shop* laws, which permit holding the owners of drinking establishments liable if they serve alcohol to intoxicated patrons who later cause crashes while legally intoxicated, has given rise to server intervention programs [Mosher 1983]. In these, servers of alcoholic beverages receive special training to prevent their customers from driving while intoxicated. There are a number of such programs, such as the six hour Training for Intervention Procedures by Servers of Alcohol (TIPS) developed by Chafetz [1984]. Russ and Geller [1987] obtained direct measures of servers' intervention behaviors and patrons' BAC levels both before and after 50% of the servers at two bars were trained in the TIPS program. Research assistants, who were unaware of which of seventeen servers had received the training, posed as regular patrons (*pseudopatrons*) and set the occasion for server intervention to occur by drinking three alcoholic beverages per hour for two consecutive hours. Using a hidden microphone, a partner taped all interactions between the server and pseudopatron, and at the end of the session measured the pseudopatron's BAC. It is found that the trained servers initiated significantly more interventions to reduce the probability of driving while intoxicated than did untrained servers, and that the pseudopatrons served by trained personnel exhibited fewer signs of intoxication and had lower BAC levels than the pseudopatrons served by untrained servers.

Server intervention is becoming increasingly popular in the US as businesses take steps to protect themselves from potentially enormous liability suites [Geller and Lehman 1988]. Individual party hosts have also been held liable for the behavior of departing guests. Server intervention has become important also in Canada, where, in 1989 the Supreme Court of Ontario ordered a tavern to pay nearly $1 million dollars in damages to a teenager disabled in a car struck by an intoxicated patron [Traffic Injury Research Foundation of Canada 1989]. The court judged that the drunk driver and the tavern were equally responsible.

COUNTERMEASURES AT THE SOCIETAL LEVEL

The above interventions have focused mainly on the individual alcohol abuser. Decisions about when, where, and how much to drink are individual; even if an individual is too drunk, or alcoholic, to make a reasoned decision about his or her next drink, it was still previous individual decisions that created this situation. Many interventions focusing on individual responsibility have reduced the harm from drunk driving. However, this in no way denies that each individual exists in a social context and environment not of his or her own creation or choosing, and that changes in this environment can unquestionably affect drunk driving. The number of drunk driving offenses depends on innumerable inputs, including, but by no means limited to, those from major institutions like government, the alcoholic beverage industry, advertising and the mass media.

Because alcohol has existed in human affairs for so long, and is considered by many to provide much benefit, institutions to produce, market, and distribute it have acquired deep roots. There are many major national companies and thousands of smaller businesses which derive all or part of their incomes from alcohol. The alcoholic beverage industry provides millions of customers with products they willingly purchase, pay taxes on, and enjoy without discernible ill-effects to themselves or others; we use the term alcohol industry for convenience, even though, as pointed out by Mosher and Jernigan [1989], it is not a monolith. Many, including physicians, claim health benefits from moderate alcohol use; in reviewing 150 literature references on the health effects of modest alcohol consumption, Colsher and Wallace [1989] find evidence that the risk of coronary heart disease is reduced by modest alcohol use, though they do not consider the relationship to be established beyond reasonable doubt.

Within countries with traditions of alcohol use there is today little sentiment that it should be prohibited; there is even less sentiment that it should be marketed freely like other products (available to all ages, free samples in the mail to attract new customers, reduced cost coupons, coin operated vending machines in public places, etc.) It is almost universally agreed that government should regulate the distribution of alcohol, and influence its cost through taxation policy. Given the toll of traffic deaths and injuries, and other ills attributable to alcohol use, one expects a natural ongoing tension between the interests of the alcohol industry and the goals of public health, particularly traffic safety.

ECONOMIC INFLUENCES

Mass media programming and advertising convey an impression that just about everyone drinks alcohol. Vingilis [1987] notes that television tends to represent alcohol consumption as normal, appropriate, glamorous, and inconsequential, citing in support research suggesting an average of 5.7 scenes per hour in which some form of alcohol was observed, and that it was the most frequently preferred drink for the characters. The alcohol industry has effectively conveyed the impression that the problems associated with alcohol arise from abuse by an aberrant few whose conversion to abstinence would be an immediate boon to everyone, especially their industry [Ross 1987b]. Such a view contradicts the basic logic that the alcohol industry, like other industries, depends heavily on its best customers.

The National Research Council [Moore and Gerstein 1981, p. 29] finds that the heaviest drinking 5% of the adult population accounted for 50% of total alcohol consumption. The heaviest drinking third accounts for over 95% of total alcohol consumed. Two-thirds of the US adult population drink three or fewer drinks per week, and one-third abstain from consuming alcohol altogether. As the number of days on which drinkers are drunk is, not surprisingly, strongly dependent on their average consumption [Moore and Gerstein 1981, p. 31], the conclusion is inescapable that a major portion of drunk driving arises from those who, on average, drink a lot. Data are not available showing the fraction of all alcohol sales that are to problem drinkers or alcoholics. However, there are over 10 million alcoholics and over 7 million alcohol abusers in the US [Williams et al. 1987]; that is, 9.8% of the US adult (18 years and older) population are either alcohol abusers or alcoholics. While the conversion of all alcoholics and problem drinkers to moderate drinking would go a long way towards solving drunk driving (and other problems), any reasonable interpretation of the data that are available suggests that this same change would generate a major loss of business to the alcohol industry.

In common with other commodities, increasing the price of alcohol is expected to decrease its consumption. Economists describe the relationship between price and consumption in terms of *price elasticity*; an elasticity of -1 means that a (say) 5% increase in price leads to an equal 5% decrease in consumption, whereas an elasticity of -0.1 implies a 0.5% decrease in consumption for the same 5% price increase. Although there is always high uncertainty in elasticity estimates, Ornstein [1980] observed that a consensus has developed for a price elasticity (for all consumers) for beer of about -0.3 to -0.4; for wine and liquor, he finds no clear consensus, although both appeared in general to be more price responsive than beer. Elasticity estimates of -0.5 to -1.0 for wine and -1.0 to -1.5 for distilled spirits are not incompatible with much of the literature. Phelps [1988a] finds that even modest increases in the tax on alcohol generate large reductions in harm from traffic crashes, because those preferentially responsible for the problem, young males [Wagenaar 1984], are the very ones most sensitive to price increases.

Satisfactory quantitative estimates of reductions in traffic losses associated with changes in prices of alcohol have not been made because the detailed knowledge necessary to make such estimates is not available. For example, there is no estimate of the price elasticity of beer as a function of purchaser age, sex, or annual consumption. Notwithstanding the absence of such specific calculations, there is nonetheless widespread agreement in the literature [Cook 1981; Phelps 1988a; b; Saffer and Grossman 1987; Walsh 1987] that increased price through increased taxation would lead to reduced drunk driving. At a more macroscopic level, Wagenaar and Streff [1989] report relations between overall economic conditions, alcohol consumption and fatal traffic crashes.

US Federal Excise Tax

US federal tax policy, rather than contributing to reducing drunk driving has been operating in the opposite direction. The federal excise tax on liquor, beer and wine remained constant in absolute dollar terms between 1 November 1951 and the end of fiscal 1985, a period during which general prices increased typically by more than a factor of 4, as indicated by the consumer price index. During that period the federal government taxed 100 proof liquor at $10.50 per gallon, beer at $0.29 per gallon and wine at $0.17 per gallon. In 1985 the tax on liquor was increased to $12.50 per 100 proof gallon, but that on wine and beer remained unchanged. These taxes add the following amounts to the price of the *typical* drinks defined in Chapter 7; liquor, 9.8 cents; beer, 2.7 cents; and wine, 0.5 cents. In addition to federal excise taxes, there are additional state and other taxes. However, the pattern has been somewhat similar, with the amount of tax declining in real terms, leading to reductions, in inflation-adjusted dollars, in the cost of alcoholic beverages [Cook 1981].

One reason why the federal excise tax is potentially important is that it applies to the whole nation, and can be changed by the US Congress. Increasingly, traffic safety is focused at the national level, through the National Highway Traffic Safety Administration. Thus it would appear that one of the most effective safety countermeasures would be a change in the federal excise tax on alcohol, especially as such changes apply nationally without the need for phase-in delays. Keeping the total amount of tax approximately fixed, but applying an equal tax on all beverage ethanol, independent of the type of drink, can be expected to benefit traffic safety by increasing the cost of the drink of choice of young males, while lowering the cost of hard liquor, which is more favored by older drinkers. Other combinations are possible, each with different sets of pros and cons; for example, raising the tax on all drinks to that currently applied to liquor, or, after equalizing on all drinks, indexing the tax to inflation. Price increases would appear to have most influence on the consumption of the young and the heavy drinker, and least on the moderate and occasional drinker.

RESTRICTING THE AVAILABILITY OF ALCOHOL

A number of investigations from Nordic countries have shown unmistakable links between abrupt interruptions in the availability of alcohol and alcohol-related harm in general. However, none found clear links with traffic crashes.

In September 1978 workers at Norway's state operated Wine and Spirits Monopoly went on strike for nine weeks. The occurrence of various events during this period was compared to their occurrence in the same period in 1977, with the following results; drunkenness, down 40%; domestic disturbances, down 22%; acts of violence against the person, down 15% [Hauge 1988]. Comparisons for non-strike affected periods for the same two years showed increases in all these cases of between 3% and 6%. No change in traffic crashes, nor in drivers killed or injured, was observed to coincide with the nine-week strike. Similar interruptions in supply in Finland in 1972 and in Sweden in 1963 also produced no observable changes in traffic losses. Closing Norway's Wine and Spirits Monopoly outlets on Saturdays in some towns but not in others led to differences in drunkenness but there were no observed differences in traffic crashes. Hauge [1988] interprets these findings as possibly specific to the cultural environment of the Nordic countries, in which strict per-se laws with low BAC limits have widespread public support. He writes that there is reason to believe that large groups of the population will in practically every situation abstain from driving after drinking. As such behavior is uncommon in the US, and automobile transport is more available to all sectors of society, it seems likely that impediments to availability might lead to reductions in traffic crashes. Such an observation is somewhat academic for the market-driven distribution system in most US states. Some states control price and availability, but laws prohibiting transportation between states (because of differing state taxes) are rarely supported by credible enforcement. It is still possible that hours of legal sale and such constraints could be used to affect consumption.

The experience of Prohibition is sometimes offered as evidence that making alcohol more difficult to obtain does not influence consumption. Prohibition extended from 1920 to 1933 when, in compliance with the 18th Amendment to the US Constitution, the manufacture or sale of any drink with more than 0.5% alcohol was prohibited. The effects of this unfortunate attempt at social engineering on a grand scale were unquestionably tragic, and many ill-effects still linger to this day. However, its catastrophic failure by nearly all measures does not mean that it did not reduce alcohol consumption. We have almost no direct knowledge about how it affected alcohol consumption because the problem of obtaining reliable information, difficult under normal circumstances, becomes impossible when extreme measures are taken to conceal it. However, time trend data for cirrhosis and alcoholism presented by Gerstein [1981, p. 195] suggest that alcohol consumption declined by about 50% during Prohibition. Traffic fatalities (Fig. 3-12) were changing too rapidly to allow any inferences about alcohol effects.

It is sometimes claimed that increasing the cost and difficulty of obtaining alcohol will simply lead to illegal manufacture and transport, as happened during Prohibition. While this is clearly true at high levels of cost and difficulty of obtaining alcohol, illegal activity will occur only if the rewards exceed the costs and risks. During prohibition there were large shipments of alcohol into the US from Canada, where manufacture was legal. Today, when Canadian taxes make alcohol substantially more expensive than in the US, there are no reports of smuggling in the opposite direction. Similarly, although state taxes on alcohol vary from US state to state, the differences do not attract illegal shipments at the wholesale level, although many individual users violate unenforced laws.

Minimum Drinking Age Laws

Perhaps the clearest indication of reductions in traffic deaths following reduced alcohol availability occurred when, from the mid 1970s to the mid 1980s, all US states increased the minimum age to purchase or consume alcohol to 21 years, from the ages of 18 to 20. Wagenaar [1984] reports that drops in crashes, arrests for alcohol driving offenses, and reduced beer consumption are associated with these changes. The National Highway Traffic Safety Administration [1989] reports a 13% reduction in fatal-crash involvements of affected drivers. Restrictions on the availability of alcohol to those under 21 years of age is politically possible because of the lack of political influence of this age group. Even though voting rights are available at 18, few in the 18 to 21 year interval choose to vote. Modest increases in the difficulty of obtaining alcohol by the much larger fraction of the population which is over 21 run into more formidable opposition.

SOCIAL NORMS REGARDING ALCOHOL USE

The decisions individuals make regarding when, what, and how much to drink are influenced by the overall social framework in which they are embedded. Their behavior is responsive to a social norm, meaning, basically, that people tend to behave in ways that are admired by those whose esteem they solicit. Alcohol use, especially by young males, who contribute so disproportionately to traffic crashes, seems to be deeply intertwined with social norms regarding masculinity and growing into manhood. Social norms arise from many inputs all interacting together. They are in a constant state of flux. Public policy unquestionably influences social norms, even if not always in the intended direction. Changes in social norms can produce changes in traffic safety. Changes in social norms with respect to drinking and driving may have the potential to generate harm reductions like those those already achieved from changing social norms regarding other health-threatening habits.

An Example of a Changed Social Norm—Smoking

One of the most dramatic changes in social norms is that which has occurred in smoking habits in the last 25 years in the US. The reasons for this are many and interrelated; the various Surgeon General's reports stressing the link between smoking and a host of illnesses; increased discussion about the nature and origins of the habit, and its culmination in chemical addiction; warnings on packages; positive testimony from those who have quit; the 1971 prohibition of television advertising. Warner [1989a; b] estimates that, without the antismoking campaign, his term for the collective effects of all of these, adult per capita cigarette consumption in 1987 would have been 79% to 89% higher than it was. He further estimates that between 1964 and 1985 approximately three quarters of a million Americans avoided or postponed smoking-related deaths; worldwide, the death toll from smoking is estimated at 2.5 million per year [Warner 1990] (compared to half a million from traffic crashes). Dramatic changes in prevailing social norms regarding smoking are readily apparent. They are easily perceived by a traveller flying from one of the many US airports which prohibit smoking except in designated areas. Smoking is prohibited on all flights taking off and landing in North America, as of 26 January 1990. In the mass media, the smoking hero has so completely disappeared from the modern entertainment scene that in older movies he looks more comical than heroic to many younger Americans.

My own view is that of all the factors which contributed to declines in tobacco consumption, the greatest contributions came from the near disappearance of smoking on television, both in advertising and in programming. The decision in programming was not mandated nor, on the whole, consciously articulated. It was more a response to changing expectations and values, this response in turn further changed these same values.

Television Advertising of Beer

Today American children see no television commercials for cigarettes. In contrast, Postman et al. [1987] estimate that American children see about 100 000 television commercials for beer as they are growing up. Such commercials appear with programs aimed especially at young males, both above and below the legal age for drinking, and associate the product with the types of positive attributes to which healthy young males aspire. While usually presented in a social atmosphere, there is generally no indication of how anyone got there, even though in the US the mode of transport almost certainly involves driving.

Atkin [1989] reports that more than $600 million was spent on television commercials for beer in 1986. Content analysis showed a wide variety of benefits are frequently linked to the product, in the following order of prevalence; social camaraderie, masculinity, delicious flavor/good taste, escape, femininity, romance, adventure, refreshment, physical relaxation, and elegance. Atkin [1989] comments, "Three advertising-promoted beliefs may disinhibit drinkers through legitimization and rationalization: the conceptions that drinking is a widespread norm, that alcohol is a harmless substance, and that deficit motivations such as escape and relief are acceptable reasons for drinking."

In contrast to the widespread advertising of beer on television, the advertising of liquor is prohibited. If a choice were to be made between the prohibition of liquor advertising and the prohibition of beer advertising, then prohibiting beer rather than liquor advertising is expected to lead to larger traffic crash reductions. Of those arrested for drunk driving in the US [Greenfeld 1988], more than twice as many had been drinking only beer as had been drinking only liquor. Specifically, of those arrested, 54% self-reported drinking only beer, compared to 23% drinking only liquor, and 2% drinking only wine. The remaining 21% reported drinking two or more drink types.

Discussions of future restrictions on the advertising or sale of such products as tobacco or alcohol are often conducted as if they involved matters of grand principle—free speech, First Amendment rights, the individual's rights to do things that are harmful or anti-social, etc. It is remarkable that such questions seem to arise prospectively, but rarely retrospectively. There is no widespread feeling, even among smokers, that prohibiting cigarette advertising on television constitutes an important diminution of their basic rights. Other drugs which, arguably, do much less harm cannot even be sold, let alone advertised. The claim that beer is a legal product, and therefore should be advertised without constraint seems to have no more logic than the claim that it is a legal product and therefore ought to be marketed without restraint. Everyone seems to accept restraints in marketing—certainly I am unaware of the industry ever pushing for vending machine sales. Prohibiting beer advertising on television involves no grand principal whatever, since advertising of a largely equivalent product, liquor, is already prohibited.

Alcohol/Tobacco Differences and Similarities

In contrasting the reduction in harm from tobacco in the last 25 years with the less dramatic reductions in harm from alcohol abuse, a number of points come to mind. There is universal agreement that both products should be subject to various types of restrictions, yet the restrictions that apply reflect haphazard developments rather than a coherent policy. For example, there are only minimal restrictions (apart from a legal fiction) on the sale of tobacco products to persons of any age, as is attested by the availability of the products in vending machines. In contrast, not only are alcohol products not available in vending machines, which would be an obvious convenience to customers, but merchants strictly enforce age limits three years above that defining legal adulthood. If young people were as effectively represented in the courts as are older people, I am sure that such restrictions would have long since been struck down as illegal age discrimination; however, legal procedures take so long that the problem for any individual young person would be solved by them reaching twenty-one years well in advance of the legal remedy. Partly in response to declining markets, tobacco and alcohol producers have each sought new purchasers, especially women. Even though there was a decrease in drunk driving arrests of men in North Carolina from 1976 to 1984, female arrests increased by 43% [Popkin et al. 1986].

There are few restrictions regarding selling cigarettes, which must not be advertised on television; a restaurant requires a difficult-to-obtain license to sell beer, which is widely advertised on television. There are widespread prohibitions against consuming alcohol in public places; in the past such restrictions against smoking were rare, but are becoming more common at a fast rate. Still, one does not find *drinking* sections in public places provided for those who have brought along their own drinks. There is a substantial body of medical and other opinion that alcohol consumed in moderate quantities might produce health benefits. There is no corresponding view regarding smoking, for which the evidence is increasing that the damage to health increases monotonically with consumption. Although the US Environmental Protection Agency estimates that second-hand smoke from the greatly reduced numbers of smokers is still responsible for the deaths of 3800 nonsmokers each year, a much larger fraction of the diseases and premature deaths resulting from smoking is still borne by those indulging in the habit than is so for alcohol abuse.

Many of the points made in defense of present policies regarding beer advertising parallel those made a couple of decades ago regarding cigarette advertising. However, the consequences bore little resemblance to the results that were feared. The advertising-supported evening news is still broadcast by all television networks, most of the producers of the product causing so much harm have been flexible enough to thrive, employees have not lost their jobs in droves, the public does not feel that it has been deprived of rights guaranteed under the US Constitution, etc. On the other side of the ledger are the dramatic benefits in health documented by Warner [1989a; b].

Influence of Citizen Activist Groups

The approach to drunk driving in the US before the 1980s was somewhat ambiguous; even when laws were stringent, enforcement tended to be lax. A major change occurred in the 1980s, largely stimulated by citizen activist groups representing the families of victims of crashes involving drunk drivers. The best known such group is Mothers Against Drunk Driving (MADD), which was founded in 1980 by Candy Lightner after her 13-year-old daughter, a twin, was struck and killed by a car driven by a drunk driver as she walked on a bicycle path in the middle of the day on 3 May 1980. The fact that the driver had prior convictions, and had been out of jail on bail only two days for another hit-and-run drunk driving crash before this fatal crash, focused attention on the judicial system as a contributor to the tragedy. A main thrust of MADD has been to advocate more severe punishments, such as more and longer prison sentences. MADD furthers these goals by *court monitoring,* in which members observe the court proceedings and encourage the judicial process to take the rights of victims, and potential victims, into account at the time of sentencing. A citizen activist group which predated MADD was Remove Intoxicated Drivers (RID), founded in 1978.

The top graph in Fig. 8-4 shows the rapid growth of citizen activist groups in the 1980s, the center graph shows the number of news stories about drunk driving, and the bottom graph shows the number of legislative changes to reduce drunk driving. Although the similarity in the patterns does not logically imply causality, a plausible interpretation is that activist groups heightened general interest in the subject, and that the activist groups and the publicity they generated played a role in generating the increased legislative activity. Note the decline in both legislative activity and in news stories in the late 1980s.

Ross [1987a] takes exception to the positions of victim's movements such as MADD, which he claims focus all their anger and grief on the individual drunk driver while ignoring other important contributory features of the society of which the drunk driver is a member. He notes, for example, that MADD was for some time heavily subsidized by a brewing company. Ross [1987a] claims further that it is probability of detection, and not severity of punishment, that deters drunk driving [Ross 1984]. Further evidence that severity of punishment has little influence on drunk driving is provided by a comparison of drunk driving in nearby jurisdictions with different severities of punishment [Ross and Voas 1989]. In a sense, the ultimate punishment for drunk driving is death in a traffic crash, and if this severity does not deter the behavior it is not surprising that increased fines or prison sentences do not generate observable changes. It is the probability of being arrested, rather than the severity of punishment after arrest, which exercises a larger control on behavior. As the probability of being arrested in the US on a drunk driving trip is about one in one thousand, even doubling the police resources devoted to detection would increase this to only one in five hundred. In the face of such miniscule levels of actual threat, the proclaimed penalties lose credibility.

While accepting that severity of punishment in itself did not play a crucial role, my own view is that the citizen activist groups are responsible for major reductions in harm from drunk driving. Their successful efforts to increase penalties have had an influence not through the increased deterrence effects of harsher penalties, but through harnessing the law in its role as educator and

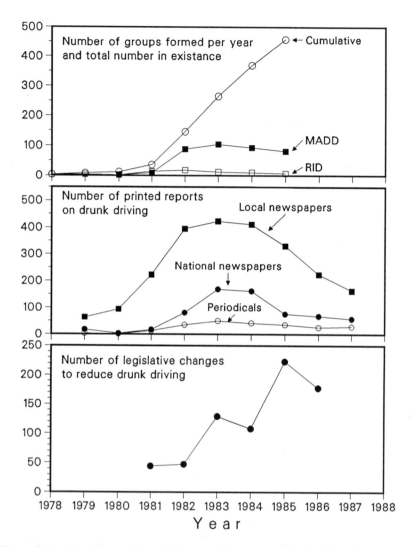

Figure 8-4. *Top:* The number of citizen activist groups. The MADD and RID curves show the number of new chapters formed each year; the cumulative curve refers to cumulative total of these plus some other less well known groups. Based on data in McCarthy and Harvey [1988]. *Center:* Print media coverage of drunk driving. Based on data in McCarthy and Harvey [1988]. *Bottom:* The number of legislative changes to reduce drunk driving. Based on the data of Hatos quoted as a personal communication by Howland [1988, p. 167].

definer of acceptable behavior. An even larger influence is through the mass media. Mercer [1985] finds reductions in drunk driving in British Columbia, Canada, to be more related to media coverage than to police roadcheck *blitz*. Increasing public awareness has become the most common program emphasis among the citizen activist groups [McCarthy, Wolfson, and Harvey 1987]. Their widespread mass media coverage, including a full length television movie on the tragedy that struck Candy Lightner's family, stimulated many people to reflect more on possible negative factors associated with drinking. Although the coverage was modest compared to the television messages associating beer with positive characteristics, I believe that the impact was important. Working on behalf of MADD provides a measure of therapeutic relief to parents who have lost a child to a drunk driver; their testimony makes it harder for society to continue to look upon the drunk as an endearing figure of amusement. Such changing attitudes make drunk driving a less acceptable form of behavior.

CHANGING ALCOHOL-RELATED CRASHES AND FATALITIES

Important and unmistakable changes have been observed in the role of alcohol in traffic crashes; in Chapter 7 we find that if alcohol had played the same role in 1987 that it did in 1982, then 1987 traffic fatalities would have been increased by over six thousand. I share the view of Howland [1988] that changing social norms relating to the use of alcohol played the largest role in such changes, with citizen activist groups playing a catalytic role in stimulating such changes. Another norm regarding alcohol use which undoubtedly changed in this period is increased concern about health in general. These changes have been associated with declining alcoholic beverage consumption per capita.

Although the reductions in harm from alcohol-related crashes have been impressive, it should be kept in mind that 47% of US traffic fatalities, or about 22 000 deaths a year, are still attributable to alcohol. Further progress in reducing harm from drunk driving will have to focus on broader interventions than the traditional one of aiming almost exclusively at the drunk driver. As Gusfield [1988, p. 119] writes "It is just as logical to control the institutions that sell alcohol, to treat chronic alcoholics or 'alcohol abusers,' and to maintain high prices on alcohol as it is to prohibit and punish driving under the influence." It should be noted that approaches aimed at alcohol use provide benefits well beyond reductions in traffic crashes. Roizen [1982] reports that up to 85% of homicide offenders and homicide victims had been drinking; The President's Commission on Law Enforcement and Administration of Justice [1967] finds 40% to 49% of all non-traffic arrests in the US were for alcohol-related offenses.

It seems to me that two simple *laws* appear to pertain to the alcohol and traffic safety problem.

Law 1. Decreased consumption of alcohol leads to decreased traffic deaths and injuries.

It is possible to imagine situations to which this law would not apply. For example, if average consumption decreased, but drinking became more concentrated among fewer people, or more concentrated at specific hours. I consider Law 1 to be so eminently reasonable that the onus must be squarely on the shoulders of anyone claiming it does not apply in some specific case to provide convincing reasons why not. The veracity of this law does not have any immediate policy implications, no more than does the equally valid law that decreasing freeway speed limits decreases fatalities. Such laws should be acknowledged factors in policy decisions. One profound difference between the speed and alcohol case is that there is no large industry whose earnings depend directly and primarily on higher speed limits.

Law 2. Alcohol consumption is decreased by:
Increasing its price
Decreasing its availability
Decreasing its advertising

It is hard to imagine any set of circumstances, even of a hypothetical nature, in which all components of Law 2 would not apply. The only disagreement with Law 2 that I have ever heard expressed is by those with an interest in selling alcohol. Given their claims that the law does not apply, it is difficult for me to understand why they still oppose applications of it! The claim that advertising is used merely to attract users of one brand to another brand is entirely unconvincing; I am unaware of such a claim ever being made for any products other than tobacco and alcohol. If such a claim were true, then a prohibition of advertising would leave the alcohol industry, collectively, richer by the amount of their entire advertising budgets. It would be in their collective economic interest to lobby for, not against, such a measure. In any event, if alcoholic beverages are competing with other beverages, advertising them would still stimulate switching from non-alcoholic to alcoholic beverages.

Any approach which has the possibility of substantially reducing drunk driving will inevitably involve a clash of opposing interests. Ross [1986, p. 503] writes as follows:

The US brewers, although faced with a relatively static market, do not give the impression of an industry in retreat. They are rich and powerful, although they acknowledge the limits of their power:

The League of Women Voters takes a position on every issue, but usually has no influence on them. We take positions on life-or-death issues such as the excise tax, especially when earmarked or if increasing beer taxes more than liquor, advertising laws, price affirmation, and franchising laws favoring wholesalers. . . . We are usually successful. . . .

CONCLUSIONS

Alcohol is responsible for more traffic deaths—about 22 000 a year in the US—than any other single factor. Large though the traffic losses due to alcohol are, they would be considerably larger were it not for implementation in the past of many countermeasures. Important among these is the development of per-se laws which proscribe driving with BAC in excess of some legally specified limit, typically 0.1% in the US, but lower elsewhere. There are a number of approaches which have the potential to further reduce losses attributable to alcohol, such as increasing the perceived probability of detection for violating drunk driving laws.

More potentially important in the future than laws aimed specifically at individuals violating drunk driving laws are changes in the broader social atmosphere. Drunk driving in the US is intrinsically linked to overall national alcohol consumption; large reductions in drunk driving necessarily require reductions in alcohol consumption. Increases in price and difficulty of obtaining alcohol, and decreases in advertising of the product, all lead to reduced alcohol consumption. The main potential for large decreases in drunk driving are in the synergistic interaction of the types of factors which led to such dramatic changes in smoking. These factors include the elimination of television advertising, and the general deglamorizing of the product in fictional representations.

REFERENCES

Allen, R.W.; Stein, A.C.; Jex, H.R. Field test of a drunk driving warning system (DDWS). American Association for Automotive Medicine, 28th Annual Proceedings, p. 261–272; 1984.

Arthurson, R.M. Evaluation of random breath testing. Rosebury, NSW, Australia: Roads and Traffic Authority, Road Safety Bureau, research note RN 10/85; 1985.

Atkin, C.K. Television, socialization and risky driving by teenagers. *Alcohol, Drugs, and Driving* 5(1):1–11; 1989.

Broughton, J. Predictive models of road accident fatalities. *Traffic Engineering and Control* 29:296–300; 1988.

Cairney, P.T.; Carseldine, D. Drink, driving and random breath testing: a survey of knowledge, attitudes, beliefs and self-reported behaviour. Rosebury, NSW, Australia: Roads and Traffic Authority, Road Safety Bureau, research note RN 3/89; July 1989.

Chafetz, M. Training in intervention procedures: a prevention program. *Abstracts and Reviews in Alcohol and Driving* 5(4):17–19; 1984.

Colsher, P.L.; Wallace, R.B. Is modest alcohol consumption better than none at all? An epidemiologic assessment. *Annual Review of Public Health* 10:203–219; 1989.

Compton, R.P. Potential for application of ignition interlock devices to prohibit operation of motor vehicles by intoxicated persons. Washington, DC: National Highway Traffic Safety Administration, report DOT-HS-807-281; May 1988.

Cook, P.J. The effect of liquor taxes on drinking, cirrhosis, and auto accidents. In: Moore, M.H.; Gerstein, D.R., editors. *Alcohol and Public Policy—Beyond the Shadow of Prohibition.* Washington, DC: National Academy Press, p. 255–285; 1981.

Donelson, A.C. The alcohol-crash problem. In: Laurence, M.D.; Snortum, J.R.; Zimring, F.E., editors. *Social Control of the Drinking Driver.* Chicago, IL: University of Chicago Press, p. 3–40; 1988.

Frank, J.F. Further laboratory testing of in-vehicle alcohol test devices. Washington, DC: National Highway Traffic Safety Administration, report DOT- HS-807-333; November 1988.

Geller, E.S.; Lehman, G.R. Drinking-driving intervention strategies: a person-situation-behavior framework. In: Laurence, M.D.; Snortum, J.R.; Zimring, F.E., editors. *Social Control of the Drinking Driver.* Chicago, IL: University of Chicago Press, p. 297–320; 1988.

Gerstein, D.R. Alcohol use and consequences. In: Moore, M.H.; Gerstein, D.R., editors. *Alcohol and Public Policy—Beyond the Shadow of Prohibition.* Washington, DC: National Academy Press, p. 182–224; 1981.

Glad, A. After 50 years with a per se law—the drinking and driving problem in Norway. In: Noordzij, P.C.; Roszbach, R, editors. *Alcohol, Drugs and Traffic Safety—T86,* Proceedings of the 10th International Conference on Alcohol, Drugs and Traffic Safety. Amsterdam, Netherlands: Elsevier Science Publishers, p. 241–244; 1987.

Greenfeld, L.A. Drunk driving. Bureau of Justice Statistics Special Report NCJ-109945. Washington, DC: US Department of Justice, Bureau of Justice Statistics; February 1988.

Gusfield, J.R. The control of drinking-driving in the United States. In: Laurence, M.D.; Snortum, J.R.; Zimring, F.E., editors. *Social Control of the Drinking Driver.* Chicago, IL: University of Chicago Press, p. 109–135; 1988.

Hauge, R. The effects of changes in availability of alcoholic beverages. In: Laurence, M.D.; Snortum, J.R.; Zimring, F.E., editors. *Social Control of the Drinking Driver.* Chicago, IL: University of Chicago Press, p. 169–187; 1988.

Howland, J. Social norms and drunk driving countermeasures. In: Graham J.D., editor. *Preventing Automobile Injury—New Findings From Evaluation Research.* Dover, MA: Auburn, p. 163–180; 1988.

Jex, H.R.; McDonnell, J.D.; Phatak, A.V. A "critical" tracking task for man-machine research related to the operator's effective delay time. Part 1: theory of experiments with a first-order divergent controlled element. NASA CR-616; November 1966.

Job, R.F.S. The application of learning theory to driving confidence: the effect of age and the impact of random breath testing. *Accident Analysis and Prevention* 22:97–107; 1990.

Jones, R.K.; Joscelyn, K.B. Alcohol and highway safety, 1978: a review of the state of knowledge. Washington, DC: National Highway Traffic Safety Administration, report DOT-HS-5-01207; 1978.

Jones, T.O.; Tennant, J.A. A critical evaluation of the Phystester: a test for driver impairment. American Association for Automotive Medicine, 16th Annual Proceedings, Chapel Hill, NC, p. 274–306; 19-21 October 1972.

Klette, H. Sweden lowers BAC limit. *ICADTS Reporter* (Newsletter of the International Committee on Alcohol, Drugs and Traffic Safety. Bethesda, MD: Potomac Press) 1(2):1–2; 1990

McCarthy, J.D.; Wolfson, M.; Harvey, D.S. Chapter survey report of the project on the citizens' movement against drunk driving. Center for the Study of Youth Development, Catholic University of America; 1987.

McCarthy, J.D.; Harvey, D.S. Independent citizen advocacy: the past and the prospects. *Surgeon General's Workshop on Drunk Driving—Background Papers,* p. 247-260. Washington, DC; 14-16 December 1988.

Mercer, G.W. The relationships among driving while impaired charges, police drinking-driving roadcheck activity, media coverage and alcohol-related casualty traffic accidents. *Accident Analysis and Prevention* 17:467–474; 1985.

Moore, M.H.; Gerstein, D.R., editors. *Alcohol and Public Policy—Beyond the Shadow of Prohibition.* Washington, DC: National Academy Press; 1981.

Mosher, J.F. Server intervention: a new approach to preventing drinking driving. *Accident Analysis and Prevention* 15:483–497; 1983.

Mosher, J.F.; Jernigan, D.H. New directions in alcohol policy. *Annual Review of Public Health* 10:245–279; 1989.

National Highway Traffic Safety Administration. Alcohol and highway safety 1984: a review of the state of the knowledge. Document DOT-HS-806-569. Washington, DC; February 1985.

National Highway Traffic Safety Administration. The impact of minimum drinking age laws on fatal crash involvements: an update of the NHTSA analysis. Document DOT-HS-807-349. Washington, DC; January 1989.

Ornstein, S.I. Control of alcohol consumption through price increases. *Journal of Studies on Alcohol* 41:807–818; 1980.

Popkin, C.l.; Rudisill, L.C; Geissinger, S.B.; Waller, P.F. Drinking and driving by women. American Association for Automotive Medicine, 30th Annual Proceedings, Montreal, Quebec, p. 1–14; 6-8 October 1986.

Phelps, C.E. Death and taxes—an opportunity for substitution. *Journal of Health Economics* 7:1–24; 1988a.

Phelps, C.E. Alcohol taxes and highway safety. In: Graham, J.D., editor. *Preventing Automobile Injury—New Findings from Evaluation Research.* Dover, MA: Auburn, p. 197–219; 1988b.

Postman, N.; Nystrom, C.; Strate, L.; Weingartner, C. *Myths, Men and Beer: An Analysis of Beer Commercials on Broadcast Television, 1987.* AAA Foundation for Traffic Safety, 1730 M. St. NW, Washington, DC; 1987.

President's Commission on Law Enforcement and Administration of Justice. Task force on drunkenness. Task Force Report, Washington, DC; 1967.

Reed, D.S. Reducing the costs of drinking and driving. In Moore, M.H.; Gerstein, D.R., editors. *Alcohol and Public Policy—Beyond the Shadow of Prohibition.* Washington, DC: National Academy Press, p. 336–387; 1981.

Roads and Traffic Authority. *Road Traffic Accidents in New South Wales 1988.* Rosebury, NSW, Australia: Road Safety Bureau; May 1989.

Roizen, J. Estimating alcohol involvement in serious events. In: Alcohol and health, monograph No. 1, Alcohol consumption and related problems, US Department of Health and Human Services; 1982.

Ross, H.L. *Deterring the Drinking Driver.* Lexington, MA: Lexington Books; 1984.

Ross, H.L. The Scandinavian Myth: The effectiveness of drinking-and-driving legislation in Sweden and Norway. *Journal of Legal Studies* 2:1–78; 1975.

Ross, H.L. The brewing industry views the drunk-driving problem. *Accident Analysis and Prevention* 18:495–504; 1986.

Ross, H.L. Reflections on doing policy-relevant sociology: how to cope with MADD mothers. *American Sociologist* 18:173–178; 1987a.

Ross, H.L. Brewers view of drunk driving: a critique. *Accident Analysis and Prevention* 19:475–477; 1987b.

Ross, H.L. Deterrence-based policies in Britain, Canada, and Australia. In: Laurence, M.D.; Snortum, J.R.; Zimring, F.E., editors. *Social Control of the Drinking Driver.* Chicago, IL: University of Chicago Press, p. 64–78; 1988.

Ross, H.L.; Voas, R.B. The new Philadelphia story: the effects of severe penalties for drunk driving. AAA Foundation for Traffic Safety, 1730 M. St. NW, Washington, DC; March 1989.

Russ, N.W.; Geller, E.S. Training bar personnel to prevent drunken driving: a field evaluation. *American Journal of Public Health* 77:952–954; 1987.

Saffer, H.; Grossman, M. Beer taxes, the legal drinking age, and youth motor vehicle fatalities. *Journal of Legal Studies* 26:351–374; 1987.

Snortum, J.R. Deterrence of alcohol-impaired drivers. In: Laurence, M.D.; Snortum, J.R.; Zimring, F.E., editors. *Social Control of the Drinking Driver.* Chicago, IL: University of Chicago Press, p. 189–226; 1988.

Tennant, J.A.; Thompson, R.R. A critical tracking task as an alcohol interlock system. SAE paper 730095. Warrendale, PA: Society of Automotive Engineers; 1973.

Thompson, R.R.; Tennant, J.A.; Repa, B.S. Vehicle-borne drunk driver countermeasures. In: Israelstam, S.; Lambert, S., editors. Proceedings of the 6th International Conference on Alcohol, Drugs and Driving. Toronto, Ontario, Addiction Research Foundation of Ontario, p. 347–363; 1975.

Traffic Injury Research Foundation of Canada. *Crossroads—A National Newsletter on Drinking and Driving* 3(1):1–1; 1989.

Vingilis, E. Drinking drivers and alcoholics—are they from the same population?. In: Smart, R.G.; Glasser, F.B.; Israel, Y; Kalant, H.; Popham, R.; Schmidt, W., editors. *Research Advances in Alcohol and Drug Problems,* Vol. 7. New York, NY: Plenum Press, p. 299–342; 1983.

Vingilis, E. The six myths of drinking-driving prevention. *Health Education Research* 2:145–149; 1987.

Voas, R.B. Cars that drunks can't drive. National Highway Safety Bureau Report HS-810 169. Washington, DC; 1969.

Voas, R.B. Emerging technologies for controlling the drunk driver. In: Laurence, M.D.; Snortum, J.R.; Zimring, F.E., editors. *Social Control of the Drinking Driver.* Chicago, IL: University of Chicago Press, p. 321–370; 1988.

Wagenaar, A.C. *Alcohol, Young Drivers, and Traffic Accidents: Effects of Minimum-Age Laws.* Lexington, MA: Lexington Books; 1984.

Wagenaar, A.C.; Streff, F.M. Macroeconomic conditions and alcohol-impaired driving. *Journal of Studies on Alcohol* 50:217–225; 1989.

Waller, J.A. *Injury Control—A Guide to the Causes and Prevention of Trauma.* Lexington, MA: Lexington Books; 1985.

Walsh, B.M. Do excise taxes save lives? The Irish experience with alcohol taxation. *Accident Analysis and Prevention Analysis and Prevention* 19:433–448; 1987.

Warner, K.E. Effects of the antismoking campaign: an update. *American Journal of Public Health* 79:144–151; 1989a.

Warner, K.E. Smoking and health: a 25-year perspective. *American Journal of Public Health* 79:141–143; 1989b.

Warner, K.E. Tobacco taxation as health policy in the third world. *American Journal of Public Health* 80:529–531; 1990.

Williams, G.D.; Stinson, F.S.; Parker, D.A.; Harford, T.C.; Noble, J. Demographic trends, alcohol abuse and alcoholism, 1985-1995. *Epidemiologic Bulletin* No. 15. *Alcohol Health and Research World* 11(3):80–83,91; 1987.

9 Effectiveness of Occupant Protection Devices When They Are Used

INTRODUCTION

Much of the focus in previous chapters has been on factors related to crash involvement. Interventions to prevent crashes have been referred to as pre-crash phase interventions, or primary safety. Here we address questions of secondary safety—occupant protection devices designed to reduce or prevent injury, given that a crash has occurred. Countermeasures in the crash phase aim at managing the energy dissipated in the crash in such a way as to reduce harm [Haddon 1980]. Occupant protection devices are active or passive. Active devices can provide protection only if the user performs some specific act, usually for each trip, such as fastening a safety belt or wearing a helmet. Passive devices, such as airbags or passive safety belts, offer protection without the user having to do anything, or in some cases, even without the user being aware of their existence.

The effectiveness of a device is defined as the fractional, or percentage, reduction in the occurrence of some specified level of injury (such as fatality) if a population of occupants changes from all not using the device to all using the device, without any other factors changing. Equivalently, effectiveness is the percentage reduction in risk an average occupant obtains when changing from non-use to use of the device without otherwise changing behavior. Three distinct effectiveness measures must be considered:

1. *Severity-specific effectiveness,* defined as the percentage reduction in injuries in crashes of a specific severity, or within a narrow range of severities.
2. *When-used effectiveness,* defined as the percentage reduction in injuries that occurs when the device is used.
3. *Field effectiveness,* defined as the percentage reduction in injuries, taking into account the use rate for the device.

The severity-specific effectiveness depends only on the engineering of the device and on the biomechanical properties of the human body. The when-used effectiveness depends on the types of crashes that occur in actual traffic. These two effectiveness measures apply to active and passive devices. Field effectiveness is identical to when-used effectiveness only when the device is always used. When the device is not used at all times, field effectiveness is less than when-used effectiveness. This is the case for manual safety belts, but also may apply to nominally passive devices which users defeat by disconnecting, modifying, or improperly using, or by not replacing deployed airbags. In this chapter we discuss only the first two of these measures of effectiveness—that is, the effectiveness of occupant protection devices when used. Chapter 10 addresses use rates.

Injury Biomechanics and Occupant Restraints

In order to understand better how restraints protect occupants, we review the basics of injury biomechanics [Viano 1988; Viano et al. 1989] and vehicle dynamics in crashes [Mackay 1987; Grime 1987]. Vehicle dynamics deals with the mechanical forces and subsequent crushing of vehicles in crashes. Injury biomechanics deals with the relationship between physical forces and injury. In the 1950s, Colonel John Stapp, MD, of the US Air Force, provided pioneering information on the forces the body could withstand by subjecting himself to deceleration forces in sled tests. Since then, biomechanical knowledge has been expanded by, for example, university studies in which human cadavers have been subjected to the more severe forces that occur in crashes. From the information gathered in such studies, instrumented anthropomorphic dummies have been designed to simulate human responses to crash forces; these dummies are used in vehicle and restraint system evaluation and certification.

Impact between a human body and a physical object can cause compression, stretching, and other deformation of tissues beyond recoverable limits. In non-biological systems this would be called mechanical failure; in the human system it is called trauma. Trauma can be either penetrating or blunt. Penetrating trauma is most typically caused by high-speed projectiles, such as bullets, or by sharp objects moving at low speeds, such as knives or daggers. Although penetrating trauma can occur in traffic crashes, blunt trauma is by far the more common cause of injury. Blunt trauma occurs when the human body strikes, or is struck by, a blunt object such as an instrument panel, a windshield, or the roadway.

Let us consider what happens to an unrestrained front-seat occupant in a car crashing head-on at a speed of 30 mph into an immovable barrier. This crash is equivalent to two identical cars crashing head-on into each other at 30 mph, as is apparent when one considers that if the barrier were an unbreakable mirror, an observer could not distinguish between the two situations (except for the steering wheel being on the passenger side); this is further equivalent to one car travelling at 60 mph crashing into an identical stationery car. On impacting the barrier, the car's speed will change rapidly from 30 mph to near zero (in fact the car achieves a negative value of about 10% to 20% of the initial speed as it bounces back from the barrier). The change in speed, perhaps about 35 mph, is an important measure of crash severity, and is often referred to in the literature as *delta-v*; a 60 mph car crashing into a stationery car would have the same delta-v as a 30-mph car crashing into a barrier.

The speed of the occupant's body is not materially affected just after the instant of impact, and in accord with Newton's first law of motion, will continue to move at about 30 mph until acted upon by a force. Factors such as frictional forces between seat and occupant, and arm and leg muscles, will reduce the occupant's speed by small amounts. No major reduction will occur until some part of the occupant's body strikes some part of the vehicle, perhaps a knee impact which might reduce the speed by about a third. The major portion of the speed reduction occurs when the occupant's head or chest strikes the steering wheel or instrument panel, typically about 120 ms (a little more than a tenth of a second) after car/barrier contact, by which time the occupant compartment is nearly stationery. To keep the situation in perspective, the occupant approaches the vehicle structure at a speed similar to that attained by an object dropped from a four story building. Any notion that the occupant can avoid harm by muscular effort alone is as unrealistic as the hope of avoiding harm in a fall from a four story building by correctly bracing for the impact.

The impact between the occupant and the vehicle interior has been referred to as the *second collision,* to distinguish it from the first collision, the one in which the car hit the barrier. There is an analogous *third collision* when soft tissue impacts the decelerating skeletal structure inside the body [Viano and Lau 1990].

If a car were perfectly rigid, the occupant compartment would change from a forward speed of 30 mph to a negative speed almost instantly. In fact it takes about 150 ms because of the time that it takes for the front structure to crush; the greater the time the vehicle takes to crush, the greater is the potential for occupant protection. An occupant restrained in place relative to the occupant compartment would then likewise take a similar time to stop; spreading the change in speed over as long a time as possible minimizes the maximum decelerations, which, from Newton's second law, likewise minimize the injury-producing forces.

Occupant restraints spread the occupant's change in speed over longer times, and thereby reduce maximum forces. In the example above, if the occupant had been wearing a lap/shoulder belt, this would have applied forces keeping the body more fixed to the occupant compartment. The belt helps the occupant *ride-down* the crash, and impact with the steering wheel or instrument panel is less likely and less severe. Safety belts also prevent occupants from being ejected from vehicles during crashes. An ejected occupant might travel outside the vehicle at close to the vehicle's pre-crash speed, and would continue at that speed until stopped by striking something.

Airbags are restraint systems that consist of a bag in front of the occupant which inflates rapidly when a frontal crash occurs with a severity exceeding some pre-set limit [Passell 1987; Maugh 1986], typically a delta-v in the range of 10 to 20 km/h. Instead of striking the steering column or instrument panel, the occupant rides down the crash in contact with the airbag, which additionally spreads the impact forces over a larger area. A lap/shoulder-belted occupant can receive additional protection from an airbag because it may reduce loading forces on the belt, and further reduce the probability of injury from an impact with the steering wheel or instrument panel. The airbag is a supplemental system—it is designed to be used in conjunction with a lap/shoulder belt.

There are many field studies illustrating the various ways in which restraint systems have prevented or reduced injury in real world crashes [Huelke and Sherman 1987], and on specific questions such as the improper use of the devices [States et al. 1987]; here we confine attention to the broader question of the overall effectiveness of the devices in preventing injury.

Conceptual Considerations Common to All Occupant Devices

A number of general concepts pertain to all devices which are designed to prevent or reduce occupant injury [Evans 1987a; Horsch 1987; Malliaris, Hitchcock, and Hansen 1985; Mertz and Marquardt 1985]. In formally examining these concepts, Evans [1987a] assumes different injury probability versus crash-severity functions for occupants using and not using protection devices. For expository convenience the formalism is summarized below in terms of driver fatalities, although the results are, in general, equally applicable to all occupants and levels of injury. The safety of drivers using and not using some occupant protection device is compared; the terms *protected* and *unprotected,* and *users* and *non-users* denote use, or non use, of the occupant protection device.

At a given crash severity, the probability of a driver fatality is defined as the number of drivers killed in crashes of that severity divided by the number of crashes at that severity. Because of the variation in survivability, and other variability, whether the driver is fatally injured or not is stochastic in nature. Crash severity, s, is considered to be a univariate variable with the property that as s increases, the probability that the driver is killed also tends to increase. For example, s could be equal to delta-v. We need not specify s in detail beyond requiring that as it increases, then so, in general, does the probability of driver fatality.

The leftmost curve in Fig. 9-1 shows how the probability of death of an unprotected driver might depend on crash severity. There is some threshold crash severity value, say s_1, at or below which no drivers are killed; the region $s <$ s_1 contains all minor crashes. As s increases beyond s_1, the probability that the driver is killed increases until at some value, say s_2, it reaches unity. That is, no unprotected drivers can survive crashes in the range $s > s_2$. The other curve,

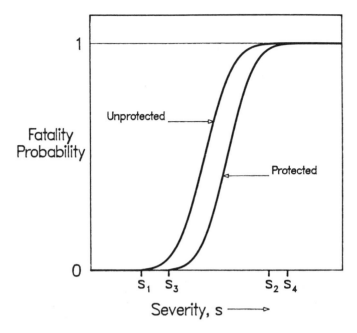

Figure 9-1. Representation of how the probabilities that a driver is killed in a crash of given severity depends on severity and on whether the driver is using or not using some protection device. From Evans [1987a].

for the protected driver, assumes that the occupant protection device reduces fatality risk at all severities. When the severity just exceeds s_1, the unprotected driver's probability of being killed just exceeds zero. If the protection device has any efficacy at this severity, then its use must reduce this probability to zero. As s increases it reaches a threshold value, s_3, at which even the protected driver's fatality risk is no longer zero. When $s = s_2$, the unprotected driver's risk of fatality is 100%. If the protection device has any efficacy at this severity, then the probability that the protected driver is killed must be less than 100%. However, as severity increases, it reaches a new threshold value, s_4, at which even the protected driver has zero chance of survival.

Dividing a value on the lower curve in Fig. 9-1 by the corresponding value on the upper curve enables us to define a severity-specific effectiveness, ε, which gives the percentage by which the device reduces driver fatality risk in crashes of severity s, as follows:

$$\varepsilon(s) = 100 \left[1 - \frac{\text{Probability that protected driver is killed}}{\text{Probability that unprotected driver is kiled}} \right]. \quad \text{Eqn 9-1}$$

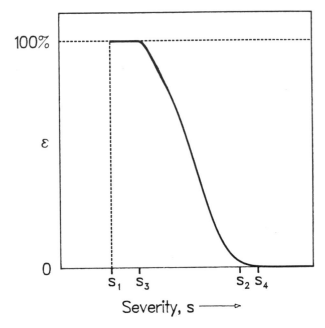

Figure 9-2. Dependence of severity-specific effectiveness, ε, in preventing fatalities versus crash severity, s; ε is not defined for severities $s \leq s_1$ because in this region the probability that the unprotected occupant is killed is zero, so that there is no opportunity for further reductions in fatality probability. From Evans [1987a].

When $s < s_1$, ε is undefined (Fig. 9-2). In this severity range, the probability is zero that the unprotected driver will be killed, so the protection device has no opportunity to reduce this probability further. It is important to stress that the device may prevent (or reduce) nonfatal injuries in this crash severity range, but if the fatality risk is already zero, the device cannot have any efficacy in preventing fatalities. When s just exceeds s_1, the protected driver's fatality risk is zero while the unprotected driver's fatality risk slightly exceeds zero, so that ε must be 100%. When severity reaches s_3, fatality risk for the protected driver becomes greater than zero, so that ε becomes less than 100%. When $s > s_2$, all unprotected drivers are killed, so ε is identical to the probability that the protected driver will survive. When $s > s_4$, all protected users are killed, so ε = 0. The functional form of Fig. 9-2, derived from the most basic formal considerations, is supported by empirical data [Campbell 1987a; b].

The severity-specific effectiveness relationship does not enable us to estimate the effectiveness of the device in preventing fatalities in actual use. If all crashes had $s < s_3$, then the overall effectiveness would be 100%. On the other hand, if all crashes had $s > s_4$, the identical device would have 0% overall effectiveness. In most of what follows we focus not on the severity-specific effectiveness, but on the when-used effectiveness, E, which is essentially the severity-specific effectiveness weighted by the number of crashes that occur at each severity level. More simply and directly, it is defined as the reduction in the number of occurrences of some level of injury to a population of occupants if all occupants change from being nonusers to users, assuming that all other factors remain the same. Formally, for equal numbers of nonuser and user occupants,

$$E = 100 \; \frac{\text{Number of non-user injuries} - \text{Number of user injuries}}{\text{Number of non-user injuries}}. \qquad \text{Eqn 9-2}$$

The when-used effectiveness of any occupant protection device depends on two factors:

1. The specific dependence of effectiveness on severity (Fig. 9-2) in crashes, which results from the engineering of the device and its relationship to human biomechanics.
2. The actual distribution of crashes by severity that occurs in real traffic.

It is the severity-specific dependence at some chosen level of severity that tends to be investigated in laboratory evaluations of occupant protection devices. As crash tests are difficult and expensive, the chosen level tends to be at severities for which the device was primarily designed; tests are less likely to be conducted at substantially higher or lower severities. Considerations such as these may have contributed to a history of disappointing field results relative to expectations based largely on laboratory tests, because in actual use there are likely to be many crashes at such extreme levels of severity that there is little opportunity for mitigation of injuries. In addition, a surprisingly large number of fatal crashes are of a bizarre nature not readily encompassed in any laboratory testing program (foreign objects entering the passenger compartment, cars being dragged for long distances along a railroad track, etc.). Based on an examination of 101 fatally-injured front seat occupants, Huelke et al. [1979] estimated that approximately 50% of the crash fatalities were unpreventable by available occupant restraints.

When a crash is of such extreme severity that death cannot be prevented, then the force reductions produced by occupant protection devices provide no benefits. In this regard, fatality is a unique level of injury, because for all other levels of injury, reduction in the forces leads to reductions in injuries. This general consideration suggests that the effectiveness of an occupant protection device is likely to be higher for injuries at severity levels less than fatality, though specific factors might lead to an opposite result. When effectiveness estimates are available only for fatalities, it is worth keeping in mind that effectiveness for lower levels of injury is more likely to be higher than lower.

Effectiveness, as defined in Eqn 9-2, implies only a reduction in injuries at some specific level—it does not imply the elimination of injury. If a device is 40% effective at eliminating fatalities, this means that for every 100 nonusers killed, 60 would still have been killed, but 40 not killed, had they been using the device. However, the 40 not killed would still likely sustain injuries, many of high severity. Thus, by reducing fatalities, the device would actually generate increases in the numbers of injuries at lower severity levels. These increases are expected to be small compared to the reductions generated by the device for injuries at these lower injury levels, assuming effectiveness at such levels. This is because the number of injuries increases steeply with declining injury severity, in keeping with many more crashes of minor than major severity [Ricci 1980].

Difficulties in Determining Effectiveness from Data

It might seem straightforward to estimate the effectiveness of an occupant protection device by simply comparing the percentage of fatally injured drivers which police reports indicate were wearing the device to the percentage of all drivers wearing the device, as determined in independent observations. Although such calculations appear in the literature, the results they provide (in some cases effectiveness estimates as high as 90%) are grossly in error. The problems are many. There is copious evidence that belt wearers are more careful drivers than nonwearers [Ashton, Mackay, and Camm 1983; Deutsch, Sameth, and Akinyemi 1980; Evans, Wasielewski, and von Buseck 1982; Evans and Wasielewski 1983; Evans 1987b; Hunter et al. 1988; O'Neill et al. 1985]. When belted drivers have crashes, they are of lower severity than crashes of unbelted drivers [Campbell 1987a, b; Ricci 1980]. Thus the simple calculation incorrectly attributes to the safety belt injury reductions that are in fact caused by belted drivers being in fewer, and less severe, crashes. In an insightful paper, O'Day and Flora [1982] address the overall question of interactions between safety belt use and other factors relevant in estimates of effectiveness, and conclude that the general answer to the question, "What other things are different between persons who wear restraints and those who don't is 'Nearly everything'."

Most of the biases resulting from differences between belted and unbelted occupants can be circumvented by applying the double pair comparison method described in Chapter 2 to FARS data. Because subject and control occupant are involved in the same crash, the differences in involvement rates and severities between belted and unbelted occupants are no longer of central importance [Evans 1986a]. Even with the double pair comparison method, a number of problems remain—problems common to all attempts to estimate belt effectiveness using field data.

One of the most difficult problems, and one which has become more difficult in recent years, is reliability of reported belt use. There is little reason to expect any bias in restraint use reporting for occupants fatally injured at the scene of the crash, especially as physical evidence is often readily visible. However, for surviving occupants, especially those who manage to get out of the vehicle, obvious physical evidence may be lacking. The coded restraint use is based largely on the occupants' own responses to police officers' questions, and may be subject to bias. There is clear evidence in FARS of large biases since the advent of mandatory safety belt wearing laws; indeed, to admit nonwearing is to confess commission of an offense to a police officer. Police officers may, understandably, uncritically accept the occupant's claim of belt wearing in order to avoid the distraction of having to write a safety-belt violation when there is more vital work to be done at the crash scene. Because of these biases, the estimates of driver and right-front passenger effectiveness [Evans 1986b; 1990; Evans and Frick 1986] are all based on FARS data only up to 1983 in order to avoid any influences from mandatory laws, the first of which in the US was implemented in New York State in 1984. When later data are included [Partyka 1989], higher effectiveness estimates are calculated.

Another general problem in inferring effectiveness of occupant protection devices is that the precise device used is often unknown. Knowing that an occupant was *belted* does not indicate whether a lap belt, shoulder belt, or lap and shoulder belt system was used. As each system has different effectiveness, it is crucial to know which one was used. This problem is particularly acute for the case of young children where child seats present additional opportunities for miscoding. Although there is strong evidence that child seats substantially reduce fatality risk [Partyka 1984; Kahane 1986], quantitative estimates in a form parallel to those presented below for other devices are unavailable. In what follows all effectiveness estimates apply exclusively to adult occupants, defined as age 16 years or older.

LAP/SHOULDER BELTS

The FARS variable indicating which specific occupant protection device was used is often incorrectly coded, especially in some states and early FARS years; unmistakable evidence of such miscoding is provided by indications of use of restraint systems not available in the specified vehicles. Such coding uncertainties make it impossible to determine the effectiveness of specific restraint systems for outboard-front occupants (drivers and right-front passengers) using data for cars manufactured before 1974. Many of these cars had separate shoulder and lap belts in the outboard-front seating positions. Some users fastened one, or the other, or both; ideally one would want to know effectiveness for all combinations. However, as it is not possible to know which was used, the data on pre-1974 model-year cars cannot be used to estimate effectiveness of specific restraint systems. All cars of model year 1974 and later were required to be equipped with integrated three-point lap/shoulder belts in outboard-front seating positions. In determining the effectiveness of lap/shoulder belts, Evans [1986b] assumes that any outboard-front occupant in a car of model year 1974 or later coded as using any restraint system was in fact using the lap/shoulder belt. Even for model year 1974 or later cars, it is possible that in some cases occupants modified the restraint system, or used it improperly, so that a FARS coding of, say, lap only, could have been correct. There are probably few errors from assuming that coding the use of any belt system implies use of a lap/shoulder belt; the assumption does require discarding all data for pre 1974 model-year cars, which does substantially reduce sample sizes, especially since FARS data for calender years 1984 and later are also discarded.

Overall Effectiveness in Reducing Fatalities

The effectiveness of lap/shoulder belts in preventing fatalities to outboard-front occupants is determined by Evans [1986b] by applying the double pair comparison to occupants in cars of model year 1974 or later coded in FARS data 1975-1983. The study used 711 belted driver and 716 belted right-front passenger fatalities, together with over 30 000 fatally injured unbelted occupants. Following the procedures described in Chapter 2, cars containing belted drivers as subject occupants and unbelted right-front passengers as control occupants were extracted from the FARS data, and the ratio of belted drivers killed to unbelted passengers killed is computed. From a second set of crashes, the ratio of unbelted drivers to unbelted right-front passengers is computed. From the ratio, R, of these two ratios, the effectiveness of the lap/shoulder belt is computed as

$$E = 100 (1 - R) .$$ Eqn 9-3

The subject and control data are disaggregated into three age categories, and occupants in all car seats (front and rear, and in center seats) are used as control occupants. In using the method to estimate restraint effectiveness it is crucial that the control occupant be disaggregated by restraint use. If this were not done, then the control occupant accompanying a restrained subject occupant would be more likely to survive a crash than a control occupant accompanying an unrestrained subject occupant, in violation of the assumptions of the method, because restraint use by one occupant in a vehicle is highly correlated with use by other occupants.

The combination of control occupants used led to 46 estimates of E. Computing weighted averages provides the following estimates of fatality-reducing effectiveness:

(42.1 ± 3.8)% for drivers

(39.2 ± 4.3)% for right-front passengers

The composite estimate for outboard-front occupants weighted in accord with occupancy rates is (41.4 ± 3.8)%, where the error is assumed identical to the smaller of the above errors (if driver and right-front passenger estimates are derived from independent, rather than the same, data the composite error would be calculated as 2.8%). Although the estimates are obtained using data containing no cars of model year later than 1984, we assume that they apply to all three-point integrated lap/shoulder belt systems, including passive ones introduced later; these passive systems automatically move belts into place around the occupant when, for example, the door is closed.

The above estimates are lower than those obtained by most other methods. Arguably, the best study using field data other than FARS is that of Campbell [1987a], who examined the probability that a crash at a given level of severity proved fatal to belted and unbelted drivers using police reported data from North Carolina. Severity was measured using the Traffic Accident Data (TAD) scale [National Safety Council 1984]. This scale is based on the police officer locating the crash on a severity scale defined by a series of photographs of crashes of increasing severity. By controlling for severity, and examining fatalities per crash, this study eliminates two of the sources of bias—the higher crash rate and the higher crash severities of unbelted compared to belted drivers. The results showed belt effectiveness not defined for the lowest of 10 severity levels used, and then varying from a nominal indication of 100% at low levels of severity, and declining systematically to 36% at the highest of the 10 severity levels (in keeping with the pattern in Fig. 9-2). The weighted average, which corresponds to when-used effectiveness, is 65%. This value is larger than Campbell's estimate of 52% for serious injuries, whereas the discussion above suggests effectiveness in fatality preventing is likely less than effectiveness for lower severity injuries. Effectiveness for right-front passengers is estimated at 54% for fatalities and 44% for serious injuries. The lack of agreement between the Campbell [1987a] and double pair comparison estimates suggests the operation of large biasing effects.

Possible Biases in Estimates

There are a number of possible sources of bias in double pair comparison estimates of belt effectiveness. It is assumed that estimates derived for drivers accompanied by right-front passengers apply also to unaccompanied drivers, who in fact constitute the majority of driver fatalities. There are two mechanisms by which belt effectiveness might be different for accompanied drivers than for lone drivers. First, in a right-side impact an unaccompanied unbelted driver may strike the right interior of the vehicle; the presence of a right-front passenger will cushion the severity of this impact. The presence of the passenger reduces the risk to the unbelted driver, but does not affect the risk to the belted driver. Hence, the effectiveness of the belt, which is calculated relative to the unbelted risk, necessarily declines, and the double pair comparison method will therefore underestimate belt effectiveness for unaccompanied drivers. The magnitude of this effect is estimated to bias the overall effectiveness estimate downwards by less that 1% [Evans 1988a]; various other biasing mechanisms relating to missing data and occupants being struck by other occupants generate even smaller effects.

The second real difference between effectiveness for accompanied and un-accompanied drivers is that each of these groups of drivers has a different distribution of crashes by direction of impact; for example, the unaccompanied driver who crashes has greater probability of a frontal crash, but lower probability of a rollover crash, than does the accompanied driver. A calculation using estimates of belt effectiveness by direction of impact (discussed later) and the distribution of crashes by impact direction for accompanied and unaccompanied drivers indicates no difference in overall belt effectiveness (the nominal indication is to bias the estimate upwards by 0.1%).

The largest potential for bias in the double pair comparison is from possible miscoding of belt use. Surviving drivers may tend to indicate that a belt was used when it was not. All belt effectiveness estimates based on field data are vulnerable to biases from this source, which will tend to bias estimates upwards. However, for two reasons the effects are likely to be less for estimates derived using the double pair comparison method than those derived using other methods.

First, the double pair comparison method uses only fatal crash data, whereas examining the fraction of drivers killed in crashes of a given severity requires use mainly of data in which no fatality occurred. It seems plausible that the less serious the crash, the greater is the likelihood that belt nonuse might be recorded as use.

Second, the double pair comparison effectiveness estimates depend mainly on individual crashes in which one occupant is coded as belted, while another occupant in the *same* crash is coded as unbelted. The increased potential of serious criminal proceedings (for example, for negligent homicide) against a surviving driver could provide increased motivation to avoid perjury by falsely claiming use, especially as nonwearing was not an offense in the 1975–1983 period in which the data were collected. The more objectively determined belt use of fatally injured occupants, together with the extreme seriousness of the situation, might discourage surviving occupants from compounding their problems by falsely indicating belt use. The presence of additional occupants is itself an additional incentive to provide truthful information.

Data in the study by Campbell [1987a] provide remarkably clear evidence supporting the above comments. These data provide the fraction of drivers and passengers coded as using a restraint for crashes categorized into 10 levels of severity. For drivers and passengers the indicated restraint use shows a strictly monotonic decrease for every increase in severity level; for drivers the percentage indicated as belted declines from 11.1% at the lowest severity level to 6.5% at the highest; for right-front passengers the corresponding values are 8.2% and 3.7%. There is no basis to expect such large declines with increasing severity to be real. A much more plausible explanation is that the influence of miscoding nonusers as users becomes greater as severity level decreases; in other studies free of crash-related tension, drivers responding to telephone surveys and questionnaires consistently self-report substantially higher use rates than are observed [Streff and Wagenaar 1989]. Even at the second most severe of the 10 severity levels, more than 97% of the crash-involved drivers were not fatally injured; given the mix of injuries involved in these crashes it is not improbable that many drivers were outside the vehicle before police arrived; the data for this case [Campbell 1987a] show that if 4% of surviving unbelted drivers had been incorrectly coded as belted, the effectiveness estimate for this level would be 39.7% rather than the 70.8% reported.

The systematically higher use rates for drivers compared to passengers in Campbell [1987a] supports the contention that accompanied occupants are more likely to provide correct indications of belt use. There are no observational or fatality data to support large differences. The large difference between the effectiveness estimates for drivers and passengers in Campbell [1987a] (65% − 54% = 11%) seems more likely a reflection of larger biases for drivers (mainly unaccompanied) than for passengers (always accompanied) than a real difference in effectiveness. The corresponding difference for the double pair comparison estimates is 42.1% − 39.2% = 2.9%.

Other possible biases can arise from comparing the outcomes from different crashes. Even after controlling for crash severity, there may be many other crucial differences between belted and unbelted occupants. For example, those with high levels of alcohol are less likely to be wearers, but are also more likely to die in a crash of the same severity (Chapter 7), an effect which would bias estimates upwards. This is unlikely to influence double pair comparison estimates as both occupants are likely to have similar alcohol consumption levels.

Although double pair comparison estimates are not free from potential biases, they appear to be far more free from them than estimates based on any other method. While a few effects could bias such estimates downwards by small amounts, by far the main concern is of miscoded belt use, which would systematically bias estimates upwards. In what follows we focus mainly on double pair comparison estimates of effectiveness in reducing fatalities.

Fatality-Reducing Mechanisms

Safety belts protect vehicle occupants in two ways: they prevent ejection, and they reduce the frequency and severity of occupant contact with the vehicle's interior. The when-used effectiveness, E, can be written as the sum of two components,

$$E = F + I,$$
Eqn 9-4

where F is the percent reduction in fatalities to an unbelted population of occupants if ejection were eliminated, assuming that those prevented from ejecting would acquire the same fatality risk as those not ejected in similar crashes, and I represents the percent reductions in fatalities from preventing the occupant from impacting the interior structure of the vehicle and reducing the severity of such impact. The equation assumes that safety belts eliminate ejection, a more than adequately correct assumption for present purposes, even though some belted occupants may be ejected. For example, a study [Green et al. 1987] of 919 crashes in the UK finds 2 cases of completely ejected belted occupants among a predominantly belted population; the authors conclude that belt use reduces the rate of ejection by a factor of 39. FARS data show that only 0.2% of fatally injured ejected occupants are coded as using any type of restraint.

The fraction of fatalities that would be eliminated if ejection were prevented is estimated by Evans and Frick [1989] by applying the double pair comparison method to 1975–1986 FARS data to estimate the ratio of the risk of death if ejected compared to the risk of death if not ejected. The ratio is investigated for various occupants as a function of many variables. For drivers, the overall result is that the risk of death if ejected is 3.82 times the risk of death in the same crash if not ejected. The FARS data show that 25.27% of unbelted drivers who were killed were ejected. If these drivers had not been ejected, then $F = (1 - 1/3.82) \times 25.27\% = 18.7\%$ of all fatally injured drivers would not have been killed. Substituting this value into Eqn 9-4 gives that the interior impact reduction component of lap/shoulder effectiveness is 23.4%. These values and their associated errors, together with the corresponding information for right-front passengers, are presented in Table 9-1. Almost half of the effectiveness of the lap/shoulder belt in preventing fatalities comes from preventing ejection.

Table 9-1. Fatality reductions from lab/shoulder belt use and from eliminating ejection for outboard-front occupants. From Evans [1990]

Fatality reducing source*	Fatality reduction, %	
	Driver	Right-front passenger
E	42.1 ± 3.8	39.2 ± 4.3
F	18.7 ± 0.5	16.9 ± 0.6
I = E - F	23.4 ± 3.8	22.3 ± 4.3

*E is lap/shoulder safety belt when-used effectiveness.
F is fatality reduction from prevention of ejection.
I is fatality reduction from reduction of impacts with vehicle interior.

Effectiveness by Direction of Impact

Table 9-2 shows belt effectiveness by direction of impact derived from 1975–1983 FARS data, and the contribution to that effectiveness of eliminating ejection derived from 1975–1986 FARS data [Evans 1990]. The effectiveness values show the same pattern as, but are lower than, those derived by Partyka [1988] using 1982–1985 FARS data, as is expected based on the earlier discussion of increasing miscoding biases in later FARS data. Lap/shoulder belts reduce fatalities for all principal impact points, much of this effectiveness being due to prevention of ejection. Even for rear impacts, lap/shoulder belts substantially

Table 9-2. Comparison of lap/shoulder belt when-used effectiveness, E, with fatality reductions from ejection elimination, F, according to principal impact point. Plus or minus one standard error is indicated for each estimate. From Evans [1990]

Principal impact points	Description	Driver		Right-front passenger	
		E, %	F, %	E, %	F, %
12	Front	43 ± 8	9 ± 1	39 ± 9	8 ± 1
1, 2	Front right	41 ± 18	21 ± 1	30 ± 20	14 ± 1
3	Right	39 ± 15	17 ± 1	27 ± 19	6 ± 1
4, 5, 6, 7, 8	Rear	49 ± 14	22 ± 1	45 ± 20	21 ± 2
9	Left	27 ± 17	8 ± 1	19 ± 20	16 ± 1
10, 11	Front left	38 ± 15	12 ± 1	23 ± 20	16 ± 1
13	Top	59 ± 10	41 ± 1	46 ± 15	41 ± 1
0	Noncollision	77 ± 6	63 ± 1	69 ± 8	61 ± 1
All principal impact points combined		42 ± 4	19 ± 1	39 ± 4	17 ± 1

Table 9-3. Results According to Rollover Status. From Evans [1990]

Rollover status (Distribution)[a]	Fatality reducing source	Fatality reductions, % Driver	Fatality reductions, % Right-front passenger
Rollover is first event[a] (8.5%)	E	82 ± 5	77 ± 7
	F	64 ± 1	64 ± 1
	$I = E - F$	18 ± 5	13 ± 7
Rollover is subsequent event (16.4%)	E	55 ± 10	57 ± 11
	F	42 ± 1	43 ± 1
	$I = E - F$	13 ± 10	14 ± 11
All rollovers[b] (24.9%)	E	69 ± 6	67 ± 6
	F	50 ± 1	50 ± 1
	$I = E - F$	19 ± 6	17 ± 6
No rollover (75.1%)	E	31 ± 8	23 ± 9
	F	7 ± 1	6 ± 1
	$I = E - F$	24 ± 8	17 ± 9

[a]Distribution of driver fatalities by rollover status based on same data used to determine F; distribution for right-front passengers is similar.
[b]Calculated from combined raw data for first event and subsequent event cases.

reduce fatalities to drivers and right-front passengers; although the effectiveness estimate has large uncertainty, the estimate that over 20% of fatalities from rear impact are prevented by ejection elimination is more precise. For far-side impacts (right for driver, left for right-front passenger), elimination ejection prevents 17% of driver fatalities and 16% of right-front passenger fatalities; for near-side impacts the corresponding reductions, 6% and 8%, are less, in part because the fatality risk inside the vehicle is so much greater in a near-side impact [Evans and Frick 1988a].

Lap/shoulder belts are (77 ± 6)% effective in preventing driver fatalities in *non-collisions*. When the 63% ejection prevention component is subtracted from this effectiveness, a value of $I = (14 ± 6)$% remains; for the right-front passenger the corresponding value is $I = (8 ± 8)$%. Noncollisions normally imply rollover not initiated by striking a clearly identifiable object, such as a tree or another vehicle.

From 1978 onwards vehicles in FARS are coded according to whether the first event was rollover, whether rollover was an event subsequent to striking some other vehicle or object, or whether no rollover was involved. The results in Table 9-3 use 1978–1983 FARS data for the estimates of lap/shoulder safety belt effectiveness, E, and 1978–1986 for the estimate of the ejection prevention component, F. Note the high effectiveness of safety belts when rollover is the

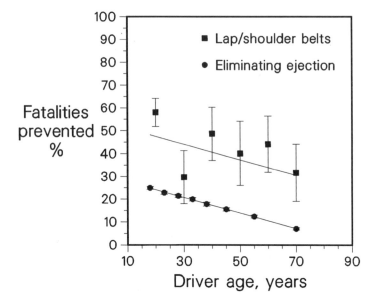

Figure 9-3. The when-used effectiveness of lap/shoulder belts in reducing fatalities (upper data) and the percent fatalities preventable by eliminating ejection (lower data) versus driver age. The lower line is a weighted least squares fit to the lower data; the upper line is parallel to the lower. From Evans [1991b].

first event (82% for the driver and 77% for the right-front passenger), and that 64% is due to prevention of ejection.

Influence of Various Other Factors

The upper data in Fig. 9-3 show lap/shoulder belt effectiveness and the lower data the fraction of traffic fatalities preventable by eliminating ejection as a function of driver age. The fit to the safety belt data is a line parallel to the fit to the ejection data. This figure, and the discussion in Evans [1991b], support the contention that front-seat lap/shoulder belt effectiveness is higher at younger adult ages.

Driver lap/shoulder belt effectiveness versus car mass (Fig. 9-4) shows no large systematic trends, in keeping with the result derived in Chapter 4 (Fig. 4-7) using the pedestrian exposure approach. A higher value at very small mass is supported by Partyka [1989], who also finds higher effectiveness for cars under 880 kg. It is possible that the higher effectiveness for younger drivers (Fig. 9-

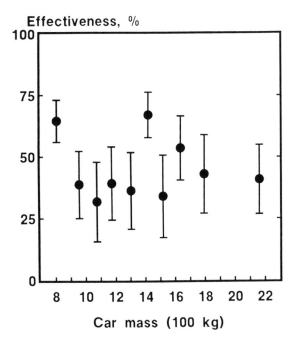

Figure 9-4.   Driver lap/shoulder belt when-used effectiveness versus car mass. From Evans and Frick [1986].

3) elevates effectiveness for the smallest cars. There are insufficient data to be justify any strong conclusions.

None of the values of effectiveness versus car model year (Fig. 9-5) indicates any departure from the overall driver effectiveness of 42%. If effectiveness for cars of fixed model year is examined using more recent FARS data than the 1975–1983 data used to produce Fig. 9-5, larger effectiveness estimates are obtained. This provides clear evidence of the increasing miscoding of belt use discussed earlier, because there is no other plausible reason why belt effectiveness of, say, a 1980 model-year car should be measured as being higher in 1987 than in 1981.

In examining the influence of various other factors, Evans and Frick [1986] find effectiveness higher in single- than in two-vehicle crashes; this reflects the larger role of rollover crashes in single-car crashes. Effectiveness is higher for 2-door than for 4-door cars, probably reflecting that the drivers of the 2-door cars were younger and that the 2-door cars were involved in more rollover crashes. FARS contains a variable indicating degree of deformation. The nominal

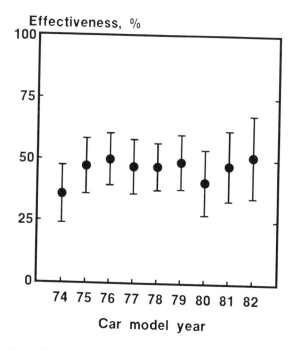

Figure 9-5.   Driver lap/shoulder belt when-used effectiveness versus car model year. From Evans and Frick [1986].

indication is of a declining effectiveness as deformation changed from minor, to moderate, to severe, in keeping with Fig. 9-2. However, as nearly all the data are in the severe category, the uncertainty in the effectiveness estimates at the two lowest severities is large. Effectiveness is not found to be systematically affected by posted speed limit (generally known), travel speed (generally not known), available lighting, season of year, type of roadway or urban compared to rural driving.

LAP BELTS ONLY (IN REAR SEATS)

Estimates of restraint system effectiveness for rear seats are more uncertain than those for front seats because two effects combine to reduce greatly the quantity of data. First, occupancy rates, and therefore fatalities, are considerably lower in rear than in front seats (Fig. 3-4). Second, restraint system wearing rates are even lower in rear than in front seats. Because data are so few, 1975-1985 FARS data are used in the study by Evans [1988b]. Rear seat occupants did not tend

Table 9-4. Fatality reductions from lap belt use and from eliminating ejection for outboard-rear passengers. From Evans [1990]

Fatality reducing source*	Fatality reduction, %	
	Left passenger	Right passenger
E	19.4 ± 10.0	17.3 ± 8.7
F	16.1 ± 0.8	17.7 ± 0.7
$I = E - F$	3.3 ± 10.0	−0.6 ± 8.7

*E is safety lap belt when-used effectiveness.
F is fatality reduction from prevention of ejection.
I is fatality reduction from reduction of impacts with vehicle interior.

to be covered by mandatory wearing laws, and biasing effects are less important in the context of the much lower precision necessitated by small sample sizes. It is assumed that any occupant coded as using any rear restraint is using a lap belt only. For the cars on the road in 1975-1985 this assumption will introduce very little error. Cars of all model years are included in the analysis.

The overall effectiveness estimates found by Evans [1988b] together with the fraction of fatalities preventable by eliminating ejection [Evans and Frick 1989] are shown in Table 9-4, which may be compared to the corresponding information for lap/shoulder belts in front seats in Table 9-1. Combining the estimates for right and left occupants gives a composite estimate of (18 ± 9)% for effectiveness of lap belts in preventing fatalities to outboard-rear occupants. This is in close agreement with the value of (17 ± 8)% derived by Kahane [1987] using similar methods and data.

For lap-only belts in rear seats, the impact severity reducing component, I, is (3 ± 10)% for the left-rear passenger and (−1 ± 9)% for the right-rear passenger, for a weighted average of (1 ± 9)%. The 18% effectiveness thus appears to flow mainly from prevention of ejection, though the high level of uncertainty precludes any more definitive conclusion. Because of the paucity of data, it is not possible to examine lap-belt effectiveness as a function of the factors examined for lap/shoulder belts. However, the discussion in Evans [1988b] indicates that effectiveness in frontal crashes is likely lower than overall effectiveness, again suggesting that the main fatality reduction mechanism of the lap belt in the rear seat may be ejection prevention.

The composite estimate, (18 ± 9)%, refers only to fatality reductions to wearers of the belt; it does not include any possible benefits that belt use by rear-seat occupants might generate for front-seat occupants. Park [1987] estimates that the presence of an unbelted rear-seat occupant increases the fatality risk to front-seat occupants by (4 ± 2)%, presumably because of the increased loading force that the unbelted rear occupant imposes on the front occupant.

SHOULDER BELTS

Although the shoulder belt alone has never been offered as an occupant protection device, it is a separate component of some passive motorized restraint systems. Because some occupants will use only this component of the system, it is desirable to estimate its effectiveness, which is also of interest in augmenting overall understanding of occupant protection device effectiveness. Motorized two-point safety belts automatically move a shoulder belt into place around the occupant when, for example, the door is closed and the ignition circuit is switched on. Occupants are advised to fasten the manual lap belt. When this is fastened, the restraint system consists of a shoulder belt and a lap belt, and is consequently expected to provide occupant protection similar to that provided by integrated three-point belts in the form of manual lap/shoulder belts or automatic lap/ shoulder belts.

Using the assumption that three-point lap/shoulder belts essentially eliminate ejection, Evans [1991a] uses published data [Esterlitz 1987] that 10 out of 56 fatally-injured occupants were ejected from one specific model car equipped with motorized belts to estimate the difference in effectiveness between the two-point motorized system and the lap/shoulder belt system. Although the number of data are small, they focus specifically on the difference in effectiveness between the two-point motorized system and the three-point system, thus allowing reasonably precise estimates to be made. From this difference, effectiveness of the two-point motorized belt system, in conjunction with whatever lap-belt use occurred in traffic, is inferred. From independently observed lap-belt use, an estimate is obtained of the effectiveness of the shoulder belt alone in preventing fatalities to outboard-front occupants.

It is found that the two-point motorized system, in conjunction with the lap-belt use that occurred in traffic, is $(9 \pm 3)\%$ less effective in the field than the when-used effectiveness of three-point belts. As the three-point system when-used effectiveness for outboard-front occupants is 41%, this gives a field effectiveness of $(32 \pm 5)\%$, with the larger error than for the difference calculation resulting from a more direct dependence on the effectiveness of the three-point system than is so for the difference. Based on observational use rates for lap belts, and for the motorized portion (some users defeated the system) [Williams et al. 1989], the effectiveness of the shoulder belt only is estimated as $(29 \pm 8)\%$.

AIRBAGS

As is the case for shoulder belts, indirect means must be used to estimate airbag effectiveness in preventing fatalities because it will be many years before there are sufficient field data to do it using the methods applied to lap/shoulder belts

Impact directions for fatally injured unbelted car drivers

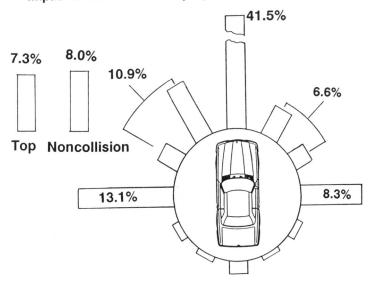

Figure 9-6. Distribution of driver deaths by principal impact point. From Evans [1990]

and lap belts. All manufacturers advise that a lap/shoulder belt should always be worn in conjunction with an airbag. The estimation of effectiveness described here [Evans 1990] is for the airbag alone, without the use of belts, and depends on the following three assumptions:

1. Airbags deploy only in frontal, or near frontal, crashes.
2. Airbags provide the same interior impact reduction effectiveness as lap/shoulder belts.
3. Airbags do not influence ejection risk, whereas lap/shoulder belts eliminate ejection risk.

These assumptions will be discussed further after the effectiveness estimate is described.

The first assumption is that airbags work only in frontal, or near frontal, crashes, which we define as those with principal impact points at 10, 11, 12, 1 or 2 o'clock (Fig. 9-6). The preponderance of left over right side deaths follows because impacts on the left, being closer to the driver, are more likely to produce driver fatalities [Evans and Frick 1988a]; the pattern for right-front passengers is approximately the mirror image of Fig. 9-6.

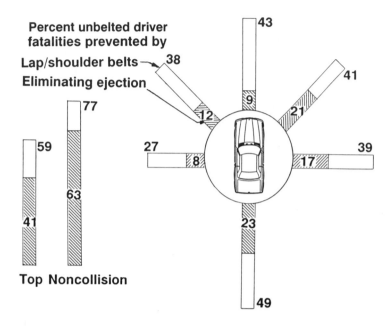

Figure 9-7. When-used effectiveness of lap/shoulder belts in preventing driver fatalities, and the fraction of fatalities prevented by eliminated ejection according to impact direction. For example, in frontal (12 o'clock) crashes, lap/shoulder belts prevent 43% of driver fatalities; 9% of this is due to elimination of ejection, so that 34% is due to interior impact reduction. From Evans [1990].

Fig. 9-7 shows driver lap/shoulder belt effectiveness, and the portion of this that is due to elimination of ejection, based on the data in Table 9-2. While the lap/shoulder belt reduces fatality risk for crashes for all impact directions, and is particularly effective for noncollisions (essentially rollovers), the airbag is designed to deploy only in frontal, or near frontal, crashes. Because of the second and third assumptions, its effectiveness in such crashes is given by the unshaded portions in Fig. 9-7 (that is, $E - F$ in Table 9-2).

In order to estimate airbag effectiveness for drivers we require the fraction of crashes that are frontal, or near frontal, and safety belt effectiveness in reducing interior impact, which is assumed to be the same for the airbag, by the same impact directions (Table 9-5). From these values, effectiveness is calculated as $0.415 \times 34 + 0.175 \times 24 = 18.3$, with a standard error of 4.2; that is, airbags are $(18 \pm 4)\%$ effective in reducing driver fatalities. Similarly, Evans [1990] estimates the effectiveness for right-front passengers as $(13 \pm 4)\%$. By weighting these values by 0.75 and 0.25 to reflect the approximate proportions of driver

Table 9-5. Summary of driver results for frontal and near frontal crashes used to infer airbag effectiveness

Principal impact (clock points)	Distribution	Fatality reductions, %		
		E	F	I
Frontal (12 o'clock)	41.5%	43 ± 8	9 ± 1	34 ± 8
Near frontal (10 + 11 + 1 + 2 o'clock)	17.5%	39 ± 11	15 ± 1	24 ± 11

and right-front passenger fatalities (Fig. 3-4), we obtain an estimate of airbag effectiveness in reducing outboard-front fatalities of $(17 \pm 4)\%$.

Automobile manufacturers advise that the airbag is a supplemental restraint, and a lap/shoulder belt should always be worn. Nevertheless, it is still possible that some lap/belt wearers might stop wearing them when they obtain airbags. Drivers who cease wearing the lap/shoulder belt exchange a 42% effectiveness for an 18% effectiveness, and thereby increase their fatality risk by $(1 - 0.18)/(1 - 0.42) - 1 = 41\%$; the corresponding calculation for right-front passengers estimates that switching from lap/shoulder belt use to airbag only protection increases fatality risk by 43%.

Each of the three assumptions on which the airbag effectiveness calculations are based has the potential to introduce bias, as discussed in Evans [1990]. The assumption that the device deploys only in frontal crashes is the least uncertain, although the definition used in the calculation is probably more inclusive than the common design goal of plus or minus 30 degrees from straight ahead, thus biasing the estimate upwards. The assumption that safety belts eliminate ejection is more than adequately correct for the estimate. The assumption that airbags do not materially affect ejection risk is based on the absence of any clear mechanism of ejection prevention. One can imagine mechanisms by which an airbag could either hinder or facilitate ejection. Elimination of all ejections in frontal crashes reduces driver fatalities by 9% (Table 9-2), so that if, for example, airbags prevented 10% of such ejections, this would increase the overall effectiveness by $0.41 \times 0.1 \times 0.9 = 0.4\%$. Ejection plays a larger role in near frontals, but as most such ejections are through side glass, it seems unlikely that airbags could make major contributions to ejection prevention.

The assumption that airbags provide protection against impact with the vehicle interior equal to that provided by the lap/shoulder belt is made in the absence of firmer quantification, although this assumption seems more likely to bias the estimate downwards than upwards. However, there are general reasons [Evans 1987a; Horsch 1987] why it is unlikely that any device can have very high effectiveness in impact protection over a wide range of crash severities. If one made the substantially different assumption that airbags provide 50% more impact protection than lap/shoulder belts (so that frontal effectiveness would become 34% × 1.5 = 51% for the driver (a value higher than this seems highly implausible) then the overall effectiveness values would similarly increase by 50%, to 27% for drivers and 19% for right-front passengers.

It is possible that some occupants, especially older ones, could be fatally injured at crash severities below the threshold at which airbags deploy, typically designed to occur at a perpendicular barrier crash equivalent of about 12 mph [Passell 1987; Maugh 1986]. There will be many just-below-threshold-severity crashes because the number of crashes at a given severity increases steeply with declining severity. On the other hand, deployment can cause or increase injury, especially to out of position occupants [Passell 1987]. Assuming no additional fatalities from either of these effects biases effectiveness estimates upwards.

There has been only one estimate of effectiveness based on field data, by Pursel et al. [1978], who find an effectiveness in preventing severe injuries (AIS ≥ 3) of 9%. This is based on comparing injuries sustained by 180 occupants in a fleet of airbag-equipped cars introduced in the early 1970s with injuries sustained in matched crashes of non-equipped cars. Design approaches to increasing effectiveness beyond this value are discussed by Mertz [1988].

The standard errors in the $(18 \pm 4)\%$ and $(13 \pm 4)\%$ effectiveness estimates for driver and right-front passenger arise only from the errors in the quantities from which they are calculated. Violations of the assumptions constitute additional sources of error. As it is not possible to quantify these factors, one has only judgment to rely on. I do not consider that the assumptions, collectively, generate any obvious systematic bias in the estimates, nor that the collective effect is to increase the stated errors substantially beyond those quoted.

The deployment of the airbag only in essentially frontal crashes raises the possibility that it could be more effective for some occupants and situations if these were characterized by a greater tendency towards frontal crashes. The analysis of Evans [1991b] shows that although the distribution of impact directions does depend on driver age and alcohol use, the fraction that are frontal is relatively unaffected, suggesting in turn that airbag effectiveness is relatively unaffected by driver age or alcohol consumption. Effectiveness is found to be higher in two-car crashes than in single-car crashes (21% compared to 16%).

MOTORCYCLE HELMETS

Helmet effectiveness in preventing fatalities to motorcycle drivers and passengers is determined by Evans and Frick [1988b], who applied the double pair comparison method to FARS data for 1975-1986. Motorcycle crashes with a driver and a passenger, at least one of whom was killed, were used. In order to reduce as much as possible potentially confounding effects due to the dependence of survivability on sex and age, the analysis is confined to male drivers (there were

Table 9-6. The when-used effectiveness of various devices in preventing fatalities to outboard occupants. Except for the lap belt, which is for rear seats, all other values are for drivers and right-front passengers

Occupant protection device	Effectiveness in preventing outboard occupant fatalities (percent)
Airbag plus lap/shoulder belt	46 ± 4
Lap/shoulder belt	41 ± 4
Shoulder belt	29 ± 8
Lap belt (rear seats)	18 ± 9
Airbag only	17 ± 4

insufficient female driver data), and to cases in which the driver and passenger age do not differ by more than three years. Motorcycle helmet effectiveness estimates are found to be relatively unaffected by performing the analyses in a number of ways different from that indicated above. It is found that helmets are (28 ± 8)% effective in preventing fatalities to motorcycle riders, the effectiveness being similar for male and female passengers, and similar for drivers and passengers. By applying essentially the same method to 1982-1987 FARS data, Wilson [1989] obtains a nearly identical effectiveness estimate of 29%.

COMPARISON OF EFFECTIVENESS OF DIFFERENT CAR-OCCUPANT DEVICES

For lap/shoulder belts in front seats and lap-only belts in rear seats, the nominal indications are for higher effectiveness for the left occupant than for the right occupant. Although the differences fall short of statistical significance, they are likely real and result from the unsymmetrical nature of traffic. The data in Evans and Frick [1988a] suggest 38% more impacts of high severity from the right than from the left, so that right occupants receive more near-side impacts, for which belt effectiveness is low. For the airbag, the effectiveness estimate is also larger for the left occupant, though in this case the difference is due mainly to cars with right-front passengers being less likely to be involved in frontal crashes.

Consistent though the nominal differences are between effectiveness for left and right occupants, they are small. It is accordingly convenient to focus on the combined estimates for outboard occupants, especially as in some cases only such combined estimates are available. The previously determined effectiveness estimates for all the devices are summarized in Table 9-6; the derivation for the estimate for airbag plus lap/shoulder belt will be explained in the next section.

If one thinks of the front-seat shoulder belt as having a 29% effectiveness, and the lap belt as having an 18% effectiveness, then, if they operated inde-

Table 9-7. Comparison of estimates of fatality reducing effectiveness for outboard occupants presented in Table 9-6 with those in three previous studies. The lap belt effectiveness in Table 9-6 is for rear seats only, whereas the other lap belt estimates are for mainly front seats. All other estimates are for front seat occupants, mainly drivers

| | Fatality reducing effectiveness estimate (percent) | | | |
Occupant protection device	Value in Table 9-6	NHTSA [1984]	Wilson and Savage [1973]	Huelke et al. [1979]
Airbag plus lap/shoulder belt	46 ± 4	45 − 55	—	—
Lap/shoulder belt	41 ± 4	40 − 50	31	32
Airbag plus lap belt	—	40 − 50	29	34
Shoulder belt	29 ± 8	—	—	28
Lap belt	18 ± 9	30 − 40	17	13
Airbag only	17 ± 4	20 − 40	18	25

pendently, their combined effectiveness would be $1 - (1 - 0.18)(1 - 0.29) = 42\%$, a value remarkably close to the observed 41% effectiveness of the lap/shoulder belt. This indicates that the shoulder belt may be mainly preventing impact with the interior of the vehicle and the lap belt mainly preventing ejection. Indeed, the component of lap/shoulder belt effectiveness found associated with interior impact reduction is 23% [Evans 1990]; if the same value applied for the shoulder belt, this would imply that the remaining 6% arose from prevention of ejection, a value about one third of that for the lap/shoulder belt.

When the analysis of Evans [1986b] is applied to cars of *all* model years (not just 1974 or later), outboard-front effectiveness of $(33.6 \pm 3.6)\%$ is computed. This lower value is compatible with a mix of lap/shoulder, lap only, and shoulder only belts, as might have been used when pre-1974 model-year cars are included.

Relationship to Prior Estimates

Because of the large biases previously discussed, nearly all prior estimates are much larger than those shown in Table 9-6. We therefore confine this comparison to three studies which appear to be relatively free from large biases, discussing first the extensive Final Regulatory Impact Analysis performed by the National Highway Traffic Safety Administration [1984] in connection with Federal Motor Vehicle Standard 208. Estimates of effectiveness, shown under the NHTSA heading in Table 9-7, were derived by synthesizing the results of many analyses, mainly based on NHTSA's national traffic crash files. This detailed and thorough study used the best methods and data then available.

Taking the midpoints of the ranges of the NHTSA values indicates an effectiveness of 50% for lap/shoulder belt plus airbag, which is five percentage points higher than their 45% value for lap/shoulder belts alone. Another way to express these values is to say that a lap/shoulder belted occupant obtains a 9.1% reduction in fatality risk by the addition of an airbag (calculated as $1 - 0.50/0.55$). The value of 46% in Table 9-6 was obtained by assuming that the same five percentage point difference could be applied to the lap/shoulder belt effectiveness estimated using the double pair comparison method; if we are considering drivers only, rather than outboard occupants, the 5% would be added to a 42% effectiveness for drivers [Evans 1986b] to give a 47% effectiveness for lap/shoulder belt plus airbag for drivers. The effect of adding the airbag now reduces fatality risk to the lap/shoulder belted outboard occupant by 8.5% (calculated as $1 - 0.54/0.59 = 0.0847$). The corresponding calculation, $1 - 0.53/0.58$, for the driver gives 8.6%. This lower value (8.5% rather than 9.1%) is appropriate in view of the general pattern of the values in Table 9-6 being lower than the NHTSA estimates. The equation given in Evans [1989] computes that a 8.5% fatality reduction can be achieved by choosing a vehicle with mass larger by 80 kg (170 pounds). The 17% fatality reduction the airbag provides the unbelted occupant can likewise be obtained by choosing a car with a mass larger by 160 kg (360 pounds). A car with increased mass provides increased protection to all occupants, whereas each airbag protects only one occupant.

If the injury reducing mechanisms of airbags and lap/shoulders belt were independent of one another, the combined effectiveness would be 51% (calculated as $1 - (1 - 0.17)(1 - 0.41)$). On the other hand, if the airbag did only what the lap/shoulder belt did, it would not add to the lap/shoulder belt effectiveness, so the net effectiveness would remain at 41%. The average of these two is 46%, the same as the estimated effectiveness.

The studies of Wilson and Savage [1973] and Huelke et al. [1979] are free from all the types of biases present in all the previously discussed studies; this is not to say that they are free from all possible biases, but only that their biases have different sources than those in all the other studies. In the Wilson and Savage [1973] study a panel of four expert engineers examined, in detail, a sample of fatal crashes in which 706 occupants were killed; 74 of these were using some type of restraint system. Using crash reports, medical and/or autopsy reports, photographs and other such information, the panel discussed the injury mechanisms for each fatally injured occupant, and arrived at a judgement about whether different restraint systems would have prevented the fatality. Their effectiveness estimate for lap belts is an average for all seating positions, so that it refers mainly, but not exclusively, to front seating positions. The nature of the method made it difficult to identify cases in which the use of a restraint would have increased, rather than decreased, injuries. So in this sense, there is a mechanism generating a systematic upwards bias. The 706 fatalities are a sample of convenience, so that they may not have been representative of fatal crashes in general. The estimate for airbags and lap belts are remarkably similar to those in Table 9-6, whereas the estimate for lap/shoulder belt effectiveness is lower.

The study by Huelke et al. [1979] is similar in approach. It is based on analysis of 101 front-seat occupants fatally injured in 80 crashes in Washtenaw County, Michigan; four occupants were wearing belts. The potential of different restraint systems to prevent the fatality was estimated by three of the authors of the study. The smaller sample size and narrower geographic location of these crashes probably renders the results less typical of effectiveness over all crash configurations. The lower value for lap belt effectiveness, and higher value for airbag effectiveness, probably indicates fewer than average numbers of crashes involving ejection. The results of Evans and Frick [1989] indicate that preventing ejection alone reduces fatality risk by 18%.

CONCLUSIONS

When a vehicle crashes, it undergoes a rapid change in speed. Occupants continue to move at the vehicle's previous speed until stopped, either by impact with objects external to the vehicle if ejected, by striking the interior of the vehicle, or by being restrained in some other way. A number of occupant protection devices have been developed which reduce the severity of impact with the vehicle's interior (for example, lap/shoulder belts and airbags) or reduce the risk of ejection (for example, lap belts). Three distinct measures of effectiveness must be defined to address the effectiveness of such devices: (1) severity-specific effectiveness, defined as the percentage reduction in injuries in crashes of a specific severity, or within a narrow range of severities; (2) when-used effectiveness, defined as the percentage reduction in injuries that occurs when the device is used; and (3) field effectiveness, defined as the percentage reduction in injuries taking into account the use rate for the device.

It is no simple matter to estimate when-used effectiveness of safety belts from field crash data because wearers and nonwearers differ in so many ways. In particular, drivers who wear safety belts have fewer, and less severe, crashes. Nonwearers who survive are more likely than those who die to be incorrectly coded in data files as wearers, especially since the advent of mandatory wearing laws. All these effects can bias estimates of effectiveness upwards, leading to many unrealistically high published values. The double pair comparison method, which is less influenced by these biases, was applied to FARS data to estimate the fatality-reducing effectiveness of various devices, giving $(41 \pm 4)\%$ for lap/shoulder belts in front seats and $(18 \pm 9)\%$ for lap belts in rear seats. Nearly all of the lap belt effectiveness, and almost half of the lap/shoulder belt effectiveness, is due to the prevention of ejection.

By assuming that airbags do not influence ejection risk, and that they provide interior impact reduction effectiveness equal to that of lap/shoulder belts, effectiveness is estimated at 17%; a different, and somewhat extreme, assumption that the airbag has an interior impact-reducing effectiveness one and a half times that of the lap/shoulder belt gives an airbag effectiveness estimate of 25%. Lap/shoulder belt plus airbag effectiveness is estimated to be (46 ± 4)%. All these results are for fatalities only, and cannot be extrapolated to lower levels of injury. There are general reasons to expect effectiveness to be higher at lower severity levels. For example, airbags are expected to have high effectiveness at preventing non-life-threatening facial injuries resulting from contact with the steering wheel. The occupant protection device expected to provide the highest level of protection is a lap/shoulder belt supplemented by an airbag.

REFERENCES

Ashton, S.J.; Mackay, G.M.; Camm, S. Seat belt use in Britain under voluntary and mandatory conditions. American Association for Automotive Medicine, 27th Annual Proceedings, San Antonio, TX, p. 65–75; 1983.

Campbell, B.J. Safety belt injury reduction related to crash severity and front seated position. *Journal of Trauma* 27:733–739; 1987a.

Campbell, B.J. The effectiveness of rear-seat lap-belts in crash injury reduction. SAE paper 870480. Warrendale, PA: Society of Automotive Engineers; 1987b. (Also included in Restraint technologies—rear seat occupant protection. SAE special publication SP-691, p. 9–18; 1987b.)

Deutsch, D.; Sameth, S.; Akinyemi, J. Seat belt usage and risk-taking behavior at two major traffic intersections. American Association for Automotive Medicine, 27th Annual Proceedings, San Antonio, TX, p. 415–421; 1980.

Esterlitz, J.R. A comparison of rates of fatal ejection from manual and automatic belt cars. Arlington, VA: Insurance Institute for Highway Safety; June 1987.

Evans, L. Double pair comparison—a new method to determine how occupant characteristics affect fatality risk in traffic crashes. *Accident Analysis and Prevention* 18:217–227; 1986a.

Evans, L. The effectiveness of safety belts in preventing fatalities. *Accident Analysis and Prevention* 18:229–241; 1986b.

Evans, L. Occupant protection device effectiveness—some conceptual considerations. *Journal of Safety Research* 18:137–144; 1987a.

Evans, L. Belted and unbelted driver accident involvement rates compared. *Journal of Safety Research* 18:57–64; 1987b.

Evans, L. Examination of some possible biases in double pair comparison estimates of safety belt effectiveness. *Accident Analysis and Prevention* 20:215–218; 1988a.

Evans, L. Rear seat restraint system effectiveness in preventing fatalities. *Accident Analysis and Prevention* 20:129–136; 1988b. (Also see Evans, L. Rear compared to front seat restraint system effectiveness in preventing fatalities. SAE paper 870485; also included in Restraint technologies—rear seat occupant protection. SAE special publication SP-691, p. 39–43; 1987.)

Evans, L. Passive compared to active approaches to reducing occupant fatalities. Proceedings of the Twelfth International Technical Conference on Experimental Safety Vehicles, Gothenburg, Sweden; 29 May–1 June 1989. US Department of Transportation, National Highway Traffic Safety Administration, Vol. 2, p. 1149–1157; 1989.

Evans, L. Restraint effectiveness, occupant ejection from cars and fatality reductions. *Accident Analysis and Prevention* 22:167–175; 1990.

Evans, L. Motorized two-point safety belt effectiveness in preventing fatalities. *Accident Analysis and Prevention* 23 (in press); 1991a.

Evans, L. Airbag effectiveness in preventing fatalities predicted according to type of crash, driver age, and blood alcohol concentration. *Accident Analysis and Prevention* 23 (in press); 1991b.

Evans, L.; Frick, M.C. Safety belt effectiveness in preventing driver fatalities versus a number of vehicular, accident, roadway and environmental factors. *Journal of Safety Research* 17:143–154; 1986.

Evans, L.; Frick, M.C. Seating position in cars and fatality risk. *American Journal of Public Health* 78:1456–1458; 1988a.

Evans, L.; Frick, M.C. Helmet effectiveness in preventing motorcycle driver and passenger fatalities. *Accident Analysis and Prevention* 20:447–458; 1988b.

Evans, L.; Frick, M.C. Potential fatality reductions through eliminating occupant ejection from cars. *Accident Analysis and Prevention* 21:169–182; 1989.

Evans, L.; Wasielewski, P. Risky driving related to driver and vehicle characteristics. *Accident Analysis and Prevention* 15:121–136; 1983.

Evans, L.; Wasielewski, P.; von Buseck, C.R. Compulsory seat belt usage and driver risk-taking behavior. *Human Factors* 24:41–48; 1982.

Green, P.D.; Robertson, N.K.B.; Bradford, M.A.; Bodiwala, G.G. Car occupant ejection in 919 sampled accidents in the U.K.—1983-86. SAE paper 870323. Warrendale, PA: Society of Automotive Engineers; 1987. (Also included in Restraint technologies: front seat occupant protection. SAE special publication SP-690, p. 91–104; 1987.)

Grime, G. *Handbook of Road Safety Research.* London, UK: Butterworth; 1987.

Haddon, W., Jr. Advances in the epidemiology of injuries as a basis for public policy. *Public Health Reports* 95:411–421; 1980.

Horsch, J.D. Evaluation of occupant protection from responses measured in laboratory tests. SAE paper 870222. Warrendale, PA: Society of Automotive Engineers; 1987. (Also included in Restraint technologies—front seat occupant protection SP-690, p. 13–31; 1987.)

Huelke, D.F.; Sherman, H.W. Seat belt effectiveness: case examples from real-world crash investigations. *Journal of Trauma* 27:750–753; 1987.

Huelke, D.F.; Sherman, H.W.; Murphy, M.J.; Kaplan, R.J.; Flora, J.D. Effectiveness of current and future restraint systems in fatal and serious injury automobile crashes. SAE paper 790323. Warrendale, PA: Society of Automotive Engineers; 1979.

Hunter, W.H.; Stewart, R.J.; Stutts, J.C.; Rodgman, E.A. Overrepresentation of non-belt users in traffic crashes. Association for the Advancement of Automotive Medicine, 32nd Annual Proceedings, Seattle, WA, p. 237–256; 12-14 September 1988.

Kahane, C. J. An evaluation of child passenger safety: the effectiveness and benefits of safety seats. Washington, DC: National Highway Traffic Safety Administration, report DOT HS-806 890; February 1986.

Kahane, C.J. Fatality and injury reducing effectiveness of lap belts for back seat occupants. SAE paper 870486; Warrendale, PA: Society of Automotive Engineers; 1987. (Also included in Restraint technologies: rear seat occupant protection. SAE special publication SP-691, p. 45–63; 1987.)

Mackay, G.M. Kinematics of vehicle crashes. *Advances in Trauma* 2:21–42; 1987.

Malliaris, A.C.; Hitchcock, R.; Hansen, M. Harm causation and ranking in car crashes. SAE paper 850090. Warrendale, PA: Society of Automotive Engineers; 1985.

Maugh, R.E. Supplemental driver airbag system—Ford Motor Company Tempo and Topaz vehicles. Proceedings of the Tenth International Technical Conference on Experimental Safety Vehicles, National Highway Traffic Safety Administration, DOT HS 806 916, p. 59–63; February 1986.

Mertz H.J. Restraint performance of the 1973–76 GM air cushion restraint system. SAE paper 880400. Warrendale, PA: Society of Automotive Engineers; 1988.

Mertz, H.J.; Marquardt, J.F. Small car air cushion performance considerations. SAE paper 851199. Warrendale, PA: Society of Automotive Engineers; 1985.

National Highway Traffic Safety Administration. Final regulatory impact analysis, Amendment of FMVSS 208, passenger car front seat occupant protection. Washington, DC; 11 July 1984.

National Safety Council. *Vehicle damage scale for traffic accident investigators*. 3rd edition. Chicago, IL; 1984.

O'Day, J.; Flora, J. Alternative measures of restraint system effectiveness: interaction with crash severity factors. SAE paper 820798. Warrendale, PA: Society of Automotive Engineers; 1982.

O'Neill, B.; Lund, A.K.; Zador, P.; Ashton, S. Mandatory belt use and driver risk taking: an empirical evaluation of the risk-compensation hypothesis. In: Evans, L.; Schwing, R.C., editors. *Human Behavior and Traffic Safety*. New York, NY: Plenum Press, p. 93–107; 1985.

Park, S. The influence of rear-seat occupants on front-seat occupant fatalities: the unbelted case. General Motors Research Laboratories, Research publication GMR-5664; 8 January 1987.

Partyka, S.C. Restraint use and fatality risk for infants and toddlers. National Highway Traffic Safety Administration. Washington, DC; May 1984.

Partyka, S.C. Belt effectiveness in pickup trucks and passenger cars by crash direction and accident year. Washington, DC: National Highway Traffic Safety Administration; 13 May 1988.

Partyka, S.C. Belt effectiveness in passenger cars by weight class In: Papers on car size—safety and trends. Washington, DC: National Highway Traffic Safety Administration, report DOT HS 807 444, p. 1–35; June 1989.

Passell, P. What's holding back air bags? In: Viano, D.C., editor. Passenger car inflatable restraint systems: a compendium of published safety research. Warrendale, PA: Society of Automotive Engineers, publication PT-31, p. 3–7; 1987.

Pursel H.D.; Bryant R.W.; Scheel J.W.; Yanik A.J. Matched case methodology for measuring restraint effectiveness. SAE paper 780415. Warrendale, PA: Society of Automotive Engineers; 1978.

Ricci, L.L., editor. NCSS Statistics: passenger cars. Report UM-HSRI-80-36, Highway Safety Research Institute, University of Michigan. Ann Arbor, MI; June 1980.

States, J.D.; Huelke, D.F.; Dance, M.; Green, R.N. Fatal injuries caused by underarm use of shoulder belts. *Journal of Trauma* 27:740–745; 1987.

Streff, F.M.; Wagenaar, A.C. Are there really shortcuts? Estimating seat belt use with self-report measures. *Accident Analysis and Prevention* 21 509–516; 1989.

Viano, D.C. Causes and control of automotive trauma. *Bulletin of the New York Academy of Medicine* 64:376–421; 1988.

Viano, D.C.; Lau, I.V. Biomechanics of impact injury. International trends in thoracic surgery—surgical management of chest injuries, Chapter 2, Volume 7; 1990 (in press).

Viano, D.C.; King, A.I.; Melvin, J.W.; Weber, K. Injury biomechanics research: an essential element in the prevention of trauma. *Journal of Biomechanics* 22:403–417; 1989.

Williams, A.F.; Wells, J.K.; Lund, A.K.; Teed, N. Observed use of automatic seat belts in 1987 cars. *Accident Analysis and Prevention* 21:427–433; 1989.

Wilson, D.C. The effectiveness of motorcycle helmets in preventing fatalities. Washington, DC: National Highway Traffic Safety Administration, report DOT HS-807 416; March 1989.

Wilson, R.A.; Savage, C.M. Restraint system effectiveness—a study of fatal accidents. Proceedings of Automotive Safety Engineering Seminar, sponsored by Automotive Safety Engineering, Environmental Activities Staff, General Motors Corporation; 20-21 June 1973

10 Restraint-Use Laws, Use Rates, and Field Effectiveness

INTRODUCTION

While equipping a vehicle with a passive occupant protection device, such as an airbag, is expected to automatically reduce risk, the same is not true for active devices such as safety belts. Adding safety belts reduces risk only if they are worn. It is only in the limit of 100% wearing rates that the field effectiveness, or actual reduction in fatalities in a population of drivers in vehicles equipped with belts, will equal the when-used effectiveness values in Table 9-6. For passive devices (assuming that they are not disabled) there is no distinction between when-used and field effectiveness.

Notwithstanding the safety benefits provided by belts, voluntary wearing rates have generally been low. Many efforts have been made to increase such rates by motivational and informational campaigns [Robertson et al. 1974; Geller 1984; Nagayama 1990]. While some such measures have generated increases in use rates, these have been small compared to use increases from mandatory belt-wearing laws.

Influence of Mandatory Belt-Wearing Laws on Use Rates

The first mandatory belt-wearing law in a jurisdiction with a substantial car population came into effect on 22 December 1970 in Victoria, one of the states of Australia [Trinca 1984]. (Malawi and the Ivory Coast appear to have had earlier laws [Grimm 1988]). The Victoria law required drivers and front passengers in seats equipped with safety belts to fasten them. In 1971 about 75% of driver seats in cars in Victoria were equipped with belts, over 90% of these being lap and shoulder belts. As all new cars were required to have belts, the rate soon approached 100%. In the first year of the law about 75% of drivers in cars equipped with belts wore them. Andreassend [1976] estimates that as a consequence of the law, deaths to drivers and left-front passengers declined by about 12% in 1971 when the overall use rate was about 50%. By January 1972, the compulsory wearing of safety belts, if fitted, for occupants over 8 years of age applied throughout all Australian states [Trinca 1984].

By mid 1990, 40 countries had mandatory wearing laws, as did all 10 Canadian provinces and 34 US states (plus the District of Columbia) [Grimm 1988; 1990]. Even though four US states (Massachusetts, Nebraska, North Dakota, and Oregon) have repealed laws by referendum, 84% of the US population lives in states with wearing laws [Campbell, Stewart, and Campbell 1988]. While belt-wearing rates in excess of 90% have been often observed in some Australian states, the UK, Japan, Finland, and West Germany, much lower rates, often under 40%, occur in other jurisdictions [Grimm 1988; 1990].

In the US from the early 1970s to the mid 1980s, before there were any mandatory wearing laws, belt-wearing rates were relatively stable at close to 14%. The first mandatory wearing law in the US became effective in New York State in December 1984, well after such laws had become widespread in the rest of the world. US wearing rates, based on daytime samples in 19 cities [National Highway Traffic Safety Administration 1989], now average 46%. The rate for cities without wearing laws is 33%, and for those with such laws the rate is 50%.

It is not as simple as it might appear to obtain an accurate estimate of belt-wearing rates. A common technique is to place observers on the sidewalk near traffic lights, so that belt use of occupants in stationery vehicles can be noted. When traffic is moving, reliable observation becomes more difficult, although in some cases rural use is estimated. Although fatality crash risks peak at night (Figs 4-12 and 7-5), it is not generally possible to obtain nighttime wearing rates. Apart from the obvious difficulty of observing in the dark, there is the possibility of danger to observers, and low traffic volumes which lead to substantially higher costs per observation. So, estimates of wearing rates for most jurisdictions are necessarily extrapolations of data from a few specific sites at restricted times.

While the influence of wearing laws on use rates is different in detail for each jurisdiction, there are some recurrent general patterns. Fig. 10-1 shows data from the UK, where belt wearing became compulsory on 31 January 1983. The law is associated with a steep increase in belt wearing from 40% to over 90%.

More modest increases in belt wearing occurred with the passage of various mandatory wearing laws in the US. Fig. 10-2 shows fairly typical data for two states, both of whose laws came into effect in July 1985 (month 0 in the graph). The increases in belt wearing that occurred before the laws went into effect in Michigan, and also in Fig. 10-1, are fairly typical, and arise because of media discussion and possible confusion about when belt-wearing is mandatory as distinct from when the legislation is passed. Also typical is an immediate increase in wearing rates just after the passage of the law, followed by a decline to a lower level, but a level still substantially above the pre-law level.

The use rate levels in Fig. 10-2 were in response to secondary enforcement, meaning that police officers were not empowered to stop vehicles solely because they observed occupants not wearing belts. Citations for nonwearing could be issued only after vehicles were stopped for some other reason, such as speeding or defective equipment. In efforts to increase wearing rates, a number of juris-

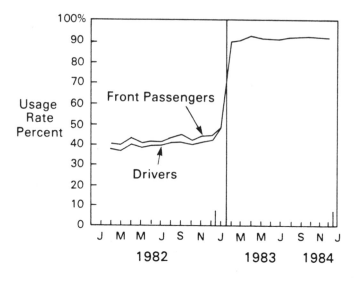

Figure 10-1. Safety belt wearing rates in the UK for occupants of cars and light vans. Reproduced, with permission, from Mackay [1985].

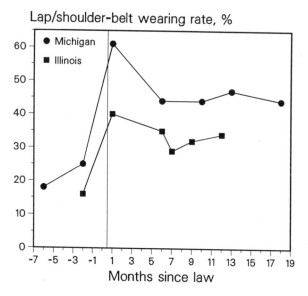

Figure 10-2. Belt-wearing rates in two US states with secondary enforcement.

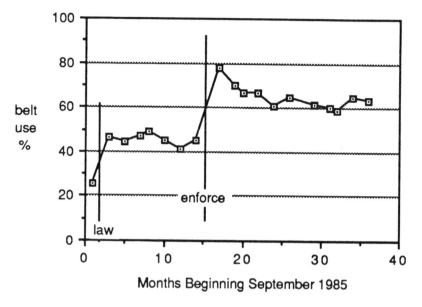

Figure 10-3. The effect of increasing enforcement on wearing rates in North Carolina, which has a primary enforcement law. Reproduced, with permission, from Campbell, Stewart, and Campbell [1988].

dictions have changed from secondary to primary enforcement, which does allow police to stop vehicles and issue citations based solely on wearing-law violations. The effect of increasing enforcement in a state with a primary law, North Carolina, is shown in Fig. 10-3.

Campbell [1987] finds considerable evidence (Fig 10-4) that increasing the level of enforcement leads to increased belt-use rates.

CALCULATING CASUALTY CHANGES FROM BELT-USE CHANGES

While changes in belt-wearing rates attributable to passing wearing laws can be measured readily, it is much more difficult to determine directly with much precision any consequent changes in casualties, as is discussed in later sections. In order to anticipate better the magnitude of effects to be expected, we first derive an equation estimating changes in driver fatalities when belt-use rates change from some initial value to a new value. (For expository convenience, the derivation is described in terms of fatalities, though the ideas and equations are applicable to all injury levels.) If belt wearers had crash rates that were the same as those for nonwearers, then estimating changes in driver fatalities as-

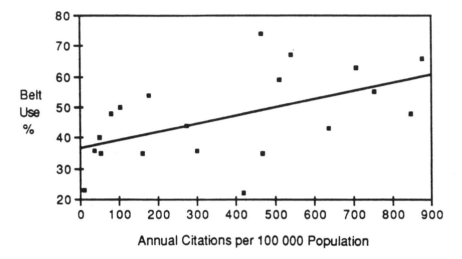

Figure 10-4.   The influence of enforcement on belt-wearing rates in 20 US states (eight using primary enforcement and 12 using secondary enforcement). Reproduced, with permission, from Campbell [1987].

sociated with changes in belt-wearing rates would be relatively simple. However, copious evidence (cited in Chapter 9) shows that belt wearers are less risky drivers than belt nonwearers. Therefore, if additional drivers are recruited to belt wearing (when belt-wearing rates are low), these drivers are likely to be of below average risk. Hence the reduction in fatalities would be less than if the same number of average drivers became wearers. The process by which it is the safer-than-average drivers who switch from non-wearing to wearing has been labelled "selective recruitment" [Evans 1985].

Simple Calculation Ignoring Selective Recruitment

To clarify the discussion of expected casualty changes from changes in belt-use rates we first develop a *simple calculation* based on the (incorrect) assumption that, apart from their decision on belt use, belted and unbelted drivers behave similarly. We introduce the following notation:

u_i = initial, or old, belt-use rate   Eqn 10-1

u_f = final, or new, belt-use rate   Eqn 10-2

$\Delta u = u_f - f_i$ = change in belt-use rate   Eqn 10-3

Table 10-1. Estimates of the involvement rate of unbelted drivers to the rate for belted drivers in various traffic incidents

Type of Event	$\dfrac{Unbelted\ rate}{Belted\ rate}$
Driver fatalities	1.57
Crashes in which pedestrians were killed	1.57
Crashes in which motorcyclists were killed	1.37
Police reported crashes (headway study)	1.32
Police reported crashes (speed study)	1.28
Traffic violations (headway study)	1.86
Traffic violations (speed study)	1.73

F = fractional reduction in fatalities   Eqn 10-4

E = when-used belt effectiveness   Eqn 10-5

Assuming that all drivers have identical crash rates, it can readily be shown [Evans 1987a; Hedlund 1986] that

$$F = E\ \Delta u/(1 - E\ u_i)\qquad \text{Eqn 10-6}$$

If an initial use rate of zero increases to 100%, Eqn 10-6 reproduces the definition of E. The simple calculation, Eqn 10-6, has the characteristic that, starting from the same initial use rate, fractional reductions in fatalities increase linearly with increases in belt-use rate. In order to obtain an estimate of F that reflects the important differences between crash rates of wearers and nonwearers that are ignored in Eqn 10-6, quantitative estimates of such differences are required.

Belted Compared to Unbelted Driver Crash Rates

The ratio R, defined as

$$R = \frac{\text{involvement rate for unbelted drivers}}{\text{involvement rate for belted drivers}},\qquad \text{Eqn 10-7}$$

is estimated in Evans [1987b] for involvements in various types of crashes, and also for traffic violations. Seven essentially independent estimates of R are obtained (Table 10-1); three use FARS data, and four use data from the State of Michigan giving crash and traffic violation records of drivers whose belt use was determined from photographs of them driving in traffic.

The first estimate is based on comparing belted and unbelted daytime driver fatalities to the number expected, based on the 14% use rate in Michigan at the time, and the when-used effectiveness of safety belts. The second (and third) estimates compare the numbers of pedestrians (motorcyclists) killed in daytime crashes with cars driven by belted drivers to the number killed in crashes with unbelted drivers.

The remaining four cases in Table 10-1 are based on studies in which approaching cars were photographed on Michigan roads [von Buseck et al. 1980; Evans and Wasielewski 1983; Wasielewski 1984]. Driver safety belt use was noted from the photograph, as was the car license-plate number, which, through the cooperation of the Michigan Department of State, yielded information on the car's registered owner, including his or her driver license number. Cases in which the photographed driver appeared different in age or sex from the one described in the driving record were excluded; if not so excluded, it was assumed that the observed driver was the one whose record was provided, and that the observed safety belt use could be associated with that driver. From the driver license file, the driver's record, including crashes and traffic violations (there was then no law requiring belt wearing) were obtained. All the observational data also included a measure of driver risk taking, either following headway or travel speed; in Table 10-1 this is used only for identification purposes.

For all seven cases studied, unbelted driver involvement rates are 28% to 86% higher than those for belted drivers. A feature not noted in the original paper [Evans 1987b] is that the seven values divide rather cleanly into the three lowest (from $R = 1.28$ to 1.37) and the four highest (from $R = 1.57$ to 1.86). The three lowest values all refer to essentially two-vehicle crashes (the great majority of police-reported crashes involve two vehicles), whereas the four highest refer more to single-vehicle incidents. This therefore presents another example of the distinction between, on the one hand, involvement, and on the other hand, responsible involvement, which is discussed in Chapter 7. Many of the safer belted drivers were crash-involved because of the actions of the drivers of other vehicles, which reduces the proportional difference between involvement rates of the safer and the less safe drivers.

The average of the seven values in Table 10-1 is 1.53, meaning that unbelted drivers are 53% more likely to be involved in crashes than belted drivers. An essentially similar value is obtained by Hunter et al. [1988] using a survey method. We therefore use $R = 1.53$ to capture quantitatively the selective recruitment phenomena in a calculation of how fatality reductions are expected to depend on changes in belt use.

Calculation Including Selective Recruitment

The central concept behind the calculation is that differences in risk taking between belted and unbelted drivers observed consistently in so many studies reflect an underlying continuous relationship between propensity to wear a belt and crash rate. Consider all the drivers in a population rank ordered from the most willing to the least willing to wear a belt. Conceptually, one can imagine any level of belt use occurring for such a population of drivers, depending on external motivation. Presumably, if wearing were heavily taxed, wearing rates would approach zero, whereas if non-wearing were severely punished, rates would approach 100%. As the motivational level is increased, more and more unwilling drivers, with ever higher and higher crash rates, become users. The only observational data is that the average crash risk for the 86% of nonusers observed in Michigan is 1.53 times the average rate for 14% of users. From this information, a fairly robust relationship between fatality changes and belt-use changes is derived in Evans [1987a], which can be expressed as

$$F = \frac{E \, \Delta u \, [1 + k \, (u_i^2 + u_i u_f + u_f^2)]}{1 + k - E \, u_i \, (1 + k \, u_i^2)}, \qquad \text{Eqn 10-8}$$

where the parameter k captures the selective recruitment effects and is given by

$$k = (R - 1)/(1 + b + b^2 - R \, b^2) = 0.4692, \qquad \text{Eqn 10-9}$$

where b is the use rate, namely 0.14, for the studies from which the unbelted to belted risk ratio $R = 1.53$ is derived.

While Eqn 10-8 might appear somewhat complicated, it is based on fairly simple assumptions. Because the fatality reductions depend on both final and initial belt-use rates, it is not possible to display Eqn 10-8 in simple graphical form. The quantitative results are relatively unchanged for different choices of plausible assumptions provided belt nonusers have crash rates 53% higher than users. If $R = 1$, meaning that there is no selective recruitment, then $k = 0$ and Eqn 10-8 reduces to the simple case, Eqn 10-6.

Fatality Changes Compared to Zero Belt Use

One case of particular interest is the determination of the total casualty reductions from belt use; that is, a comparison of the reduction in fatalities for some belt-use rate compared to zero belt use. If $u_i = 0$, and $u = u_f = \Delta u$, then Eqn 10-8 gives

$$F = E \, u \, (1 + k \, u^2)/(1 + k). \qquad \text{Eqn 10-10}$$

Figure 10-5 shows F plotted versus u. Also shown as a straight line is the simple model calculation.

The data points plotted are estimates of fatality reductions reported by Partyka and Womble [1989] (the numerical values appear later in Table 10-2). These are estimated using data on fatally-injured driver and right-front passengers coded in FARS as using a restraint system. These fatality data, together with the known effectiveness of the belts, are used to estimate the number of belted occupants

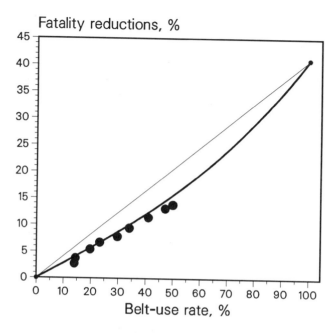

Figure 10-5. Fatality reductions versus belt-use rate (compared to zero use) calculated using Eqn 10-10 (the curve) and Eqn 10-6 (the straight line). The data points show fatality reductions estimated from FARS data by Partyka and Womble [1989].

who, but for the belt, would also have been killed, from which the percentage reduction in driver and right-front passenger fatalities is estimated.

It is clear that the curve (Eqn 10-10) provides a much superior fit to the data than the straight line (Eqn 10-6). The data are systematically lower than the curve, but by fairly small amounts. Partyka and Womble [1989] show that these same data fitted well a quadratic function of u. It should be stressed that the curve in Fig. 10-5 is not a fit to the data—the equation was published *before* the availability of the data.

While the agreement between the data and Eqn 10-10 is good, one must keep in mind that the data are not directly-observed fatality reductions, but inferences from fatalities. If there were 100% belt use, then the calculated data are con-strained to agree identically with the curve (ignoring differences that arise because Partyka uses a 45% effectiveness whereas the equation uses 41%). Thus there is sufficient overlap in the computations required for the data and for the curve that each does not provide an entirely independent check on the other. However, the closer agreement with the curve than with the straight line does reflect real agreement which increases confidence that the more general form, Eqn 10-8, may also be reasonably accurate.

OBSERVED CASUALTY CHANGES FROM CHANGES IN BELT USE

The ideal evaluation of a public health measure would be a clearly observed change in the harm that the measure was enacted to reduce. It is rarely possible to provide such evaluations, which are generally not even contemplated. For example, a new heart operation, no matter how successful, cannot be expected to generate observable changes in the total number of deaths from heart disease, because that total number is far too large, and therefore subject to large random variation. The only feasible (even if flawed) evaluation of such an intervention is the standard one of comparing recovery rates of patients undergoing and not undergoing the procedure. Such an evaluation cannot address the possibility that improved heart surgery might encourage increased smoking, and thereby generate a net increase in heart and other disease. However, it would be unreasonable to interpret the lack of a measured decline in heart disease deaths as indicating that this did indeed happen. Such data would argue that the intervention was ineffective only if they did not show a decline larger than that calculated in terms of the likely efficacy of the operation, when applied, and the number of operations.

The tradition of expecting directly observable casualty reductions from passing safety belt wearing laws became established because unrealistically large, readily observable, casualty reductions were promised. Such promises were based on assuming unrealistic when-used effectiveness, assuming unrealistically large and sudden increases in belt use, and more understandably, ignoring selective recruitment effects. If a halving of fatalities is promised, then a change should be readily apparent. However, laws have typically increased use rates from about 20% to about 40%, which Eqn 10-8 calculates will reduce fatalities by 6.7% for those covered, who typically constitute well under half of all road users. It is exceedingly unlikely that such a difference can be measured using data from a typical jurisdiction with a few hundred relevant fatalities per year; it is even more improbable that a 3% reduction in total fatalities can be detected. Early promises of large reductions, followed by no discernible decrease, gave rise to many explanations, including the explanation that compulsory belt wearing laws induce collective increases in driver risk taking that reduce the benefits to the belted occupants while at the same time place other road users at increased risk [Adams 1985].

Directly Observing Casualty Changes—Difficulties and Methods

From the point of view of ease of evaluation, one would like use rates to increase overnight from 0% to 100%, have no other factors change, and to have as large a population as possible affected by the law. These conditions cannot be attained even approximately. Even before wearing laws are discussed, use rates are well above zero; laws are introduced only after much debate and media coverage, which usually generates increases in use rates before the passage of the law (Figs. 10-1 to 10-3). Thus, increases in belt use occur in the pre-law period. After belt wearing is required, rates may increase only modestly (Fig. 10-3) until another law increasing penalties is enacted. Thus, instead of a steep step function increase in use rates, a more gradual increase generally occurs, which makes evaluation difficult. In federal nations like Australia, Canada, and the US, laws are introduced in one state or province at a time, so that sample sizes are generally inadequate relative to the size of the effects.

Even without changes in laws, casualties change for a variety of reasons. Note particularly the seasonal effects in Figs 4-8 to 4-10; US traffic fatalities in July and August are typically 50% higher than in January and February. In the face of such large monthly variation, a 7% effect from a belt-wearing law is going to be exceedingly difficult to observe. Taking periods of whole years before and after enactment will remove effects due to monthly variation, but will introduce variation from other sources, such as economic changes (Fig. 11-3), or a general change in time (Figs 13-1 to 13-4). In addition to variation from sources that can be to some extent explained, there is of course additional unexplained random variation.

There is no entirely satisfactory solution to these formidable difficulties. We can identify five approaches to estimate the casualty changes from wearing laws.

1. *Interrupted time-series analyses.* Apply statistical time series analyses to the pre-law casualties, and generate equations which predict what post-law casualties would have been if the pre-law trends had continued. A comparison with the observed post-law data gives an estimate of the effect of the intervention. Among the difficulties here is that the method usually relies on monthly data, which, for fatalities, provide relatively small sample sizes. Another difficulty is the inherent complexity of the models. It is difficult for anyone other than the researchers actually doing the work to get a feel for the source of the estimates.

2. *Control jurisdiction.* Compare the ratio of post- to pre-law casualties to a corresponding ratio for the same periods in a control jurisdiction which had no law change. The aim here is that all effects due to seasonal, economic, etc. factors will be taken into account by the control jurisdiction, so that any remaining difference can be attributed to the law. This approach has been applied to US and Australian states, and to Canadian provinces; it has little possibility of application to the majority of countries, which have nation-wide traffic laws. The negative features of this approach are that the choice of the control juris-

diction is arbitrary, and control jurisdiction sample sizes place additional constraints on precision.

3. *Control occupant.* Compare the ratio of casualties to affected road users (say car drivers) to those for non-affected, or control, road users. There are various choices for control road users, such as truck drivers (if not affected by the legislation). Pedestrian and motorcyclist fatalities can be used only if it is assumed that the wearing laws do not influence casualties to these road users. Other occupants in the same car as the driver cannot be used to estimate the effect of the mandatory wearing law on total driver fatalities, but instead can be used to estimate the effectiveness of the belts in crashes (Chapter 9).

4. *Simple before versus after count.* This has the advantage of transparency and simplicity. While estimates for one specific jurisdiction might have substantial errors, there is no reason to presume that the average value obtained for many jurisdictions would not tend towards an unbiased estimate of the true effect.

5. *Count and examine crash victims admitted to hospital.* This approach has been more successful at identifying changes in character and types of injuries when belt laws are passed than in evaluating overall field effectiveness.

The UK's Mandatory Belt-Wearing Law

Of the more than 80 mandatory belt-wearing laws passed, the one that came into effect on 31 January 1983 in the UK has three factors favoring effective evaluation which are not available for any other jurisdiction. First, belt use was closely monitored before and after the law came into effect at 55 Department of Transport traffic census sites, generally from 8:30 a.m. to 4:30 p.m. Second, a large increase in belt use occurred quickly, from about 40% to 90% (Fig. 10-1). Third, the UK, with over 16 million cars in 1983, provides about the largest population of occupants affected by a single law. While France and West Germany have somewhat more cars, their laws did not lead to such sharp increases in belt use. In France, use was required only on rural roads in 1973, and on all roads in 1979. When belt wearing was made compulsory in West Germany in 1976, use rates rose only modestly, from 32% to 50%. In 1985 the instigation of more severe penalties led to an increase from 58% to 92%. While Japan has had a law since December 1971, with a increase in penalty for non-compliance in September 1985, eventually generating compliance of over 90%, I am not aware of any estimate of its effect on fatalities.

Despite uniquely favorable conditions, evaluating the UK's law has not been without difficulties or controversy, especially regarding possible driver behavior

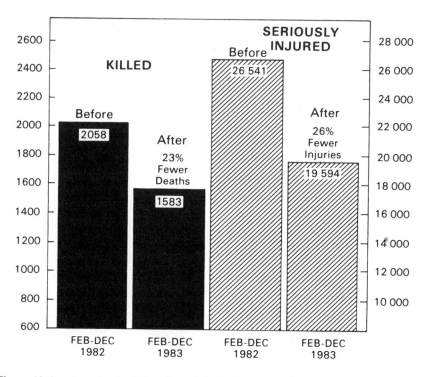

Figure 10-6. An estimate of the effect of the UK's belt-wearing law based on a simple count of casualties before and after the law. Reproduced, with permission, from Mackay [1985].

changes induced by the law [Adams 1985]. The simplest evaluation, a count of casualties in an 11-month period before the law compared to an 11-month period after the law [Mackay 1985] is shown in Fig. 10-6; January is excluded because of the rising belt use in the month of introduction. The somewhat higher reductions in serious injuries compared to fatalities (26% compared to 23%) is consistent with the discussion in Chapter 9 suggesting that when-used belt effectiveness is likely higher for levels of injury lower than fatality. Adams [1985] argues that changes in other factors could have produced the declines, a view he supports by fitting a multivariate function to a time series for all UK fatalities without invoking any influence from the law. However, annual changes as large as 23% are simply not vulnerable to being explained away by other factors; only major inputs, like the energy changes after the 1973 Arab oil embargo, generate effects of such magnitude.

   A somewhat more complex time-series analysis was applied to the UK data by Scott and Willis [1985]. They conclude that there was an approximately 20%

reduction in fatal and serious casualties to car drivers and van occupants; for front-seat car passengers they find a larger 30% reduction. More recently, Broughton [1988], in examining long term trends in total British fatalities per unit distance of travel, finds a 6.2% decrease (90% confidence limits from 1.9% to 10.3%) associated with the law; as affected occupants were 37% of all road users, this result implies a 17% reduction.

Despite the relative agreement between the inference from the simple numbers and the Scott and Willis [1985] time-series analysis, various questions continued to be raised, especially about possible effects on pedestrians and pedalcyclists. Accordingly, two distinguished statisticians without previous involvement with the Department of Transport, the body responsible for both implementing and evaluating the intervention, were invited to examine the monthly time series of casualties to various road users. Their paper, which is at the cutting edge of statistical theory, and accordingly understandable only to a few, was presented to the Royal Statistical Society [Harvey and Durbin 1986]. The discussion (printed after their paper) is uninhibited by the politeness that often does such disservice to the search for truth in North America.

For the large samples of those seriously injured (including fatally injured), Harvey and Durbin [1986] find a reduction of 23% for car drivers and a 30% reduction for front-seat passengers, showing large reductions for those directly affected by the law. For those not affected, they find a 3% increase for rear-seat passengers, a 0.5% decrease for pedestrians and a 5% increase for pedal-cyclists, all these values being not statistically significant. The uncertainties surrounding injury definitions (Chapter 1) are not likely to cause a major problem for a study of this type unless important changes in data collection procedures coincide with the introduction of the wearing law.

For fatalities they find reductions of 18% for drivers and 25% for front-seat passengers. For those not directly affected by the law, they find increases of 27% for rear-seat passengers, 8% for pedestrians and 13% for cyclists. The value for rear-seat passengers is highly statistically significant and the other two values are on the borderline of significance. Harvey and Durbin [1986] conclude that there was an increase in fatalities to those not directly affected, but write that they cannot explain its origin. They specifically state their reluctance to accept changes in driving behavior as an explanation because of, among other reasons, the inconsistency of the fatality and injury findings.

As a possible explanation for part of the increase in rear-seat fatalities, Jones [1986] provides data suggesting possible migration of passengers unwilling to wear belts from front to rear seats, which were not covered by the legislation. I find this convincing for three reasons. First, I know with certainty of one specific case of its occurring. As it is hard to imagine anyone moving to the front seat because belt wearing was required in it, the direction, if not magnitude, of the effect is established. Second, interpreting the 27% increase as an identical increase in severe crash involvement by belted drivers in the face of an 18% reduction in driver deaths implies a when-used belt effectiveness that is unrealistically high. The third reason is the consistent finding of higher fatality reductions for passengers than drivers for essentially similar use rates, implying substantially higher when-used effectiveness for passengers, in contrast to a small difference in the opposite direction in Table 9-1; some of the reduction in front-passenger deaths may have occurred because of fewer front passengers.

The Harvey and Durbin [1986] estimates of reductions of 18% for drivers and 25% for front passengers give a weighted average of 20% as the estimated reduction in fatalities to affected occupants. This is quite close to the simple fatality count calculation of 23% in Fig. 10-6. Substituting $u_i = 40\%$ and $u_f = 90\%$ into Eqn 10-8 generates an estimate of 26%, which is in reasonable agreement with the observed value.

The medical effects of the UK's law were determined by Rutherford et al. [1985] by examining crashed-car occupants requiring hospital treatment. Patients arriving at 15 hospitals (eight in England, four in Northern Ireland, two in Scotland, and one in Wales) the year before and the year after the law were compared. The hospitals were chosen because of their high standards of data collection. The study finds a 15% reduction in patients brought to hospital, a 25% reduction in those requiring admission to wards, and a similar fall in bed occupancy. Larger reductions are found for front-seat passengers than for drivers.

Are There Cases in Which the Use of a Safety Belt Increases Injury?

I cannot conceive of any medical or other safety intervention which, in some cases, may not increase rather than decrease harm. Let us illustrate with an example from traffic. Every year a number of pedestrians walking on the sidewalk are killed by out of control vehicles. The existence of specific instances in which walking on the sidewalk led to death, while walking in the center of the fastest traffic lane would have been safer (well, certainly not less safe), while undoubtedly true, hardly has any bearing on whether one should walk on the sidewalk or the center of the fast lane. We choose the sidewalk not because it is always, under all circumstances, safer, but because it is, on average, safer. The same reasoning applies to all safety interventions, including use of safety belts.

Some types of injuries may increase with safety-belt use. Rutherford et al. [1985] concluded that fractures of the sternum and sprained necks appeared to have increased. Salmi et al. [1989] report increases in tharaco-lumbar spine injuries and serious cervical spine injuries following the French mandatory belt-wearing law. However, the decrease in injuries in general was much greater than these specific increases. Indeed, the injuries that increased in frequency might be substitutes for more serious injuries if no belt had been worn.

Casualty Changes in Other Jurisdictions

Wagenaar, Maybee, and Sullivan [1988] list 101 estimates of fatality reductions associated with introducing mandatory belt wearing in 27 jurisdictions, thus providing an average of over three estimates per jurisdiction. However, unlike the three estimates for the UK discussed above, these different estimates often vary widely. For example, for France from 21% to 50%; for New York State from 5% to 27%; for North Carolina from −7% (an increase of 7%) to 5%. Because the methods used to obtain some of the estimates (usually the high ones) are not technically defensible (six of them exceed the when-used effectiveness of 41%!) one cannot simply take the average as the best estimate. Accordingly, with present knowledge, there is no effective way to compare what actually happened in most jurisdictions with the values calculated using Eqn 10-8.

The main reason we do not have reliable estimates for fatality changes after wearing laws are introduced is because of the difficulty of measuring small effects in insufficiently large samples of data that are additionally changing for various other reasons. While estimates for individual US states are uncertain, a number of authors have estimated the effects for all states combined. The results obtained are: 7% by Partyka [1988]; 7% by Campbell, Stewart, and Campbell [1988]; 6% by Hoxie and Skinner [1987]; and 9% by Wagenaar, Maybee, and Sullivan [1988]. These estimates use several of the techniques mentioned earlier. The relatively good agreement between the overall national estimates, even though estimates for different states varied by large amounts, shows the advantage of combining states. Collectively, the studies show no change in the risk to non-affected road users. Use rate typically changed from about 16% to 45% when laws were passed [Wagenaar, Maybee, and Sullivan 1988]. Substituting these values into Eqn 10-8 calculates a reduction of 9.7%, similar to, but higher than, the reductions estimated directly from the data.

In addition to estimating reductions for individual US states, and for all states, Wagenaar, Maybee, and Sullivan [1988] also estimated reductions for two groups of states, those using secondary and those using primary enforcement, by applying an interrupted time-series analysis which included the use of adjacent states for control of other sources of variability. They find a 6.8% reduction for secondary enforcement states and a 9.9% reduction for primary enforcement states. Assuming a use rate increase from 16% to 40% for the secondary and from 16% to 55% for the primary states gives calculated fatality reductions of 7.8% and 13.6%, respectively, values reasonably close to, but larger than, those observed.

Switzerland provides a particularly interesting case, because the law that became applicable in January 1976 was repealed because of voter petition in July 1977 and subsequent court action, leading to wearing being no longer required after October 1977 [Grimm 1988; Huguenin 1988]. However, a new law became effective on November 1980, providing a unique natural experiment in which the independent variable (the law) changed from off to on, from on to off, and from off to on again. The results in Fig. 10-7 show clear effects at every law change.

COMPARISON BETWEEN OBSERVED AND ESTIMATED FATALITY REDUCTIONS

The fatality reductions estimated quantitatively are compared to the values calculated using Eqn 10-8 in Table 10-2. (Let us use *observed* to refer to estimates from field data, even though such estimates involve analyses and assumptions.) The first point to note is the extent of agreement; selective recruitment goes a long way to explain the actual changes in fatalities from changes in belt use, a point previously made [Evans 1988a] in comparing estimates for four US states [Williams and Lund 1988] with Eqn 10-8. Any additional factors, such as behavioral change, cannot be all that large, insofar as the observed effects are reasonably well explained without invoking them.

Beyond the relatively good agreement between the observed and estimated reductions, the next most striking feature of Table 10-2 is that all observed values, except one, are lower than estimated; for the exception, the values are identical. The most likely reason for this is that actual belt-use rates are systematically lower than those shown in Table 10-2, which are based on daytime observations. Mackay [1985] indicates that observational data suggest lower rates when pubs are closing. The data in Evans [1987b] show that belt use in fatal crashes is consistently lower at night than in the day. For example, FARS 1975-1983 data show 5.59% of fatally-injured drivers in crashes from 6:00 a.m. to 6:00 p.m. coded as belt users. The corresponding rate for 6:00 p.m. to 6:00 a.m. is 3.41%. Thus, for these pre-law data, the nighttime driver is only 60% as likely as the daytime driver to be wearing the belt. Other data in Evans [1987b] show similarly large effects. If one assumes, as an approximation, that half the fatalities are at night, and that use rates at night are 60% what they are during the day, then all use rates in Table 10-2 should be set to 80% of their observed daytime values (this means that for the UK the change is from 32% to 72% instead of from 40% to 90%). After such a use rate adjustment, 12 of the 14 estimated fatality reductions become lower than observed. The pre-law results in Evans [1987b] may overestimate differences when use rates increase. If one instead assumes that nighttime wearing rates are 80% of daytime rates, so that all wearing rates should be 90% of the values in Table 10-2, then agreement between the observations and calculations is remarkably close. No deviation is as large as 2 percentage points, and most are substantially less.

Thus, modestly lower wearing rates during nighttime hours accounts for the systematic differences between the observed and estimated reductions. There is

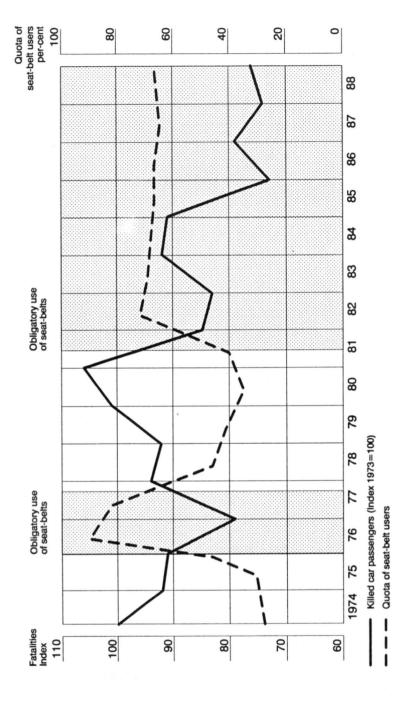

Figure 10-7. Car occupants killed and safety belt use rates in Switzerland, where a belt-use law was passed, repealed, and another law passed. Provided through the courtesy of R.D. Huguenin [1990].

Table 10-2. Comparisons of fatality reductions estimated using field data to the reductions calculated using Eqn 10-8

| | | | Fatality reductions | |
| | | Belt-use | From | |
Study	Population	change	data	Eqn 10-8
Wagenaar,	US states	16% to 45%	8.7%	9.7%
Maybee, and	US states (secondary)	16% to 40%	6.8%	7.8%
Sulivan [1988]	US states (primary)	16% to 55%	9.9%	13.6%
Harvey and Durbin [1986]	UK	40% to 90%	20%	25.8%
Partyka and	1983—all US states	0%* to 14.0%	2.7%	3.9%
Womble [1989]	1984—no-law states	0% to 14.4%	3.7%	4.1%
	1985—no-law states	0% to 19.8%	5.4%	5.6%
	1986—no-law states	0% to 23.3%	6.7%	6.7%
	1987—no-law states	0% to 29.7%	7.8%	8.6%
	1988—no-law states	0% to 34.0%	9.4%	10.0%
	1985—law states	0% to 40.9%	11.4%	12.3%
	1986—law states	0% to 47.1%	13.1%	14.5%
	1987—law states	0% to 49.8%	13.8%	15.5%
	1988—law states	0% to 50.0%	13.8%	15.6%

*Fatalities at observed belt-use rate compared to estimate for zero belt use.

no need to invoke other explanations, such as crash rates increasing more steeply with unwillingness to use belts than in Eqn 10-8 (or Fig. 10-4), or changed user risk taking.

REPEAL OF MANDATORY MOTORCYCLE HELMET-WEARING LAWS

Following the Highway Safety Act of 1966, the US federal government made passage of mandatory helmet-wearing laws for motorcycle drivers and passengers a precondition for the states to receive highway construction funds. All but three states passed such laws. In 1976, in response to pressures from many states, the US Congress revoked the financial penalties for nonenactment of helmet-wearing laws. In the next few years, just over half of the states repealed their laws; half repealing and half not repealing provides the optimum *natural experiment* to compare repeal and nonrepeal states.

The results of such a comparison are shown in Fig. 10-8, computed from the data in Chenier and Evans [1987]. The numbers along the horizontal axis give the states ordered by date of repeal, from 21 May 1976 for Rhode Island to 1 January 1982 for Louisiana. There are 27 data points for 26 states in Fig. 10-8; Louisiana appears twice as a result of repealing its law, passing another, and subsequently repealing this also. All the states may be identified from Table 2

Increase in motorcyclist fatalities, %

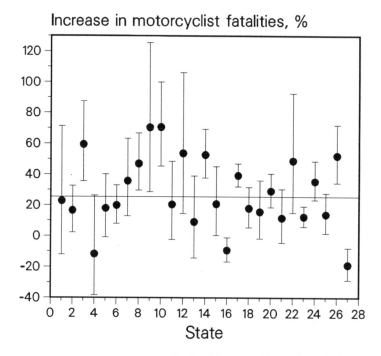

Figure 10-8. The change in motorcyclist fatalities after 27 mandatory helmet-wearing laws were repealed in the US. Based on data in Chenier and Evans [1987], which source identifies the states plotted.

of Chenier and Evans [1987], which presents them in the order plotted. The fatality change for each state is estimated by dividing the ratio of the number of fatalities in a period after the law was put into effect to the number in a period before the law by the corresponding ratio for all the fatalities in the nonrepeal states. Thus each estimate, and its corresponding error, is computed from four fatality frequencies in a manner similar to the calculations in Eqns 7-2 and 7-4. A minor difference is that the log transformation (Eqns 6 and 7 of Evans [1988b]) is used, as is required for large errors, because, logically, changes cannot be less than -100%, but can have any positive value. The pre-law period is from 1 January 1975 (the beginning of FARS) to three months before repeal; the post-law period is from three months after repeal to 31 December 1982. As the laws were repealed at haphazard times, and the repeal states show no obvious geographic groupings, taking the average over all the jurisdictions should eliminate spurious effects and provide a reliable estimate for the fatality change associated with repeal.

Nominally, 24 of the points indicate fatalities increased after repeal, compared to 3 indicating a decrease, so the data provide extremely strong evidence that repeal led to a substantial increase in fatalities. The weighted average of all 27 values, indicated by the horizontal line in Fig. 10-8, is $(25 \pm 4)\%$. The error limits for 17 values (or 63% of the 27 values) cross this value. As the error limits are one standard error, 68% of them are expected to include the true value, thus perhaps indicating weakly that a few data may depart more from the average than would be expected by chance.

There have been a number of other estimates of the effect of repeal on fatalities. Watson, Zador, and Wilks [1981] report a 40% increase using methodology criticized by Adams [1983], who claims that the data can also support a value close to zero. De Wolf [1986] reports an effect in the range of 4% to 10%, which might reasonably be interpreted as a point estimate of 7%. Fatality increases of 14% and 22% are reported by Graham and Lee [1986] after controlling for changes in registrations; the two values reflect different calculation assumptions. A 24% increase is reported by Hartunian et al. [1983].

Helmet Use Rates

An attempt to calculate increases in fatalities expected from repealing mandatory wearing requires estimating helmet-wearing rates in law and no-law states. Helmet use is observed as part of the 19 city survey sponsored by the National Highway Traffic Safety Administration. Over 18 000 observations in 1984 gave the following estimates:

	Helmet wearing rates	
	Drivers	Passengers
Daytime city use in law states	99.7%	98.4%
Daytime city use in no-law states	51.3%	34.8%

Consulting FARS data indicates lower wearing rates in crashes; for example, in law states, one in three motorcyclists killed was unhelmeted. By using the 28% when-used effectiveness of the helmet (Chapter 9), one can estimate (as previously done by Partyka [1988] and Evans [1987b] for safety belts) the number of helmeted motorcyclists involved in crashes of sufficient severity to kill unhelmeted motorcyclists, and thereby infer the wearing rates in crashes of the same severity. The results are:

	Helmet wearing rates	
	Drivers	Passengers
Severe crash involvement in law states	76%	61%
Severe crash involvement in no-law states	32%	12%

The use rates inferred from the fatality data are in all cases substantially lower than those observed directly in cities in daylight, although there is qualitative correspondence between all differences. The use rates inferred from FARS do not represent use rates averaged over the times and places that fatal crashes occur, because, as in the case of safety belts, there is every reason to expect that the non-users have higher crash rates than the users. However, such effects cannot come close to explaining the magnitude of the discrepancy, especially given the near 100% observed helmet use in the law states. With present knowledge there is no satisfactory resolution of these differences. Let us therefore take the simple average of both estimates, thereby obtaining:

	Helmet wearing rates	
	Drivers	Passengers
Best estimate for law states	88%	80%
Best estimate for no-law states	42%	23%

Comparison of Estimates with Observed Increases

Although there is no quantitative information available for selective recruitment in motorcycle helmet wearing, we use Eqn 10-8 in the absence of anything more specific for helmets. Substituting the best estimates gives fatality increases of 18% for drivers and 19% for passengers, for a weighted average of 18% (compared to 17% and 21%, for a weighted average of 18% from the simple calculation, Eqn 10-6).

The estimated reduction is in reasonable agreement with, but somewhat less than, the $(25 \pm 4)\%$ value from Chenier and Evans [1987]. It is also in reasonable agreement with three of the other estimates discussed earlier which are 14%, 22% and 24% (the other three estimates, 40%, 7% and 0% appear to be outside the general pattern).

MANDATORY USE LAWS AND BEHAVIOR CHANGES

In many cases road users react to safety changes in ways that lead to safety changes which are quite different from those intended (Chapter 11). It is therefore not surprising that such an explanation arose when large promised reductions in casualties from belt laws were not apparent in data. Adams [1985] claims that safety-belt laws induced increased driver risk taking that greatly diminished the safety benefits to those wearing the belts while increasing the risks to other road users. Adams [1983] also claims that the repeal of motorcycle helmet-wearing laws induced increased caution, so that the repeal did not affect motorcyclist fatalities.

When one takes into account selective recruitment, and the clear evidence that observed daytime use rates are higher than those during the nighttime high crash-risk hours, then estimated fatality reductions from increases in belt wearing are in satisfactory agreement with those few observed values based on sufficiently large populations to be estimated reliably. While the comparison provides no evidence of a behavioral change in response to the introduction of mandatory belt wearing, the weak nominal indication is that an increase in caution is more likely than a decrease. While there are suggestions of increases in deaths, but not injuries, of pedestrians and pedalcyclists following the UK's mandatory wearing law, no such effects are found in other jurisdictions [Wagenaar, Maybee, and Sullivan 1988; Huguenin 1988].

The observed increase in motorcyclist fatalities after repeal of helmet-wearing laws is in agreement with increases estimated assuming realistic changes in helmet wearing rates. Again, the weak nominal indication is that repealing the laws is more likely to have increased than decreased recklessness. Another possibility is that repeal made motorcycling more appealing, thereby increasing the exposure to risk.

Observational Studies

If compelling drivers to wear belts did indeed increase their risk taking, this ought to lead to observable consequences. Evans, Wasielewski, and von Buseck [1982] examined driver risk taking, as indicated by close following, for belt wearers and nonwearers in two jurisdictions. One was Michigan in 1978, with no belt law and a use rate observed in the study at 14%. The other was Ontario, Canada in 1980, with a mandatory wearing law and a use rate observed in the study of 51%, compared to a pre-law rate of 14%. Thus, 37% of the Ontario users were compelled users. In both jurisdictions, belt nonwearers were found to take higher driving risks. Making the assumption that behavior in Ontario before the law could be estimated by observed behavior in Michigan generated no evidence of any increase in risk taking in response to the law; indeed, the weak nominal indication was of a reduction in risk taking.

Lund and Zador [1984] and O'Neill et al. [1985] compared a number of driver behaviors in Newfoundland, Canada before and after that province acquired a mandatory law to the same behaviors in Nova Scotia, which did not have a law during the observation period. The behaviors examined were travel speeds, following headways, turning headways, and responses to yellow signals. None showed any indication of increased risk taking after the law. O'Neill et al. also report that drivers in England travelled significantly slower around sharp curves eight to nine months after the law than a year earlier, whereas other measures showed no evidence of change. They conclude that the evidence does not support any increase in driver risk taking.

Ideally, one would prefer to compare behavior in the same driver belted and unbelted than to look for differences between populations of belted and unbelted drivers. Streff and Geller [1988] attempted to do this by having the same subjects drive a five-horsepower go-cart around an oval test track. Four groups of subjects drove in two phases, each consisting of 15 circuits of the track. One group drove phase one unbelted and phase two belted, another the opposite, while a third group drove all trials unbelted and a fourth all belted. The behavioral measure was the average time to drive around the track (the reciprocal of the speed, which was typically about 20 km/h). The paper includes a graph showing this measure for each of the group's 30 circuits, plus two initial warm-up circuits.

Streff and Geller's [1988] plotted data show two dominant effects. First, a systematic learning effect (the time to complete the 30th lap is typically 10% less than the time to complete the first lap). Second, the group that changed from unbelted to belted contained a consistently slower group of drivers (with a shallower learning curve) than the other three groups. While the nominal indication from the graph is that those who switched from using belts to not using belts increased their speed more than those who did not change their belt-wearing status (that is, they are more cautious using the belts), the effect is small compared to the two dominant effects mentioned, and the authors conclude it is not statistically significant. However, they claim a statistically significant increase in speed (compared to the other groups) for those who changed from not wearing to wearing, an effect which seems to result mainly from speed increases that occurred some number of trials after the subjects first fastened the belts, rather than as a result of the belts. Their claim of a statistically significant effect due to the belts seems to me as unconvincing as their claim of no statistically significant difference between the speed of this same group and the others, notwithstanding that this group was the slowest of the four in 32 trials out of 32. I think that the only important conclusion from these interesting data is that they exclude the possibility that switching from belt use to non use (or vice versa) changed the speed at which the go-cart was driven by more than about two percent in either direction. A more general question than whether the results support that belt wearing influenced go-cart speed is whether the results of such a test have realistic transferal to the overlearned task of normal driving.

Based on reason alone, it is essentially certain that users change behavior in some ways in response to an intervention as clearly visible as wearing a belt or helmet. The empirical evidence collectively establishes that any such change is of small magnitude, and of unknown sign. The evidence suggests very weakly that a behavioral change in the direction of driving more carefully after belt laws are introduced is more likely than one in the opposite direction.

While the evidence cannot determine the sign of the behavioral response, it can dismiss beyond reasonable doubt any suggestions that users react in such a way to as to negate, or almost negate, expected casualty changes. There is no scenario of biases or changes that could plausibly suggest that the data in Fig. 10-8 are compatible with zero effect, or that the evidence on belt laws is so flawed that the effects are zero, or near zero. Following the point of Farber [1985], if former belt non-wearers are to retain their fatality risk unchanged after becoming wearers, they would have to increase their severe crash involvement rate by $1/(1 - E)$, where E is when-used belt effectiveness, assumed to be 42% (Chapter 9); that is, a 72% increase in crash rate would be required. Any increase approaching this would be observed readily, by, for example, insurance companies when jurisdictions experience large increases in belt use. An effect even 20% of this size would long since have been observed reliably, and the consequent approximate 15% increase in insurance premiums would have generated considerable public debate.

DIFFERENCES BETWEEN JURISDICTIONS

While over 80 mandatory belt-wearing laws are in effect, daytime use rates vary widely from over 90% in Australia, Finland, Japan, the UK, and West Germany to under 40% in some US states. Many jurisdictions, including 16 US states, have no laws and wearing rates of 20% or less are not uncommon. These differences have invited all sorts of interesting explanations in terms of differing national characteristics. I have often heard (fortunately less frequently in recent years) citizens from nations with no laws or low use rates invoking national or cultural characteristics as explanations. Examples are that the citizens are too independent thinking and individualistic to allow the government to tell them what to do (the explanation favored by those inclined towards chauvinistic jingoism) or too lawless and stupid to know what is good for them (favored by those inclined "to praise every century but this and every country but his own." [Gilbert, 1885])

Rather than being due to differences in national temperaments, it seems to me that the variations between jurisdictions result from legislative decisions responding to pressures from specific institutions, or in many cases, just one or two individuals. Victoria, Australia, had the first important mandatory wearing law largely because a few individuals, mainly physicians, vigorously sought it. Because of the esteem of those advocating mandatory belt wearing, and the favorable media coverage, wearing rates were high. After passage, there was widespread agreement of substantial reductions in casualties (some estimates now seem to have been clearly too high). With such positive experience it is not surprising that other Australian states soon passed similar laws.

I see no indications that the US has any greater or lesser intrinsic tendency to mandatory laws than Australia, or anywhere else. The first child restraint law in the US came into effect in Tennessee in January 1978 at a time when there were only a few comparable laws in effect in the world. The driving force was two Tennessee pediatricians. By June 1985, child restraint laws were in force throughout the entire US, whereas many of the countries which had passed adult belt-wearing legislation had no laws covering children and infants. No prediction based on stereotypical views of the role of government or political attitudes in different US states would have identified Tennessee as the most likely state to have the nation's first car-occupant restraint law. A similar comment applies to mandatory safety belt laws. In 1985 the US state with the highest belt-wearing rate was Texas; Massachusetts does not have a mandatory wearing law.

Wearing rates seem largely determined by the way laws are introduced and by media coverage, in addition to enforcement policies. Ireland required mandatory wearing in February 1979, yet wearing rates remained below 50% [Hearne 1981]. However, in adjacent Northern Ireland, rates reached the same high levels of over 90% observed in the rest of the UK after the mandatory wearing law came into effect in January 1983 [Rutherford et al. 1985, Table 18]. The high UK rates seem more related to positive media coverage and public acceptance than to enforcement, which is modest and non-obtrusive. A publicity campaign in Elmira, New York raised wearing rates from 49% to 77% [Williams et al. 1987]; there are other examples of public information increasing compliance with traffic laws [Shinar and McKnight 1985].

Campbell and Campbell [1988, p. 24–25] explain why mandatory belt-wearing was introduced into the US so much later than in other countries as follows:

One reason for the delay in passing seat belt legislation in the United States may have been a lack of early advocacy on the part of traffic safety leadership groups. In the absence of vigorous support by leadership groups, there was little movement toward seat belt laws during the 1960s and 70s. Illustrative is the fact that in the late 1960s, the newly created National Highway Safety Bureau (NHSB) of the US Department of Transportation (DOT) promulgated 17 different state standards touching almost every area of highway safety, none of which had anything to do with seat belt use. It was not until 1984 that, for the first time, DOT publicly endorsed seat belt laws.

According to Campbell and Campbell [1986; 1988], a factor that almost certainly delayed consideration of wearing laws was the debate centered on choosing between automatic passive restraint systems, such as airbags, and belt laws. This point is also made by Trinca [1984, p. 4], representing the Royal Australasian College of Surgeons, which played a pivotal role in Victoria making belt wearing mandatory, who writes (before the US had any mandatory laws):

The arguments for passive restraint, for air bags as an alternative to seat belts, for exemption against seat belt wearing produce a smoke screen that has successfully delayed in many countries and in the U.S.A. actually prevented, the introduction of mandatory seat restraint laws.

Eventually all cars in the US were required to to be equipped with passive devices for the driver and right-front-passenger seats. Graham [1989] gives a fascinating account of the over two decades of squabbling that culminated in this decision. In reviewing Graham's [1989] book, Campbell [1989] writes:

Another irony: the sight of people long associated with highway safety and the need for occupant restraint standing in opposition to seat belt laws. I am still dumbfounded that both [former NHTSA Administrators] Claybrook and Haddon presented barriers to belt laws.

Almost totally absent from the airbag versus safety belt debate [Graham 1989] was any focus on the relative effectiveness of these different approaches to occupant protection. It seems that the technical question of which approach would save more lives was not an important ingredient of the debate, because many of the key participants had neither the interest nor the competence to address it. Yet one early well-designed study [Wilson and Savage 1973] showed the fatality-reducing effectiveness of airbags to be about half that of lap/shoulder belts (Table 9-7), devices then already being fitted to all new cars. It is therefore not surprising that airbags are now offered not as complete restraint systems, but as supplements to the primary restraint system, the lap/shoulder belt. There is even a product liability case pending in New York in which an automobile manufacturer is being sued in the death of an unbelted occupant, the claim being that the installed airbag discouraged the deceased from wearing the belt that it is claimed would have prevented her death. In many more cases manufacturers are sued for non-installation of airbags, and it is entirely within the rules of the game for the same manufacturer to lose one case of each type on the same day. The degree to which product-liability litigation in the US bears no resemblance to that anywhere else in the world is effectively documented by Babcock [1988], who compares how the same injury in the same crash would be handled in a number of US states, compared to how the same situation would be handled in eight other Western democracies.

The different handling of occupant protection legislation in the US compared to the handling of occupant protection legislation in all other countries also is probably related to the uniquely powerful role of the legal industry in the US, and its dominance over technical and other considerations. As Lamm [1989] points out, the US has 5% of the world's population, but almost 70% of its lawyers (there are 700 000 lawyers in the US); the US has 25 times as many lawyers per capita as Japan. Even just one portion of the burden the legal industry imposes on US society, what Huber [1988] calls the "tort liability tax," he estimates costs the nation $300 billion per year—more than the cost of defense, and four times the total cost of traffic crashes (Chapter 1). Comparing the US with other nations, none of which has a situation which is remotely comparable, shows no discernible benefit from such staggering expenditures. Essentially everything that happens in the US leads to wealth on a grand scale being transferred to the legal industry. The situation does not seem susceptible to remedial measures because the benefactors define and administer the rules.

If the energies and resources of the airbags versus belts debate had been focused on passing mandatory belt-wearing laws, and on increasing use rates, there can be no doubt that large numbers of lives would have been saved. Partyka [1988] estimates that in 1984, 1985, 1986, 1987, and 1988 US belt-wearing laws prevented 239, 850, 2016, 2551, and 2956 occupant deaths, respectively (assuming a 40% effectiveness, her lower-bound estimate). The increasing numbers reflect the increasing numbers of states with laws, and increasing use rates in these states as well as increases induced in the no-law states by increases in the law states. If, rather than starting in 1984, this sequence had started in 1978 (Canada's two most populous provinces, Ontario and Quebec, have had compulsory wearing since 1976), then by 1984 over 8000 lives would already have been saved. This is of course based on the relatively low US wearing rates. If the US had national wearing rates comparable to those in Australia or the UK, rather than pre-law rates, there would be a decrease of 8300 deaths per year. Whatever plausible scenario one considers leads to the inescapable conclusion that the delay in introducing mandatory wearing laws in the US compared to most other nations, and the uncertainty raised regarding their value, has led to the deaths of tens of thousands of occupants. It seems improbable that such losses will be balanced by future reductions from the passive approach adopted after so much debate, effort, and litigation [Graham 1989] by the US, an approach that has found no adherents in any other nation in the world.

CONCLUSIONS

Over 80 jurisdictions have laws compelling drivers and some passengers to wear safety belts. Wearing rates vary widely, from over 90% in Australia, the UK, and West Germany to under 40% in some jurisdictions. Among the factors influencing wearing rates is publicity and level of enforcement. The highest precision evaluation is for the UK's law, where belt use rose rapidly from 40% to 90% in a large population of affected occupants. The law reduced fatalities to drivers and front-seat passengers by 20%. For smaller use rate increases, and for smaller populations (that is, in nearly all other cases), it is not possible to directly measure fatality changes. They can be reliably estimated using an equation based on the known when-used effectiveness of the belts together with a quantification of *selective recruitment* effects—the tendency of those changing from non-use to use to be safer than average drivers. The equation fits well the few data points that are reliably known. The repeal of mandatory helmet-wearing laws in the US increased motorcyclist fatalities by about 25%. If realistic assumptions are made about nighttime use rates for belts and helmets, the agreement between predicted and observed changes is sufficiently close to preclude any possibility that mandatory use laws induce substantial changes in driver behavior; the weak nominal indication is that such laws more likely decrease than increase driver risk taking.

REFERENCES

Adams, J.G.U. Public safety legislation and the risk compensation hypothesis; the example of motorcycle helmet legislation. *Environment and Planning C: Government and Policy* 1:193–203; 1983.

Adams, J.G.U. Smeed's law, seat belts and the emperor's new clothes. In: Evans, L.; Schwing, R.C., editors. *Human Behavior and Traffic Safety*. New York, NY: Plenum Press, p. 193–248; 1985.

Andreassend, D.C. Victoria and the seat belt law, 1971 on. *Human Factors* 18:563–600; 1976.

Babcock, C.W. Could we alone have this? Comparative legal analysis of product liability law and the case for modest reform. *Loyola of Los Angeles International and Comparative Law Journal* 10:321–359; 1988.

Broughton, J. Predictive models of road accident fatalities. *Traffic Engineering and Control* 29:296–300; 1988.

Campbell, B.J. The relationship of seat belt law enforcement to level of belt use. Chapel Hill, NC: University of North Carolina Highway Safety Research Center Report HSRC–TR72; June 1987.

Campbell, B.J. Review of Graham, J.D. *Auto Safety—Assessing America's Performance. Accident Analysis and Prevention* 21:595–596; 1989.

Campbell, B.J.; Campbell, F.A. Seat belt law experience in four foreign countries compared to the United States. Falls Church, VA: AAA Foundation for Traffic Safety; December 1986.

Campbell, B.J.; Campbell, F.A. Injury reduction and belt use associated with occupant restraint laws. In: Graham, J.D., editor. *Preventing Automobile Injury—New Findings from Evaluation Research*. Dover, MA: Auburn House, p. 24–50; 1988.

Campbell, B.J.; Stewart, J.R.; Campbell, F.A. Changes with death and injury associated with safety belt laws 1985–1987. Chapel Hill, NC: University of North Carolina Highway Safety Research Center Report HSRC–A138; December 1988.

Chenier, T.C.; Evans, L. Motorcyclist fatalities and the repeal of mandatory helmet wearing laws. *Accident Analysis and Prevention* 19:133–139; 1987.

de Wolf, V. A. The effect of helmet law repeal on motorcycle fatalities. Washington, DC: National Highway Traffic Safety Administration, report DOT HS 807 065; December 1986.

Evans, L. Human behavior feedback and traffic safety. *Human Factors* 27:555–576; 1985.

Evans, L. Estimating fatality reductions from increased safety belt use. *Risk Analysis* 7:49–57; 1987a.

Evans, L. Belted and unbelted driver accident involvement rates compared. *Journal of Safety Research* 18:57–64; 1987b.

Evans, L. Comments (on two papers on mandatory safety belt use laws, and reflections on broader issues). In: Graham, J.D., editor. *Preventing Automobile Injury—New Findings from Evaluation Research*. Dover, MA: Auburn House, p. 73–83; 1988a.

Evans, L. Rear seat restraint system effectiveness in preventing fatalities. *Accident Analysis and Prevention* 20:129–136; 1988b.

Evans, L.; Wasielewski, P. Risky driving related to driver and vehicle characteristics. *Accident Analysis and Prevention* 15:121–136; 1983.

Evans, L.; Wasielewski, P.; von Buseck, C.R. Compulsory seat belt usage and driver risk-taking behavior. *Human Factors* 24:41–48; 1982.

Farber, E.I. Comment on p. 111 of Evans, L; Schwing, R.C., editors. *Human Behavior and Traffic Safety*. New York, NY: Plenum Press; 1985.

Geller, E.S. A delayed reward strategy for large-scale motivation of safety belt use: a test of long-term impact. *Accident Analysis and Prevention* 16:457–463; 1984.

Gilbert, W.S. *The Mikado*. 1885.

Graham, J.D. *Auto Safety—Assessing America's Performance*. Dover, MA: Auburn House; 1989.

Graham, J.D.; Lee, Y. Behavioral response to safety regulation: the case of motorcycle helmet-wearing legislation. *Policy Sciences* 19:253; 1986.

Grimm, A.C. International restraint use laws. University of Michigan Transportation Research Institute, Ann Arbor, MI: *UMTRI Research Review* 18(4):1–9; 1988.

Grimm, A.C. Update to Grimm [1988], personal communication; 1990.

Hartunian, N.S.; Smart, C.N.; Willemain, T.R.; Zador, P.L. The economics of deregulation: lives and dollars lost due to repeal of motorcycle helmet laws. *Journal of Health Politics, Policy and Law* 8:76; 1983.

Harvey, A.C.; Durbin, J. The effects of seat belt legislation on British road casualties: a case study in structural time series modeling. *Journal of the Royal Statistical Society* A149:187–227; 1986.

Hearne, R. The initial impact of the safety-belt legislation in Ireland. Dublin, Ireland: An Foras Forbartha, technical report RS 255; 1981.

Hedlund, J. Casualty reductions: results from safety belt use laws. In: *Effectiveness of Safety Belt Use Laws: A Multinational Examination*. Washington, DC: National Highway Traffic Safety Administration, report DOT HS 807 018; October 1986.

Hoxie, P.; Skinner, D. Fatality reductions from mandatory seatbelt usage laws. Cambridge, MA: Transportation Systems Center; 1987.

Huber, P.W. *Liability: The Legal Revolution and Its Consequences*. New York, NY: Basic Books; 1988.

Huguenin, R.D. The concept of risk and behaviour models in traffic psychology. *Ergonomics* 31:557–569; 1988.

Huguenin, R.D. Personal communication; 1990.

Hunter, W.H.; Stewart, R.J.; Stutts, J.C.; Rodgman, E.A. Overrepresentation of non-belt users in traffic crashes. Association for the Advancement of Automotive Medicine, 32nd Annual Proceedings, Seattle, WA, 237–256; 12–14 September 1988.

Jones, D.H. Comment on the paper by Harvey and Durbin. *Journal of the Royal Statistical Society* A149:219–219; 1986.

Lamm, R.D. Lawyers and lawyering—the legal system and its cost to American society. *Vital Speeches of the Day* 55:206–209; 1989.

Lund, A.K.; Zador, P. Mandatory belt use and driver risk taking. *Risk Analysis* 4:41–53; 1984.

Mackay, M. Seat belt use under voluntary and mandatory conditions and its effect on casualties. In: Evans, L.; Schwing, R.C., editors. *Human Behavior and Traffic Safety*. New York, NY: Plenum Press, p. 259–278; 1985.

Nagayama, Y. The effects of information and education on traffic accident decrease, behavior change and attitude change. *IATSS Research—Journal of International Association of Traffic and Safety Sciences* 14(1):(in press) 1990.

National Highway Traffic Safety Administration. Occupant protection trends in 19 cities. Washington, DC; November 1989.

O'Neill, B.; Lund, A.K.; Zador, P.; Ashton, S. Mandatory belt use and driver risk taking: an empirical evaluation of the risk-compensation hypothesis. In: Evans, L.; Schwing, R.C., editors. *Human Behavior and Traffic Safety*. New York, NY: Plenum Press, p. 93–107; 1985.

Partyka, S.C. Lives saved by seat belts from 1983 through 1987. Washington, DC: National Highway Traffic Safety Administration; June 1988.

Partyka, S.C.; Womble, K.B. Projected lives savings from greater belt use. Washington, DC: National Highway Traffic Administration Research Notes; June 1989.

Robertson, L.S.; Kelly, A.B.; O'Neill, B.; Wixom, C.W.; Eiswirth, R.S.; Haddon, W., Jr. A controlled study of the effect of television messages on safety belt use. American Journal of Public Health 64:1071–1080; 1974.

Rutherford, W.H.; Greenfield, T.; Hayes, H.R.M.; Nelson, J.K. The medical effects of seat belt legislation in the United Kingdom. London, UK: Her Majesty's Stationery Office, Department of Health and Social Security, Office of the Chief Scientist, Research Report number 13; 1985.

Salmi, L.R.; Thomas, H.; Fabry, J.J.; Girard, R. The effect of the 1979 French seat-belt law on the nature and severity of injuries to front-seat occupants. Accident Analysis and Prevention 21 589–594; 1989.

Scott, P.P.; Willis, P.A. Road casualties in Great Britain the first year with seat belt legislation. Crowthorne, Berkshire, UK: Transport and Road Research Laboratory report 9; 1985.

Shinar, D.; McKnight, A.J. The effects of enforcement and public information on compliance. In: Evans, L.; Schwing, R.C., editors. Human Behavior and Traffic Safety. New York, NY: Plenum Press, p. 385–415; 1985.

Streff, F.M.; Geller, E.S. An experimental test of risk compensation: between-subject versus within-subject analyses. Accident Analysis and Prevention 20:277–287; 1988.

Trinca, G.W. Thirteen years of seat belt usage—how great the benefits. SAE paper 840192. Warrendale, PA: Society of Automotive Engineers; 1984. (Also included in Restraint technologies: front seat occupant protection. SAE special publication P-141: p. 1–5; 1984).

von Buseck, C.R.; Evans, L.; Schmidt, D.E.; Wasielewski, P. Seat belt usage and risk taking in driving behavior. SAE paper 800388. Warrendale, PA: Society of Automotive Engineers; 1980. (Also included in Accident causation. SAE special publication SP–461, p. 45–49; 1980).

Wagenaar, A.C.; Maybee, R.G.; Sullivan, K.P. Mandatory seat belt laws in eight states: a time-series evaluation. Journal of Safety Research 19:51–70; 1988.

Wasielewski, P. Speed as a measure of driver risk: observed speeds versus driver and vehicle characteristics. Accident Analysis and Prevention 16:89–103; 1984.

Watson, G.S.; Zador, P.L.; Wilks, A. Helmet use, helmet use laws, and motorcyclist fatalities. American Journal of Public Health 71:297–300; 1981.

Williams, A.F.; Lund, A.K.; Preusser, D.E.; Blomberg, R.D. Results of a seat belt use law enforcement and publicity campaign in Elmira, New York. Accident Analysis and Prevention 19:243–249; 1987.

Williams, A.F.; Lund, A.K. Mandatory seat belt use laws and occupant crash protection in the United States: present status and future prospects. In: Graham, J.D., editor. Preventing Automobile Injury—New Findings From Evaluation Research. Dover, MA: Auburn House, p. 51–72; 1988.

Wilson, R.A.; Savage, C.M. Restraint system effectiveness—a study of fatal accidents. Proceedings of Automotive Safety Engineering Seminar, sponsored by Automotive Safety Engineering, Environmental Activities Staff, General Motors Corporation; 20–21 June 1973.

11 User Responses to Changes in Traffic Systems

INTRODUCTION

It has been recognized as obvious since antiquity that humans change their behavior in response to the perceived probability and severity of harm. We walk more carefully when the ground is wet or icy than when it is dry; we walk more carefully on rough surfaces when barefoot than when wearing shoes. A warrior clad in armor may accept a greater risk of being struck by a weapon than one not so clad, and so on. Shakespeare writes, "Best safety lies in fear" [*Hamlet*, Act I, Scene 3]. The question of road users responding to changes in the safety of traffic systems has also long been recognized. More than half a century ago, in a paper entitled "A theoretical field-analysis of automobile driving," Gibson and Crooks [1938, p. 458] write:

> More efficient brakes on an automobile will not in themselves make driving the automobile any safer. Better brakes will reduce the absolute size of the minimum stopping zone, it is true, but the driver soon learns this new zone and, since it is his field-zone ratio which remains constant, he allows only the same relative margin between field and zone as before.

A decade later Smeed [1949, p. 13] writes:

> It is frequently argued that it is a waste of energy to take many of these steps to reduce accidents. There is a body of opinion that holds that the provision of better roads, for example, or the increase in sight lines merely enables the motorist to drive faster, and the result is the same number of accidents as previously. I think there will nearly always be a tendency of this sort, but I see no reason why this regressive tendency should always result in exactly the same number of accidents as would have occurred in the absence of active measures for accident reduction. Some measures are likely to cause more accidents and others less, and we should always choose the measures that cause less.

This chapter is devoted to examining user reactions that were observed following various safety changes in traffic systems. A formalism to organize such user responses systematically is developed. Some explanations of user reactions to safety interventions, and broader attempts to model driver behavior, are then discussed.

HUMAN BEHAVIOR FEEDBACK

Let us suppose that some change is introduced into a traffic system that is expected to change safety by some fraction, say ΔS_{Eng}, assuming users continue to behave exactly as they did before the change. The subscript denotes that the change is of an engineering nature. For example, if design changes to a guardrail are estimated by engineering methods to reduce the probability of driver death on impact by 10%, then ΔS_{Eng} would be 10% for drivers killed crashing into the guardrail. We use ΔS_{Eng} more generally to indicate fractional reductions in some harm measure (crashes, fatalities) expected from systems changes if users do not alter their behavior in response to these changes. The change might be a higher or lower speed limit, equipping vehicles with devices aimed at reducing fatality or injury risk, transferring to heavier vehicles which have lower fatality and injury risks, or mandating belt or helmet wearing. While safety interventions always aim at producing positive values of ΔS_{Eng}, there are other changes motivated by different considerations, such as saving fuel in the case of smaller cars, for which the values of ΔS_{Eng} are negative.

Because road users may alter their behavior, the actual realized percent safety change, represented by ΔS_{Act}, may differ from ΔS_{Eng}. These quantities can be considered to be related in the following simple way:

$$\Delta S_{Act} = (1 + f)\, \Delta S_{Eng}, \qquad \text{Eqn 11-1}$$

where f is a feedback parameter which characterizes the degree to which users respond to the safety change. In this context feedback is synonymous with user reaction, behavior change, or interactive effects in the system. If users do not change behavior in response to the safety change, then $f = 0$, and the safety change is just as expected on engineering grounds. If the safety change is in the expected direction, but of lesser magnitude than expected, then $-1 < f < 0$, and the safety change is discounted compared to the expected amount. If the safety change has no effect, then $f = -1$.

In order to discover what values of f really occur, we consult the literature. There we find responses in ranges beyond those illustrated above. Because of this rich variety, I recommend the term *human behavior feedback* rather than the many other terms, such as risk compensation and danger compensation, which have appeared; every one of these other terms implies that user reactions are confined to a narrower spectrum than evidence shows to be the case. A stronger reason why such terms should not be used is that they go beyond describing the phenomenon, but rather, without justifiable evidence, also imply a knowledge of the mechanism leading to the effect. The progression in science is first to organize what is observed, and then to try to explain it, rather than name the observations with the explanation.

The studies reviewed in the literature are placed in two broad categories; first, those with $\Delta S_{Eng} > 0$, which are aimed at increasing safety; second, those with $\Delta S_{Eng} < 0$ which are expected to decrease safety, but are introduced for other reasons. We use *expected* to mean the change expected in the absence of user response, even if we know enough to really expect user response. From a formal point of view, there is no need to treat changes expected to increase and changes expected to decrease safety as separate cases; Eqn 11-1 applies equally to positive and negative values of ΔS_{Eng}. Because treating them together would involve using language that flows awkwardly against common usage we instead treat positive values first, and then treat negative values.

Another advantage of treating positive and negative values of ΔS_{Eng} separately is that it facilitates graphical representation (Figs 11-1 and 11-2). As we read up the page, f increases in Fig. 11-1, but decreases in Fig. 11-2, so that safety increases as we go up the page for both figures. These figures build on those in Evans [1985a], and include only effects supported by the discussion below or the reference cited; a ? indicates my judgment of an uncertain result or interpretation. Interventions reviewed below are associated with one of five regions of the human behavior feedback parameter, f, as indicated in the figures; the level of uncertainty is generally too high to estimate specific numerical values of f.

INTERVENTIONS AIMED AT INCREASING SAFETY

1. Safety Increase Greater Than Expected ($f > 0$)

There are various indications that when the nationwide 55 mph speed limit was imposed in the US in 1974, various crash, injury, and fatality rates on roads unaffected by the change also declined. As such changes were coincident with many other major disruptions, it is not possible to associate them confidently with the 55 mph speed limit (which was instigated as a fuel-saving measure). However, the possibility that reducing a speed limit on the Interstate system could generate spillover effects of the type discussed in Chapter 5 raises the possibility of safety increases beyond those computed for the intervention.

2. Safety Increase as Expected ($f = 0$)

It is exceedingly improbable that any intervention of which road users are aware can have $f = 0$ exactly. However, this value is of particular interest because of its interpretation, even though the probability is essentially zero that any specific

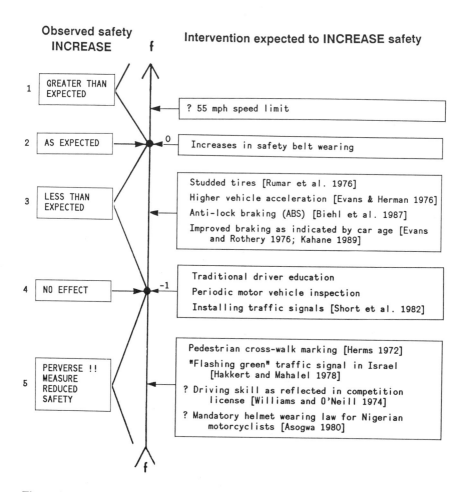

Figure 11-1.   Human behavior feedback for safety changes expected to *increase* safety.

exact numerical value of *f*, including *f* = 0, will occur. Some values of *f* very close to zero must arise for cases in which most road users are unaware of the safety intervention, such as side-guard beams in car doors. Although some road users might react to the national fatality data or to news reports, it is difficult to see how such inputs could affect net harm (in the short term) by more than a microscopic amount.

One area in which there has been much focus over possible user reactions is that of driver-restraint use (Chapter 10). It seems to me essentially impossible that such prominently visible and widely discussed items as safety belts and

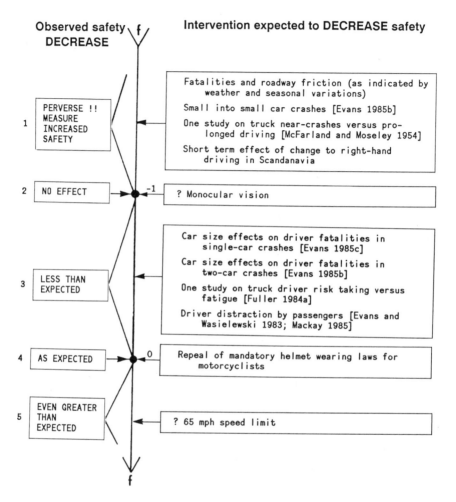

Figure 11-2. Human behavior feedback for safety changes expected to *reduce* safety.

helmets would not induce some change in user behavior. Thus, on logical grounds, it seems almost impossible that f would be exactly equal to zero. Such an observation is little more than a truism of no practical importance. What is important is the magnitude (including of course the sign) of *f*.

In Chapter 10 we find that observed fatality reductions from increases in safety belt use rates are in essential agreement with reductions calculated based on realistic estimates of changes in belt use, selective recruitment, and the effectiveness of belts in crashes. Such agreement between actual and expected changes precludes the possibility that f can differ much from 0. This finding is further corroborated by field studies in which the behavior of drivers compelled to wear belts is found indistinguishable from estimated behavior of non-wearers, and by a test track study in which the change from wearing to non-wearing, and from non-wearing to wearing, produced no observable systematic changes in chosen speed. Collectively, the evidence suggests weakly that drivers obliged to wear belts are more likely to increase than to decrease caution; that is, f is more likely to be positive than negative. While available evidence does not lead to a calculated numerical value for f, I believe it does place f in the region $-0.1 < f < 0.2$. The evidence (Chapter 10) precludes beyond doubt that f could be close to -1. If $f > 0$, an explanation could be that the act of fastening the belt reminds the driver of the possibility of crashing, and thereby induces more careful driving. As the evidence places f close to 0, we assume $f = 0$ for the case of mandatory belt-wearing laws.

3. Safety increase less than expected ($-1 < f < 0$)

Rumar et al. [1976] unobtrusively measured speeds maintained on a curve by Swedish drivers in cars with studded or unstudded tires under actual highway conditions. They find that cars with studded tires were driven faster, but that the overall safety margin, taking account of estimated frictional forces, was still greater for these vehicles than for cars with unstudded tires. Thus, cars with studded tires were less likely to skid than those without, but not as much less as the increased friction of the studded tires alone would indicate.

Evans and Herman [1976] investigated how a car's acceleration capabilities affected the last moment a driver in a stationary car was willing to cross in front of an oncoming car. The study was performed on two nonpublic roads intersecting at right angles, with the oncoming car driven at constant speed. The acceleration capabilities of the car driven by the subjects could be set by the experimenter at normal (high performance) or restricted (low performance). The same subject performed a number of series of trials alternatively under these conditions, with each series being preceded by a number of standing starts to familiarize the subject with the condition. Under the higher acceleration condition, subjects were prepared to cross with a gap 0.37 s shorter than under the lower acceleration condition. This compares to a physical safety margin difference of 0.50 s. Thus most, but not all, of the 0.50 s increase in safety margin was consumed by accepting shorter gaps.

Anti-lock braking systems (ABS) use electronic controls to maintain wheel rotation, and thereby maximum vehicle control with near optimal braking, rather than allowing the wheels to lock under hard braking, as in non-ABS. This increases vehicle stability, especially when tire/roadway friction is reduced or varying, as when the pavement is wet, and generally reduces the minimum stopping distance. The technical advantages of such systems is demonstrated clearly by Rompe, Schindler, and Wallrich [1988] in test track experiments using two instrumented cars, one with and one without ABS, but otherwise similar. Shorter braking distances and superior obstacle avoidance are found for five driving tests simulating driving maneuvers with a high crash risk element (straight line braking, braking on a slippery curve, etc.). Based on an analysis of historical traffic crash data for a non-ABS vehicle fleet, Langwieder [1986] predicts that all vehicles having ABS in Germany could diminish severe crashes by 10 to 15%, which, in the present formalism is an estimate of ΔS_{Eng}. Biehl, Aschenbrenner, and Wurm [1987] estimated ΔS_{Act} by comparing the crash experience of groups of Munich taxi drivers randomly assigned vehicles with and without ABS. They report decreases in the numbers of some types of crashes, but increases in others, for no net overall change. It appeared that the ABS was inducing behavioral changes, such as reductions in caution on snow and ice, beyond those justified by the advantage of ABS under such circumstances. Because the severity of such apparently induced crashes was less than that for the crashes prevented, the study suggests that the ABS reduces harm, but by less than expected. Additional data from German insurance companies show that vehicles equipped with ABS tend to have higher crash rates than similar vehicles not so equipped, possibly due to riskier drivers choosing to purchase the ABS [Huguenin 1990].

Two other studies indirectly suggest that improved braking may be used for purposes other than safety. In both studies, car age serves as a surrogate for braking, because it is plausible that as vehicles age, their stopping distances increase as tires and brakes deteriorate. Evans and Rothery [1976] examined observational data on traffic behavior at two signalized intersections and find that, when cars stopped, newer cars used higher levels of deceleration than older cars. When cars proceeded, drivers of newer cars were more likely than were drivers of older cars to enter the intersections after the onset of red (that is, to be in violation of the traffic code). They comment, "It is possible that the drivers of older vehicles are adjusting their behaviour to compensate for the reduced mechanical condition of their vehicles" (p. 569). Kahane [1989] examines rear-end crashes, and finds a highly regular pattern in which the probability that a car was struck in the rear, given that it was involved in a crash, declines systematically with car age. If a seven-year-old car was involved in a crash, the probability that it was struck on the rear is about 30% lower than the corresponding probability for new cars. Thus the findings of Evans and Rothery [1976] and Kahane [1989] suggest behavioral responses to cars being in newer condition, with better braking likely being the dominant factor. Although it is not possible to infer whether the newer vehicles still lead to a net safety increase, we assume this to be the case, and therefore categorize improved braking, as indicated by car age, as $-1 < f < 0$. Even more difficult to categorize, and therefore not shown in Fig. 11-1, is a simulator study which finds that improved roadway delineation is associated with faster curve entry speed [Ranney and Gawron 1986].

4. Safety Measure Has No Effect ($f = -1$)

In principle, one can never show that an intervention has no effect, only that its effect is less than some value. Indeed, as stressed in Chapter 1, it is almost inconceivable that one variable will be entirely unaffected by another for which there is any conceivable avenue of influence. The inclusion of driver education and mandatory vehicle inspection in this category is based on an absence of any indication of a safety effect, although many studies have examined such questions, usually with a view to showing efficacy. Haddon [1980, p. 51] writes, "No one has yet shown with the required formal research if periodic motor vehicle inspection makes any clear difference." Findings of reductions in specific types of crashes, such as those in which bald tires were a major factor, do not constitute proof of efficacy, because the compelled purchase of new tires will likely increase other types of crashes. As in the case of better brakes, bald tires affect the mix of crashes, but with an unknown influence on the total number. The inclusion of traffic signals (which are introduced mainly to reduce delay) is based on the study of Short, Woelfl, and Chang [1982], who find that introducing traffic signals influences the types of crashes without affecting the total number.

5. Perverse Effect—Safety Measure Reduces Safety ($f < -1$)

Herms [1972] investigated the effect on pedestrian safety of painted pedestrian crosswalks. During a five-year observation period, 177 pedestrians were hit in 400 marked (or painted) crosswalks compared to 31 hit in 400 unmarked crosswalks. This included 18 fatalities in the marked crosswalks versus 3 fatalities in the unmarked crosswalks. Part of the difference was due to more pedestrian traffic at the marked crosswalks. However, relative to the numbers of pedestrians using the crosswalks, approximately twice as many pedestrians were struck in the marked crosswalks as in the unmarked crosswalks. This large-scale, well-executed study provides clear evidence of a case in which a safety improvement led to a dramatic reduction in safety. It would appear that the painted crosswalk induced a sense of security in the pedestrians that was not justified by any increase in caution on the part of the drivers approaching it.

Hakkert and Mahalel [1978] examined the effect of the *blinking green* phase of signals in Israel on crash rates. The green light is set to blink for the last two or three seconds of the green phase to warn drivers of the impending yellow phase, and thereby reduce the probability that drivers are trapped in the so-called *dilemma zone* [Gazis, Herman, and Maradudin 1960; Herman, Olson, and Rothery 1963].

Based on various before versus after comparisons, Hakkert and Mahalel [1978] conclude that the installation of the blinking green phase led to an increase rather than the intended decrease in crashes. Klein, Zaidel, and Mahalel [1983], using a movie film technique, conclude that the blinking green places additional decision pressure on the driver and creates greater opportunity for error. It is also tempting to surmise that the drivers were attempting to use the additional information provided by the blinking green to increase their chances of clearing the intersection before the onset of red, rather than to increase their safety, as intended. The blinking green stimulated an early decision to proceed, which sometimes had to be changed to a decision to stop, hence precipitating increased numbers of rear-end crashes. These findings have implications relative to recurrent proposals for *count-down* traffic signals that indicate the amount of green time remaining.

As discussed in Chapter 6, Williams and O'Neill [1974] find that on-the-road crash rates of Sports Car Club of America national competition license holders are higher than those of matched comparison drivers. This would be an example of a safety measure (increased skill) producing a perverse safety effect only under the assumption that the increased skill acquired in obtaining this license led to higher risk driving, and consequently higher crash rates. However, another interpretation is that high risk, high crash rate, drivers sought the special license, and without the skills honed in obtaining it, their crash rates might have been even higher; hence the ? in Fig. 11-1.

Asogwa [1980] examined motorcyclist fatalities in Anabra State, Nigeria, before and after the introduction of a law mandating the wearing of helmets. A substantial increase in fatalities (from 5 to 18) and injuries (70 to 145) occurred in a two-year period after the legislation, compared to a two-year period before the legislation. The number of registered motorcycles also increased from 5303 to 7071 giving before and after rates of 94 and 255 fatalities per 100 000 registered motorcycles per two years, and 13.2 and 20.5 injuries per thousand registered motorcycles per two years. Thus, after the introduction of the law, the data indicate that the fatality rate increased by 171% and the injury rate by 55%. Taken at face value, the data indicate large reductions in safety following a change expected to increase safety. However, given uncertainties in the data (for example, ongoing improvements in data collection completeness could generate a false indication of increased casualties), and how surprising the result is in the context of studies discussed in Chapter 10 of helmet-use laws involving enormously more data, I have characterized the study with a ? in Fig 11-1. It is possible that it could be a real effect, but highly jurisdiction dependent.

CHANGES EXPECTED TO REDUCE SAFETY

In many cases it is arbitrary whether we think of a change in one direction as increasing safety or in the opposite direction as reducing safety. Thus we can think of switching to a larger car as increasing safety, or switching to a smaller car as decreasing safety. In the same way, a number of items in Fig. 11-1 could be transferred to Fig. 11-2, and vice versa.

1. Perverse Effect—Safety Actually Increases ($f < -1$)

In Chapter 4 we saw that serious injury and fatality risk decline as roadway friction declines, a finding corroborated by lower fatality rates in winter than summer months. While the number of crashes may increase, this finding still identifies inclement weather (though not man-made, like all the Fig. 11-1 items) as a fatality and injury reducing factor, contrary to the intuitive impression that it should have the opposite effect. This is probably another manifestation of the braking effects discussed earlier—when braking capabilities decline, whether due to vehicles aging, the absence of ABS, or to roadways becoming more slippery, drivers take more care.

Large user behavior feedback effects as a function of car mass in two-car crashes are shown in Evans [1985b] (see also in Chapter 4). Relative to the numbers of vehicles registered, and correcting for driver age effects, 30% fewer injuries and fatalities resulted from small cars crashing into small cars than from large cars crashing into large cars. This occurred despite a driver in a small-small crash being 2.35 times as likely to be seriously injured or killed as a driver in a large-large crash. Thus, the more dangerous case, from an engineering point of view, turns out to be safer because of its reduced occurrence.

Prolonged driving can undoubtedly reduce safety [Brown 1982; Hertz 1988]. However, one study [McFarland and Moseley 1954, p. 240–248] provides a counterexample. The study was conducted by placing trained observers in 17 long-haul trucks on 20 trips travelling some 8000 km. The numbers of *near accidents* (as judged by the observers) for the first, second, third . . . and ninth hours of driving were, respectively, 11, 11, 6, 4, 4, 4, 4, 3 and 1. This may have occurred because of reduced risk taking with increased duration of driving [Fuller 1984a]. It is possible that effects in experiments of this type could be different from normal driving because higher arousal levels are likely when drivers know their performance is being monitored.

Short-term safety decreases were anticipated in two Scandinavian countries when they changed from driving on the left- to the right-hand side of the road. However, for both Sweden [Näätänen and Summala 1976, p. 139] and Iceland [Wilde 1982, p. 215], the changeover was in fact followed by substantial drops in traffic fatalities.

2. No Effect on Safety ($f = -1$)

The evidence available on the safety of drivers with only one eye (Chapter 5) does not support the contention that they have crash rates different from average drivers, suggesting $f = -1$ for monocular vision; the evidence is so flimsy that the value is qualified by a ? in Fig. 11-2. The nominal indication from the data is in fact lower crash rates for monocular drivers, suggesting $f < -1$.

3. Safety Reduction Less Than Expected ($-1 < f < 0$)

The car mass effects summarized in Table 4-2 show that, for single car crashes and for two-car crashes, the effect of decreased mass on the risk of death, given a crash, is larger than is reflected in the number of fatalities per registered car. These results imply [Evans 1985c; 1984] that drivers are reducing some of the larger fatality risk of the smaller car by lower involvement rates, findings that are further supported by observational data associating lower risk taking with smaller cars [Wasielewski and Evans 1985]. In an experiment, Noguchi [1990] finds that the larger of two cars was driven faster (each car was driven by different subjects) and Wasielewski [1984] finds higher speeds for drivers of larger cars in traffic.

Fuller [1984a] had 12 army truck drivers drive one truck following another for 11 hours on each of four consecutive days. Drivers reported symptoms of performance deterioration, drowsiness, and exhaustion, and often desired to stop driving. However, time headways systematically increased with driving time and self-reported performance deterioration, providing evidence of compensatory adjustments in following distance when fatigued. Evans and Wasielewski [1983] find that drivers adopt longer following headways when passengers are present than when driving alone. Mackay [1985] reports that accompanied drivers choose lower speeds than those travelling alone. Thus the potential deterioration in driving performance due to being distracted by passengers is compensated for by more cautious driving as reflected in longer headways and slower speeds. The compensatory responses to fatigue and distraction only establish that $f < 0$. Assigning them to $-1 < f < 0$, rather than other $f < 0$ regions, is little more than a guess.

4. Safety Reduction as Expected ($f = 0$)

In Chapter 10 we find that observed fatality increases in the states in the US that repealed mandatory motorcycle helmet-wearing laws are in satisfactory agreement with increases calculated using realistic estimates of reductions in helmet use and the when-used effectiveness of helmets. Such agreement between actual and expected changes indicates that the most likely value for f is close to 0, though the evidence does not preclude small negative or positive values, positive being somewhat more likely. Mechanisms that could give rise to larger than expected fatality increases are increased use of the motorcycle, or the removal of the safety reminder that the helmet might have provided. The data convincingly reject $f = -1$.

5. Safety Reduction Even Greater Than Expected ($f > 0$)

Earlier in this chapter we discussed the possibility that the introduction of the 55 mph speed limit in the US in 1974 may have induced reductions in casualties on roads with unchanged speed limits. A parallel phenomenon may have occurred when the speed limit on portions of the rural Interstate system was increased to 65 mph in 1987. Brown, Maghsoodloo, and McArdle [1989] find evidence that property damage crashes increased on stretches of Alabama Interstate highway on which the speed limit remained fixed at 55 mph when the speed limit on other sections increased to 65 mph. Such spillover effects would mean that reductions in safety from speed limit increases would exceed those experienced only on the affected roadways.

SUMMARY OF HUMAN BEHAVIOR FEEDBACK EFFECTS

Figs 11-1 and 11-2 show 24 comparisons of actual safety changes to the changes expected assuming no road-user behavior change. For changes made to increase safety, examples were presented in which

1. Safety increased even more than expected
2. Safety increased as expected
3. Safety increased, but less than expected
4. No change in safety
5. The change actually decreased safety—a perverse effect.

For changes expected to decrease safety, examples were presented in which

1. The change actually increased safety—a perverse effect
2. No change in safety
3. Safety decreased, but less than expected
4. Safety decreased as expected
5. Safety decreased even more than expected.

The results show that the noninteractive calculation may give not only an erroneous estimate of magnitude, but sometimes may give even the incorrect sign. While a case could be made to reclassify some of the entries in Figs 11-1 and 11-2 into adjacent categories, the overall finding that behavior feedback effects are widespread in traffic safety systems seems beyond reasonable dispute.

The widespread occurrence of behavior feedback poses a difficult problem in estimating the expected benefits of proposed countermeasures. All countermeasures have associated values of f which, if much different from zero, will crucially influence their efficacy. The only way to determine f is empirically; this can be done only after implementation, and usually with great difficulty. However, prior experience does suggest some sufficiently robust patterns to provide substantial guidance.

Because of the self-paced nature of the driving task, technical changes that are readily apparent to the driver are very likely to induce user responses. Thus improved braking, handling, tire-road friction, headlights, and so on, are likely to induce increases in speed, enjoyment, relaxation, etc. One can anticipate with considerable confidence that safety increases from such measures will be lower than expected. (As an additional piece of anecdotal evidence, I consider that my own greatest risk of rear-end collision was experienced as a passenger in a car demonstrating an experimental radar-braking device designed to prevent rear-end collisions!)

There is no case of a safety change invisible to road users which has generated a measurable user response. The aggregate influence of such inputs as drivers reading about the changes seems obviously miniscule, as is the possibility of effects due to observing reductions in injuries to their acquaintances or from studying data.

For highly visible safety changes which influence only the probability of death or serious injury, but not the probability of crashing, there is little evidence of important behavior response. This is consistent with the prevailing view in criminology that it is probability of something unpleasant happening, rather than the degree of unpleasantness, that has the much larger influence on behavior. In the traffic safety context, the view that probability of detection is more important than severity of punishment in deterring undesired behavior has been persuasively presented by Ross [1984a; 1984b]. A high probability of a minor adverse consequence exercises a much larger influence on driver behavior than, say, the factors influencing the probability of being killed or injured. The prospect of a $20 fine (and other associated ramifications) controls traffic speeds more than does the relationship between fatality risk and speed. The probability of death is so improbable and abstract that its reduction through the use of a device such as a safety belt or airbag is unlikely to exert much influence on driver behavior. The empirical evidence shows little indication of changes in driver behavior with the introduction of mandatory safety-belt-wearing laws, or the repeal of helmet-wearing laws. The evidence (Chapter 10) convincingly precludes the possibility that such measures generate large user responses.

For the case of car mass effects, the cars with the higher fatality risk have lower crash rates. This more likely results from directly observed differences in performance, handling properties, stability, and noise levels than in the expectations of outcome, given that a crash occurs. Rothengatter [1988] suggests that a tendency of drivers with inclinations towards higher speeds to choose larger (more powerful) cars could also contribute to such effects. Scenarios in which outcome is expected to affect behavior can be imagined; it seems highly likely that a car loaded with dynamite set to explode at the smallest impact would be driven more carefully than an average car. However, this is because the probability of death has been elevated to a real possibility rather than the distant abstract concept which it is in normal driving.

MODELS OF DRIVER BEHAVIOR

The information summarized in Eqn 11-1 and Figs 11-1 and 11-2 does not constitute a model of driver behavior. The formalism is an attempt to classify observed effects into an organized framework. Its focus is phenomenological rather than explanatory, listing what happens rather than why it happens.

Attempts to find unifying principles or models underlying driving behavior go back over half a century [Gibson and Crooks 1938]. Given the diversity of responses to interventions, the task is clearly a formidable one. Despite the difficulties, a number of researchers have made serious attempts to shed light on processes underlying driving behavior, as discussed below.

Accident Proneness

The notion of *accident proneness* has been controversial in traffic safety [Haight 1964; Shaw and Sichel 1971; McKenna 1983] since first introduced by Greenwood and Woods [1919], who compared the distributions of various mishaps with several hypothetical distributions. If all individuals were equally likely to be involved, then the distributions would be Poisson, whereas greater involvement likelihood on the part of some would generate different types of distributions, as was indeed found to be the case. Some interpreted this to imply that individuals have a stable trait that defines their involvement rate. Such a notion finds support in any casual examination of the distribution of crashes—it always turns out that a small fraction of drivers accounts for a large fraction of crashes. However, this is what randomness alone (as reflected in the Poisson distribution) would generate, even if all drivers had identical expected crash risks. Because crashes are so infrequent, an individual driver's prior crash rate would not be an effective predictor of future crash rates even if some individuals did have expected rates higher than others. While correlations of high statistical significance can be obtained, they are of only modest practical use; most high crash-rate drivers in one period will be average in subsequent periods, while most high-crash rate drivers in subsequent periods will have previously been average [Peck, McBride, and Coppin 1971; Gebers and Peck 1987].

Some have misinterpreted this fundamental lack of high predictability to mean that all drivers are almost equally likely to crash. Nothing could be further from the truth. One can conclude with the utmost confidence (insurance companies do it every day) that some groups of drivers (young males) have crash rates well above average. At the individual driver level, some factors, such as previous driving violation record [Peck and Kuan 1983], are useful predictors of future crash rates. The term *accident proneness* has been so controversial, and used to mean so many different things, that I share McKenna's [1983] recommendation that it be abandoned entirely, and that traffic safety be discussed using more clearly defined terms, such as *differential crash involvement.*

Skill Model

Before the 1970s most efforts to increase understanding of driver behavior focused on driving as a perceptual-motor skill. Crashes were interpreted as failures of driver skill. This approach implies that safety is determined mainly by the driver's level of skill in relation to the situational demands on that skill. Thus safety is increased by increasing driver skill and reducing environmental demands.

The skill model of driver behavior is incompatible with many of the central findings in Chapter 5; driver training and education have not been shown to have much influence on crash rates, drivers with the highest perceptual-motor skills and interest in driving (young males) also have the highest crash rates, and high-skill drivers have above average crash rates. The clear failure of the skill model underlines the need to consider motivational models [Summala 1988] that incorporate the self-paced nature of the driving task [Näätänen and Summala 1976] in which drivers select their own levels of task difficulty. Because the chosen level of task difficulty depends on drivers' evaluation of their own skill levels, and of their own evaluation of environmental demands, changes in skill, vehicle, and roadway do not exercise a straightforward influence on safety.

Utility Maximizing

Utility theory has its origins with Jeremy Bentham and John Stuart Mill at the beginning of the 19th century. It occurs in economic theory, often in the form of benefit/cost analysis. In applying the theory to driving, the basic assumption is that the driver has a goal that can be written as a *utility function* in which desired quantities have positive signs and unwanted consequences have negative signs. The driver strives to maximize this utility function [Bloomquist 1986], which can be solved mathematically if all quantities are expressed as functions of simple variables. Most mathematical efforts, starting with the insightful paper by O'Neill [1977], have concentrated on the single variable speed; the desired goal is to save time, and the unwanted consequence is harm from crashes, which is expressed as an assumed function of speed. The ideal, or optimum, speed is the one which maximizes the utility function. At this ideal speed the expected benefits and costs are in equilibrium balance; a slightly slower speed leads to a greater increase in delay than is considered worth the corresponding decrease in crash risk. Safety improvements modify the expected harm versus speed function, leading to higher optimum speeds. A hypothetical *rational* driver uses the increased safety to reduce travel time as well as to increase safety, and in choosing the optimal mix will increase safety, but by less than the amount of the safety improvement.

Such models are mathematically interesting, and offer insights into the region $-1 < f < 0$. Their major inadequacy is largely captured in the quip, "Economics is the science of how people ought to behave." The unitary goal of minimizing trip time seems to be given a far more central role in traffic (not just safety) than it merits. While an employer paying a driving employee by the hour has no trouble measuring the value of time, it is not clear what the concept means in general. Most driving is substituting one activity for another, and may be more or less desired than the alternative. The value-of-time concept seems based on some underlying notion that driving is disliked, and that every second of driving is spent desiring to do something else. When I see people leaving work, relaxed, waiting for elevators that are much slower than using the stairs, ambling to their cars, and so on, I find it implausible that when they enter their cars they are in any sense balancing a few seconds less in this activity for some increased risk of death or injury. Mackay [1990] mentions an origin and destination study conducted in August in Kuwait which finds that 30% of car occupants were not going anywhere in particular but were just driving around in their air-conditioned cars to keep cool! Assuming a time-minimizing goal seems to suggest, implausibly, that such drivers have zero crash risk; my guess is that their crash risks are lower, but not dramatically lower, than those of other drivers in the same traffic.

The mental construct of utility maximizing also seems inappropriate for the typical fatal traffic crash involving an intoxicated driver in the early hours of Saturday or Sunday morning. It is difficult to imagine such a driver consciously increasing his speed in order to arrive home at 1:42 a.m. rather than 1:45 a.m. To claim that the utility maximizing equation included decisions on how much to drink which were solved prior to, or during, drinking is merely to underline the intrinsic complexity of the problem. As American drivers spend, on average, about 7.5 hours per week driving [Horowitz 1986], it is similarly difficult to conceive that most of this time is spent, even to a modest approximation, or even in some collectivist sense, maximizing utility functions.

Driver Risk

The need for drivers to estimate risk is central to utility maximizing models, and also to other approaches to modelling traffic safety. While risk may play a central role in controlling behavior in some driving situations, it may be less important in others. Risk estimation likely plays a crucial role in the behavior of a racing driver who derives enormous benefit by travelling just a little faster. Historical data show that drivers in the Indianapolis 500 race had fatality rates (per unit distance of travel) 1400 times that of the average on-the-road driver (Chapter 13); if the racing rate applied to the US driver population, there would be over 30 million annual driver fatalities! It seems implausible that the same basic processes governing racing-driver behavior would apply, in dramatically scaled down form, to normal driving. What other relationships governing social phenomena apply over three orders of magnitude?

The term *risk* covers many distinct meanings [Haight 1986]. Most driver models focus on *subjective* risk, or what the driver perceives the risk to be, in contrast to *objective* risk, as measured using data. While this is conceptually orderly, it can raise insurmountable practical problems. If subjective risk is to have any validity as an explanatory variable, it must be measurable. Attempts have been made to render the variable measurable by physiological monitoring [Taylor 1964], but apparently not in recent decades. If subjective risk is estimated using such objective data as crash rates, then one is likely to end up with no more than the tautology that crash rates are related to crash rates. On the other hand, conceding that subjective risk is not really measurable discounts its use as a factor in a scientific explanation. Models based on speculations about what goes on inside the driver's head are of minimal value unless they can explain observed effects better than less speculative models.

Do Drivers Seek Risk?

Examples of drivers actively seeking risk have encouraged the notion that drivers essentially always seek some level of risk. Such an inference from specific examples to the general is not justified. For example, unquestionably some individuals (generally of the sex and age associated with high traffic-crash rates) actively seek high levels of pain on some occasions. A scene in the movie *Lawrence of Arabia* comes to mind; T.E. Lawrence extinguishes a lit match by slowly engulfing the flame between his thumb and index finger. An unlooker attempts to copy the action, screams out in pain, and asks, "What is the trick?" Lawrence answers, "The trick is not minding that it hurts." (Lawrence died in a motorcycle crash). It is of course arguable whether it is indeed the pursuit of pain that motivates such behavior. However, even conceding the fact that some people seek pain on some occasions does not imply that all people seek some desired level of pain at all times, nor that there is some pain threshold below which life gets so boring that people seek to elevate pain to above that level. Similarly, rather than seeking some level of risk, it seems more plausible that most of the time most drivers seek the lowest possible, or zero, level of risk. Fuller [1989] writes, "Only very special road users, such as homicidal maniacs, putative suicides . . . *intentionally* opt for a greater chance of collision," and he quotes Shakespeare [*Macbeth,* Act 3, Scene 1] in support, "To be thus is nothing; but to be safely thus." Speed and high performance are sought for the sensations of pleasure and excitement they induce, as discussed by Rothengatter [1988], and with unrestrained gusto by Bayley [1986] in his book *Sex, Drink and Fast Cars*. To claim that the risk of crashing somehow encourages fast driving seems to me barely more plausible than claiming that the risk of contracting a sexually transmitted disease encourages sexual activity.

Comment on "Risk Homeostasis Theory"

Risk homeostasis theory claims that drivers have a target level of risk per unit time, so that physical changes to the traffic system stimulate user reactions that reset safety to its previous level [Wilde 1982; 1986]. The finding that most values of f in Figs 11-1 and 11-2 are not equal to -1 is sufficient to dismiss this claim, which is even more definitively refuted by crash data [Shannon 1986; Evans 1986]. The claim has nonetheless found willing debaters for two decades. The tone of advocacy for the claim has been largely philosophical, metaphysical, and theological in nature, unencumbered by the standards, methods, or norms of science, and at times happily abandoning the rigors of Aristotelian logic and the multiplication table. One can but marvel that repeated claims so clearly devoid of face validity have been debunked in such respectful tones by so many of us [Slovic and Fischhoff 1982; Graham 1982; Orr 1982; McKenna 1982; 1985; Shannon 1986; Evans 1986; Summala 1985; 1988; Rothengatter 1988; Michon 1989]. The journal *Ergonomics* justifies devoting much of a whole issue (April 1988) to airing the issue yet again on the grounds that there is somehow a legitimate debate; to me this seems as plausible as devoting an issue to the proposition that the earth is flat simply because a few adherents, who conjure up *ad hoc* explanations for every piece of contrary evidence, still claim it is, and that the issue must not be considered settled until these believers concede.

Fatalities per unit distance of travel on nonfederal aid rural arterial roads is over 800% higher than on urban Interstates (Table 4-4), and for total US travel was over 900% higher in 1921 than in 1988 (Fig. 13-2); applying reasonable corrections to convert fatalities per unit distance of travel to fatal crashes, injury crashes, or property damage crashes per unit time of travel will in some cases increase, and in other cases decrease, these differences, but cannot conceivably reduce them to values anywhere close to zero. Such large differences show beyond doubt that average driver risks are different on different roads, and change in the long term. Risk also changes by large amounts during an individual trip; the risk of crash, injury, and death is enormously higher when driving through intersections than when driving between intersections. Although most drivers must surely be aware of this, they are in little better position to equalize these risks than is a pilot to equalize the risk per unit time at landing to that when cruising at 35 000 feet. Replacing roads containing intersections and junctions by limited-access freeways reduces crash risk as certainly as eliminating the take-off and landing risk would reduce air travel risk.

When the homeostasis notion first appeared over two decades ago, it played a positive role in stimulating thinking about interactive effects, and highlighted the importance of motivational as well as engineering factors. Even though copious data have always been available to dismiss specific claims, one paper on homeostasis might have been of sufficient interest to merit publication. As criticisms multiplied, the *theory* changed and became a moving nebulous target claiming everything and nothing. When every re-interpretation was refuted by observation, claims of observable consequences were abandoned, and with them all possibility of experimental refutation (a requirement of any scientific theory). At the internal motivational level, drivers could be maintaining something constant. It is not impossible that belted drivers travelling today on Interstate freeways in some sense *feel* as safe as did drivers travelling on rural two-lane roads in 1920. However, if the notion of a possible constancy in perceived risk is to be discussed sensibly, it is imperative to use some term different from one previously used to refer to a long series of convincingly refuted propositions.

The endless regurgitation, fixing-up, and ignoring of the basic issues has regrettably flourished because traffic safety research has not yet (see Chapter 14) acquired the methods, style, values, attitudes, and institutional structures which have proved so successful in the traditional sciences, especially the tradition of requiring publications to be peer-reviewed. In science, a coherent rational explanation, or theory, of things that happen may well be incorrect. Science has no term for explanations of things that do not happen! The use of the word *theory* is without justification; the claim that risk per unit time is a constant is no more a theory than the claim that all people are the same height, or think they are the same height. Haight [1986] comments:

> There is some question as to whether the theory is meaningless (since incapable of testing) or simply false. Evans' [1986] conclusion that "there is no convincing evidence supporting it and much evidence refuting it" is if anything generous. In my view, a sufficient argument against the validity of risk homeostasis is provided by the incoherence of its "theoretical" formulation.

Motivational Approaches

The zero-risk model [Näätänen and Summala 1976; Summala 1988] avoids some of the difficulties surrounding estimation of risk by assuming that drivers aim at zero subjective risk. The two starting points of the model are, first, the motivational basis of driver behavior, and, second, the adaptation to perceived risks on the road. Drivers seek increasing speeds for a variety of motivations in addition to saving time, such *extra motives* include pleasure, showing-off, and competitive urges. In terms of the example of driving around a curve [Summala 1988, p. 498], the driver has a subjective estimate of the maximum possible speed at which the curve can be negotiated. Because of the changes in various factors, such as coefficients of friction, the objective maximum speed will vary by more than the driver's subjective estimate of it. The driver chooses a speed lower than the subjective maximum by an amount judged to generate a safety margin that is associated with an essentially zero risk of crashing. Because the chosen speed relates to the perceived maximum safe speed, this chosen speed will increase in response to roadway and vehicle improvements. Each time the driver safely negotiates the curve, there is positive reinforcement that the chosen safe speed was risk-free, encouraging speeds to creep upwards. Even as speeds creep upwards, they will still be perceived subjectively to be as risk free as earlier lower speeds, assuming that no incident has occurred to provide the driver feedback that the chosen speed was too high. Because of variations of the driver's actual speed around the selected chosen speed, and variations of the maximum physical safe speed around the subjective estimate of the maximum safe speed, the probability that the driver's actual speed will exceed the maximum safe speed will increase steeply as the driver's speed creeps upwards. In order to counteract the tendency of speeds to drift upwards, Summala [1988] recommends external constraints in the form of enforced speed limits, and underlines this by pointing out that large casualty reductions can reliably be attributed to speed limits. Speed limits reflect society's accumulated knowledge about a safe speed for the curve which the driver cannot satisfactorily acquire by trial and error, because the errors are too costly.

Fuller [1984b; 1988] explains aspects of driving in terms of a threat avoidance model. He uses *threat* because most of the time on the roadway the driver is not dealing with aversive stimuli but *potential* aversive stimuli or threats; he uses *avoidance* because for much of the time the driver seems to be either avoiding aversive stimuli (for example, steering around obstructions) or avoiding the possibility of aversive stimuli arising (for example, reducing speed or selecting a clear lane). The driver is not so much trying to avoid crashes, but trying to avoid unpleasant experiences, which in some cases might be precursors to crashes. By analogy with animal experiments, Fuller [1988] discusses the concept that drivers might have a bias towards postponing taking unwelcome actions (such as slowing down) when confronted with potentially unpleasant experiences. When postponing undesired responses leads to no undesired consequence, the habit of postponing can be reinforced. The later a response, such as slowing down, to a potentially hazardous traffic situation, the greater is the actual crash risk.

Boyle and Wright [1984] discuss *accident migration,* the notion that when a stretch of roadway with a high crash rate (a *blackspot*) is treated, crash reductions at the blackspot lead to increases elsewhere. For example, if a road has a sharp curve, then drivers are going to slow down to negotiate it, thereby travelling more slowly both before and after the curve; some are going to experience fear or loss of control, and a few of these will crash, with consequent influences on subsequent behavior. If the curve is straightened and widened, it seems inevitable that safety must be less on the roadway portions near the curve. Although, in principle, it is possible that correcting some blackspots could even increase crashes overall, it is exceedingly difficult to examine such possibilities empirically. The worst blackspots still have only a handfull of crashes per year, so that it would be almost impossible to find convincing evidence of an increase in crashes over the number expected. Even aggregating many blackspots cannot provide clear cut evidence because of the many other factors involved, though Boyle and Wright do report a 10% increase in adjacent links and nodes. It appears that these differences [Maher 1990] may have been due to other causes. The roadways with the fewest (or zero) blackspots, namely, limited access freeways, have substantially lower crash, injury, and fatality rates than average roadways, which have more blackspots. This demonstrates that, in the limit, removing all blackspots generates a system with higher aggregate safety, even if the safety increase might not be as great as expected ignoring changes in user behavior.

Many authors (for example, Howarth [1987]) have stressed the potential safety benefits of decreasing objective risk without altering subjective risk, or of increasing subjective risk without changing objective risk. Denton [1973] provides an interesting example of reducing crash rates by painting a geometric pattern of bars with decreasing spacing on a roadway to reduce speeds by convincing drivers they are travelling faster than they are.

Michon [1985] expresses the hope that the cognitive revolution that has swept psychology will greatly illuminate the driving task, and further suggests [Michon 1988] that it can be implemented in production systems. Michon [1989] claims that rule-based modeling, using some advanced production system architecture is the most promising approach to better theories of driver behavior. He considers it particularly effective in the context of driver training, in which specific learned rules are of more value than general admonitions to, say, drive carefully.

Economic Models

Partyka [1984] explains much of the variation in fatalities from 1960 through 1982 in terms of various economic indicators (Fig 11.3). This provides another illustration of the importance of factors other than engineering. The finding that fatalities increase (more than travel) when economic activity increases does not

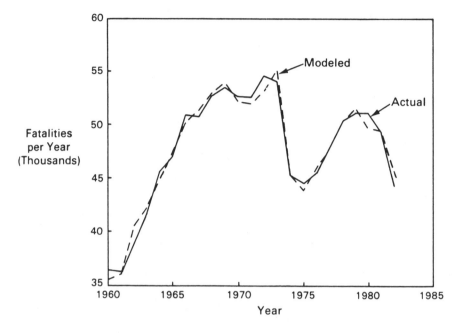

Figure 11-3.   US fatalities estimated using a model with five (mainly economic) variables compared to actual fatalities. Data of Partyka [1984] as presented by Hedlund [1985]; reproduced with permission.

identify the mechanism leading to such effects. It has been speculated that discretionary travel depends more strongly on the economy than travel in general, and that discretionary travel involves higher fatality risk than more work-related nondiscretionary travel. This might be part of the reason why fatality rates are so much higher in the summer than in the winter months (Figs 4-8 to 4-10). Joksch [1984] finds that the index of industrial production is an effective explainer of changes in US traffic fatalities from 1930 to 1982, and concludes that, as a rule of thumb, the annual percentage change in traffic fatalities is about two thirds the annual percentage change in the index of industrial production.

Peltzman [1975] used time-series fatality data in a study aimed at estimating the influence of vehicle safety standards, and concludes that they have little net effect. He interprets this to indicate that drivers used the extra safety mandated by the standards partly to drive faster (thus killing additional other road users), and partly to increase their own safety, an explanation along the lines of utility maximizing. However, the data are susceptible to a variety of interpretations

(Chapter 4). As most of the safety standards were relatively invisible to drivers, a substantial driver response is improbable.

Some Thoughts on Driver Modelling

While many models offer insight into specific aspects of driver behavior (realistic ones do not claim more), it seems unlikely that general models offering much more can be formulated. The problem arises from an intrinsic dilemma. For a model to be elegant, and have derivable quantitative values of parameters, it must be simple. Yet the commuter going home at 5:00 p.m. and the drunk going home at 2:00 a.m. are unlikely to be describable by the same model; two sober drivers of the same age and sex may still have basic differences which frustrate simple explanations. The quest for simplicity leads to monist models which focus on one aspect of driving, while ignoring others factors which are much too important to be ignored, thereby violating Albert Einstein's advice that "Everything should be as simple as possible, but not simpler."

The most common monist choice has been risk, often being narrowed even further to subjective risk of crashing. There are many problems associated with affording risk a central role in controlling driver behavior. Individuals are extremely poor at accessing risk based on personal experience. There is no reason to expect that people would avoid X-rays or foods containing cholesterol were it not for information from the mass communication media. Yet news stories and the reactions to them can be extraordinary. Reaction in the US to two Chilean grapes containing a non-health-threatening 3 μg of cyanide resulted in 17 000 Chileans losing their jobs; enormous quantities of apples and apple products were discarded after essentially baseless claims regarding the chemical alar [*Wall Street Journal* 1989]. People misjudge the risk of common hazards; for example, a group of 30 college students underestimated the number of deaths due to smoking by a factor of 62, due to traffic crashes by a factor of 5, but overestimated the number of skiing deaths by a factor of 4 [Slovic, Fischhoff, and Lichtenstein 1980]. Zeckhauser and Viscusi [1990] point out that large risks are ignored while some small ones are regulated stringently. Adams [1985, p. 145] suggests that, on average, people may be able to rank order risks because they can rank order weights, as illustrated in experiments that showed the average rank-orderings of many subjects approached the correct rank ordering with increasing number of subjects. This is nothing more than an illustration of the high sensitivity that subjects exhibit in two-category forced choice judgments, as well documented in the psychological literature [Woodsworth and Schlosberg 1954]. The fact that slightly more than 50% of a large number of subjects forced to chose will correctly judge a 101 gram weight to be heavier than a 100 gram weight says nothing about how large numbers of subjects will judge which is riskier—taking a bite from an alar-treated apple or violating the 55 mph speed limit.

Even if drivers could somehow accomplish the improbable, and collectively estimate risk, there is still little reason to conclude that this is the only important factor controlling driver behavior. Rothengatter's [1988] conclusion that motivations for speed choice involve many factors, and that risk can account for only part of the variance found in road-user behavior seems beyond reasonable dispute. He further suggests that seeking pleasure may be as plausible a controlling factor as risk. Rumar [1988] also considers that risk plays no more than a minor role. When late for an appointment, the need to save time can elevate risk to a central factor in speed choice. On other occasions, quite different motivations clearly seem to apply, such as a young man's desire to impress or frighten a girl friend with his driving, absent both destination and time schedule, or the same young man's desire to impress the same girl's mother with his responsible prudent behavior. In Chapter 13 we discuss social norms as exercising an influence on driving—in part drivers drive at the speed that they think those whose esteem they crave would expect. In the US in November 1973 motorists reduced speeds to conserve fuel, with risk not entering into consideration as a factor. It seems entirely implausible to think that risk (of crashing, or receiving a police violation, etc.) can, even as the crudest approximation, be conceived as the sole determinant of driver behavior. As risk is not necessarily a dominant, and certainly not the sole, determinant of driver behavior, terms like *risk compensation* to describe user responses in the range $-1 < f < 0$, should be avoided. All that is observed is a user response; to call it risk compensation is to imply knowledge of why it happened, an implication without justification.

While attempts to describe driver behavior in terms of a single stimulus, such as risk, are too simple to be realistic, attempts using large numbers of decision-based rules requiring computer processing seem to me to be too complicated. Poincaré wrote (in 1903) that, "Science is built up with facts as a house is with stones. But a collection of facts is no more a science than a heap of stones is a house." My own feeling is that driving is more than a collection of specific steps—it is more of a holistic process not explainable in terms of a collection of reductionist details.

In Chapter 6 we encountered the Tillmann and Hobbs [1949] conclusion: "Truly it may be said that a man drives as he lives." Insofar as driving reflects much of the complexity of life, perhaps a useful general model of driving is almost as unattainable as a general model of life. Rather than focusing on models which attempt to explain more than can realistically be explained, it might be more fruitful to attempt to model more specific driving situations. Two types of crashes which are not understood at the perceptual and cognitive level might benefit from such attention; multiple vehicle crashes in dense fog, some involving over 50 cars and more than half a dozen deaths, and older drivers' over-involvement in intersection crashes.

CONCLUSIONS

Human behavior feedback, or user response, to changes in safety systems may greatly alter safety outcomes. In some cases the outcome may even be of an opposite sign to that which is expected; some changes made to increase safety have actually reduced safety, while other changes which were expected to reduce safety, but made for other reasons, have actually increased safety. While no predictive model of how users react to changes is available, some general patterns are apparent. If the safety change affects vehicle performance, it is likely to be used to increase mobility. Thus, improved braking or handling characteristics are likely to lead to increased speeds, closer following, and faster cornering. Safety may also increase, but by less than if there had been no behavior response. When safety changes are largely invisible to the user, such as improvements in vehicle crashworthiness, there is no evidence of any measurable human behavior feedback. Likewise, when measures affect only the outcomes of crashes, rather than their probability, no user responses have been measured. In principle, it is almost certain that users respond in some degree to just about everything of which they are aware. Empirical studies can never show no user response, but only that user response is less than some amount.

REFERENCES

Adams, J.G.U. *Risk and Freedom—The Record of Road Safety Regulations*. Nottingham, UK: Bottesford Press; 1985.

Asogwa, S.E. The crash helmet legislation in Nigeria: a before-and-after study. *Accident Analysis and Prevention* 12:213–216; 1980.

Bayley, S. *Sex, Drink and Fast Cars*. London, UK: Faber and Faber; 1986.

Biehl, B.; Aschenbrenner, M.; Wurm, G. Einfluss der Risikokompensation auf die Wirkung von Verkehrssicherheitsmassnahmen am Beispiel ABS. Unfall-und Sicherheitsforschung Strassenverkehr, No. 63, Symposion Unfallforschung '87, Köln; 1987.

Bloomquist, G. A utility maximization model of driver traffic safety behavior. *Accident Analysis and Prevention* 18:371–375; 1986.

Boyle, A.J.; Wright, C.C. Accident migration after remedial treatment at blackspots. *Traffic Engineering and Control* 25:260–267; 1984.

Brown, I.D. Driving fatigue. *Endeavour* (New Series) 6(2):83–90; 1982.

Brown, D.B.; Maghsoodloo, S.; McArdle, M.E. The safety impact of the 65 mph speed limit: a case study using Alabama accident data. Washington, DC: National Highway Traffic Safety Administration, report DOT HS 807 425; April 1989.

Denton, G.G. The influence of visual pattern on perceived speed at Newbridge M8 Midlothian. Crowthorne, Berkshire, UK: Transport and Road Research Laboratory; 1973.

Evans L. Accident involvement rate and car size. *Accident Analysis and Prevention* 16:387–405; 1984.

Evans, L. Human behavior feedback and traffic safety. *Human Factors* 27:555–576; 1985a.

Evans, L. Involvement rate in two-car crashes versus driver age and car mass of each involved car. *Accident Analysis and Prevention* 17:155–170; 1985b.

Evans, L. Driver behavior revealed in relations involving car mass. In: Evans, L.; Schwing, R.C., editors. *Human Behavior and Traffic Safety*. New York, NY: Plenum Press, p. 337–352; 1985c.

Evans, L. Risk homeostasis theory and traffic accident data. *Risk Analysis* 6: 81–94; 1986. (Also see reply by Wilde and response by Evans. *Risk Analysis* 6:95–103; 1986).

Evans, L.; Herman, R. Note on driver adaptation to modified vehicle starting acceleration. *Human Factors* 18:235–240; 1976.

Evans L.; Rothery, R. Comments on effects of vehicle type and age on driver behaviour at signalized intersections. *Ergonomics* 19:559–570; 1976.

Evans, L.; Wasielewski, P. Risky driving related to driver and vehicle characteristics. *Accident Analysis and Prevention* 15:121–136; 1983.

Fuller, R.G.C. Prolonged driving in convoy: the truck driver's experience. *Accident Analysis and Prevention* 16:371–382; 1984a.

Fuller, R.G.C. A conceptualization of driving behaviour as threat avoidance. *Ergonomics* 27:1139–1155; 1984b.

Fuller, R.G.C. On learning to make risky decisions. *Ergonomics* 31:519–526; 1988.

Fuller, R.G.C. To be safely thus? Conditions for risk-compensation and its modification. Paper presented to the 1st European Congress of Psychology, Amsterdam, Netherlands; 2–7 July 1989.

Gazis, D.C.; Herman, R.; Maradudin, A.A. The problem of the amber light in traffic flow. *Operations Research* 8:112–232; 1960.

Gebers, M.A.; Peck, R.C. Basic California traffic convictions and accident record facts. Sacramento, CA: California Department of Motor Vehicles, report CAL-DMV-RSS-114; December 1987.

Gibson, J.J.; Crooks, L.E. A theoretical field-analysis of automobile driving. *American Journal of Psychology* 51:453–471; 1938.

Graham, J.D. On Wilde's theory of risk homeostasis. *Risk Analysis* 2:235–237; 1982.

Greenwood, M.; Woods, H.M. A report on the incidence of industrial accidents upon individuals with special reference to multiple accidents (1919). Reproduced in Haddon, W.; Suchman, E.A.; Klein, D., editors. *Accident Research*. New York, NY: Harper and Row; 1964.

Haddon, W., Jr. Advances in the epidemiology of injuries as a basis for public policy. *Public Health Reports* 95:411–421; 1980.

Haight, F.A. Accident proneness, the history of an idea. *Automobilismo & Automobilismo Indusriale* 4:3–15; 1964.

Haight, F.A. Risk, especially risk of a traffic accident. *Accident Analysis and Prevention* 18:359–366; 1986.

Hakkert, A.S.; Mahalel, D. The effect of traffic signals on road accidents—with particular reference to the introduction of a blinking green phase. *Traffic Engineering and Control* 19(5):212–215; 1978.

Hedlund, J.H. Recent US traffic fatality trends. In: Evans, L.; Schwing, R.C., editors. *Human Behavior and Traffic Safety*. New York, NY: Plenum Press, p. 7–19; 1985.

Herman, R.; Olson, P.L.; Rothery, R.W. Problem of the amber signal light. *Traffic Engineering and Control* 5:298–304; 1963.

Herms, B.F. Pedestrian crosswalk study accidents in painted and unpainted crosswalks. Highway Research Record no. 406, Highway Research Board, p. 1–13; 1972.

Hertz, R.P. Sleeper berth use as a risk factor for tractor-trailer driver fatality. *Accident Analysis and Prevention* 20:431–439;1988.

Horowitz, A.D. Automobile usage: a factbook on trips and weekly travel. Warren, MI: General Motors Research Laboratories, research publication GMR-5351; 2 April 1986.

Howarth, C.I. Perceived risk and behavioural feedback: strategies for reducing accidents and increasing efficiency. *Work and Stress* 1:61–65; 1987.

Huguenin, R.D. Personal communication; 1990.

Joksch, H.C. The relation between motor vehicle accident deaths and economic activity. *Accident Analysis and Prevention* 16:207–210; 1984.

Kahane, C.J. An evaluation of center high mounted stop lamps based on 1987 data. Washington, DC: National Highway Traffic Safety Administration, report DOT HS 807 442; July 1989.

Klein, T.; Zaidel, D.; Mahalel, D. The influence of a "flashing green" on stopping and crossing decisions at approaches to signalized intersections. Haifa, Israel: Technion, Israel Institute of Technology, technical report 83–22; 1983.

Langwieder, K. Der Problemkreis Bremsen in der Unfallforschung. VII.-Symposium. HUK-Verband, Büro für kfz-technik, München; 1986.

Mackay, M. Seat belt use under voluntary and mandatory conditions and its effect on casualties. In: Evans, L.; Schwing, R.C., editors. *Human Behavior and Traffic Safety*. New York, NY: Plenum Press, p. 259–278; 1985.

Mackay, M. Towards a unified traffic science. *IATSS Research—Journal of International Association of Traffic and Safety Sciences* 14(1):(in press) 1990.

Maher, M.J. A bivariate binomial model to explain traffic accident migration. *Accident Analysis and Prevention* 22:487–498; 1990.

McFarland, R.A.; Moseley, A. L. Human factors in highway transport safety. Harvard School of Public Health. Boston, MA; 1954.

McKenna, P.F. The human factor in driving accidents; an overview of approaches and problems. *Ergonomics* 25:867–877; 1982.

McKenna, P.F. Accident proneness: a conceptual analysis. *Ergonomics* 15:65–71; 1983.

McKenna, P.F. Discussion on "Risk homeostasis in an experimental context". In: Evans, L.; Schwing, R.C., editors. *Human Behavior and Traffic Safety*. New York, NY: Plenum Press, p. 143–144; 1985.

Michon, J.A. A critical view of driver behaviour models: what do we know, what should we do? In: Evans, L.; Schwing, R.C., editors. *Human Behavior and Traffic Safety*. New York, NY: Plenum Press, p. 485–520; 1985.

Michon, J.A. Should drivers think? In: Rothengatter, J.A.; de Bruin, R.A., editors. *Road Users and Traffic Safety*. Assen/Maastricht, Netherlands: Van Gorcum, p. 508–517; 1988.

Michon, J.A. Explanatory pitfalls and rule-based driver models. *Accident Analysis and Prevention* 21:341–353; 1989.

Näätänen, R.; Summala, H. Road-user behavior and traffic accidents. Amsterdam, Netherlands: North Holland; 1976.

Noguchi, K. In search of optimum speed: from the users viewpoint. *IATSS Research—Journal of International Association of Traffic and Safety Sciences* 14(1):(in press) 1990.

O'Neill, B. A decision-theory model of danger compensation. *Accident Analysis and Prevention* 9:157–166; 1977.

Orr, L. Goals, risks and choices. *Risk Analysis* 2:239–242; 1982

Partyka, S.C. Simple models of fatality trends using employment and population data. *Accident Analysis and Prevention* 16:211–222; 1984.

Peck, R.C.; Kuan, J. A statistical model of individual accident risk prediction using driver record, territory and other biographical factors. *Accident Analysis and Prevention* 15:371–393; 1983.

Peck, R.C.; McBride, R.S.; Coppin, R.S. The distribution and prediction of driver accident frequencies. *Accident Analysis and Prevention* 2:243–299; 1971.

Peltzman, S. The effects of automobile safety regulation. *Journal of Political Economy* 83:677–725; 1975.

Ranney, T.A.; Gawron, V.J. The effects of pavement edgelines on performance in a driving simulator under sober and alcohol-dosed conditions. *Human Factors* 28:511–525; 1986.

Rompe, K.; Schindler, A.; Wallrich. M. Advantages of an anti-wheel lock system (ABS) for the average driver in difficult driving situations. Proceedings of the Eleventh International Technical Conference on Experimental Safety Vehicles. Washington, DC: National Highway Traffic Safety Administration, report DOT HS 807 223, p. 442–448; November 1988.,

Ross, H.L. *Deterring the Drinking Driver*. Lexington, MA: Lexington Books; 1984a.

Ross, H.L. Social control through deterrence: drinking-and-driving laws. *Annual Review of Sociology* 10:21–35; 1984b.

Rothengatter, T. Risk and the absence of pleasure: a motivational approach to modelling road user behaviour. *Ergonomics* 31:599–607; 1988.

Rumar, K. Collective risk but individual safety. *Ergonomics* 31:507–518; 1988.

Rumar, K.; Berggrund, U.; Jernberg, P.; Ytterbom, U. Driver reaction to a technical safety measure—studded tires. *Human Factors* 18:443–454; 1976.

Shannon, H.S. Road accident data: interpreting the British experience with particular reference to the risk homeostasis theory. *Ergonomics* 29:1005–1015; 1986.

Shaw, L.; Sichel, H.S. *Accident Proneness—Research in the Occurrence, Causation and Prevention of Road Accidents*. Oxford, UK: Pergamon Press; 1971.

Short, M.S.; Woelfl, G.A.; Chang, C.J. Effects of traffic signal installation on accidents. *Accident Prevention and Analysis* 14:135–145; 1982.

Slovic, P.; Fischhoff, B. Targeting risk. *Risk Analysis* 2:227–234; 1982.

Slovic, P.; Fischhoff, B.; Lichtenstein, S. Facts and fears: understanding perceived risk. In: Schwing, R.C.; Albers, W.A., editors. *Societal Risk Assessment—How Safe is Safe Enough?* New York, NY: Plenum Press, p. 181–214; 1980.

Smeed, R. Some statistical aspects of road safety research. *Journal of the Royal Statistical Society, Series A* 112:1–34; 1949.

Summala, H. Modeling driver behavior: a pessimistic prediction? In: Evans, L.; Schwing, R.C., editors. *Human Behavior and Traffic Safety*. New York, NY: Plenum Press; 43–61; 1985.

Summala, H. Zero-risk theory of driver behaviour. *Ergonomics* 31:491–506; 1988.

Taylor, D.H. Driver's galvanic skin response and the risk of accident. *Ergonomics* 7:439–451; 1964.

Tillmann, W.A.; Hobbs, G.E. The accident-prone automobile driver. *American Journal of Psychiatry* 106:321–331; 1949.

Wall Street Journal. Fruit frights. Page A12, 17 March 1989.

Wasielewski, P.F.; Evans, L. Do drivers of small cars take less risk in everyday driving? *Risk Analysis* 5:25–32; 1985.

Wasielewski, P. Speed as a measure of driver risk: observed speeds versus driver and vehicle characteristics. *Accident Analysis and Prevention* 16:89–103; 1984.

Wilde, G.J.S. The theory of risk-homeostasis: implications for safety and health. *Risk Analysis* 2:209–255; 1982.

Wilde, G.J.S. Notes on the interpretation of traffic accident data and of risk homeostasis theory: a reply to L. Evans. *Risk Analysis* 6:95–101; 1986.

Williams, A.F.; O'Neill, B. On-the-road driving records of licensed race drivers. *Accident Analysis and Prevention* 6: 263–270; 1974.

Woodsworth, R.W.; Schlosberg, H. *Experimental Psychology*. New York, NY: Holt, Rienhart and Winston; 1954.

Zeckhauser, R.J.; Viscusi, W.K. Risk within reason. *Science* 24:559–564; 1990.

12 How You Can Reduce Your Risk

INTRODUCTION

At a White House news conference in 1960 a reporter asked President Eisenhower, "Sir, do you realize that on your upcoming birthday you will be the oldest President ever to serve?" Ike smiled and answered, "I believe it's a tradition in baseball that when a pitcher has a no-hitter going for him, nobody reminds him of it" [Humes 1975, p. 155]. Perhaps I would be wise to take note of that tradition, and not start this chapter by stating that, at the time of writing, this researcher of traffic crashes has never actually experienced one in 34 years of driving. It is, of course, not possible to determine with confidence whether this is merely the result of sheer blind luck, or whether it reflects safer than average driving. One might, however, note that if a specific individual's crash risk remained constant at the overall average of one per 10 years (Table 13-2), then Eqn 1.1 with $x = 3.4$ indicates that the probability of having 34 consecutive crash-free years is 3.3%; an assumed rate of one crash per five years gives a corresponding probability of 0.1%.

There is no reason to believe that my experience is typical of traffic safety researchers in general, based on the finding in Chapter 6 that knowledge is not the most central factor in crash involvement rates. An informal (and not too confidential) survey I conducted at an international traffic safety meeting provided clear evidence that some of those studying the subject had involvement and violation rates well above the average. Although the average rates reported by the researchers were lower than average rates for the general public, I consider this an unreliable indication because of two large biases—imperfect memory, and a tendency towards more socially acceptable answers. Both biases operate in the direction of lowering self-reported rates. My casual observation is that those of us who attend meetings on traffic safety, including meetings that focus on the role of alcohol, are not dramatically more sober than the general run of humanity. More objective data on the behavior of safety researchers were obtained by Summala [1987], who measured the speeds of Finnish road-safety researchers as they approached a hotel in which a national road safety meeting was to be arranged. Of the 13 researchers who could be tracked by radar in a 60 km/h speed-limit zone, nine exceeded 70 km/h, six of these exceeded 80 km/h, and three of these reached 90 km/h! The researchers' speeds were, on average, higher than those of the general public.

In the previous chapters many results relating to aggregate effects have been presented, and interpretations offered of factors that affect overall traffic safety. Here we address the more personal question of what steps an individual driver can take to reduce his or her personal crash risk. We do not cover the whole range of driving situations featured in many "How to drive safely" books. Rather, we treat in detail a few specific aspects of driving with a view to gaining insight into general approaches to increasing personal safety.

AVERAGE BEHAVIOR GENERATES AVERAGE CRASH RISK

A theme we touched on in Chapter 6 is that direct experience continuously reinforces an impression that driving is extremely safe. Let us invoke the mental construct of a hypothetical *average driver,* who has a 0.1 probability of crashing per year. Such an individual has a better than even chance of driving six and a half years without crashing (or over 100 000 km, assuming 16 000 km per year); in the same period, this driver also has a 14.0% probability of being involved in two or more crashes, which is how the average comes out to be one per 10 years (computed using Eqn 1.1 with x = 0.65). The rich repetitive feedback from frequent driving corroborates the impression that appropriate and safe driving behavior is being used, and fits the *zero-risk* interpretation of Näätänen and Summala [1976]. This average driver has no direct way of knowing that a natural and essentially inevitable consequence of such average driving is involvement in one crash per 10 years, or 6 crashes in a 60-year driving career.

As the probability that our hypothetical driver experiences at least one crash over a driving career is greater than 99.7%, one might view it as a near certainty that this driver will be involved in a crash. A common reaction of drivers involved in crashes is to view such incidents as rare unpredictable events outside reasonable human control, and of such a unique nature that nothing like them will ever recur. Yet, for our hypothetical driver, rather than being unpredictable, a crash is essentially inevitable. To realistically expect less than six crashes over a driving career, our hypothetical driver must adopt changed driving behavior so that it no longer matches that same average behavior which copious direct feedback indicated to be appropriate. A crash rate of 0.1 per year would be an unthinkable average for airline pilots, yet flying a plane appears to involve intrinsic risks far exceeding those associated with driving. In my view, it is within the control of the ground-vehicle driver to approach the same low crash risks which commercial pilots achieve when flying (although it is conventional wisdom that pilots have above-average crash risks on the road). Before addressing how a driver might greatly reduce individual crash risk, it is helpful to divide all crash-involved drivers into categories.

AVOIDABLE AND UNAVOIDABLE INVOLVEMENT

Police procedures generally categorize drivers involved in crashes as being either *at fault* or *not at fault*. Our use of these terms does not deny that each crash has many antecedents, nor that vehicle, roadway or environmental conditions may have played a role. Nor does it suggest that countermeasures other than changed driver behavior could not have prevented the crash. Replacing all rural two-lane roads by divided highways greatly reduces crashes for unchanged driver behavior. The focus of the present chapter is on how an individual driver can reduce personal crash risk within the present infrastructure, which includes as a given the behavior of all the other drivers.

Placing a crash-involved driver in the *at fault* category implies some violation of traffic law, while the *not at fault* category implies an absence of evidence of a traffic-law violation. Although such a categorization is tidy for legal purposes, it tends to convey an erroneous impression that not-at-fault drivers are helpless victims of crashes which occurred entirely outside their control. It may be more illuminating to place all crash-involved drivers into three categories, although this is also a simplification:

1. At fault
2. While not legally at fault, the driver could still have avoided involvement
3. Unavoidably involved

Of these categories, the first and third are the easiest to determine. Most would agree that the majority of single-vehicle crashes could have been avoided by more prudent driver behavior. The presence of vehicular or environmental factors does not necessarily imply no possibility of driver control. If the vehicle has worn tires or brakes, the roadway is icy, or the weather is foggy, the driver could still have adjusted behavior accordingly. Chapter 11 presents considerable evidence that drivers do in fact adjust their behavior for changed conditions. Much of the content of driver education and public service messages focuses on correcting behavior that tends to involve drivers in *at fault* crashes.

In contrast to cases in which the driver has control, there are cases in which drivers are involved in crashes in which their involvement is unavoidable, given that they had decided to drive. Cases of vehicles driving over bridges which collapse because of structural failure or earthquake, or vehicles stopped in traffic being struck by crashing airliners provide unmistakable, if extreme, examples. Indeed, such crashes are not even included in the FARS data if judged to have resulted directly from an "act of God" [National Highway Traffic Safety Administration 1989, Chapter 5, page 3]. Drivers involved in such crashes are victims of largely random events over which they have essentially no control. There are no realistic changes they can make in their driving behavior to reduce such risks. In my view only a very small fraction of drivers involved in crashes have involvements which can be characterized as entirely outside their control. Although the fraction is small, one must always remember that, because of the enormous magnitude of the traffic crash problem, the absolute number of drivers fatally injured in such events still exceeds deaths from many other causes which command much more public attention and resources.

There has been some tendency to view not-at-fault involvement in multiple-vehicle crashes as possessing characteristics in common with the same random model outlined above. Basically, the driving environment, in the form of the other drivers, is judged to have visited upon the hapless driver some unfortunate event over which no measure of control is possible. Many drivers seem to have a view that because they cannot control the behavior of other drivers there is little they can do beyond driving carefully and obeying the law to prevent themselves from being struck.

Rather than accepting this, I believe that the individual driver can reduce crash risk substantially by taking various steps to avoid not-at-fault involvement. Indeed, I consider that a large majority of not-at-fault drivers involved in multiple-vehicle crashes fit into the second category, with only a small fraction being in the third category (again, their absolute numbers are large). Below we discuss some ways in which drivers in the first two categories might reduce crash risk by specific behavior modifications; we discuss rear-end crashes in detail, and leave it to the reader to apply similar notions to other driving situations.

REAR-END CRASHES

In most jurisdictions, when a rear-end crash occurs, the following driver is presumed to be at fault, whereas the driver of the lead vehicle is presumed to be not at fault. Legally, this is how it should be—it is the responsibility of following drivers to not rear-end vehicles they are following, whereas drivers are entitled to slow down or stop, as the need arises, without incurring legal jeopardy. Close following, or tailgating, places a minimum of two vehicles at risk of rear-end collision.

What Can a Following Driver Do?

Figure 12-1 shows the distribution of following headways on a US urban Interstate freeway in Michigan in 1978 [Evans and Wasielewski 1982]. For this figure, headway is defined as the elapsed time between the front of the lead vehicle passing a point on the roadway and the front of the following vehicle passing the same point; various headway definitions are used in the literature, but the differences are unimportant in the present discussion. The figure shows data for drivers in two groups, based on their driving records from police files. One group had one or more violations of any type (most commonly a speed limit violation) in a seven-year period, whereas the other group was violation free; 27.5% of the drivers with violations were observed following at headways less than one second, compared to 21.6% for the violation-free drivers. Although

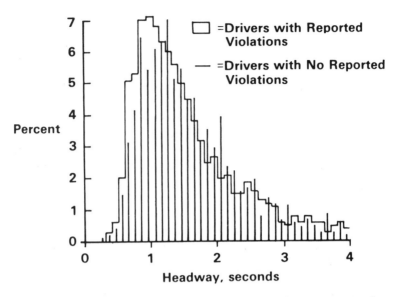

Figure 12-1. The distribution of following headways on a US urban Interstate freeway in Michigan in 1978. Reproduced from Evans and Wasielewski [1982].

short headways indicate risk taking, the reverse is not necessarily so; in any stream of traffic there will be many vehicles sufficiently distant from others that it is inappropriate to consider them in a vehicle-following mode [Wasielewski 1979].

Relative to the reaction times mentioned in Chapter 5, and to the advice in most driving manuals that headways should be at least two seconds, driving with a headway of less than one second must be viewed as behavior that greatly increases rear-end crash risk. Indeed, most drivers choose following headways less than the recommended two seconds. Wasielewski [1979] finds that drivers who are following other vehicles do so with an average headway of 1.32 seconds; that is, the average headway is considerably shorter than the recommended minimum!

Sivak et al. [1989] investigate differences in driving risk perception in the US, West Germany, Spain, and Brazil by inviting 80 subjects from each of these countries to estimate subjectively the degree of risk implicit in 100 traffic scenes presented in color slides, 50 of which were photographed from the driver's viewpoint. The subjects from Brazil judged that close following did not play an important role in increasing risk. Close following is given the highest risk-increasing rating by the subjects from the US, followed by those from West Germany, Spain, and as mentioned, Brazil. These results are consistent with the notion that the danger thought to be associated with close following increases through a collective, rather than individual, learning experience as nations have more historical experience of widespread motorization.

There are two likely reasons why drivers tend to become comfortable following at headways that unreasonably increase the risk of involvement in rear-end collisions. First, a dominant cue when following is the relative speed between your vehicle and the one in front. In normal vehicle following, relative speed is very close to zero. There is no risk of a rear-end collision if both vehicles maintain identical speeds, no matter how high that speed is. I believe that the largely static visual impression in vehicle-following tends to lower awareness and concern regarding speed. If the speed of the vehicle in front changes suddenly, then the ensuing dynamical behavior of both vehicles is strongly speed-dependent, with the amount of energy to be dissipated in the event of a crash even more so. The second reason why drivers become comfortable when following too closely is that they have learned, from repeated experience, that it is safe to do so, in the sense that they have been doing it for years without adverse consequences. Experience teaches that the vehicle in front does not suddenly slow down.

Why do drivers choose to follow so closely? It seems to me that it becomes largely a driving habit, rather than being reasoned conscious behavior. Drivers appear to do many things more for their own sake than for any utility benefit; Katz [1988] suggests that even some criminal behavior is indulged in, not for the expected gain, but for the enjoyment of the activity. Given that there are some workers in every type of job who would work even if they were not paid, why should some burglars not also enjoy their work without regard to the normally modest material gain? Returning to the driving question, we have all observed one vehicle dangerously tailgating another on a stretch of multi-lane freeway containing no vehicles other than our own and these two. Such tailgaters could often reduce their risk by passing the followed vehicle, and thereby in fact save time. Unlike many other forms of increased risk-taking in driving, such as speeding, overtaking, or running red lights, tailgating generally provides the driver very little in the way of time savings. Following at a headway of 2.0 seconds instead of 0.5 seconds means that you arrive 1.5 seconds later, assuming that no vehicles cut into the gap in front of you. If the 1.5 seconds is critical, it can all be recaptured by, say, closing up on the vehicle in front just before exiting from the freeway. In that way the risk of a closer following gap is incurred for just a few seconds, rather than for the entire freeway trip. Larger gaps do increase the probability that another vehicle will cut in front of you. With a gap of two seconds, this probability is still low, and only arises at high flow levels. If you are in a slower lane, drivers in a faster lane would rarely want to come in front of you so that they could also travel more slowly. If you are in the faster lane, drivers in the slower lane may be more cautious and thereby less likely to perform the risky maneuver of merging into a two second gap. Even if a few vehicles do cut into the gap in front (my guess is about one per 10 km of freeway travel), this adds only about 2 seconds per such incident to the overall trip time.

Drivers probably object to other vehicles cutting in front of them not because it delays them a couple of seconds, but because it is interpreted as some sort of personal affront, an assault on manhood or womanhood. If detached rationality cannot dispel such feelings, comfort might be sought in the confident expectation that the offending driver is likely to be experiencing more than the average crash rate of one per 10 years. Let such drivers have their fun—they are paying a high price for it; recapture your two seconds by walking faster to your vehicle.

A case in which changing behavior can increase safety and save time arises in single-lane vehicle following when the lead vehicle signals an intention to turn right. Many following drivers maintain an almost constant headway in such situations, so that the following vehicle's trajectory largely matches that of the lead vehicle, even though the lead vehicle will normally have to reduce speed substantially to execute a tight right turn; if the lead vehicle slows more than expected, the following driver may have to reduce speed even more than the lead vehicle. A better following practice, from the perspective of both safety and efficiency, is to aim at reducing speed as little as possible by allowing a wider gap to open as soon as the lead vehicle indicates the intention to turn. When the lead vehicle completes the turn, your vehicle, although travelling more slowly than before the initiation of the turn signal, is still travelling faster than the turning vehicle, thereby saving you time and fuel; by being further from the lead vehicle during its main deceleration, you have also increased your safety margin.

An individual driver can dramatically reduce the risk of being involved in an at-fault rear-end crash by developing the habit of adopting more generous following headways than experience teaches. The experience that the vehicle in front does not suddenly slow down must be replaced by the intellectual appreciation that for it to do so is not an event of miraculous rarity. As Summala [1985, p. 51] comments, the traffic system is not as deterministic as the driver's internal representation of it. There is simply nothing to be gained, commensurate with the potential cost by driving in such a way that you will certainly crash into the vehicle in front if it brakes unexpectedly for some rare, but not cosmically rare, event such as a small animal unseen by you running onto the roadway.

Tailgating and Platoons of Vehicles

Tailgating can produce particularly catastrophic results when a platoon of many consecutive tailgaters forms. This is because of intrinsic platoon dynamics which may amplify disturbances as they propagate down a line of vehicles [Herman et al. 1959]. If the lead vehicle of a many vehicle platoon slows down gently and then regains its previous speed, the second vehicle may respond by slowing down more rapidly (depending on parameters such as reaction time and headway). The third vehicle will then be confronted with a more rapidly decelerating lead vehicle, so that as we progress down the platoon, each driver produces a larger deceleration, until eventually braking capability is exceeded. For a sufficiently long platoon of vehicles with identical following parameters, a multiple-vehicle pile-up becomes inevitable.

Figure 12-2 shows results from a mathematical model of a situation in which a stream of identical cars follow each other, initially all travelling at the same speed and separated by 40 feet. The position of each car is shown relative to the position of the first car (labelled 1), assuming that this first car continued at a constant speed. At time zero the first car reduces speed, but then returns to its initial speed. The curves show how all the following cars respond. As we proceed down the platoon, each car approaches closer to the one in front, until the trajectories for cars 7 and 8 intersect. In other words, car 8 crashes into car 7. One dear lady confessed that after being exposed to this figure she always made sure she was never car number 7 in a platoon with more than 7 cars!

Naturally, her concerns should not have been so specific, as Fig. 12-2 represents model output based on assumed parameters, and different choices would have predicted crashes involving other vehicles in the platoon. However, it does illustrate the intrinsic instability of rows of tailgaters, which manifests itself in the real world in the form of multiple-vehicle pile-ups, sometimes with multiple fatalities. Crashes involving the largest number of vehicles generally occur in fog where rather different principles (such as the lead vehicle suddenly appearing, rather than being followed) may apply.

An individual driver in a platoon following at a large headway may damp out the disturbance so that no collisions occur. If you find yourself following many consecutive tailgaters, and are yourself closely followed, then adopt a headway larger than the normally safe two seconds. Drivers choosing safer headways for themselves may thus make safety contributions to the system, and thereby prevent harm to drivers who will be entirely unaware that somebody else prevented them from being involved in a crash.

The system-wide effects of safe headways are not necessarily all positive. If all drivers were so selfish as to reduce their personal risk of rear-end crash involvement by choosing two-second headways, the capacity of freeways would decline, and would indeed have a theoretical upper limit flow of 1800 vehicles per lane per hour; incredibly, flows of 2650 vehicles per lane per hour, which corresponds to an *average* headway of 1.36 seconds, have been recorded on a British motorway [Wasielewski 1974]. As this chapter is intended for the individual driver, the wise individual decision is to protect yourself by choosing a safe following headway of about two seconds, and let other more altruistic

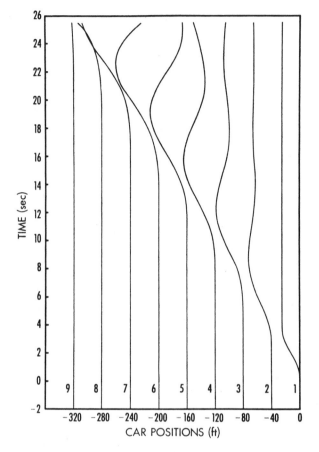

Figure 12-2. Mathematical representation of a stream of identical cars, initially all travelling at the same speed and separated by 40 feet. The eighth car crashes into the seventh as a consequence of the lead car (number 1) reducing speed and then returning to its initial speed. Reproduced from Herman et al. [1959].

drivers bear the personal risk of keeping congested traffic flow high by following at headways which place them at personal risk with, as we have discussed, little personal benefit.

What Can a Lead-Vehicle Driver Do?

When another driver follows you too closely, you bear the risk of being involved in a rear-end crash without enjoying even the modest time savings of the tailgater.

In many cases you can reduce or avoid this risk by using a variety of techniques to discourage other drivers from following you too closely. To do so involves frequent use of rear-view mirrors, which is in general a good driving practice. If a vehicle follows mine too closely on a non-crowded freeway, I simply speed up to get away from it, or slow down to encourage it to pass. If traffic is congested, increasing your own headway and level of attention is indicated. Generally, your attention, or mental load assigned to the driving task, is a factor which is under your control. Uncrowded freeway driving in which you are neither following nor being followed requires only a fraction of maximum driving mental load. It is not necessary, or desirable, to apply this maximum mental load at all times. Indeed, to attempt to do so may reduce safety by generating fatigue. Novice drivers tire quickly because the task, in its pre-autonomous state, does consume most mental capacity. Maximum attention should be invoked when circumstances, as might be identified by glancing in a rear view mirror, merit it.

One situation in which being tailgated is particularly unacceptable is merging onto a freeway. Here you may have to change speed abruptly, and the possibility of having to abort an attempt to merge between two vehicles cannot be excluded. The tailgater's need to share attention between the merging and following tasks places you at additional risk. If I am tailgated on a freeway entrance ramp I monitor the tailgater, reduce my speed substantially well before the freeway, and when a potentially acceptable gap comes along, accelerate rapidly, observing the tailgater recede into the distance in my rear view mirror. The time lag before the tailgater responds to the acceleration is readily observed, and provides an interesting indication of his or her likely time lag if the lead car had instead braked!

Another effective way to deter tailgaters is to flash your brake lights; this is most satisfying if it is followed by braking by the following vehicle. This approach should not be used if the tailgater is also being tailgated; you don't really want to play the role of vehicle 1 in Fig. 12-2! When in a particularly feisty mood, I have occasionally applied the brakes mildly, followed by acceleration, with most satisfying results. If the following driver concludes you are crazy, and unsafe to drive close to, then you have achieved your goal of increased safety. When being tailgated on quiet rural two-lane roads, I have pulled onto the shoulder forcing the tailgater to pass. It is not uncommon for the tailgater to then proceed at a slower speed than that used previously to tailgate me, providing additional indications that the source of the behavior is habit rather than time savings. In congested city traffic, slowing down and using a sweeping hand gesture to invite a tailgating driver, who can see you clearly, to back off usually produces the intended result. You occasionally get satisfying indications that the offending driver receives additional helpful comments from a spouse wise enough to share your views on the subject.

The risk of being struck in the rear while approaching a red light, or the risk of being struck while stationary waiting at the light, can be influenced by behavior approaching the light. Rather than proceeding at your prior cruising speed and braking strongly just in front of the stop line, you can reduce crash risk by gently coasting towards the stop line while maintaining only enough pressure on the brake pedal to activate the brake lights; a moving vehicle is more visible than a stationary one. Basically, the goal should be to arrive in front of the the the stop line just as the light turns green having reduced your speed as little as possible. This strategy minimizes vehicle wear and saves fuel [Chang et al. 1977; Evans 1979]. Such an approach is not possible if you are already close to the signal when the light turns red. Then a brisk deceleration followed by a period of stationary waiting is unavoidable. For the period when your vehicle is the only one waiting, you are at some risk of being struck in the rear. Although there is not a great deal you can do, it is still worth keeping an eye on the rear view mirror. If any vehicle approaches in a threatening way, it might be helpful to flash your brake lights off and on because visual sensitivity to dynamic cues is greater than to static cues, especially in peripheral vision. Some cases of being struck in the rear fall clearly into the category of events unpreventable by the struck driver.

OTHER TRAFFIC SITUATIONS

We treated rear-end crashes in detail to emphasize a number of points which also arise in other situations. Experience teaches us to adopt inadequate safety margins. To avoid crashes over long periods of time requires adopting safety margins that incorporate the possibility of events of much greater rarity than are encountered in everyday driving. In a driving career, we will encounter a number of extremely rare and unexpected events. The aim is to behave so that we do not convert such rare events into crashes. In particular, there are many steps we can adopt to avoid involvement in crashes for which we have no legal culpability. Below are offered a few comments, based largely on personal experience, on a number of such situations.

Intersections

It is not an event of extreme rarity for a vehicle, especially a large truck [Evans and Rothery 1983], to proceed after a traffic light has turned red (to *run the red*). If you are the first vehicle in line, it is prudent to glance left, and then right, before proceeding when the light turns green. The presence of stationary, or stopping vehicles, in each lane crossing in front of you confirms that it is safe to proceed. Such increased caution is particularly important if you are able to approach the intersection without stopping just as the light turns green. In this case, by reaching the center of the roadway in less time than an initially stationary vehicle, you could surprise a driver running the red light. The increased incidence of side impact crashes to older drivers [Viano et al. 1990] should motivate the older driver to increase vigilance and attention when at intersections, and when turning in the face of oncoming traffic. It may be that the subjective safety margins learned in youth continue to be applied even as the senses and information processing capacities decline.

In city streets faith should not be placed in other drivers obeying stop signs, or adhering to right-of-way rules. Many drivers seem to attack stop signs at high speed, and brake at the last moment, even when they can clearly see traffic on the major road. If the pavement turns out to be unexpectedly slippery, such behavior can be disastrous. This seems to be another driving behavior rooted in habit, rather than the pursuit of a goal of minimizing trip time. When I, and many other drivers, travelling on a major road see such a driver heading for our path, we slow down to see what develops. After the driver on the minor road makes the required legal stop, we regain our previous speed, and proceed with caution. Thus aggressive drivers delay themselves (as well as the prudent drivers on the major road). It is another case in which more dangerous, aggressive driving is rewarded by increased crash risk, increased vehicle wear, increased fuel use, and increased delay! Pedestrians often similarly increase delays to themselves and others by standing so near the curbside that prudent approaching motorists slow down.

Overtaking

Many drivers tailgate a vehicle they desire to overtake. Assuming that such behavior does not influence the lead vehicle, it will generally increase overtaking risk. The maximum overtaking risk occurs when the overtaken and overtaking vehicle are adjacent, so that the overtaking vehicle cannot quickly return to its original lane. The time the vehicles are adjacent is reduced if the relative speed between the vehicles when they are level is increased. If the following vehicle starts very close to the lead vehicle, then, the initial relative speed at the commencement of the overtaking maneuver is zero. If the following vehicle is further back, its speed can exceed substantially that of the overtaken vehicle by the time the vehicles draw level. Just prior to drawing level, the following vehicle can abort if there is any reason to do so. This method may lead to missing some overtaking opportunities, but it makes others available.

On relatively deserted freeways I often observe vehicles driving alongside each other on adjacent lanes. Such behavior increases crash risk for no apparent reason. If you find yourself alongside another vehicle, especially a long truck, then speed up or slow down. Be particularly wary of drivers who locate themselves behind your vehicle in positions in which they cannot be seen in your rear-view mirrors. In general, keep as much space around you as possible; major driving errors, skids, tire blow-outs, and such incidents are far less likely to lead to crashes if your vehicle is not close to any other vehicles or objects. If a crash does occur, lots of object-free space surrounding the vehicle is the safest occupant protection environment. In moments of lax concentration, drivers do drift out of lanes, change lanes without sufficient care, etc. Such threats cannot always be avoided in high flow traffic, but there is no point incurring them unnecessarily.

Speed

The above comments on methods for reducing risk all involved minimal, or no, delay. As speed involves a clear trade-off between safety and mobility, it is something on which different rational drivers might make different decisions on different occasions. Increased average speed can be obtained with the least increase in risk by focusing the speed increases preferentially on the least risky portions of the trip. Roadway portions with wide shoulders pose less risk than those with close guardrails, and guardrails pose less risk than solid structures such as walls, utility poles or trees. However, the basics should be kept firmly in mind. Increased speed increases crash risk, and given that a crash occurs, injury severity increases steeply with speed (Eqns 6-1 to 6-3).

DRIVERS' PERCEPTION OF RISK

The simplicity of the earlier claim that average driving leads to average crash risk is complicated by drivers' misconceptions about their own driving ability.

Most Drivers Think They Are Better Than Other Drivers

Svenson [1981] had groups of subjects from the US state, Oregon, and from Stockholm, Sweden, rank their own safety and driving skill relative to that of other members of the group, each of whom could be seen performing the same ranking task concurrently in the same room. The results for both groups of subjects combined are shown in Fig. 12-3. The interpretation is that the highest bar in the top distribution indicates that 28% (21 out of 75 subjects) claimed that they drove more safely than 80% of the drivers, but less safely than the safest 10% of the drivers; one subject (the lowest bar at the extreme left) claimed to be less safe than 90% of the other members of the group. The bottom distribution, for driving skill, is for 86 subjects (all different from those in the safety study). Both distributions would be horizontal lines at 10%, as shown by the dashed line, for any objectively measured characteristic; by definition, 10% of drivers are more skilled than (say) the least skilled 30%, but less skilled than the 60% most skilled, and so on for all values. The dominant feature of both distributions is the subjects' greater likelihood of ranking their safety and skill

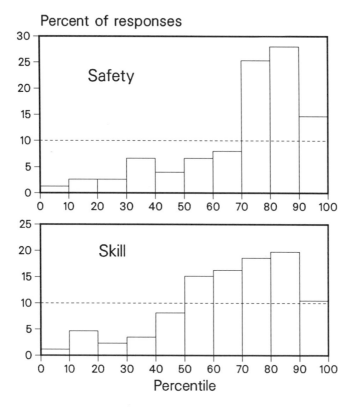

Figure 12-3. Driver self-evaluation estimates. Most drivers estimated their own safety and skill above that of the 50th percentile (or median) driver. For any objectively measured characteristics, both distributions would be horizontal lines at 10%. Data from Svenson [1981].

to be well above the 50th percentile, or median, value; 76% of the drivers considered themselves safer than the driver with median safety, and 65% of the drivers considered themselves more skillful than the driver with median skill.

In a study in which Australian drivers were interviewed at home, Job [1990] finds that drivers systematically self-rate their abilities as higher than average. The overestimation is greater for older than younger drivers, and is greater for males than for females of the same age, the sex differences being large and systematic over all the seven age categories investigated. The subjects similarly overrated their abilities, compared to the average, to drive safely after consuming alcohol. A study in New Zealand [McCormick, Walkey, and Green 1986] finds that up to 80% of drivers rate themselves above average on a number of important characteristics, but also tended to rate themselves below *a very good driver*. Of US students participating in the study of DeJoy [1989], 75% considered themselves to be safer than others, 89% to be more skillful, but only 54% to have lower crash likelihood. Matthews and Moran [1986] find that young and old Canadian drivers systematically rate their overall driving ability, and their abilities at specific driving tasks, as above average, but, unlike the New Zealand study, slightly greater overconfidence is exhibited by the younger drivers.

These systematic misjudgments are not necessarily corrected by personal experience. Preston and Harris [1965] compared 50 drivers whose driving involved them in crashes which were serious enough to require hospitalization with 50 crash-free drivers matched in relevant variables. When asked about how skillful they were, the two groups gave similar answers, indicating that most drivers, irrespective of crash records, considered themselves to be more skillful than most other drivers. On the other hand, Matthews and Moran [1986] report that estimates of personal crash risk increase and estimates of driving ability decline with crash involvement, and DeJoy [1989] reports that optimism regarding crash noninvolvement increases with experience. It is possible that driver attitudes and knowledge have changed in the time that has elapsed since the Preston and Harris study.

It should be kept in mind that over 50% of all drivers do in fact have crash rates lower than the average. While this might appear paradoxical, it is a necessary consequence of the skewed nature of the distribution of crashes discussed in Chapter 1; some drivers have crash rates many times the average value, whereas no driver can have a rate below zero. (Similarly, more than half of salaried workers earn less than the average salary.) By definition, half of all drivers have crash rates lower, and half higher, than the median crash rate, which is lower than the average crash rate. The focus of most of the studies reviewed is on medians; the public tends to think of average as meaning median, so the distinction is of little practical importance in those few studies which asked subjects to compare themselves to average drivers.

Why Do Most Drivers Think They Are Better Than Average?

Groeger and Brown [1989] extended the investigation of Svenson [1981] by asking subjects to rank themselves not only for safe driving and skillful driving, but also for eight additional abilities or dispositions (gardening, clumsiness, house painting, intelligence, happiness, cooking, competitiveness, and musical ability). Their finding of a similar general tendency for subjects to consider themselves better than most for many attributes led the investigators to consider the result for the case of driving to be expected on more general principles, and therefore of reduced importance. Weinstein [1989] reports on a body of research showing that people have a systematic bias in favor of thinking that their personal risk is lower than that of others for a wide range of hazards; he further cites research emphasizing the benefits of illusions, such as reduced depression. Counterbalancing such benefits can be substantial costs in specific instances. People betting on horse races often think that they know better than the odds-makers. As in the case of drivers, experience does not often change this view. The tendency of drivers to think that they are safer than other drivers, whatever its source, tends to move driver behavior in the direction of less prudent safety margins.

Job [1990] mentions some mechanisms by which experience actually teaches us that we are better than most drivers. Reports of fatalities rather than inducing fear tend to confirm our perceptions of driving superiority, because other people are being killed and we have not been killed. Most drivers have not been injured, so reports of serious injuries similarly confirm that we drive better than others. While fear is present when learning to drive, the goal is to eliminate it; good driving is relaxed and confident. The longer one drives, the greater is the accumulation of evidence that all the really bad things happen to others. Fuller [1988] writes:

> From behavioural theory we can predict that every time a driver takes risks, either knowingly or unknowingly, and "gets away with it" without any undesirable consequence, then that behaviour will be reinforced; that is, made more probable in similar circumstances in the future.

We receive day-to-day feedback that we drive better than others. We notice when other drivers maintain poor lane position, or turn corners with inappropriate trajectories, or without signalling. We are generally unaware when others are making similar judgments about us. As Robert Burns laments, "O wad some Pow'r the giftie gie us—To see oursels as others see us!" The mechanism that systematically biases our perceptions about our own driving is somewhat akin to people's perception that they find more coins than they lose, because they are aware of finding but generally unaware of losing. As Brehmer [1980] points out, experience can be a false teacher.

Implications for the Individual Driver

The above findings suggest two points for the individual driver. First, the majority of drivers you encounter in traffic consider themselves to be better than most drivers, and thus pose a greater threat to you than they think they do. Second, it is possible that your self-evaluation of driving skills and safety may be biased in the same direction as that of most drivers.

CHOICE OF VEHICLE AND OCCUPANT PROTECTION DEVICES

Before the need for continuous decision making in traffic, the driver makes a more long-term decision regarding the choice of vehicle; this decision influences safety, to some degree, in all traffic circumstances. Let us first consider motorcycles. Since FARS data have been collected, annual US motorcycle rider fatalities have varied from a high of 5144 in 1980 to a low of 3661 in 1988. In 1988 there were 4.58 million motorcycles driven an average of 2188 miles per year [Federal Highway Administration 1989, p. 172], for a fatality rate of 36.5 deaths per hundred million miles of motorcycle travel. The corresponding data for cars are 26 069 occupant deaths in a fleet of 141.25 million cars driven an average of 10 118 miles per year, giving a fatality rate of rate of 1.82 deaths per hundred million miles. That is, the motorcycle fatality rate is 20 times that for cars. While the types of drivers who choose motorcycles are likely to have higher crash risks, even when driving cars, than the average driver, the major portion of the fatality risk difference is due to the limited occupant protection a motorcycle provides in a crash. A car is involved in a crash every 10 years or so; most crashes involve only minor, or no, injury. If one makes the assumption that a motorcycle is about as likely to be involved, per year, in a crash as is a car, then we would expect a motorcyclist to be involved in one crash per 10 years. However, the outcome to motorcyclists is likely to be much more severe than to car occupants. Perhaps any young person contemplating motorcycle travel should find out how many of his friends have been involved in car crashes, and become familiar with the generally injury-free, or minor injury, outcomes of most such crashes. If the same crashes had occurred to motorcyclists, what would the outcomes have been? If the decision to choose a motorcycle is made despite the high risk, then certainly a helmet should always be worn. These reduce fatality risk by 28% (Chapter 9), which, using the use rates in Chapter 10, enables us to calculate that the fatality risk per unit distance of travel for the helmeted motorcyclist is about 17 times what it is for car occupants (typically unbelted), compared to 24 times for the motorcyclist without a helmet. The intrinsic higher risk to motorcycle riders, with or without helmets, inspired one wit to grossly overstate the situation by quipping, "Buy your son a motorcycle for his last birthday."

We first discussed motorcycles because they constitute the low end of the distribution of vehicles by size and mass. Many goals and constraints other than safety enter into the choice of a vehicle. However, it should be kept in mind that vehicles obey the laws of physics. Other factors being equal, the greater a vehicle's mass, the lower is the expected injury severity in a crash. Other factors being equal, the lower a vehicle's center of gravity, the greater is its resistance to rollover. There is little evidence of important differences in safety between vehicles of the same model year, type, and mass. Differences

in overall injury rates (injuries per registered vehicle) for different models relate mainly to use factors. This is particularly apparent in the stable observation that station wagons have lower rates than the corresponding four-door
version of the same vehicle, which in turn has a lower rate than the corresponding two-door version (Chapter 4). Clearly, the message here is that different types of users choose different types of vehicles, and not that adding a
couple of doors increases crashworthiness.

The more careful the driver is, the greater is the relative importance of vehicle
mass. This is because the proportion of all crashes that involve more than one
vehicle increases with declining driver crash risk, and car mass has a larger
influence on fatality and injury risk in multiple-vehicle crashes than in single-
vehicle crashes. In the limit, if the risk of single-vehicle crash is reduced to zero
so that the only risk is being struck by another vehicle, then the results in Chapter
4 suggest that the occupant in a 1800 kg car might have a fatality risk as much
as 75% lower than an occupant in a 900 kg car.

For occupants who always fasten manual safety belts, motorized or other types
of passive belts offer no discernible advantages. If a motorized two-point belt
is used, then the manual lap belt should always be fastened. Any decision
regarding whether to purchase the additional occupant protection provided by
airbags is subject to the same economic and other considerations that apply to
vehicle choice. It is worth noting that, in terms of reducing fatality risk, the
additional protection the airbag provides to an occupant wearing a three-point
belt system is provided equally by choosing a vehicle with mass 80 kg greater
(Chapter 9).

INCENTIVES TO DECREASE OR INCREASE CRASH LIKELIHOOD

The notion of incentives to decrease the likelihood of involvement in traffic
crashes may seem absurd. After all, involvement in even a very minor crash is
an extremely unpleasant experience, involving a ruined day, bureaucratic en-
tanglements, and the loss of hundreds of dollars. A major crash may involve
the loss of tens of thousands of dollars, the loss of transportation, criminal
prosecution, jail, a long stay in hospital, permanent injury, or death. What
penalties beyond these could possibly further motivate drivers to avoid crashes?
Such an analysis fails to include the fact that behavior still tends to be influenced
by changes in the perceived cost (monetary and other) of outcomes. All drivers
I have questioned admit that they would drive more carefully if their vehicles
contained high explosives set to detonate on impact; dramatically increasing the
harm from a minor crash can clearly reduce the probability of a minor crash. I
suspect that the potential embarrassment of losing my own crash-free record,
which I so foolhardily announced at the beginning of this chapter, has further
increased my own driving caution.

Does Collision Insurance Increase Collisions?

If increasing the cost of crash involvement tends to reduce crash involvement, then the following corollary seems inescapable; reducing the cost of crash involvement increases crash involvement. Insurance sharply reduces the cost of involvement in a specific crash by transferring most of the monetary cost away from those directly involved. Based on the discussion above, it seems almost certain that insurance must increase the number of crashes, although there is no direct evidence of this, let alone any quantification of the presumed effect. I would certainly feel safer driving amongst drivers required to pay the full property damage cost of any crash in which they were involved rather than the actual situation in which much of the cost is borne by those uninvolved.

The nonpurchase of collision insurance is a safety measure which does slightly reduce mobility by encouraging more careful driving; the trade-offs here are a reduction in crash risk, a small reduction in mobility, but a large saving in money. If you judge that your risk is average, and possess resources that would allow you to pay the vehicle-repair or replacement costs of a crash without unbearable pain, then there is no investment that I can conceive of which has an expected return even approaching the investment decision of changing from purchasing to not purchasing collision insurance. (Perhaps the decision to change from betting on horses to not betting on horses has a comparable pay off.) If your risk is below average, then the return is all the greater. My casual observation is that I and other motorists who carry little insurance beyond that required by law have crash involvement rates well below average, while motorists with abnormally high crash rates tend to shy away from driving even around the block without collision coverage, their premium for which reflects their driving record. Such patterns are not reflecting the influence of insurance on driver behavior, but of self-knowledge about driver behavior on insurance purchase decisions; those who know they are safer than average tend to prefer to spend their money themselves rather than give it to the insurance company, while those who have been *unlucky* in the past fear more bad luck.

The remarks above have focused exclusively on the monetary and safety benefits of not purchasing insurance to cover the repair or replacement of your own vehicle, provided you can absorb such losses yourself. Discharging obligations to others is a quite different matter, for which the law rightly requires every driver to carry insurance. Those driving illegally without insurance tend to be high risk drivers, often at the fringes of society.

Pleasure

While poor assessment of risk can lead to poor driving decisions, it cannot be denied that riskier driving is often indulged in because it is fun; driving has motivations other than transportation (Chapter 6). Driving is only one of many activities in which pleasure and safety are in conflict. Many people have been denying themselves the pleasures of fried bacon or ice-cream sundaes, not to mention double martinis, in the expectation that they will stay healthier and live longer. Pursuing the food analogy, it is worth noting that the restaurant industry did not go broke because of changes in eating habits which emphasized reduced consumption and simpler food; quite the reverse happened. When people become more concerned about something, they are creative enough to find ways to spend more money on it. Many people are willing to endure what, to many of us, seems the agony of jogging. Part of their motivation is the desire to live longer, a motivation which never seems to stigmatize them as being more cowardly than others less afraid of dying. It seems to me that a convincing case can be made that taking a little more care in traffic is a substantially less unpleasant and less time consuming way to increase longevity. Basically, the costs of risky driving seem out of all proportion to the benefits, especially when considered in the context of the sacrifices so many people are willing to make for more modest life expectancy gains.

CONCLUSIONS

Average driving is perceived by drivers to be safe, a view repeatedly confirmed by copious direct feedback. Experience teaches drivers to adopt safety margins which, on average, generate about one crash involvement per 10 years. When a crash does occur there is a tendency to view it as a rare unpredictable event outside reasonable human control, and of such a unique nature that nothing like it will ever recur. It is not normally interpreted as the natural and largely inevitable consequence of average driving behavior. Indeed, whether they have crashes or not, most drivers consider themselves to be safer than the majority of drivers on the road. There is no intrinsic reason why a driver has to behave in such a way as to generate one crash per 10 years, or about six over a 60-year driving career; such a rate could not be contemplated for airline pilots. The airline pilot does not learn mainly by personal experience, but by a process involving a greater degree of collective learning and intellectualization of the requirements of safe driving. For road vehicles, we discussed in some detail the example of rear-end crashes. The driver of a following vehicle can increase headway to values greater than experience indicates is safe, and to do so without incurring appreciable additional delay. Even though drivers struck in the rear are judged to be not-at-fault, drivers who are followed can and should still exercise control over the behavior of following drivers, and basically refuse to be placed at risk because of the driving habits of others. To avoid crashes over long periods of time requires adopting safety margins that acknowledge the possibility of events of much greater rarity than are encountered in everyday driving. In a driving career, we will encounter a number of extremely rare and unexpected events. The aim of a safe driver is to behave so that such rare events are not converted into crashes.

Increasing the cost of crash involvement tends to reduce the likelihood of crashing; purchasing collision insurance very likely increases crash risk because it insulates drivers from some of the immediate monetary costs of crash involvement.

REFERENCES

Brehmer, B. In one word: not from experience. *Acta Psychologica* 45:223–241; 1980.

Chang, M-F.; Evans, L.; Herman, R.; Wasielewski, P. Gasoline consumption in urban traffic. *Transportation Research Record* 559:25–30; 1977.

DeJoy, D.M. The optimistic bias and traffic accident risk perception. *Accident Analysis and Prevention* 21:333–340; 1989.

Evans, L. Driver behavior effects on fuel consumption in urban driving. *Human Factors* 21:389–398; 1979.

Evans, L.; Rothery, R. Influence of vehicle size and performance on intersection capacity. In: Hurdle, V.F.; Hauer, E.; Steuart, G.N., editors. Proceedings of the Eighth International Symposium on Transportation and Traffic Theory. Toronto, Ontario: University of Toronto Press; 1983.

Evans, L.; Wasielewski, P. Do accident involved drivers exhibit riskier everyday driving behavior? *Accident Analysis and Prevention* 14:57–64; 1982.

Federal Highway Administration. Highway statistics 1988. Washington, DC: US Department of Transportation, document FHWA-PL-89-003; October 1989.

Fuller, R. Psychological aspects of learning to drive. In: Rothengatter, J.A.; de Bruin, R.A., editors. *Road Users and Traffic Safety*. Assen/Maastricht, Netherlands: Van Gorcum, p. 527–537; 1988.

Groeger, J.A.; Brown, I.D. Assessing one's own and others' driving ability: influence of sex, age, and experience. *Accident Analysis and Prevention* 21:155–168; 1989.

Herman, R.; Montroll, E.W.; Potts, R.B.; Rothery, R.W. Traffic dynamics: analysis of stability in car following. *Operations Research* 7:86–106; 1959.

Humes, J.C. *Podium Humor: A Raconteur's Treasury of Witty and Humorous Stories*. New York, NY: Harper and Row; 1975.

Job, R.F.S. The application of learning theory to driving confidence: the effect of age and the impact of random breath testing. *Accident Analysis and Prevention* 22:97–107; 1990.

Katz, J. *Seductions of Crime*. New York, NY: Basic Books; 1988.

Matthews, M.L.; Moran, A.R. Age differences in male drivers' perception of accident risk: the role of perceived driving ability. *Accident Analysis and Prevention* 18:299–313; 1986.

McCormick, I.A.; Walkey, F.H.; Green, D.E. Comparative perceptions of driver ability—a confirmation and expansion. *Accident Analysis and Prevention* 18:205–208; 1986.

Näätänen, R.; Summala, H. *Road-user Behavior and Traffic Accidents*. Amsterdam: North Holland; 1976.

National Highway Traffic Safety Administration. Fatal Accident Reporting System 1988. Washington, DC: US Department of Transportation, document DOT HS 807 507; December 1989.

Preston, C.E.; Harris, S. Psychology of drivers in traffic accidents. *Journal of Applied Psychology* 49:284–288; 1965.

Sivak, M.; Soler, J.; Tränkle, U.; Spagnhol, J.M. Cross-cultural differences in driver risk-perception. *Accident Analysis and Prevention* 21:355–362; 1989.

Summala, H. Modeling driver behavior: a pessimistic prediction? In: Evans, L.; Schwing, R.C., editors. *Human Behavior and Traffic Safety*. New York, NY: Plenum Press, p. 43–61; 1985.

Summala, H. Young driver accidents: risk taking or failure of skills? *Alcohol Drugs and Driving* 3(3–4):79–91; 1987.

Svenson, O. Are we less risky and more skillful than our fellow drivers? *Acta Psychologica* 47:143–148; 1981.

Viano, D.C.; Culver, C.C.; Evans, L.; Frick, M.C.; Scott, R. Involvement of older drivers in multivehicle side-impact crashes. *Accident Analysis and Prevention* 22:177–199; 1990.

Wasielewski, P. An integral equation for the semi-Poisson headway distribution model. *Transportation Science* 8:237–247; 1974.

Wasielewski, P. Car following headways on freeways interpreted by the semi-Poisson headway distribution model. *Transportation Science* 13:36–55; 1979.

Weinstein, N.D. Optimistic biases about personal risks. *Science* 246:1232–1233; 1989.

13 An Attempt to Estimate the Relative Importance of Factors

INTRODUCTION

This chapter discusses the main factors that have contributed to traffic safety in the past, and might contribute to safety in the future. One goal of such a discussion is to help identify and clarify approaches worthy of the most attention in the future. I believe that the problem is far too multidimensional and complex to be susceptible to any tidy analytical solution using such techniques as multivariate analysis, especially as such methods are inadequate to address even much simpler and narrower problems (Chapter 4). As progress using the reductionist scientific method seems unlikely, we instead compare and combine judgmentally various of the factors discussed in the earlier chapters, and seek analogies with other fields. The approach adopted is somewhat similar in spirit to that used in historical and social analysis.

An appropriate starting point for an attempt to estimate which factors are likely to contribute to future increases in traffic safety is to examine broad historical trends in traffic safety in different countries.

TIME-DEPENDENCE OF FATALITY RATES

Figure 13-1 shows, on a log scale, fatalities per unit distance of travel for 12 industrialized countries from the late 1960s through the late 1980s. All fatality rates show essentially log-linear declines, indicative of a constant percentage decline per year. The fitted log-linear relationships explain more than 90% of the variance in the rates for each of the countries, and indicate fatality rate declines ranging from 4% per year to 10% per year (Table 13-1). Because national distance of travel is estimated only after motorization becomes firmly established, comparable rates are unavailable for less economically developed countries, but are expected to be much higher in view of the pattern exhibited in Table 1-1.

The association between larger annual declines in rates (Table 13-1) and higher rates (Fig. 13-1) might suggest that, as rates decline, further declines become less likely. The examination below of the trend over a much longer period suggests that this may not be so, thereby adding plausibility to an alternative explanation that countries with higher rates are learning from countries with lower rates.

In order to examine the trend over a longer period we use US data, which are more numerous, and available for a longer period than data for any other country.

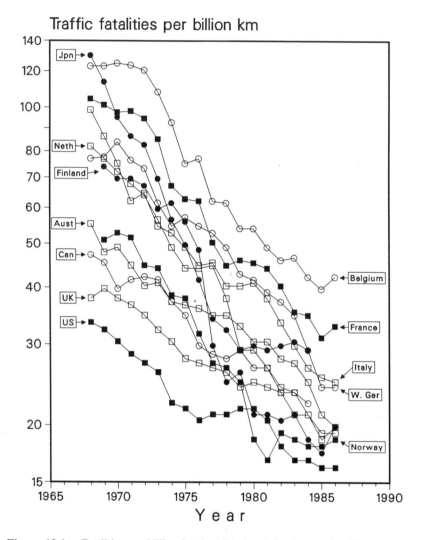

Figure 13-1. Fatalities per billion km in 12 industrialized countries. The parameters from least squares fits to the data for each country are shown in Table 13-1. Based on Motor Vehicle Manufacturers Association [1989] data.

Table 13-1. Fit of the data for the 12 countries in Fig. 13-1 to $\log_e R = \alpha + \beta t$, or $R = A \exp (\beta t)$, where R is the fatality rate in deaths per billion km, t is time in years since 1900, and $A = \exp(\alpha)$

Country	Regression parameters			Percent decline per year	Time for rate to halve
	α	β	r^2		
Belgium	10.01	−0.0747	0.954	7.5 ± 0.4	9.3 years
France	9.74	−0.0740	0.964	7.4 ± 0.4	9.4
West Germany	9.09	−0.0676	0.959	6.7 ± 0.3	10.3
Italy	9.20	−0.0699	0.968	7.0 ± 0.3	9.9
Japan	11.67	−0.1022	0.910	10.2 ± 0.8	6.8
Australia	7.23	−0.0480	0.958	4.8 ± 0.2	14.5
Canada	7.13	−0.0479	0.953	4.8 ± 0.3	14.5
Netherlands	10.34	−0.0867	0.985	8.7 ± 0.3	8.0
Finland	11.31	−0.1001	0.908	10.0 ± 0.8	6.9
Norway	9.28	−0.0765	0.924	7.6 ± 0.6	9.1
UK	6.46	−0.0409	0.976	4.1 ± 0.2	16.9
USA	6.15	−0.0396	0.927	4.0 ± 0.3	17.5

The upper curve in Fig. 13-2 shows fatalities per unit distance of travel from 1921, the earliest year for which distance of travel data are available, through 1988. The fatality data, compiled by the National Highway Traffic Safety Administration, include only deaths occurring within 30 days of the crash; National Safety Council [1989] data use a one year definition. The 1988 rate of 14.45 fatalities per billion km is 90.3% below the 1921 rate of 149.7 fatalities per billion km, equivalent to a uniform decline of 3.5% per year. The data in Fig. 13-2 closely fit a log linear trend ($r^2 = 0.979$), with the slope indicating a 3.2% per year decline over the 68-year period. (The lower than 3.5% value occurs because the actual 1921 value is higher than the linear fit.) The data for the last couple of decades (Fig. 13-1), rather than indicating saturation, in fact show a larger, 4.0%, decline. For UK data from 1949 to 1985, Broughton [1988] obtains $r^2 = 0.993$ and a decline rate of 4.8% per year, with little indication that the rate of decline in the most recent data is less than the historical trend.

The lower curve in Fig. 13-2 shows fatalities per registered vehicle from 1900 through 1988; this rate, although a less satisfactory traffic safety measure than fatalities per unit distance of travel, is available for more years and more countries (Table 1-1). The log-linear fit to the 89 years' data ($r^2 = 0.949$) gives an annual rate of decline of 3.1%, essentially the same as the 3.2% decline for fatalities per unit distance of travel. For UK fatalities per vehicle from 1930 to 1985, Broughton obtains $r^2 = 0.984$ and an average decline of 4.7% per year. Currently, most less-economically-developed countries have rates per vehicle corresponding to those at some earlier period in US history, while some have rates many times higher than were ever recorded in the US (Table 1-1).

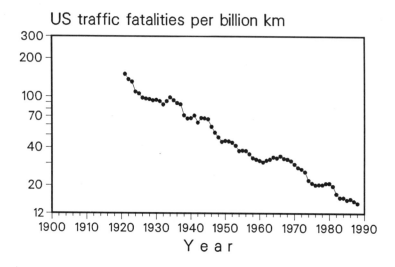

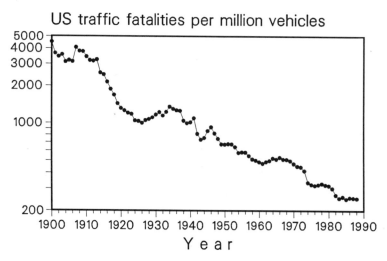

Figure 13-2. Fatalities per billion km and per million vehicles for the US. The scales are such that equal percent changes are identical in each graph. Data from the National Highway Traffic Safety Administration.

Percent change in fatality rate

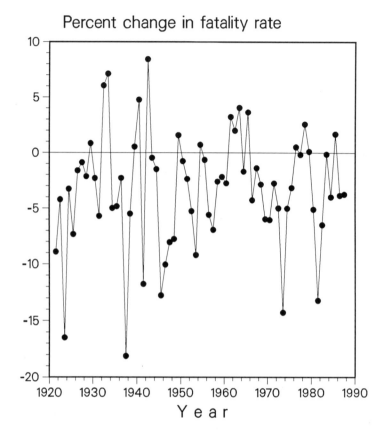

Y e a r

Figure 13-3. The percent change in fatalities per unit distance of travel from one year to the next (that is, the slope of the top curve of Figure 13-2).

Figure 13-3 shows the annual change in fatalities per unit distance of travel (that is, the percent difference between the 67 pairs of consecutive points plotted in Fig. 13-2). For 16 of these the rate increased, compared to 51 decreases. The largest increase, 8.4%, occurred from 1942 to 1943. Decreases exceeding 10% have occurred seven times, including two affected by energy supply problems (1973 to 1974, and 1981 to 1982). The percent declines per year show no discernible trend away from the long term average of 3.5%. The two most recent values are a declines of 3.85% from 1986 to 1987, followed by a decline of 3.75% from 1987 to 1988.

Another way of looking at the declines in fatality rates is the time it takes for the rate to halve, as shown in Table 13-1. All the halving times in Table 13-1 are in the range of 6.8 to 17.5 years, with a mean of 11.1 years and a standard deviation of 3.8 years. The halving time over the longer period covered in Fig. 13-2 is 21.4 years (22.5 years for the fatalities per vehicle rate).

Comments on Declining Fatality Rates

Improvements in medicine and emergency medical services have undoubtedly contributed to declines in traffic fatality rates, although no quantitative estimates are available. The ability of medical advances to reduce traffic fatalities is limited by the substantial fraction of victims who die during or immediately after the crash; recent FARS data indicate almost 50% of fatalities occur at the scene.

Steeper declines in fatality rates than in the rates for other levels of injury could indicate greater probability of surviving crashes because of medical advances. Thomas and Gallon [1988] present data showing injury crashes per unit distance of travel declined by about 3.5% per year in the UK from 1950 to 1985, compared to the previously mentioned 4.8% decline for fatalities; Hauer [1988] and Koornstra [1989] report that injury rates have declined less steeply than fatality rates. Two factors tend to increase the number of injuries reported relative to the number that occur, thus biasing downwards estimates of rates of decline in injury rates. First, the definition of injury is somewhat arbitrary, and likely becomes more inclusive as societies mature. Second, in the past it was more likely that patients had to pay medical costs directly out of their own pockets, leading to many injuries being self-treated or ignored. Today such injuries are counted in official records. As discussed in Chapter 1, fatality is the level of injury least susceptible to problems of definition and reporting bias.

Some generalizations appear to apply to the evolution of motorization in all countries. In the early stages, fatality rates (per vehicle or per unit distance of travel) are high, with pedestrians comprising a large fraction of the victims. Although fatality rates decline during the period of rapid motorization, the number of fatalities increases, with particularly steep increases in vehicle occupant fatalities. When the (proportionate) rate of growth of motorization slows, continuing declines in fatality rates lead to a reduction in the total number of fatalities. The number of traffic fatalities per unit distance of travel shows a remarkably consistent and stable time trend in country after country, and in decade after decade, as shown in Figs 13-1 to 13-3 (and the UK experience). Given this previous experience, it is difficult to understand why Trinca et al. [1988] and Mackay [1990] are so inclined to discount the likelihood of continuing declines, or why predictions of future fatalities have been made assuming a constant rate [Sivak 1987, discusses an earlier prediction which, as one would expect, turned out to be extremely high].

The total number of fatalities is the product of distance of travel and fatality rate (fatalities per unit distance of travel). If distance of travel increases proportionately faster than the fatality rate declines, the number of fatalities will increase, and vice versa. In the US, traffic fatalities peaked in the mid 1960s (Fig. 3-12, p. 57). Various attempts have been made to model the increase, and later decline, in fatalities that seems to be a characteristic of the evolution of fatalities [Oppe 1989; Koornstra 1988]. There was a particularly large decline of 45% in Japan, from 22 059 in 1970 to 12 186 in 1985.

The variation in halving times, from 6.8 years to 21.4 years, with the standard deviation about a third of the value, probably reflects real variability from country to country [Jacobs 1982]. Similar variability occurs around relationships between fatalities per vehicle and vehicles per capita [Smeed 1949; 1968]. While such relationships offer insights into underlying processes, they have too much uncertainty to be useful for specific comparisons between countries or periods.

The finding that fatality rates tend to halve every 7 to 21 years should not be misinterpreted to indicate that the process is in any sense spontaneous or natural. To so interpret such findings would be just as incorrect as to interpret Smeed's relationship between fatalities per vehicle and vehicles per capita as indicating that interventions are largely irrelevant, as has been suggested [Adams 1985]. Such relationships reflect not spontaneous effects, but rather the collective influence of all the processes, including interventions to increase safety, that tend to accompany evolving motorization. It is the primary purpose of this chapter to discuss what these main processes might be.

ANALOG WITH HEALTH

Traffic fatalities have sometimes been held to be comparable to some specific disease. I consider such an analogy unhelpful because it tends to encourage the belief that the problem of fatalities might be solved by the sort of elegant knockout blow that eliminated smallpox or scurvy. Any such hope can tend to deflect attention and resources from realistic to unrealistic approaches. A more appropriate and fruitful analogy is to all diseases, with traffic safety and public health having the same broad goal of reducing death and morbidity. One of the simplest measures of overall public health is longevity. This has been increasing in nearly all industrialized countries, in many cases more than doubling in 75 years [Sagan and Afifi 1978]. Longevity increases have been related to some single variables, such as energy consumption per capita [Sagan and Afifi 1978] or wealth per capita [Chapter 3 of Wildavsky 1988, "Richer is sicker versus richer is safer"]. Zeckhauser and Viscusi [1990] write that sustained economic development seems to be the principal factor in explaining longevity gains in the US. Explanations involving wealth also help explain longevity declines in the Soviet Union [Holding 1981] and similarly structured countries. Explaining longevity in terms of such broad measures as energy consumption or economic development is similar to explaining reductions in fatality rates in terms of increases in motorization, in that specific mechanisms are not identified.

It seems universally accepted that many factors have made major contributions to increasing longevity. Many are technological in nature—surgery, antibiotics, vaccines, organ transplants, etc. Many involve improved physical and institutional infrastructure—better housing, sewage, ambulance service, refrigeration. Many are legislative—food inspection, hygienic requirements for commercial food preparation. Many come from changes in collective human behavior regarding hygiene, diet, exercise, alcohol and tobacco use. Traffic fatality rate declines reflect contributions from these same four broad inputs—technology, infrastructure, legislation and behavior change. In the public health arena I have never heard it alleged that that any of these factors are unimportant; a less balanced tradition has arisen in traffic safety in which, from time to time, claims have been made alleging that some of these factors have never made, nor can ever make, any contribution.

ISOLATING ONE FACTOR USING US RURAL INTERSTATE FATALITIES

The ideal way to determine if one factor influences traffic safety would be to vary that factor while all others remained constant, the method used in the physical sciences. Because many factors vary concurrently in traffic, it is rarely possible to attribute a change in casualties unambiguously to just one factor. However, fatality rates on US Interstate freeways do indeed provide one example which approaches an ideal natural experiment.

Figure 13-4 shows the fatality rate for the US rural Interstate system from the first year for which such data were available, 1966, through 1988. From 1966 to 1986 the rate declined by 66% (but it has been increasing lately—see Chapter 6). Although safety improvements (better guard rails, break-away sign supports, etc.), are being incorporated continuously into existing roads, and designs for new roadways are subject to additional refinements, the broad characteristics of the rural Interstate system are relatively similar over its entire length, and have not changed much in time. Thus the 66% decline in fatalities per unit distance of travel occurred on roadways with essentially similar characteristics, and cannot therefore be attributed to improved roads.

A 34% decline in fatality rate occurred in one year, from 1973 to 1974, the period following the October 1973 Arab oil embargo. This decline could not have been due to engineering changes because the roadway facility was fixed, and about 90% of the vehicles on the road in 1974 were on the road in 1973. Therefore, even large improvements in the safety of newer vehicles could have had little effect on aggregate rates. Similarly, overall national medical procedures cannot have changed much in one year. The reduced travel which occurred in this same period should,

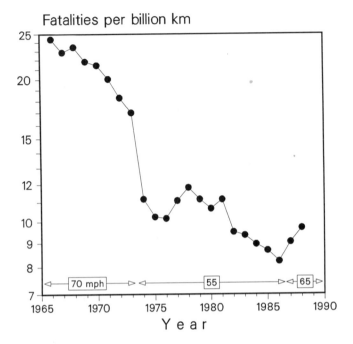

Figure 13-4. Fatalities per billion km on the US rural Interstate system. Until 1973 maximum speed limits were 70 mph (in some cases greater). From 1974 to 1987 there was a nationwide 55 mph speed limit. In 1987 some states increased limits on some portions to 65 mph. Data from Federal Highway Administration.

nominally, have had no effect on fatalities per unit distance of travel because this rate is already normalized for distance of travel. The decline therefore results clearly from changes in collective driver behavior induced, in part at least, by the introduction of the nationwide 55 mph speed limit.

   Koornstra [1989] interprets the drop in 1974 in Fig. 13-4 as a temporary perturbation in an otherwise log-linear decline, suggesting that even without the perturbation the present rate would be pretty much where it is now. The data are certainly compatible with such an interpretation. Even if this were so, there still remains the basic question of why the log-linear decline should persist for this essentially unchanged roadway environment, a question central to the present discussion.

A HIERARCHICAL ORDERING OF FACTORS

Figure 13-5 shows factors ordered judgmentally in a hierarchical structure suggested by the discussion in the previous section, and by additional discussion in

Human infrastructure

Individual human behavior

Social norms

Risk estimation

Legislative interventions

Engineering infrastructure

Roadways

Vehicles

Traffic control system

Figure 13-5.   Schematic categorization of factors.

Evans [1987]. Of the two broad categories, human infrastructure (or human factors) is considered to have a larger influence than engineering infrastructure. Under each of the two major headings, a number of more detailed factors is listed in what I consider to be their order of importance. There are many factors which are not shown which influence traffic safety; here we concentrate only on those with the largest influence. While medical advances are important, they are best considered separate from the more specifically traffic-related factors, and they fall outside the scope of this book.

Let us stress something of the utmost importance that applies in all which follows. All the factors interact, in some cases very strongly. In the interests of simplicity, we shall neither dwell on this nor repeat it; all the pieces of the system are connected in some way to all the others. When any effect is discussed, we have in mind the actual observed effect, which already includes the collective influences of all the interacting effects. Clearly, safety on different roadway types (Table 4-4) would be quite different in the absence of speed limits. Any safety differences attributed to different roadway types are for the actual speeds used.

The engineering factors, and the relative importance indicated, is based on the detailed discussion in Chapter 4. Here we discuss only the human infrastructure component.

INDIVIDUAL HUMAN BEHAVIOR

The enormous influence of driver age (Chapter 3) and driver personality (Chapter 6) on crash rates can leave little doubt that the most important factor influencing traffic safety is individual human behavior. Hence this item is placed first in Fig. 13-5. It is subdivided into two broad categories; the one judged to be the less important of the two is discussed first.

Risk Estimation

The threat of adverse outcomes certainly influences driver behavior, as discussed in Chapter 11. The near loss of control on a curve or a near rear-end crash may generate an immediate increase in driver caution. Drivers continuously react to their understanding of how conditions affect their vehicle's handling, thus exhibiting some properties characteristic of closed loop compensatory feedback control systems, as described formally by Cownie and Calderwood [1966].

While risk is omnipresent in driving, this does not mean that it forms the basis of the large numbers of decisions, or choices between alternatives, a driver is required to make. Almost every decision made in life involves choosing between alternatives with different degrees of risk, even choosing between reading a book, watching television, or driving to a movie theatre. The choice to watch television is orders of magnitude more dangerous (risk of electrocution, picture tube implosion, radiation) than the choice to read a book, yet such a choice is still orders of magnitude safer than driving to the movie theatre. Although the risks differ greatly, they exercise almost no influence on the relative popularity of books, television, and movies. In order to gain insight into the role of risk estimation in such choices as whether to drive slower or faster in normal driving, we examine a type of driving in which risk does play a more central role.

The Indianapolis 500-mile race has been held every year since 1911, except for the war-affected years 1917–1918 and 1942–1945. Figure 13-6 shows the number of various adverse outcomes per unit distance of travel versus year (plotted at the midpoint of, typically, 10 years' data combined) for data through 1986. The data show a downward trend in injuries per unit distance of travel. The downward trend in the fatality rate must be interpreted in the light of the

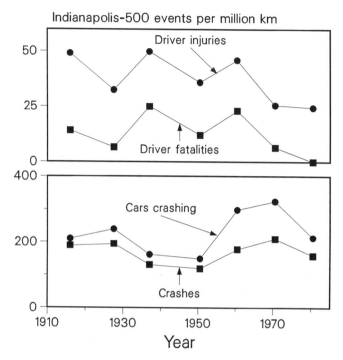

Figure 13-6.   The occurrence of various adverse events per unit distance of travel during the Indianapolis 500-mile car race. Adapted from Evans [1987].

sample size of 14 for the entire time series (7 pre- and 7 post-World War II). The most recent fatality occurred in 1973, so, as of 1990, there have been 17 consecutive fatality-free runnings covering a total driving distance of somewhat under 0.3 million km; on US roads, the average driver-fatality rate is one per 120 million km. The number of crashes, and cars crashing, has remained remarkably stable since the race began. Figure 13-6 is compatible with the interpretation that crash rates have remained constant, but injuries and deaths per crash have declined (by about a factor of two), perhaps because of improvements in occupant protection and medical treatment. If one examines time rather than distance rates, then because speeds have more than doubled, crashes per unit time of driving have increased by more than a factor of two, whereas injuries and fatalities are relatively trend free. The absence of large trends suggests that risk taking has increased approximately in step with physical changes in vehicles and the roadway. Notwithstanding dramatic improvements in driver protection, vehicle reliability, braking, suspension, tire traction, roadway surface, etc., the

adverse consequences per unit distance of travel have remained relatively unaffected in racing driving, quite unlike the large declines (Fig. 13-2) for normal
driving. Racing drivers have used these *safety* improvements to increase winning
average speeds from 120.0 km/h in 1911 to the recent record of 299.3 km/h set
on 27 May 1990. Average speed is total travel distance (500 miles, or 804.7
km) divided by the race time, including pit stops; maximum average lap speeds
are much higher, and maximum instantaneous speeds even higher.

That risk considerations should dominate racing driver behavior is plausible.
Presumably, the human desire to excel and win is relatively invariant. As risk
taking is increased, so is the chance of the glory of victory (not to mention the
winner's million dollar purse). A conscious, or near conscious, balancing of the
risks of, perhaps, taking a corner a little faster than previously, versus the
potential rewards, is likely to lead to similar rates of adverse outcomes today as
was the case in 1911.

One can think of risk having an influence that varies from almost zero when
deciding between watching television and going to a movie, to an almost total
influence in deciding whether to drive faster in the Indianapolis 500. In order
to evaluate its influence on normal driving, let us compare the racing driver
fatality rate to the rate for normal driving. In 1988 in the US there were 27 260
drivers (of any vehicle) killed travelling 3260 billion km, giving 0.0084 driver
fatalities per million km. The average rate (through 1986) for the Indianapolis
500 race is 12.0 driver fatalities per million km [Evans 1987]. In other words,
on a per unit distance of travel basis, the racing rate is 1400 times that for average
driving. If the racing rate applied to the US driver population, there would be
over 30 million annual driver fatalities!

These data illustrate fundamental differences between normal and racing driving. The normal driver does respond to perceived risk, and changes in perceived
risk influence behavior. However, the difference in the magnitude of risks between normal driving and racing driving suggests that risk estimation is not the
dominant controlling factor for normal driving. If the normal driver is not primarily reacting to the changes in risk, and feels essentially unthreatened most
of the time, then what does control driver behavior, and why do fatality rates
decline? As a consequence of present average driver behavior in the US, drivers
experience adverse consequences at the rates shown in Table 13-2. These rates
may not indicate much of a problem to the individual driver, who has a subjective
impression of driving safely, in an essentially risk-free environment, most of
the time. Even when one of the adverse events occurs, it is rarely interpreted to
be a natural consequence of many replications of aspects of normal driving
behavior. Interpretations involving unpreventable bad luck are quite prevalent.
Notwithstanding the individual driver's perception of no risk, a by-product of
current US average driving is over 40 000 traffic fatalities per year. In a para-

Table 13-2. The approximate average frequencies with which various adverse consequences occur, expressed relative to an individual driver

Event	Number per year	Average travel between events (km)	Average time between events (years)
Driver killed	27 260[a]	120 million	7100
Driver involved in fatal crashes	62 237[a]	52 million	3100
Driver injured	1.4 million[b]	2.3 million	140
Police reported crash			10–21[c]
Insurance claim			10[d]
Police violation			6[c]
Involvement in any crash	36.2 million[e]	90 thousand	5

Data sources
[a]Fatal Accident Reporting System data for 1988 [National Highway Traffic Safety Administration 1989]
[b]Estimated from National Safety Council [1988 p. 55] by assuming that all injuries not to pedestrians or pedalcyclists are to vehicle occupants, and that average vehicle occupancy is 1.2
[c]21 year value from the State of California—values in other states generally lower as indicated by range.
[d]Highway Loss Data Institute
[e]National Safety Council [1988 edition, p. 48]
The distance rates are calculated taking 3260 billion km per year as the total travel by all the vehicles in the US [Federal Highway Asministration 1990].
The time rates (when calculated) are obtained by assuming that the average vehicle travels 16 800 km per year [Motor Vehicle Manufacturers Association 1988, p. 52].

doxical sense, individuals may not perceive there is a problem, although at the national level there clearly is.

Social Norms

Long term declines in fatality rates appear to reflect mainly a broad evolution in social norms related to driving [Evans 1987; 1990]. Newly licensed drivers growing up in societies in which they and all their friends have been travelling in family-owned cars since birth, and who see much of a car's use for such boring utilitarian functions as going to work or buying groceries, acquire different average views of driving than newly licensed drivers in societies in which the owning of a vehicle sets one aside from the average citizen. An ongoing collective maturation process occurs as the vehicle evolves more in the direction of utilitarian use rather than use for *other motives*, somewhat analogous to the process that occurs as an individual driver matures from age 18 to 40.

As a society becomes more motorized, institutional changes are initiated in response to increasing casualties, which in turn influence driving social norms. Adherence to many traffic safety measures eventually evolves into habit, or autonomous behavior, without any conscious safety consideration. One obvious, and in many ways remarkable, example is that drivers tend to stop at red lights even in the absence of either traffic or police. Society abounds in examples of behavior of this type. Original motivations for improved personal hygiene were partially rooted in disease prevention. Such motivation rarely plays a role today. Rather, we find it difficult to conceive that earlier highly civilized societies (like Elizabethan England) did not share our fastidiousness. Automatic safe driving may be a goal more worth pursuing than expecting drivers to always choose only prudent risks from the mix of available risks. That is, safety may best be advanced by drivers not having to choose between driving habits more likely to lead to crashes than those less likely to lead to crashes than choosing whether to wash or not wash, or for that matter, to wear shirts or togas.

Long-term downward trends in fatality rates are interpreted somewhat differently by Minter [1987], who considers that the dominant feature of the traffic safety system is that drivers learn from accumulated driving experience, as measured by the total national distance of travel. He supports this by showing that traditional formulas from learning theory generate relationships similar to the Smeed [1949] relationships between deaths per vehicle and vehicles per capita. Michon [1989] considers the analogy farfetched, in that no mechanism generating the learning at the individual level can be identified. Minter's [1987] conclusion that, "Road casualties are going to improve irrespective of what is done (or is not done!)," although not false, is grossly overstated. Even if the evolution towards lower casualty rates is due in part to learning, the various traffic safety interventions are likely major contributors to such learning; there is no motorized jurisdiction that has simply ignored traffic safety. If one were to do so, my guess is that fatality rates would indeed decline, but at a much lower rate than observed for real jurisdictions.

Koornstra [1989] invokes community learning as contributing to the decline in traffic casualties per unit distance of travel, rather than Minter's [1989] focus on the learning of individual drivers. Through community learning, changes aimed at increasing safety are introduced into the road network, vehicles, and the rules (as distinct from self motivation) governing individual behavior. He refers to this as *adaptation,* and finds various similarities with adaptation theory as formulated by Helson [1964]. The notion of community learning seems to have much in common with the present interpretation in terms of social norms.

Many, perhaps most, traffic crashes are caused by individuals whose norms differ from the mainstream (for example, driving while intoxicated). However, these norms are subject to the same evolutionary processes as the overall norms. Indeed, it seems plausible to think that the extremes of behavior will move in directions similar to changes in the average.

LEGISLATIVE INTERVENTIONS

Legislative interventions partly reflect social norms, and partly influence them; it is often unclear which is the cart and which is the horse. Koshi comments [1985, p. 38] that safety belt wearing rates in the early 1980s were not sufficiently high in Japan that a mandatory wearing law could be passed. The 34% drop in the fatality rate from 1973 to 1974 (Fig. 13-4) is largely due to the legislative intervention of the 55 mph speed limit, while the increases after 1987 reflect speed limit increases to 65 mph on portions of the system (Chapter 6). Large casualty reductions are found to be associated with strict drunk-driving laws in the UK and in New South Wales, Australia (Figs 8-1 and 8-2). Legislative intervention is society's response to a problem that society recognizes, based largely on crash data. Individual drivers are unlikely to be able to identify major traffic risks from direct experience because of the sparsity of useful personal feedback (Table 13-2). If a driver is behaving in such a way as to double the chances of being killed, he or she has essentially no way of knowing this directly. When properly applied, legislative interventions can play an important role in increasing feedback to drivers behaving in ways likely to cause harm.

Even though the probability that a speeding motorist will receive a police citation is higher than for other adverse consequences of such behavior, it is nonetheless still low. Van Houten and Nau [1983] describe a series of experiments in which different approaches to speed limit enforcement in Nova Scotia, Canada, are compared. They find that police handing out nonpunitive location-specific informational warnings to speeding motorists led to larger, and more lasting, speed reductions than the normal speeding ticket approach. They explain that because the warning approach involved less paper work and checking, and did not open the possibility that the police officer might have to appear in court, warnings could be handed out at a much greater rate (in one location, a factor of 6.7) than conventional speeding tickets. They also report positive public reaction to the warning approach, writing: "Several drivers, who were interviewed informally, stated that they did not mind having been stopped and felt that the police were doing a good job on behalf of the community as a whole." Geller [1984] claims that positive incentives are more effective than punishments. Although a police warning could hardly be interpreted as a positive incentive, it at least moves in that direction especially when compared to the expected alternative.

Van Houten and Nau [1983] also report that the police preferred to hand out the warning messages rather than issue tickets because it entailed more positive interaction with the public. More frequent, but less unpleasant, interactions between police and drivers might also prove an effective drunk-driver counter-measure because frequency of adverse consequences influences behavior more than does severity.

Legislative interventions should reflect society's accumulated technical knowledge. Legislative standards for food purity, for example, do not imply that ordinary citizens cannot, or should not, check to see if food has putrefied before consuming it. The standards augment informal learning, and offer a better approach than just letting the individual's fear of sickness and death be the sole monitor of food quality. Legislative interventions can be effective in providing drivers with more frequent feedback to unsafe driving actions than the natural consequences of such actions can provide. Measures which further increase the frequency of such feedback have potential. For example, police stopping vehicles for violations of existing anti-tailgating laws might help lead drivers to the broader safety goal of increasing spacing between their vehicles and other objects or road users likely to harm them, or be harmed by them. The stress should be on increasing the frequency of interaction, with the details of the punishment, if any, being a lesser consideration.

APPROACHES TO INCREASING TRAFFIC SAFETY

The formalism in Fig. 13-5 is intended to clarify the relative importance of the few largest factors which have contributed to the dominant features of traffic safety, especially the long term declines in fatality rates with time. A formalism containing additional details aimed more specifically at identifying interventions is shown in Table 13-3.

All interventions are characterized as occurring before (that is, crash avoidance) or during the crash. The third phase of the matrix introduced by Haddon [1972], namely post crash, is not included. This phase relates mainly to medicine and emergency medical service, which is better considered separately from the factors more specifically related to traffic.

High technology refers mainly to new applications of electronics, such as antilock braking, radar obstacle detection, enhanced night vision, driver fatigue detection, computer control of traffic, navigational aids and the like. Traditional technology includes mechanical engineering, electrical engineering, and civil engineering. Mechanical and electrical engineering contribute to crash avoidance by enhancing the performance and reliability of such safety related systems as brakes, tires, lights, etc. Civil engineering, in the form of roadway construction, and to a lesser extent the overall traffic control system, makes even larger contributions.

By behavior modification we mean changes in behavior with consequent changes in safety, independent of what motivated the changes. For example, economic

Table 13-3. Attributes of different approaches to protecting road users

| | Crash-Phase Protection | | Crash Avoidance | | | |
| | | | Technology | | Behavior Modification | |
	Passive	Active	High	Traditional	Specific	Social norm
Decision makers	Few	Many	Few	Few	Few/ Many	Many
Who is protected	Vehicle occupants	Vehicle occupants	All road users	All road users	All road users	All road users
Can individual beneficiaries be identified?	Often	Often	Rarely	Rarely	Almost never	Never
Typical effectiveness per crash	About 20%	About 40% if used: 0% if not used	100%	100%	100%	100%
How well can it be evaluated quantitatively?	Fairly well	Fairly well	Poorly	Mostly poorly	Some fairly well	Very poorly
Judgmental ranking of past effects	4	5	6	2	3	1
Ranking of future potential benefits	6	5	4	3	2	1

downturns are associated, through behavior change, with reduced crashes [Joksch 1984; Partyka 1984], but are not initiated for that purpose. By specific changes we refer to more focused measures aimed specifically at increasing safety, such as campaigns to increase belt-wearing rates or to change laws.

Attributes of Harm Reduction Approaches in Table 13-3

The possibility that a small number of decision makers (manufacturers, legislators, regulators) could cause passive occupant protection devices to be installed on all vehicles figures as a central element in the thinking of many of those who have advocated them [Haddon 1974; 1980a;b; Ross 1988]. In contrast, universal safety belt use in the US requires over a hundred million occupants to belt up each time they get into a vehicle. Technological decisions usually involve a relatively small number of decision makers, although issues like freeway-building often involve a wider public. While focused attempts to modify driver behavior might involve a small number of decision makers, broad changes in social norms involve a large fraction of the population.

One of the most crucial elements in public attitudes towards different interventions is that of the identifiable survivor, or beneficiary, of the intervention. It can often be concluded definitively that, were it not for some specific device such as an airbag or a lap/shoulder belt, a surviving occupant would have been killed. A television interview with the survivor, together with pictures of a severely damaged vehicle, presents a potent message. Corresponding illustrations of the benefits of crash avoidance technology are rarer, and less definitive, but still possible in some special cases, such as an emergency stop with antilock braking compared to what would have been expected to happen without such technology. In contrast, it is almost impossible to identify specific persons saved by broader behavior modification approaches. This parallels the medical case in which a patient who is alive because of a heart transplant speaks eloquently for heart transplants, but there are no identifiable beneficiaries providing equally eloquent testimony for the much larger numbers who survived because they stopped smoking or modified their diet. No family can know that, were it not for changes in the availability of alcohol, their now healthy teenager would be dead or seriously injured. An intervention which saves one or two identifiable lives may attract far more public support than one which saves thousands of anonymous lives.

Conceptually, the easiest countermeasures to evaluate quantitatively are passive crash-phase devices. Such evaluations depend only on the biomechanical effectiveness of the device, assuming that its introduction does not induce behavior changes, such as driving faster or not wearing safety belts. Evaluating active devices involves all the practical difficulties of evaluating passive ones, plus the additional problems of estimating not only use rates, but the extent to which users and nonusers differ in other ways (Chapter 10). The effectiveness of crash-phase occupant devices, whether passive or active, is expressed as the percent reduction in some level of injury, such as fatality (Table 9-6). These benefits are necessarily less than the benefits of reducing crash involvement rates by the same percentages, because when the crash is avoided all injury is prevented, whereas crash-phase devices convert injuries to lower (but in many cases still severe) levels of injury.

Quantifying the effects of crash-avoidance vehicle-borne technology has, with few exceptions, proved difficult. One exception is the high mounted stop light, which studies show has reduced the probability of being struck in the rear while braking by 17% (Chapter 4). Because of the difficulties in evaluating human behavior feedback (Chapter 11) and other intrinsic difficulties, it is hard to estimate the system-wide effects of such measures as improved brakes.

Harder still is the task of linking changes in safety to broad changes in social norms regarding driving. The intrinsic difficulty here is that even if large permanent changes do occur, they occur gradually over extended periods. There is no possibility of a simple *before* and *after* comparison. The problem of evaluating any process occurring continuously over many decades against a background of innumerable other changes seems intractable.

Judgmental Ranking of Previous Approaches

As we are forced to use judgment, I feel that the purposes of this chapter are best served by stating my own judgmental ranking, based in part on the discussions, above and below, of the contributions of the six harm-reducing approaches in Table 13-3.

Even though the long term slow evolution of behavior change in driving is the factor about which we have least specific quantitative information, it is the one I rank as having contributed most, followed by road building, although such legislative interventions as speed limits undoubtedly also contributed. High technology interventions are current or future, so they have not influenced previous safety conditions.

Passive protection is ranked above active protection because the various safety improvements incorporated in vehicles are estimated (Chapter 4) to have provided cumulative benefits far in excess of the estimated 7% occupant fatality reduction (Chapter 10) associated with present safety belt use in the US. Even the benefits of proceeding from present to higher wearing rates are still unlikely to exceed those associated with the accumulated effectiveness of all previous passive improvements.

Judgmental Ranking of Future Potential Benefits

My judgmental rankings for approaches that will provide the largest safety increases in the future place greater emphasis on behavioral factors. This is because many of the technologies are reaching saturation, or levels of diminishing returns. This same point is emphasized by Koshi [1985], who attributed most of the decline in Japan's fatalities from 1970 to 1983 to road-building, but now that that process is reasonably complete, he looks to behavior changes for further fatality reductions.

The future potential of passive protection to reduce harm is ranked lower than that of active protection because the half-dozen or so most effective passive improvements are already in place (Table 4-3), while universal belt use has not been achieved anywhere. Unless the technical community has overlooked something obvious, it is hard to conceive of other passive improvements that could contribute much more than the lowest values in Table 4-3. Apart from contributions from airbags, which reduce fatality risk to belted drivers by 8.6% and to unbelted drivers by 18% (Chapter 9), and from car mass which can have larger effects (Chapter 4), other passive improvements confront ever diminishing returns. On the other hand, there are still large gains to be achieved from increased safety belt wearing rates; additional smaller gains can occur from increasing safety belt use rates in rear seats, especially when augmented by the increasing availability of lap/shoulder belts in outboard-rear seats. Fatality reductions from universal belt use, compared to present US levels of use, exceed those achievable from airbags.

THOUGHTS ABOUT INCREASING TRAFFIC SAFETY IN THE FUTURE

My conclusion that social norms play the largest role in reduction of harm suggests where future countermeasure emphasis should be placed. I believe that when one makes comparisons with other activities, such as public health, there is convincing evidence that such approaches have generated large effects. Indeed, when considering traffic safety there is the example of changes in alcohol use related to driving. In Chapter 7 we find that if alcohol had played the same role in 1987 that it did in 1982, the 1987 fatality total would have been increased by 6000. These changes probably are due, in part, to the cumulative interactive effects of many factors, including the activities of citizen activist groups such as MADD, and many legislative changes relating to the availability of alcohol to young drivers who contribute so large a fraction of the fatalities (Chapter 8). Arguably, the most important factor was the widespread serious discussion of the tragic dimensions of the problem in the media, with the consequent deglamorizing of the drunk as a likeable humorous character. The large fatality reduction was probably due not to any one of these ingredients, or even to the sum of their effects, but to the synergistic results of the interactions among them.

An even more striking change in social norms related to a safety issue is the change that has occurred in the last 25 years in the US concerning smoking, as discussed in Chapter 8. Dramatic changes in prevailing US social norms about smoking are readily apparent. The smoking hero has so totally disappeared from the modern entertainment scene that in older movies he looks more comical than heroic to many younger Americans. Who in 1965 could have predicted that after 26 January 1990 smoking would be prohibited on all commercial airline flights throughout the North American continent?

While smoking has been largely deglamorized in the mass media, this is not the case for driving behavior that is likely to cause harm. Many movies and weekly television series specifically aimed at young people contain scenes that depict unrealistic occupant kinematics under crash conditions; for example, an unbelted driver, often the hero, may crash into an oak tree at 60 km/h, jump out, and uninjured and undaunted, pursue the chase by other means. In such entertainments car crashes may be presented as humorous events; the possibility that they can destroy lives is often ignored. Young people already have a social norm relative to driving that differs from the overall norm. A change in the norms of this group towards increasingly responsible use of the automobile would probably generate larger safety benefits than changes of the norms in any other group.

Greenberg and Atkin [1983] performed a content analysis of 223 prime-time television programs broadcast in the US during the 1975-1980 seasons. They find that *irregular* driving acts (quick braking, brakes screeching, speeding beyond the apparent limit, leaving the ground or road, etc.) occurred at a rate of 7.5 per hour. Based on these findings, together with less extensive content analysis of 1988 television programs, Atkin [1989, p. 10] writes:

Each year, TV viewers see several thousand irregular driving acts and hundreds of instances where people are endangered, typically performed in an engaging manner by attractive characters who suffer minimal harm. Based on the content analytic findings and television effects theories, the following influences may be expected for the viewing audience. First, viewers can acquire and possibly imitate an array of unique and novel driving acts that are depicted on television but seldom observed first-hand. Second, inhibitory constraints may be reduced as viewers learn that irregular or dangerous driving practices are commonplace and normative (and perhaps justified in various circumstances); external inhibitions may be minimized by the relatively infrequent portrayal of serious negative consequences such as legal punishment, social disapproval, and physical harm resulting from illegal or high-risk behavior.

Flora, Maibach, and Maccoby [1989] conclude that the media hold a potential for profound influences on health behaviors in general. In traffic safety, the media have been shown to enhance safety in such areas as increasing safety-belt use [Sleet 1984; Sleet, Hollenbach, and Hovell 1986; Nagayama 1990], and in such circumstances as illustrated in the following example. In the mid 1970s in Japan there were a number of particularly tragic crashes involving riders of two-wheeled vehicles being struck by left-turning traffic (equivalent to right-turning in America and Europe). In one incident, a left-turning truck struck a mother transporting her two children to kindergarten by bicycle, killing all three. These incidents generated widespread media coverage and discussion of left-turn crashes, leading to changes in truck design, and probably more importantly, changes in awareness on the part of all road users of the possibility of such crashes. The fraction of all fatalities due to left-turn crashes declined by a factor of two from 1977 to 1988 [Nagayama 1990].

Another aspect of driving closely related to that of social norms is that of courtesy on the road. In early stages of motorization driving is an adventurous and macho activity, often characterized by competitiveness and a *king of the road* attitude. As motorization matures, and driving becomes more universal, it seems to me that drivers might become more receptive to the notion that the other drivers they take such pleasure in intimidating might be on the way to pick up their grandchildren. Drivers should become more aware of the problems that older, and handicapped, drivers face, and take pride in the same courteous behavior they would exhibit to the elderly or handicapped when, for example, getting into an elevator. If the type of courtesy that applies in most walks of life were applied more on the road, it seems likely that substantial safety benefits would result.

Young male drivers are substantially overrepresented in fatal crashes and alcohol is responsible for 47% of US traffic fatalities. Beer, the alcoholic beverage of choice of young males, is widely advertised on television in programming, especially sports, aimed specifically at young males. Postman et al. [1987] estimate that American children see about 100 000 television commercials for beer as they are growing up; such commercials tend to associate the product with the types of positive attributes to which a healthy young male aspires. In contrast hard liquor, which is favored more by older consumers, who are substantially safer drivers, is not advertised on television.

Education can make a contribution mainly by influencing attitudes and by imparting knowledge that will not be acquired by direct experience (Chapter 6). Most of the task of driving is learned by direct feedback from the task itself; safety must be imparted by less direct means because direct feedback is far too sparse. To expect drivers to learn safety by driving is somewhat akin to expecting people to learn the value of smoke-detectors by having their houses burn down. Despite the enormous reinforcement given by the facts that houses do not generally burn down, that child pedestrians do not normally dart into the road, and that bicyclists do not normally fall off their bicycles, safety requires that people behave as if such events may in fact occur. More progress seems to have been made in sensitizing people to the possibility of the house fire than to the unexpected event in traffic, perhaps because of the greater feeling of control in traffic, and the absence of a marketable product in the traffic-crash case.

The central role given to the mass media in the above discussion is based more on its influence on overall attitudes than on its ability to promote specific safety behaviors through, for example, public service messages. The agents of change, such as government or citizen advocacy groups, have influence only insofar as people are aware of their activities. The overall role of the mass media is difficult to establish, let alone quantify. Individuals rarely change their behavior because of one specific input, just as they rarely purchase products in response to one specific advertisement. However, the general belief that advertising does influence purchases is rarely contested. The finding of null results in specific focused efforts to change behavior, such as the one aimed at increasing belt use [Robertson et al. 1974], is to be expected. Broad changes of the type required to increase safety arise from the synergistic interactions of many factors. A specific set of advertisements aimed at reducing smoking is unlikely to generate any observable effect, yet as discussed in Chapter 8, behavior changes stimulated in large measure by information the public received through the mass media, accumulated over a 25-year period, have been large.

CONCLUSIONS

From 1921 to 1988 the number of traffic fatalities per unit distance of travel in the US declined by over 90%, equivalent to an average reduction of 3.5% per year. Similar, though generally larger annual reductions, are found for other countries. Changes in engineering in the form of improvements in roads, in vehicles, and in traffic engineering have made major contributions (as have advances in medical science). Because engineering and medical changes alone seem incapable of explaining such large effects, especially as some of the safety benefits of engineering are consumed in mobility increases and increased driver risk taking, it is concluded that human behavior changes have made the larger contributions. While drivers increase their safety by reacting to traffic laws, and to their own perceptions of risk, the human behavior component judged to have had the largest effect is a general evolution in social norms pertaining to driving. Societies react to the total number of fatalities, whereas individual drivers cannot react to them because they have no direct experience of them. Safety cannot be learned from direct experience alone because useful feedback is too infrequent. Many safety behaviors are eventually performed by habit; for example, drivers nearly always stop at red traffic lights, even in the absence of traffic or police. Safe driving habits are acquired by a social process not all that different from that generating hygienic habits.

It is clear that large improvements in public health have been generated by collective human behavior changes in smoking, exercise, diet, and alcohol use. This leads to the conclusion that the largest potential gains in traffic safety can be achieved by encouraging and stimulating changes in the social norms related to driving towards practices more conducive to safety, and away from practices which are inimical to safety. The following three factors seem likely to have important influences on social norms relating to driving:

1. Fictional television and movie portrayals of the life-threatening use of motor vehicles as heroic, glamorous, humorous, or non-dangerous,
2. Encouragement of increased courtesy on the road, and

3. Alcohol taxation and advertising policy, especially its influence on beer consumption by young male drivers.

REFERENCES

Adams, J.G.U. Smeed's law, seat belts and the emperor's new clothes. In: Evans, L.; Schwing, R.C., editors. *Human Behavior and Traffic Safety*. New York, NY: Plenum Press, p. 193–248; 1985.

Atkin, C.K. Television, socialization and risky driving by teenagers. *Alcohol, Drugs and Driving* 5(1):1–11; 1989.

Broughton, J. Predictive models of road accident fatalities. *Traffic Engineering and Control* 29(5):296–300; 1988.

Cownie, A.R.; Calderwood, J.H. Feedback in accident control. *Operational Research Quarterly* 17:253–262; 1966.

Evans, L. Factors controlling traffic crashes. *Journal of Applied Behavioral Science* 23:201–218; 1987.

Evans, L. An attempt to categorize the main determinants of traffic safety. *Health Education Quarterly* 5:111–124; 1990.

Federal Highway Administration. Fatal and injury accident rates on public roads in the United States. Publication FHWA-SA-90-029, Washington, DC; June 1990.

Flora, J.A.; Maibach, E.W.; Maccoby, N. The role of media across four levels of health promotion intervention. *Annual Reviews of Public Health* 10:181–201; 1989.

Geller, E.S. A delayed reward strategy for large-scale motivation of safety belt use: a test of long term impact. *Accident Analysis and Prevention* 16:457–464; 1984.

Greenberg, B.; Atkin, C. The portrayal of driving on television, 1975–1980. *Journal of Communication* 33:44–45; 1983.

Haddon, W., Jr. A logical framework for categorizing highway safety phenomena and activity. *Journal of Trauma* 12:193–207; 1972.

Haddon, W., Jr. Strategy in preventive medicine: passive vs. active approaches to reducing human wastage. *Journal of Trauma* 14:353–354; 1974.

Haddon, W., Jr. Advances in the epidemiology of injuries as a basis for public policy. *Public Health Reports* 95:411–421; 1980a.

Haddon, W., Jr. Options for the prevention of motor vehicle crash injury. *Israel Journal of Medical Sciences* 16:45–64; 1980b.

Hauer, E. Fatal and injury accidents: some interesting trends. *The Safety Network* 4(3), Canadian Association of Road Safety Professionals, Toronto, Canada; December 1988.

Helson, H. *Adaptation-Level Theory*. New York, NY: Harper and Row; 1964.

Holding, C. Health care in the Soviet Union. *Science* 213:1090–1092; 1981.

Jacobs, G.D. The potential for road accident reduction in developing countries. *Transport Reviews* 2:213–224; 1982.

Joksch, H.C. The relation between motor vehicle accident deaths and economic activity. *Accident Analysis and Prevention* 16:207–210; 1984.

Koornstra, M.J. Development of road safety in some European countries and the USA—a theoretical and quantitative mathematical analysis. Paper presented to Road Safety in Europe, Gothenburg, Sweden; 12–14 October 1988.

Koornstra, M.J. A general system approach to collective and individual risk in road safety. Paper presented to the International Symposium on Driving Behaviour in a Social Context, Paris, France; 16–18 May 1989.

Koshi, M. Road safety measures in Japan. In: Evans, L.; Schwing, R.C., editors. *Human Behavior and Traffic Safety*. New York, NY: Plenum Press, p. 27–36; 1985.

Mackay, M. Towards a unified traffic science. IATSS Research—Journal of International Association of *Traffic and Safety Sciences* 14(1):(in press) 1990.

Michon, J.A. Explanatory pitfalls and rule-based driver models. *Accident Analysis and Prevention* 21:341–353; 1989.

Minter, A.L. Road casualties—improvement by learning processes. *Traffic Engineering and Control* 28:74–79; 1987.

Motor Vehicle Manufacturers Association. *MVMA Motor Vehicle Facts and Figures.* Detroit, MI (issued annually).

Nagayama, Y. The effects of information and education on traffic accident decrease, behavior change and attitude change. *IATSS Research—Journal of International Association of Traffic and Safety Sciences* 14(1):(in press) 1990.

National Highway Traffic Safety Administration. Fatal Accident Reporting System 1988. Document DOT HS 807 507. Washington, DC; December 1989.

National Safety Council. Accident facts. Chicago, IL. 1989 edition (issued annually).

Oppe, S. Macroscopic models for traffic and traffic safety. *Accident Analysis and Prevention* 21:225–232; 1989.

Partyka, S.C. Simple models of fatality trends using employment and population data. *Accident Analysis and Prevention* 16:211–222; 1984.

Postman, N.; Nystrom, C.; Strate, L.; Weingartner, C. *Myths, Men and Beer: An Analysis of Beer Commercials on Broadcast Television.* Washington, DC: AAA Foundation for Traffic Safety; 1987.

Robertson, L.S.; Kelly, A.B.; O'Neill, B.; Wixom, C.W.; Eiswirth, R.S.; Haddon, W., Jr. A controlled study of the effect of television messages on safety belt use. *American Journal of Public Health* 64:1071–1080; 1974.

Ross H.L. Deterrence-based policies in Britain, Canada, and Australia. In: Laurence M.D.; Snortum J.R.; Zimring F.E., editors. *Social Control of the Drinking Driver.* Chicago, IL: University of Chicago Press, p. 64–78; 1988.

Sagan, L.A.; Afifi, A.A. Health and economic development II: longevity. Research memorandum RM-78-42. Laxenborg, Austria: International Institute for Applied Systems Analysis; August 1978.

Sivak, M. A 1975 forecast of the 1985 traffic safety situation: what did we learn from an inaccurate forecast? In: Rothengatter, J.A.; de Bruin, R.A., editors. *Road Users and Traffic Safety.* Assen/ Maastricht, Netherlands: Van Gorcum, p. 13–25; 1987.

Sleet, D.A. Reducing motor vehicle trauma through health promotion programming. *Health Education Quarterly* 11:113–125; 1984.

Sleet, D.A.; Hollenbach, K.; Hovell, M. Applying behavioral principles to motor vehicle occupant protection. *Education and Treatment of Children* 9:320–333; 1986.

Smeed, R. Some statistical aspects of road safety research. *Journal of the Royal Statistical Society,* Series A 112:1–34; 1949.

Smeed, R. Variations in the pattern of accident rates in different countries and their causes. *Traffic Engineering and Control* 10:364–371; 1968.

Thomas, R.; Gallon, C.A. Motorway accidents: associations between characteristics—related variables. *Traffic Engineering and Control* 29(9):456–465.

Trinca, G.W.; Johnston, I.R.; Campbell, B.J.; Haight, F.A.; Knight, P.R.; Mackay, G.M.; McLean, A.J.; Petrucelli, E. *Reducing Traffic Injury—A Global Challenge.* Melbourne, Australia: A.H. Massina; 1988.

Van Houten, R.; Nau, P.A. Feedback interventions and driving speed: a parametric and comparative analysis. *Journal of Applied Behavior Analysis* 16:253–281; 1983.

Wildavsky, A. *Searching for Safety.* New Brunswick, NJ: Transaction Books; 1988.

Zeckhauser, R.J.; Viscusi, W.K. Risk within reason. *Science* 24:559–564; 1990.

14 Traffic Safety in Broader Contexts

INTRODUCTION

This book, in keeping with its primary goal, has so far focused exclusively on the subject of traffic safety. In this chapter we place traffic safety in various broader contexts.

TRAFFIC SAFETY IN THE CONTEXT OF SAFETY

There are more than two million deaths per year in the US [National Center for Health Statistics 1989]. About 140 000 of these are due to injury [Injury in America 1985], about 45 000 being traffic fatalities. The numbers of deaths due to the two leading causes of death, three quarters of a million from heart disease and half a million from cancer, far outnumber those due to injuries. Such a comparison ignores the crucial question of the ages at which death occurs. The risk of death from disease increases rapidly with age, whereas the risk of death from injury peaks at young ages; specific functional dependencies are given in Cerrelli [1989]. The comparison also ignores the inevitability of death; every US death certificate cites some trauma or disease, so independent of safety or medical advances, every mortal must eventually increase the total listed under some cause of death.

When one takes into account the ages at which the deaths occur, a different picture emerges. Figure 14-1 shows that about twice as many preretirement years of life are lost as a result of injury as from each of the two leading causes of death. The figure also makes the point that research expenditures for the two leading diseases greatly exceed those for research on injury. Later in this chapter I suggest that the resources that are available for traffic safety research tend not to be as wisely used as they might be.

Given that a death occurs, the probability that it was the result of any type of motor vehicle crash is shown in Fig. 14-2. Although many more males than females die in traffic crashes (Figs 2-5 and 2-15), there is little difference dependent on sex in Fig. 14-2 because males are also more likely to die from other injury causes (the main reason for early death) at the ages at which motor vehicle deaths are high. Given that a 19-year-old dies, there is an approximately even chance that the death was due to a traffic crash. The large increase after the minimum at age 15 is not due solely to the commencement of driving; a corresponding increase also occurs in pedestrian deaths (Figs 2-15 and 2-16). The

358

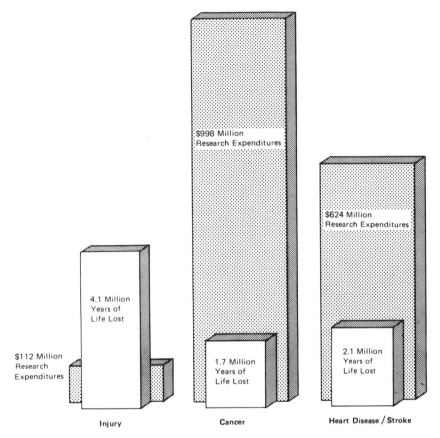

Figure 14-1. Years of preretirement life lost from different causes, and the research expenditures on these causes. Reproduced from *Injury in America* [1985, p. 14].

steep decline with increasing age occurs because traffic fatality risk declines at the same time that the risk from other causes increases. Given that death occurs, it is about 50 times more likely to be due to a motor vehicle crash at age 20 than at age 65.

Effects on Longevity

Figure 14-3 shows calculated increases in longevity arising from the elimination of all traffic fatalities, without anything else changing [Evans 1988a; Evans and

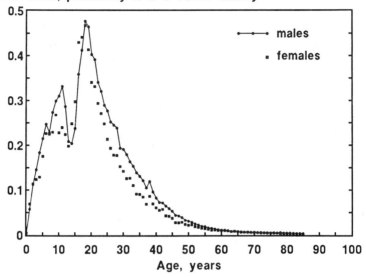

Given death, probability it is a traffic fatality

Figure 14-2. The probability that a given death is due to a motor vehicle crash, using FARS 1983-1985. From Evans [1988a].

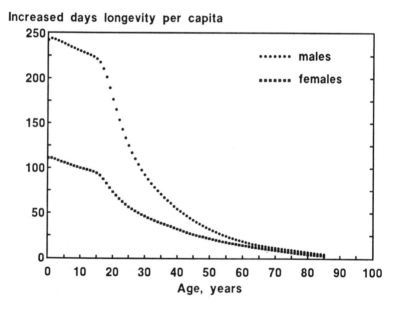

Increased days longevity per capita

Figure 14-3. Calculated increases in longevity per capita (days) assuming the elimination of all motor vehicle fatalities, using FARS 1983-1985. From Evans [1988a].

US thousands of life-years added

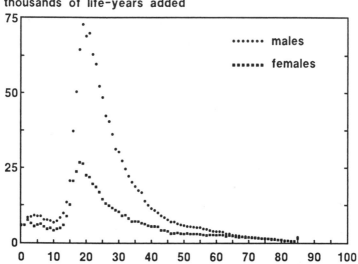

Figure 14-4. Calculated increases in total longevity to all individuals in the US of a given age and sex if motor vehicle fatalities to that group could be eliminated, using FARS 1983-1985. From Evans [1988a].

Blumenfeld 1982]. For boys at birth the increase is 242 days, or two thirds of a year; for girls 111 days. At age 65 the increases are 15 days for males and 12 days for females.

Figure 14-4 shows the total increase in longevity in the US which would result if all fatalities to individuals of one age were prevented. For example, if all fatalities to 20-year-olds were prevented, this would eliminate 1309 male deaths; as life expectancy for a 20-year-old male is 52.7 years, the elimination of these traffic fatalities generates an additional 1309 × 52.7 = 69 000 years of total longevity in the US. The corresponding calculation for 65-year-old males is 173 × 14.6 = 2500, so that the increased longevity from eliminating fatalities to 20-year-old males is 28 times as great as from eliminating fatalities to 65-year-old males.

Car Safety Compared to Safety Using Other Modes of Travel

Airline passengers awaiting take-off are sometimes told that they have already completed the most dangerous part of their trip—the drive to the airport. The impression that air travel is so much safer than car travel arises from the most widely quoted death rates per billion miles for each means of travel—0.6 for air travel compared to 24 for road travel. There are three reasons why such a comparison is inappropriate. First, the airline rate is passenger fatalities per passenger mile, whereas the road rate is all fatalities (any occupants, pedestrians, etc.) per vehicle mile. Second, road travel that competes with air travel occurs on the rural Interstate system, not on average roads. Third, driver and vehicle characteristics, and driver behavior, lead to car-driver risks that vary over a wide range. In contrast, airline fatality risk is similar for all travellers. Evans, Frick, and Schwing [1990] investigate the influences of driver age, alcohol use, safety belt use, car mass, and roadway type. The age distribution of airline passengers fatally injured in the eight worst 1975–1985 US airline crashes is used to infer car-driver fatality risk for drivers with the age distribution of airline passengers. Because risk of death on a flight does not depend on flight distance, airline fatality risk per mile decreases with flight distance. Expressions derived to compare risks for drivers with given characteristics to those on airline trips of given distance show that 18-year-old, unbelted, intoxicated, male drivers of cars 700 pounds lighter than average are substantially more likely to be killed on the trip to the airport than on the flight. However, drivers with the age distribution of airline passengers are less likely to be killed on the trip to the airport than on the flight. It is further concluded that 40-year-old, belted, alcohol-free drivers of cars 700 pounds heavier than average are slightly less likely to be killed in 600 miles of rural Interstate driving than in regularly scheduled airline trips of the same length. For 300-mile trips, the air travel fatality risk is about twice that for driving. Hence, for this set of particularly safe drivers, car travel provides a lower fatality risk than air travel for trips in the distance range for which car and air travel are likely to be competing modes.

Many sources compare safety for different travel modes; data on p. 87 of National Safety Council [1989] are typical. The data for 1987 show 9.7 car and taxi occupant deaths per billion miles of travel; the comparison rates for passengers using other modes are: for busses 0.3, for passenger railroads 1.3, and for scheduled airlines 0.7. In examining such averages, the massive contribution to the car rate from intoxicated youths should be kept in mind; if you are not one of them, then the relative risks are quite different. If you are as safe a driver as a bus driver, you are still at lower risk in the bus because of vehicle mass (including rollover) and seating position effects (Chapter 4). However, if you are a safer driver than the bus driver, you may be safer travelling in your car than by bus, especially as the bus trip necessarily involves some additional travel. As in the study by Evans, Frick, and Schwing [1990], the wide variation in driving risk should be kept in mind when comparing travel risks in different modes. In the words of an old adage noted by Feinstein [1988], "Statistics are like a bikini bathing suit: what is revealed is interesting; what is concealed is crucial."

TRAFFIC SAFETY IN THE CONTEXT OF MOBILITY

Traffic safety is all too often discussed as if the only goal in creating traffic systems were safety, as has been noted by Haight [1985]. On the contrary, the goal is mobility; crashes are an unwanted by-product which are to be minimized in the context of this primary goal. While the goals of safety and mobility are often in conflict, this is not always the case. It is helpful to discuss safety changes with regard to whether they reduce mobility, do not appreciably affect mobility, or actually increase mobility. Such categorization does not imply anything about the relative desirability of different interventions. An intervention which reduces mobility, such as drunk driving laws, might be more desirable than an intervention which increases both mobility and safety, such as building freeways. In the discussion we generally ignore the effect of crashes on mobility. Thus, we assume that decreasing speed decreases mobility without taking into account the additional mobility enjoyed by those not killed or injured as a result of the lower speeds.

Safety Measures Which Reduce Mobility

Safety measures which reduce mobility include:

Speed restrictions
Driver licensing
Drunk driving laws

The safety intervention which is most in conflict with mobility is speed regulation. Equatons 6-1 to 6-3 show that crash risk, and the probability of injury and death in a crash, increase steeply with speed. There is no reason to think that similar relationships do not apply at all speeds. Therefore, the safest speed is zero. This safest speed would indeed eliminate all harm from traffic crashes, and also eliminate all traffic. As expected harm increases steeply with increasing speed, but mobility increases more slowly, optimum speeds exist which can be estimated in terms of various assumptions. Miller [1989] performs such an examination for the US rural Interstate system and finds that the 55 mph speed limit may be close to the optimum choice. He further estimates that the higher 65 mph may not even save time when all the delays associated with injuries and crashes are added to the years of life lost through fatalities.

Driver licensing reduces the mobility of some individuals by denying them the right to drive. The main reasons for such denials are age (per se, before a specified age, but by less straightforward means for older drivers), performance impairment (for example, blindness), or criminal sanction. There are many studies which show that denying some group of individuals (usually the young) the right to drive reduces crashes. Successfully prohibiting any fraction of the population from driving is naturally expected to reduce crashes. The percent reduction in crashes will exceed the percent reduction in drivers if those prevented from driving have above average crash rates. However, this in itself does not justify denying driving privileges to a group of people. If it did, the logical consequence would be to prohibit males from driving (Fig. 2-7). If one had sufficiently detailed knowledge about all drivers, successive application of such a philosophy would eventually eliminate all except the one safest driver.

Drunk driving laws do not have the catastrophic effect on mobility which speed or driver licensing do when taken to hypothetical limits. They do, however, still inhibit the mobility of those who would otherwise drive and drink. Although increasing the minimum drinking age does not affect mobility as such, it does amount to a *selective prohibition,* in which the majority musters enough political muscle to force on a relatively weak political minority a policy which they would not accept for themselves, notwithstanding its potential contribution to traffic safety. The majority are presently unwilling to pass other laws relating to alcohol which are expected to reduce traffic crashes. In the case of alcohol use, as for driver licensing and speed laws, it is the legitimate role of the political process to balance the goals of mobility and safety when they are in conflict.

Safety Measures Which Have Little or No Effect on Mobility

Measures which have little or no effect on mobility include:

Active occupant protection devices
Passive occupant protection devices
Vehicle safety improvements
Safer highway furniture (break-away signs, etc.)
Improved emergency medicine
Passengers sitting facing rearwards
Passengers selecting rear rather than front seats

While passive occupant protection devices such as airbags do not influence mobility, it could be argued that devices which require action on the part of the occupant do. Fastening and unfastening safety belts does take some time, as does the deployment of motorized belts. These delays have such trivial effects compared to, for example, a change in the speed limit, or modest changes in the chosen speed, that it seems more appropriate to ignore them than to think of them as actual impediments to mobility. Motorcycle helmets might have a sufficiently larger effect on mobility to justify inclusion in the mobility reducing category. Not only do they take longer to put on, but they might be stored separately from the vehicle. If required by law, trips could be cancelled if helmets were lost, stolen, or not available for a passenger.

In Chapter 11 it is concluded that devices which reduce injury given that a crash occurs, but which are relatively invisible to the road user, have little or no influence on behavior. As all the other items listed above fit this definition, they are considered unlikely to influence mobility. Facing rearward, or sitting in a rear compared to in a front seat, are choices related to convenience, comfort, pleasure, etc., under which heading they are discussed later.

Safety Measures Which Can Increase Mobility

Safety measures which can increase mobility include:

Upgrading roads (for example, replacing two-lane roads by freeways)
Improved brakes, tires, headlights, and other technical equipment
Improved vehicle performance and handling
New technological approaches to night vision, drowsiness detection, etc.

The largest changes in safety associated with technical differences are those associated with different types of roads (Table 4-4). Thus upgrading a rural two-lane roadway to a divided freeway is expected to reduce crash, injury, and fatality risk by large amounts. Upgrading roads is accompanied by reduced delays due to congestion and traffic control devices, and by higher speed limits. Thus, upgrading roads sharply increases both safety and mobility. Mobility is sufficiently increased that a natural consequence is the generation of more traffic [Mackie and Bonsall 1989] which will discount some of the expected safety increases.

Insofar as improved brakes, tires, headlights, and other changes in technical equipment are used to increase mobility, their safety-increasing influence is discounted (Chapter 11). Increased acceleration reduces the time taken to reach cruising speed after stops, and reduces the time to merge into freeway traffic. It also increases overtaking opportunities. Unquestionably, for a fixed level of safety, the greater the performance characteristics, in terms of acceleration, handling, and braking, the shorter is the trip time.

Devices being developed to provide the driver with a view of what is ahead under extreme visual conditions, such as fog, have the potential to increase mobility; this is also true for devices to alert the driver of the onset of sleep. While it is not possible to apportion benefits between safety and mobility without actual experience with the devices, it does seem probable that they would permit more exhausted drivers to drive in worse weather, leading to benefits more in the realm of increased mobility than in the realm of increased safety.

TRAFFIC SAFETY IN THE CONTEXT OF OTHER VALUES

While most discussions of factors which are in conflict with safety focus on trade-offs with mobility, this is by no means the only goal which may clash with safety.

Freedom

Traffic laws regulating behavior by such measures as speed limits and requiring the use of restraints (belts, helmets) have been criticized as diminishing personal freedom. Such issues tend to arise more in prospect than in retrospect. Little concern is expressed because drivers are legally prohibited from driving on whatever side of the road they wish. The rule, rigorously enforced by custom and law, that all motorists drive on the same side of the roadway expands the freedom of mobility for all. That we all drive on one side of the road is a particularly interesting case, because the choice is arbitrary, as there are no convincing reasons for choosing one side over the other. Some nations choose the left, some the right, but there are none which have opted to allow their citizens to choose freely for themselves each time they drive. Having to stop at a red traffic light is a similar apparent impediment to freedom, yet traffic signals increase mobility.

The argument that mandatory restraint use laws are of a different nature has more merit, in that they primarily affect the safety of only the involved individual. There are some secondary effects. Unbelted rear occupants pose increased threats to front-seat occupants. Unbelted front-seat occupants pose increased threats to other front-seat occupants in side-impact crashes. It has been suggested that belted drivers may be able to control their vehicles better when crashes are imminent, but there is no supporting evidence. Apart from these considerations, the use of a belt or helmet affects mainly the user's risk. However, the nonuse of restraints imposes additional economic burdens on society. It could even be argued that unrestrained occupants increase the fatality and serious injury risks faced by restrained occupants by diverting away from them limited emergency medical resources. There does not appear to be any feasible mechanism by which the increased economic burden the unrestrained place on the restrained could be avoided. It is not conceivable, apart from any questions of desirability, that any modern society would recognize a contract by which a motorcyclist would sign away his right to medical care in return for permission to ride without a helmet. It seems to me that the society that pays the medical bill does have some legitimate right to take reasonable measures to reduce that bill. Each such issue is intrinsically political in nature; the only way to decide whether to require helmets or safety belts, impose speed limits, ban heroin or skiing is through the political process. The argument that it is nobody's business seems to me to have lost credibility as the members of society become increasingly intertwined.

The claim that motorists have a right to own and operate devices to warn them of the proximity of police radar speed monitoring devices seems devoid of any of the valid points which can be raised in favor of allowing occupants to please themselves about restraints. The only purpose of such devices is to facilitate the breaking of laws which are (formally, at least) supported by the majority. The manufacture, sale, and use of such devices seems to me about as legitimate as the manufacture, sale, and use of burglary tools.

Unlike refusing to wear restraints, there is no question that speeding kills road-users other than the speeder. Radar detectors are advertised in airline magazines, presumably because airline passengers desire to save time, and can afford such devices. I wonder how these purchasers, whose time seems so precious, would react if the pilot of their plane walked on board surreptitiously carrying an electronic black box which facilitated circumventing government regulations promulgated to increase safety, but which increase flight time as an unavoidable by-product. The pilot could explain that the flight would of course be safer, because monitoring the additional sensor would prevent boredom, and the exhilaration of the sport would ensure high adrenaline levels. I suspect that the speeding driver, who seems unconcerned at putting other road users at risk because of his or her own law breaking, may not necessarily find this make-believe situation so appealing.

Equity

Adams [1981; 1985] discusses many ways in which increased mobility for vehicle occupants may be in conflict with other human values. One of these is the relative emphasis placed on the safety and freedom of different categories of road user. In the sense in which I have been using safety in this book, a reduction in pedestrian fatalities is interpreted as an increase in safety. However, such a reduction may be obtained by preventing children from even crossing roads in which they may have played with relative safety in earlier decades. Indeed, the main mechanism which reduces the number of children playing in the road is the very increase in danger brought about by increased traffic and increased speeds. It is another example of a perverse effect in which factors adverse to safety generate safety increases because of large human behavior responses on the part of the children and their parents. While increasing motorization expands the mobility of those who can drive, it stimulates other processes which tend to diminish the mobility of those who cannot, mainly the old, those too young to have licenses but old enough to seek independence from adult control, and those with physical handicaps.

There are other approaches, such as separating pedestrians and vehicles, and building limited-access freeways which enhance safety and mobility but may diminish a sense of community and interaction between people. All these considerations place such decisions properly in the political process; they are not to be decided by technocrats with narrow goals, even those as laudable as saving lives and reducing injury. The goal of traffic safety research is to inject into the discussions objective estimates of the most likely safety effects.

Convenience, Comfort, Pleasure, etc.

Because frontal impact is the most common crash impact direction, injury risk to passengers would be less if they were seated in appropriately designed rearward-facing seats. Such a change has little direct effect on mobility, except insofar as it could affect navigation and also remove the benefit of other pairs of eyes looking for danger; such considerations have little applicability to rear-seat passengers. The desire for human interaction, and the greater pleasure of looking forward overwhelm an otherwise substantial safety increase available, in principle, at essentially no monetary cost. Rearward-facing seats in trains and aircraft, despite their increased safety, have never proved to be popular.

Passengers can presently choose between seats with substantial differences in fatality risk. A passenger who does not wear safety belts and makes the normal choice of sitting in the right-front seat, rather than an outboard-rear seat, thereby increases fatality risk by a substantial 35%. Even if the front seat is protected by an airbag, it still has an 18% higher fatality risk than the rear seat (Fig. 3-5 and Chapter 9). If the passenger uses belts, and there is a lap/shoulder system in the front and a lap-belt only in the rear, then each seat has a similar fatality risk. If both front and rear seats have lap/shoulder belts, the rear is expected to have a lower fatality risk. Notwithstanding the greater safety of rear seats, passengers are likely to continue to chose the front because of such considerations as closer interaction with the driver and a better view.

Devices like radios and telephones may compromise safety, though each of these may also contribute to safety under particular circumstances. As in the discussion on freedom, concerns seem much more intense in prospect than in retrospect. While nearly all cars have radios, which undoubtedly distract drivers to some extent, there is little desire to prohibit them, or restrict their use to when the vehicle is not in motion.

THE FUTURE

Any cursory examination of the success of those making predictions invites the following advice:

Never make predictions—especially about the future.

Such advice assumes a goal of accuracy. If, however, the goal is to become rich and famous, then different advice applies: make lots of predictions, the more unconstrained, outrageous, and alarmist the better, and keep in mind that the market for bad news far exceeds that for good news. Notwithstanding the pitfalls surrounding any attempt to estimate what will happen in the future, I offer below a few thoughts on where I think traffic and traffic safety are heading.

The Future of Traffic

In the past many interesting predictions about the field of transportation have been made. In 1979 a group of experts predicted the US price of unleaded gasoline in 1990 using a computer-interactive approach called the Delphi method [UMTRI Research Review 1987]. Their estimate, over $4.00 per gallon in 1990 dollars, is 300% higher than the 92.9 cents to $1.089 per gallon I have paid (in southern Michigan) from January to July in 1990! I have paid up to $1.359 in the period following Iraq's invasion of Kuwait on 2 Aug 1990. Macrae [1988, p. 18] reports that, in 1903, Mercedes thought there would never be a world market for more than one million automobiles, because there were not one million artisans in the world trainable as chauffeurs (also quoted in slightly different form by Mackay [1990]). Between then and now there have been a succession of predictions of saturation levels of vehicle ownership that have been over-whelmed by a reality reflected in a world now containing about 700 million vehicles [Mackay 1990]. Many mechanisms in addition to the difficulty of train-ing artisans have been invoked to infer asymptotic saturation levels; these have included limited amounts of roadway, economic constraints, energy constraints, and natural limits, such as one vehicle per family. Recently Haight [1987], Mackay [1990], and Lave [1990] have included in their thinking saturation levels of vehicle ownership similar to present US levels, with the implication that motorization in the US has saturated, and other parts of the world approaching the same level will also saturate.

The upper graph in Fig. 14-5 shows the growth of all vehicles, and of privately owned cars, in the US since the beginning of the century. Because growth in the human population contributes to the growth of vehicles, it is more illuminating to examine the growth in vehicles per capita, which is shown as the lower graph in Fig. 14-5. Apart from declines during the depression and the Second World War, the curves show increases almost every year. There is no hint of a kink corresponding to one vehicle per family, or one privately-owned car per family. The curves evince no indication of becoming horizontal, nor does the value one appear to constitute any particular impenetrable barrier.

One interesting attempt to address saturation phenomena in general is that of Marchetti [1987] who finds that a three parameter equation identical to one describing the time dependence of many ecological systems can be applied to

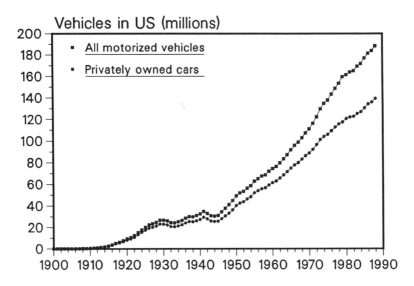

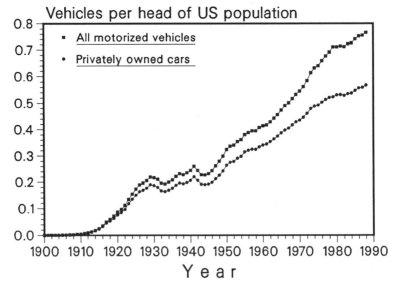

Figure 14-5. The growth of vehicles (top graph) and of vehicles per capita (bottom graph) in the US.

the evolution of such manufactured items as telegraph wires and roads. One of the parameters derived from historical time series is an estimate of a future saturation level. In applying the approach to cars, Marchetti [1983] estimates a saturation level of 200 million for the US (the 1988 total is 139.5 million). However, he points out that the goodness of fit to the equation is relatively insensitive to the choice of final saturation level. Because a simple linear equation, with only two parameters, fits the US data substantially better than the more complex three parameter equation, the third parameter, the estimated saturation level, is of questionable validity.

It seems to me there is no more a *natural* limit on vehicle ownership than there is a natural limit on the ownership of radios, televisions, bathrooms, shoes, or houses. In the early days of radio, one radio per family might have seemed a natural limit. A stronger case could have been made for one per person, given that we each have only one pair of ears. The number of products of any type sold depends on such factors as how much they are desired, how much they cost, how conveniently they can be stored, and how much money people have; it cannot be inferred from an abstract general principle. I see no reason why this should not also be the case for vehicle ownership. US evidence shows clearly that there is nothing special about one vehicle per family. There is likewise nothing magical about an average of one vehicle per person—many families now possess more than one vehicle per family member. My guess is that US vehicle ownership per capita will continue to grow without any natural upper bound, although in future decades the rate of growth might slow down. If history is any guide, motorization in other countries will tend to follow the US pattern. Vehicle registrations in the US are presently increasing at about two and a half million per year.

The total distance of travel, which is the denominator in the fatality rates plotted in, for example, Fig. 13-2, is the number of vehicles times the average distance of travel per vehicle. This (Fig. 14-6) has been remarkably stable at close to 16 000 km/year since World War II, although there is an indication of an increasing trend in the late 1980s. Figures 14-5 and 14-6 suggest continuing increases in total US travel.

In the mid 1970s there were dire predictions that the world's energy resources could not support increasing motorization, and that by now catastrophe would long since have overwhelmed us. While we know that petroleum resources are limited, as is the life of the Earth and of the solar system, the earlier noted present price of gasoline (in real terms less than the price in 1950) speaks eloquently to the immediacy of this problem. The 1970s' *energy crisis* has been replaced by the 1990s' *congestion crisis,* the concern that all these vehicles are going to be locked in *gridlock,* meaning immobilization in some gigantic traffic jam. Such concerns yet again ignore the enormous feedback that characterizes large complex social structures. Congestion today is not demonstrably worse in New York City than it was a hundred

Figure 14-6. Average distance of travel per vehicle per year since data were first collected in the US in 1921.

years ago, nor worse in London than it was three hundred years ago, nor worse in Rome than it was two thousand years ago. Congestion is caused by people's desire to have access to amenities that require large concentrated populations; it is regulated by how much aggravation they are willing to pay for such benefits, not by the number of vehicles. When congestion reaches a certain level of unpleasantness, a natural balance arises between those willing and those not willing to suffer it. The tolerable level does not seem to have changed much over the centuries, or for that matter, the millennia. It is based on the number of hours in the day, and the desire of humans to use their time in productive and pleasant ways. I see no reason why it should change in future decades. Places which are already as congested as the human spirit can bear, and there are a great number of them, will not become more congested. Because all market equilibrium processes are imperfect and have time lags, there may be some fluctuations above and below what people will tolerate; however, any net increase in congestion in the world's 100 most congested cities seems implausible, although the fraction of the city subject to congestion could increase. What is much more likely is that more cities will join the already long list of those that have reached just bearable levels of congestion. Although congestion impedes mobility, it increases safety, as measured by serious injuries and fatalities.

When land is available, road-building is the most effective way to reduce congestion, although the increased mobility thereby provided likely attracts additional traffic. Even when land is unavailable, building double-decker roads could be economically attractive in some circumstances. Although road-building has become politically unpopular in recent years, I suspect that this will change when the effectiveness of other approaches, such as electronic measures to better control traffic, are found to be modest and far less cost-effective than building roads.

Most of the increase in traffic will occur in areas which are presently less congested than the maximum tolerable level. In the US context, when life in California becomes a little less attractive because of increased congestion and other ills associated with high population density, the population of that state may stabilize in favor of growth in such less populated states as Michigan and Ohio. Even many countries with much higher population densities than the US still have large uncongested areas; in many cases the reason why people will not move to them is that they contain too few people!

The Future of Traffic Safety

Increasing motorization has led to expectations of ever increasing numbers of traffic fatalities. In 1975, when US traffic fatalities were 44 525, the National Highway Traffic Safety Administration [1975] estimated that traffic fatalities in 1985, one decade later, would be 72 300. The actual number turned out to be 43 825. In other words, a 62% increase over a 10 year period was forecast, compared to the 2% decline that actually occurred. While Sivak [1987] comments on many of the details of the calculation, it seems to me that details are rarely crucial in making predictions. In the face of high uncertainty, adding complexity generally conceals the truly crucial one or two assumptions, which often out of necessity, are little more than educated guesses. It seems particularly inappropriate to invoke computers in attempts to predict the future, as if the ability to do lots of multiplications quickly (about the only thing a computer does) is of any more relevance than would be the use of a crystal ball. The most one can hope to do is have some broad understanding of the processes, and some general view of some factors which exhibit some degree of historical stability.

The decline in fatalities per unit distance of travel (Figs 13-2 and 13-3) shows long term stability. Assuming that the logarithm of the rate declines linearly with time would rarely have generated large errors. Broughton [1988] finds a similarly scatter-free relationship for British data. Trinca et al. write, "In the most motorized countries of the world, the traffic safety rate is already nearly stabilized, so that even if percentage improvement in rate is forthcoming, the possibility for decline in absolute numbers is limited." [Trinca et al. 1988, p. 30] The fatality rates in Figs 13-1 and 13-2, and those reported by Broughton [1988] show no stabilizing tendency; the simplest interpretation of the data is of a constant percentage decline per year. If the fatality rate declines faster than the distance of travel increases, then a reduction in fatalities necessarily follows; if the human population increases, then fatalities per capita necessarily declines more. Thus, although Trinca et al. [1988] in the above quotation and elsewhere appear to suggest otherwise, reductions in fatalities can occur in motorized countries even as mobility increases. In the US, distance of travel doubled in the two decades from 1968 to 1988, yet fatalities in 1988 were 5000 less than in 1968.

Hutchinson [1987, p. 6] reproduces the following 1979 statement from the World Health Organization: "Little change may be expected in road accident rates within the next 5–10 years because alterations in the behaviour of road users and improvements in the environmental infrastructure of roads can come about only gradually." Hutchinson writes, "Happily, this prediction has turned out to be overly pessimistic," and points out that 22 of 28 jurisdictions for which he displays data show a decline in traffic deaths per million population from 1980 to 1985, with the average change being a 14% decline in the five year period.

While total distance of travel in the US increased at an average rate of 2.85% per annum from 1979 to 1988, the fatality rate (fatalities per unit distance of travel) decreased at 3.69% per annum in the same ten-year period. The slightly greater decline in the fatality rate compared to the increase in the distance of travel suggests that total fatalities are more likely to drift downwards than up-wards. However, fluctuations depending on economic conditions are to be ex-pected, as discussed in Chapter 11. In the absence of any dramatic discontinuity, such as occurred in October 1973, and based on the 1989 total of 45 500, I would expect US fatalities to remain in the range 40 000 to 51 000 throughout the remainder of the twentieth century.

The above discussion, in focusing on broad trends, has ignored details. How-ever, details are of the utmost importance, and it is the combined effects of many details that generate the broad trends. Interventions that change fatalities by 1% are not going to be visible in the broad trend. However, such an inter-vention prevents over 400 deaths annually in the US. The extent to which reductions beyond the general trend are achieved depends crucially on better understanding and knowledge; in other words, on research in traffic safety.

THE STATE OF TRAFFIC SAFETY RESEARCH

In the more than 50 years since driving behavior and traffic safety were first analyzed in a technical way, much has been learned. However, when compared to advances in the traditional sciences, increases in knowledge about traffic safety are less impressive. Below I offer some thoughts on why this is so, and offer suggestions for changes, building upon comments in three previous articles [Evans 1985; 1988b; 1988c]. I hope that my occasional oversimplifications in the interests of brevity and clarity will not be mistaken for naivety.

The comments focus mainly on hopes that traffic safety research might in the future acquire more of the method, style, values, attitudes, and institutional structures which have proved so successful in the traditional sciences, and that in the decades ahead understanding might increase at a greater rate than in the past. In advocating the application to traffic safety research of what might be called the normative model of science, I am not claiming that this model is in fact all that closely followed, even in the physical sciences. Even ignoring outright fraud, which Broad and Wade [1982] indicate is more common than is generally recognized, the normative model of science is one which is subject to many critisms [Kuhn 1970; Feyerabend 1975], rarely being the model used in the discovery process, but more likely being used to organize events after they have occurred. My claim is not so much that traditional science really follows this normative model, but that it is an understandable ideal standard. I believe that activities that have such an idealized goal will make more progress than those that do not, because possession of such a standard enables more effective evaluation of contributions.

The Goal is Knowledge

The primary motivation in science is curiosity, a desire to know. All too often in traffic safety there appears to be insufficient recognition of the difference between knowledge and what might be done with it. When Karl Marx draws the distinction in stating, "Philosophers have merely interpreted the world; the point, however, is to change it," he is stressing action over understanding. The goal of science is understanding; hopefully, increased understanding will illuminate the process of making changes.

The scientific community should be dispassionately knowledgeable about, for example, the effect of alcohol on the probability that a driver will crash and on the probability that an intoxicated driver will be arrested. On the other hand, those pursuing the policy goal of trying to reduce harm from drunk driving may legitimately publicize the first of these items more than the second. It would be counterproductive to their goal to publicize that the probability of arrest for this offence is typically about one in a thousand, and that doubling police enforcement is consequently expected to increase the chances of arrest to one in five hundred. While the scientist as a human being may indulge in activities that try to change the world, it is imperative that this entirely different activity be recognized as something separate from science.

Objectivity

Advocacy, by its very nature, implies making as good a case as you can. This involves selecting supporting evidence, and leaving the task of presenting contrary evidence to opponents. Although it is argued that advocacy performs some functions well, it is nonetheless a process which is different from, and indeed inimical to, the normative processes in science. The goal aspired to in science is that all relevant evidence be evaluated in a detached and objective manner, and that the inquirer be *disinterested* in the result.

The question of objectivity is often confounded by questions of organizational affiliation. For good or ill, the days of the gentleman/scholar of independent means are gone; essentially all researchers are paid for their efforts by somebody. To admit this is not to conclude that therefore all research is but a mere affirmation of the interests and beliefs of the body supporting it, and even less to assume that such a model applies to some bodies but not to others. All institutions, including universities (and the government bodies supporting them) and government-supported laboratories develop their own interests. As effectively pointed out Hauer [1989] in his paper "The reign of ignorance in road safety: a case for separating evaluation from implementation," the notion that government bodies charged with evaluating safety countermeasures are focused solely on the public good, without any agenda of their own, does not withstand much scrutiny.

There is little basis for judging the quality or objectivity of research based on the type of organization in which it was performed. Research is primarily an individual effort; the individual researchers within any large institution differ in such characteristics as ability, understanding, compassion, and integrity by amounts that are much greater than any possible differences in these same characteristics between types of institutions. In this book, quality research from many types of institutions has been cited; in many cases the same institutions have also supported blatantly self-seeking and incorrect studies. Research must be judged by its content, and the reputation—especially the long term track record—of the researcher. Work with the outward appearance of being technical is sometimes used purely for advocacy purposes and to buttress ideological beliefs. Some social *science* is little more than political advocacy packaged in unintelligible jargon. The question "What change in fatalities is associated with the passage of a mandatory belt-use law in some jurisdiction?" is, in its structure, a simple factual question. Most would agree that there is an objective answer. Although the answer may be difficult, or even impossible, to determine, it does not depend on the belief system, discipline, or training of the inquirer. This is not to suggest that science operates in a social vacuum; complex social factors determine what individuals, if any, are addressing this particular question, what methods they use, and what resources are available to them.

In contrast, the question "Ought we to pass (or more strictly enforce) mandatory belt-wearing laws?" is of a quite different nature, and cannot be answered by science. Questions of this type are properly addressed through the workings of the political process, in which personal philosophies and legally-pursued self-interest are legitimate ingredients. It is not the role of safety research to prescribe what is good for society, but to provide reliable information for more informed choices.

Flawed Approaches and Techniques

Although mentioned briefly in the introduction, the misunderstanding and misapplication of statistics seems to be one of the most pervasive flaws in research on traffic safety (and other fields). The impression is inescapable that there is a large army of so-called researchers, and what is much worse, an army of *teachers* of researchers, who think that the goal of their work is to test if data reject non-quantitative hypotheses. Unbelievable numbers of studies end by concluding that A is (or is not) statistically significantly different from B. It is difficult to see of what possible use any such conclusion can be, given that, with the possible exception of some elementary particles, all As are different from all Bs. If the conclusion is that A is bigger than B, then this is new information, but of extremely limited value; without knowing anything, such a statement has a 50% chance of being correct. The only answer of any real scientific value is how much bigger A is than B is. Comments parallel to the above apply equally if the question is, "Does A affect B?" The answer is yes; everything affects everything. When I spit in the ocean it affects the length of the day. The only question of any real interest is "How much?"

The following example illustrates how focussing on statistical significance can conceal important results and lead to incorrect conclusions. Suppose data collected in four studies support the following four independent estimates of some quantity: $(10 \pm 6)\%$, $(-1 \pm 8)\%$, $(7 \pm 5)\%$, and $(9 \pm 7)\%$. No individual result is statistically significantly different from zero, even at the low $p < 0.1$

level. If all that is reported for each study is that the effect is not statistically significant, then surely the naive reader must be forgiven for interpreting the consistent finding of no effect in each of four studies to constitute overwhelming evidence supporting no effect! A quite different picture emerges if the four quantitative values are combined using the calculation in Young [1962, p. 109] to obtain an overall composite estimate of $(7.0 \pm 3.1)\%$. As additional measurements become available they should contribute to composite estimates, thus increasing the precision with which quantities are known as more data are collected [Hauer 1983]. The need to present and combine quantitative estimates, rather than focussing on statistical significance, has recently been presented persuasively by Hauer [1990] who comments, "Nowadays tests of significance are often little more than a ritual used to feed the Moloch of journal etiquette."

Many papers show detailed results of many statistical tests, but display no raw data; in some cases a table of all the data analyzed would consume less page space than is consumed by the statistical analysis. Some claim that applying statistical tests is necessarily more objective than displaying data and making reasonable inferences from them. This point loses much of its impact when one realizes that there is a rich variety of statistical tests and transformations to select from, some combination of which can often produce any desired answer. Most of the key discoveries in science predate the field of statistics, which originated mainly in the early decades of the twentieth century. The main uncertainty in traffic safety research is usually in interpretation; the focus on statistical detail often obscures this. In many cases there are more than enough data to, say, determine a rate to high precision, but the meaning of the rate relative to traffic safety is subject to various alternative interpretations. Statistical procedures are vital to many studies, especially those involving large numbers of variables, but should not be at the core of all studies involving observational or experimental data.

When questions arise in traffic safety there is often a clarion call to collect more data. Such a call is often without regard to how the sought-after data can be used to address the question. In the era before the birth of experimental science, Greek philosophers thought that nature could be understood by pure thought alone, without the need for data. Nowadays there seem to be people who think that it can be understood with data alone, without the need for thought. Over half a century ago Gibson and Crooks [1938, p. 453] wrote, "Accident statistics are now widely publicized." Basically, traffic safety is one of many fields that can be characterized as data rich, understanding poor. The main thing that has been missing from traffic safety research is the appropriate scientific tradition to extract meaning from copious data that already exist; the answers to many key questions are embedded in existing data. Somewhat similar to the call for more data is the call for better driving simulators, as discussed in Chapter 5.

Flow charts appear constantly in the literature, showing boxes with labels such as *deviation from desired direction* and *driver reaction* connected by lines and arrows, relating actions to inputs, and showing all sorts of feedback. While such diagrams have application to engineering systems for which so-called *transfer functions* are known, I have yet to encounter one in traffic studies which contained any more information than could have been more succinctly stated in words. It is trivial to produce such flow charts if there is no requirement that we know anything about any of the ingredients (including whether or not they exist), or what observed output is being related to what observed input. In a minute one could produce such a chart with any arbitrary level of detail on, perhaps, how one adds sugar to one's coffee.

Creating a Scientific Literature

All the traditional sciences accumulate knowledge in a clearly identifiable peer-reviewed, or refereed, literature. It is even more crucial for peer-reviewed literature to be at the core of a subject such as traffic safety research, where so much is written for so many diverse purposes. Authors should feel reasonably comfortable (but not complacent) quoting results from such literature without the need to review all papers in detail. To require that all papers be read critically (which would involve similarly examining the work they cite, and so on) before citing would largely deny the field the possibility of advancing much beyond what one human mind can encompass. Work performed too recently to be published in a peer-reviewed article makes a strong claim to be cited because of its currency; however, authors have a greater responsibility to examine un-refereed reports before using them, or even providing them the increased credibility of a citation.

Increasing the importance of peer-reviewed literature is the most effective way to discard the plethora of nonscientific *results* which overwhelm this field. The value of many papers is very negative; not only do they spread misinformation, but they may oblige competent researchers to squander their time refuting nonsense. Many deserve to be handled with the clarity with which the great physicist Wolfgang Pauli once dealt with a particularly poor paper; he said, "That paper isn't even good enough to be wrong." [Segal 1990].

My advocacy that all published research results be archived in peer-reviewed literature does not imply that work in peer-reviewed journals is necessarily of high quality, or even free from grievous error arising from incompetence, or worse. The peer-review process is subject to all the frailties to which humans succumb. It is still surprising that the *American Journal of Public Health,* a peer-reviewed journal, has consistently opposed treating traffic crashes as a public health problem, and has instead advocated that the only countermeasures worthy of consideration are engineering changes to vehicles. This position has resulted in the publication of many conspicuously incorrect *technical* papers masquerading as science, while at the same time it has offered spurious reasons (subject not important) for refusing to publish technically correct work demonstrating the roles of nonengineering factors, such as alcohol; the journal is, however, willing to publish papers on behavioral interventions provided they *prove* that they do not work! The editor of *Science,* the peer-reviewed journal of the American Association for the Advancement of Science, declines to publish any research on traffic safety, yet uses its pages for his own uninformed opinions on the subject; he seems unaware of any relationship between car size and safety [Koshland 1989a]. Hamm [1989; 1990] takes him to task for writing, "Motor vehicle accidents, which kill more people each year than were killed during all the Vietnam war," [Koshland 1989b] by pointing out that an estimated 1.3 million people were killed in that war, 56 000 of them Americans. Even if interpreted to apply only to Americans, the statement is still false; in none of the seven years prior to his writing did traffic fatalities exceed 48 000, which falls short of being larger than 56 000!

Stressing the importance of reviewed literature is not to deny that many important contributions have appeared in nonrefereed sources. Some unrefereed literature is very good, and some peer-reviewed literature is very bad, but the *average* quality, importance, objectivity, and technical correctness of the peer-reviewed literature is substantially higher.

It seems to me that we should strive for the eventual goal that all work more than a few years old that has not been accepted in a peer-reviewed journal should be ignored. Meeting proceedings, such as the many quoted here, and papers from SAE meetings should be regarded as texts of oral presentations. It is common in the physical sciences for the proceedings of a meeting to be specifically annotated that the papers contained in it should not be cited. Unconstrained oral presentations and discussion should be encouraged as essential for scientific exchange, and a written record can facilitate this process. However, the written record of such activities should not be considered part of the scientific literature. Publication and presentation should be perceived as separate processes. One of the most regrettable practices is that some journals that review general articles publish special issues devoted to papers presented at a conference; the unwary reader may mistakenly think that such papers are reviewed. Peer review means that each paper is reviewed in as much time as is necessary (and usually a whole lot more!); it is not possible to review papers for inclusion in a meeting with scheduling constraints. Individual researchers anonymously review papers; such reviews cannot be done by committees.

Specialization

Science (and scholarship in general) advances mainly because individuals devote whole careers to fairly narrow specialized areas. Traffic safety has not acquired this tradition. Although there are hundreds of traffic safety researchers world-wide, there is not one who has devoted a substantial portion of a career to such clearly defined areas as, for example, the influence of speed, or the influence of vehicle mass or size. Yet these are areas of substantial intellectual challenge which could be advanced by applying the methods of science to organize and interpret diverse evidence available in many countries, and accumulated over decades. Greater understanding of such areas is crucial to traffic safety. Such understanding will advance much more rapidly under the sustained effort and intense focus of a few researchers who are attracted by it than by generalists picking it up from time to time, as is our current practice.

Governments usually want research that addresses some current crisis, or is *important*. Both criteria are flawed. Even if the research is good, by the time it is completed another crisis is in center stage. Importance is not a reason for researching some area, as would be readily realized if the subject were not traffic safety. The most important medical problems are probably that people don't feel good, and that they die, yet I am not aware of any project specifically aimed at developing a feel-good pill or an immortality pill. The edifice of science is built from a large number of specific results. Physics does not advance by many people addressing such broad questions as what is the nature of matter, but by intense specialization. The choice of which research to undertake is not based on the importance of the problem, but on the product of importance times the probability of making useful progress. This is obviously the most difficult problem to address as it is steeped in high uncertainty, but the researcher who is immersed in a subject is far more likely to make a wise choice than someone who is less knowledgeable.

Institutional Framework

Many of the reasons that have prevented traffic safety research from acquiring more of the values and methods of science are related to the institutional framework in which the subject is generally pursued. Much of the work is undertaken after a government defines a problem and offers contracts for institutions to complete specific projects. Institutions become dependent on such contracts. The professionals employed in them spend a good deal of their time preparing material to bid for contracts. If successful, there will be a fixed sum of money made available to the researchers and a specified time for completion of the investigation. The main point about research is that the researcher is supposed to be finding out things not previously known. This is difficult enough under the best of conditions, but almost impossible to do according to a schedule. Even if the people doing the work are competent to do it, they must divide their time between completing the present contract and obtaining the next one. Given that researchers must eat, it is perhaps excusable that the only *conclusion* in some such studies is that more research is necessary. No scientific study would ever come to so vacuous a conclusion, which was obviously known before the start; it implies that nothing was learned in the study, which is often correct but rarely stated.

The situation described above could be ameliorated by creating a half dozen or so well-endowed professorial chairs in distinguished universities throughout the world. Appointments to such positions would be based on distinguished careers doing quantitative research, and the holders would be free to pursue safety as a science, letting their curiosity determine their research agenda. Their next year's resources would not be contingent on pleasing somebody by this year's offerings. They could therefore provide more detached council on safety questions than is presently available to policy-making bodies. They could also offer that sense of historical perspective that is presently often lacking, and help policy-makers avoid travelling down identical blind alleys every ten years or so.

The cost of such an undertaking would be only a modest portion of what is currently spent. While it could not bear fruit for at least five years (more likely ten, and possibly never), such an investment has a far greater chance of increasing traffic safety knowledge than spending enormously larger amounts on the types of things that have been supported traditionally.

REFERENCES

Adams, J.G.U. *Transportation Planning: Vision and Practice*. London, UK: Routledge and Kegan Paul; 1981.

Adams, J.G.U. *Risk and Freedom—The Record of Road Safety Regulations*. Nottingham, UK: Bottesford Press; 1985.

Broad, W.; Wade, N. *Betrayers of the Truth*. New York, NY: Simon and Schuster; 1983.

Broughton, J. Predictive models of road accident fatalities. *Traffic Engineering and Control* 29:296–300; 1988.

Cerrelli, E. Older drivers, the age factor in traffic safety. Washington, DC: National Highway Traffic Safety Administration, report DOT HS 807 402; February 1989.

Evans, L. Post symposium reflections (comments on problems and issues in traffic safety research). In: Evans, L.; Schwing, R.C., editors. *Human Behavior and Traffic Safety*. New York, NY: Plenum Press, p. 525–529; 1985.

Evans, L. Older driver involvement in fatal and severe traffic crashes. *Journal of Gerontology: Social Sciences* 43:S186–S193; 1988a.

Evans, L. The science of traffic safety. *Physics Teacher* 26:426–431; 1988b.

Evans, L. Comments (on two papers on mandatory safety belt use laws, and reflections on broader issues). In: Graham, J.D., editor. *Preventing Automobile Injury—New Findings From Evaluation Research*. Dover, MA: Auburn House, p. 73–83; 1988c.

Evans, L.; Blumenfeld, D.E. Car occupant life expectancy: car mass and seat belt effects. *Risk Analysis* 2:259–268; 1982.

Evans, L.; Frick, M.C.; Schwing, R.C. Is it safer to fly or drive?—a problem in risk communication. *Risk Analysis* 10:239–246; 1990.

Feinstein, A.R. Scientific standards in epidemiologic studies of the menace of daily life. *Science* 242:1257–1263; 1988.

Feyerabend, P.K. *Against Method: Outline of an Anarchistic Theory of Knowledge*. Atlantic Highlands, NJ: Humanities Press; 1975.

Gibson, J.J.; Crooks, L.E. A theoretical field-analysis of automobile driving. *American Journal of Psychology* 51:453–471; 1938.

Haight, F. A. The place of safety research in transportation research. *Transportation Research* 19A:373–376; 1985.

Haight, F.A. International cooperation in traffic safety. *IATSS Research—Journal of International Association of Traffic and Safety Sciences* 11:11–16; 1987.

Hamm, R.M. Statistical mortality (Letter to the Editor). *Science* 245:111–111; 1989.

Hamm, R.M. Cognitive impediments to a statistical consideration of war's consequences. Boulder, CO: Institute of Cognitive Science, U. of Colorado, technical report #90–3; 1990.

Hauer, E. Reflections on methods of statistical inference in research on the effect of safety countermeasures. *Accident Analysis and Prevention* 15:275–285; 1983.

Hauer, E. The reign of ignorance in road safety: a case for separating evaluation from implementation. In: Moses, L.N.; Savage, I, editors. *Transportation Safety in an Age of Deregulation*. Oxford, UK: Oxford University Press, p. 56–69; 1989.

Hauer, E. Should stop yield? Matters of method: safety. University Studies Group, Department of Civil Engineering, University of Toronto, Toronto, Ontario, Canada, 1990.

Hutchinson, T.P. *Road Accident Statistics*. Adelaide, Australia: Rumsby Scientific Publishing; 1987.

Injury in America: A Continuing Public Health Problem. Washington, DC: Committee on Trauma Research, Commission on Life Sciences, National Research Council and Institute of Medicine; 1985.

Kamerud, D.B. Evaluating the new 65 mph speed limit. In: Graham, J.D., editor. *Preventing Automobile Injury—New Findings from Evaluation Research*. Dover, MA: Auburn House, p. 231–256; 1988.

Koshland, D.E., Jr. A tax on sin: the six-cylinder car. *Science* 243:281–281; 1989a.

Koshland, D.E., Jr. Drunk driving and statistical morality. *Science* 244:513–513; 1989b.

Kuhn, T.S. *The Structure of Scientific Revolutions*. Chicago, IL: University of Chicago Press; 1970.

Lave, C. Things won't get a lot worse: the future of U.S. traffic congestion. Paper 890603, presented to the 69th Annual Meeting of the Transportation Research Board, Washington DC; 7–11 January 1990.

Mackay, M. Towards a unified traffic science. *IATSS Research—Journal of International Association of Traffic and Safety Sciences* 14(1):(in press) 1990.

Mackie, P.J.; Bonsall, P.W. Traveller response to road improvements: implications for user benefits. *Traffic Engineering and Control* 29:411–416; 1989.

Macrae, N. The next ages of man. *Economist*, p. 5–20; 24 December 1988.

Marchetti, C. Infrastructures for movement. *Technological Forecasting and Social Change* 32:373–393; 1987.

Marchetti, C. The automobile in a system context: the past 80 years and the next 20 years. *Technological Forecasting and Social Change* 23:3–23; 1983.

Miller, T.R. 65 mph: does it save time. Association for the Advancement of Automotive Medicine, 33rd Annual Proceedings, Baltimore MD, p. 73–90; 2–4 October 1989.

National Center for Health Statistics. *Monthly Vital Statistics Report*. Washington, DC: US Department of Health and Human Services, vol. 38, no. 5; 26 September 1989.

National Highway Traffic Safety Administration. *National Highway Safety Forecast and Assessment: A 1985 Traffic Safety Setting*. Washington, DC: Department of Transportation; 1975.

National Safety Council. *Accident Facts*. Chicago, IL; 1989 edition.

Segal, I.E. The unscientific charm of the big bang. Letter to the Editor, *New York Times*; 4 May 1990.

Sivak, M. A 1975 forecast of the 1985 traffic safety situation: what did we learn from an inaccurate forecast? In: Rothergatter, J.A.; de Bruin, R.A., editors. *Road Users and Traffic Safety*. Assen/ Maastricht, Netherlands: Van Gorcum, p. 13–25; 1987.

Trinca, G.W.; Johnston, I.R.; Campbell, B.J.; Haight, F.A.; Knight, P.R.; Mackay, G.M.; McLean, A.J.; Petrucelli, E. *Reducing Traffic Injury—A Global Challenge*. Melbourne, Australia: A.H. Massina; 1988.

UMTRI Research Review. Forecast and analysis of the U.S. automotive industry through 1995—Delphi IV. University of Michigan, Ann Arbor, MI; March–April 1987.

Young, H.D. *Statistical Treatment of Experimental Data*. McGraw-Hill; 1962.

15 Conclusions

This final chapter summarizes what I think are the most important overall conclusions arrived at in the earlier chapters.

Traffic crashes constitute one of the largest public health problems in industrialized countries. In the US almost half of the deaths of 19-year-olds are caused by traffic crashes; the total number of preretirement years of life lost because of traffic crashes is approximately equal to deaths caused by the combined effects of the two leading diseases, cancer and heart disease.

Age and sex have a large influence on essentially all variables important in traffic safety, such as the number of driver or pedestrian fatalities per capita. One important finding for traffic safety, as well as for many areas unrelated to traffic, is that the risk of death from the same impact, or physical insult, depends strongly on age and sex. From about age 15 to age 45, the same physical insult is approximately 25% more likely to kill a female than a male of the same age. For ages greater than about 20, fatality risk grows at an approximately uniform rate of 2.3% per year for males and 2.0% per year for females; at age 70 the risk is about three times what it is at age 20. Thus, as drivers become older, they face increasing risk of death in crashes of the same severity. Although the risk of crashing increases as age increases beyond 40, older drivers still have fewer crashes per capita than do 20-year-old drivers. Older drivers are involved in fewer crashes in which pedestrians are killed than are younger drivers. The main reason why older drivers pose a reduced risk to other road users is that they drive less. Thus the problem faced by the ageing driver may be more one of reduced mobility than of reduced safety.

Vehicular factors are difficult to examine because, for example, more injuries per vehicle for one type of vehicle than another may reflect a difference in the types of drivers choosing one of the vehicles rather than a difference in vehicle crashworthiness. Vehicle mass, or size, is the one vehicle characteristic that has the largest effect on injury and fatality risk in crashes. Mass effects are large for single-car crashes as well as for multiple-vehicle crashes. A driver switching to a heavier car receives a larger safety increase than the safety reduction sustained collectively by the other road users into which the heavier car might crash. Federal motor vehicle safety standards appear to have reduced occupant fatality risk by about 15 to 20%. The magnitudes of differences in fatality rates between different types of roads, in some cases more than a factor of nine, suggest strongly that replacing a stretch of rural two-lane roadway with a divided freeway reduces casualties substantially. Fatalities per unit distance of travel are lower in the winter months, notwithstanding more hours of darkness, snow and ice. Indeed, fatality risk is less on wet and snow-covered roads than on dry roads because drivers alter their behavior to reduce crash risk; crash rates still increase, but fatalities decrease more because of lower speeds. Thus inclement weather reduces mobility by deterring travel or reducing speeds more than it changes safety. Fatality rates are dramatically higher at night than in the day, an effect largely due to such road-user characteristics as alcohol use. Multidisciplinary post-crash investigations in the US and UK identify road-user characteristics as factors in 94% and 95% of crashes, respectively.

One of the most remarkable features of the driving task is that in a few months just about everybody can learn to perform it in at least a rudimentary fashion. There is no clear relationship between safety and driving skill or knowledge. The very groups with the highest levels of perceptual-motor skills and interest in driving, racing drivers, young drivers, and male drivers, are the very groups with higher than average crash rates. What is crucial is not how the driver *can* drive (driver performance), but how the driver *does* drive (driver behavior). The overinvolvement of youth, and males, in traffic crashes is quantitatively similar to the overinvolvement of youth, and males, in criminal activity unrelated to traffic. Observations of actual drivers show higher levels of risk taking are associated with these same groups. Many studies provide evidence supporting the general contention that people drive as they live. Involvement in traffic crashes is correlated with being emotionally unstable, unhappy, asocial, antisocial, impulsive, aggressive, unmarried, under stress, or other similar conditions.

Alcohol plays a larger role in traffic safety than does any other single factor. About 10% of property damage, 20% of injuries, and 47% of fatalities from traffic crashes would not occur were it not for alcohol. Large though the losses due to alcohol are, they would be considerably larger were it not for the implementation in the past of many countermeasures. Important among these is the development of *per-se* laws which proscribe driving with an amount of alcohol in the blood in excess of some specified legal limit, typically 0.1% in the US, but lower almost everywhere else, and in some cases substantially lower (Sweden uses 0.02%). Potentially more important in the future than laws aimed specifically at individuals violating drunk driving laws are changes in the broader social attitude. Drunk driving in the US appears intrinsically linked to overall national alcohol consumption; large reductions in drunk driving necessarily require reductions in alcohol consumption. Increases in the price of, and difficulty in obtaining alcohol, and decreases in the advertising of alcohol, all lead to reduced alcohol consumption.

Given that a crash occurs, a driver wearing a lap/shoulder belt is 42% less likely to be killed than a driver unprotected by any restraint system. If the same driver is also protected by an airbag, the risk is reduced by 47%; that is, the airbag prevents about 9% of the belted-driver deaths. The airbag alone reduces fatality risk by 18% for drivers not wearing belts; all manufacturers advise that lap/shoulder belts must still be worn in airbag equipped cars. A formerly belted driver who switches to airbag-only protection increases fatality risk by 41%. Laws mandating the use of belts reduce fatalities, but by lesser amounts than a simple back-of-the-envelope calculation indicates.

Road-users often react to safety changes in traffic systems. Examples in the literature show that, because of such reactions, interventions aimed at increasing safety have produced observed effects that have varied all the way from larger than expected safety increases to perverse effects (actual decreases in safety). Similarly varied responses have been observed for changes, instituted for economic or other reasons, which were expected to reduce safety. Some such interventions decreased safety more than expected while others generated perverse effects (actual increases in safety). Although no model exists which can predict the actual safety effect of a new intervention, the results of previous interventions suggest some fairly stable patterns. Vehicle technology changes which reduce crash risk in ways readily apparent to drivers are almost certain to be used to increase mobility. Thus better brakes and handling, poor-weather vision, and drowsiness detection are expected to lead to faster driving, faster cornering, faster speeds under low visibility, and longer-duration driving; there is no way to know, short of empirical determination, whether any such specific technology will lead to a net increase or decrease in safety. There is no evidence in the literature of measurable user responses to interventions that influence only the outcome of crashes, such as the use of safety belts or motorcycle helmets. The possibility of user response is particularly implausible when the user is unaware of the safety intervention, as in the case of such crashworthiness features as energy-absorbing steering columns and side-guard beams in doors.

Traffic crashes should not be considered analogous to any specific disease, because this can invite the false hope that the problem might be solved by the sort of elegant knockout blow that eliminated smallpox or scurvy. Any such hope can tend to deflect attention and resources from realistic to unrealistic approaches. A much more fruitful analogy is to all diseases. Improvements in traffic safety, as in public health, are produced by a rich variety of interventions, a few making large contributions, but many more making important small contributions. Any intervention which reduces US traffic fatalities by 1% prevents 450 deaths per year, a total that in contexts other than traffic would be considered enormous, not small.

I consider that the largest potential for increases in traffic safety is in the realm of stimulating changes in social norms pertaining to road-user behavior. While this is extremely difficult to quantify, it offers the possibility of larger increases than would be attainable by specific interventions. For example, if all US motorcyclists who do not wear helmets were to become wearers, US traffic fatalities

388 TRAFFIC SAFETY AND THE DRIVER

would be reduced by under 1%. Equipping all cars with driver airbags, compared to no cars being so equipped, would reduce US traffic fatalities by 5%. In contrast, changes in the consumption of alcohol in the US from 1982 to 1987 are estimated to have already generated a 12% reduction in traffic fatalities. These changes are partially due to legislation, but are even more likely to have been due to changing social norms brought about by the synergistic effects of law changes and widespread discussion of the problem, all of which have made drinking and driving increasingly unacceptable behavior.

It is clear that large improvements in public health have been generated by collective human behavior changes in smoking, exercise, diet, and alcohol use. This leads me to conclude that the largest potential gains in traffic safety can be achieved by encouraging and stimulating changes in the social norms relating to driving in ways that are more conducive to safety, and away from directions which are inimical to safety. The following three factors seem likely to have important influences on social norms relating to driving; (1) fictional television and movie portrayals of the life-threatening use of motor vehicles as heroic, glamorous, humorous, or nondangerous; (2) the encouragement of increased courtesy on the road, and (3) alcohol taxation and advertising policy, especially its influence on beer consumption by young male drivers.

It is well recognized that good health is not just the business of doctors, hospitals, and medical researchers. No matter how good the medical infrastructure, people cannot expect to be healthy if they smoke, overeat, abuse drugs, and do not exercise, in the expectation that the system will take care of them. It must similarly become recognized that traffic safety is not just the concern of road and vehicle builders, police departments, legislators, and government regulators. This is in no way to undervalue the importance, let alone responsibility, of such bodies, but to stress that traffic safety, like health, depends also on the deep involvement of those whose lives are at stake. While efforts to improve vehicles, roadways, regulations, legislation, and law enforcement will continue to reduce harm from traffic crashes, the main opportunity for substantial reductions is through people taking steps to protect themselves from this large source of harm. It will certainly not be easy to induce large numbers of people to stop doing things that are intrinsically enjoyable, such as high speed driving, high risk driving, and drunk driving. It was not easy to induce people to abandon or moderate, to the extent that they have, such enjoyments as cigarettes, alcohol, the sedentary life, salt, sugar, and cholesterol-rich foods. The considerable success achieved in these health areas shows that it can be done, and such success offers an appropriate model for traffic safety.

Indexes

Author Index

Adams, B.D., 109
Adams, J.G.U., 7, 82, 86, 87, 89, 144, 260, 263, 271, 272, 304, 338, 367
Afifi, A.A., 338
Akinyemi, J., 226
Allain, A.N., 187
Allen, R.W., 200
Allsop, R.E., 180
American Association for Automotive Medicine, 4
An Foras Forbartha, 186
Anderson, T.E., 172
Andreassend, D.C., 251
Andreasson, R., 168
Arthurson, R.M., 196
Aschenbrenner, M., 288
Ashton, S.J., 226
Asogwa, S.E., 285, 290
Atkin, C.K., 208, 353
Automotive News, 65
Avolio, B.J., 111

Babarik, P., 123
Babcock, C.W., 277
Baker, C., 125
Baker, S.P., 20, 26, 143, 144
Barry, H., 164, 167
Baum, H.M., 154
Bayley, S., 149, 299
Berenyi, J.S., 112
Bergman, A.B., 87, 144
Biehl, B., 105, 285, 288
Black, S., 149
Blomberg, R.D., 185
Bloomquist, G., 296
Blumenfeld, D.E., 361
Boehly, W.A., 76
Boff, K.R., 100
Bollen, K.A., 8, 150
Bonsall, P.W., 84, 365
Boor, M., 147
Borkenstein, R.F., 166, 177, 179, 180, 181, 182, 187

Boyle, A.J., 302
Brantley, P.J., 187
Brehmer, B., 325
Broad, W., 375
Broome, J., 7
Broughton, J., 193, 264, 334, 374
Brown, D.B., 113, 293
Brown, I.D., 103, 105, 107, 133, 291, 324
Brownlie, A.R., 166
Brunse, A.J., 176
Buckenmaier, C.C., 125
Bureau of the Census, 29
Burns, R., 325
Buttigliere, M., 176

Cairney, P.T., 198
Calderwood, J.H., 342
Camm, S., 226
Campbell, B.J., 52, 66, 69, 224, 226, 229, 231, 252, 254, 255, 266, 276, 277
Campbell, F.A., 252, 254, 266, 276
Campbell, K.L., 117, 123
Carseldine, D., 198
Carsten, O.M.J., 86, 93, 105, 137, 186
Casali, J.G., 120
Case, H.W., 176
Casey, S.M., 113
Casserly, H.B., 149
Cerrelli, E., 3, 358
Chafetz, M., 202
Champagne, F., 105
Chang, C.J., 289
Chang, M-F., 320
Charness, N., 31
Chenier, T.C., 269, 270, 272
Cirillo, J.A., 155
Clark, C.C., 52
Cohen, J., 175
Colsher, P.L., 203
Compton, C.P., 52
Compton, R.P., 201
Conley, J.A., 106
Conn, L.S., 125

Subject Index

About the Author

Leonard Evans is a Principal Research Scientist at General Motors Research Laboratories. He has a B.Sc degree in Physics from the Queen's University of Belfast, and a D.Phil degree in Physics from Oxford University, England. Dr. Evans' many technical publications cover such diverse subjects as physics, mathematics, traffic engineering, transportation energy, human factors, trauma analysis and traffic safety. He is a Fellow of the Human Factors Society and Past President of the Southeastern Michigan Chapter of the Human Factors Society; other memberships include the Society of Automotive Engineers (Past-Chairman of SAE Human Factors Committee), the Association for the Advancement of Automotive Medicine (Life Member), Sigma Xi, Society for Risk Analysis, editorial advisory boards of Accident Analysis and Prevention and Human Factors. His main professional interests focus on traffic safety research.